FEMINIST INTERPRETATION OF THE HEBREW BIBLE, I

Recent Research in Biblical Studies, 5

Series Editor
Alan J. Hauser

General Editors
Scot McKnight and Jonathan Klawans

FEMINIST INTERPRETATION OF THE HEBREW BIBLE IN RETROSPECT

I. BIBLICAL BOOKS

Edited by
Susanne Scholz

SHEFFIELD PHOENIX PRESS

2017

Copyright © 2013, 2017 Sheffield Phoenix Press
First published in hardback, 2013
First published in paperback, 2017

Published by Sheffield Phoenix Press
Department of Biblical Studies, University of Sheffield
45 Victoria Street
Sheffield S3 7QB

www.sheffieldphoenix.com

A CIP catalogue record for this book
is available from the British Library

Typeset by Forthcoming Publications
Printed by Lightning Source

ISBN 978-1-909697-07-2 (hardback)
ISBN 978-1-910928-31-8 (paperback)

To my favorite proto-feminist Bible interpreter from the Middle Ages,
fearless and independent,

Christine de Pizan
(1363–1430)

CONTENTS

PREFACE

Some projects take unusual paths, needing various developers, rescuers, and caretakers to see them through. This volume is such a project. The idea for it came from Dr Rachel Magdalene. She invited me to come aboard when her personal and professional situation had become difficult and soon made it impossible for her to stay on. She had to face what feminist scholars often have to experience, and I thank her for her trust in me to get done what we meant to finish together.

I also want to thank my contributors, who kept plugging away when deadlines shifted and more changes were requested. The assignment was different from what Bible scholars usually write on, and so it took some extra tweaking here and there. I believe our efforts were worthwhile and I am grateful to have such cooperative, skillful, and knowledgeable colleagues.

Above all, I wish to express my enormous gratitude to the mothers, aunts, and sisters and some brothers of feminist Hebrew Bible studies. We have studied with you, read your work, and joined you in your effort to theorize gender justice in the context of the field of the Hebrew Bible. It is impossible to agree with every nook and corner of the many different exegetical proposals, insights, and interpretations you made, and this volume demonstrates the diversity and wide range of argumentations produced in the past forty years. But overall, I cannot image where our work as feminist Bible scholars would be without your efforts. Together and over many years of long and hard work, we have been producing something that the intellectual world has never seen before. Certainly there were some feminist ancestors to feminist biblical interpretation, and I am dedicating this volume to one of them, Christine de Pizan, whose hermeneutical independence in interpreting Genesis 2–3 is stunning even today. Yet never before have feminist Bible scholars examined the biblical canon with such breadth and depth. It is truly a remarkable and historic accomplishment of extraordinary proportions, even though conservative and androcentric forces in academia in general and in biblical studies in particular do not adequately acknowledge the accomplishments and changes that feminist Bible scholars have made and called for in the past forty years. As obstacles accumulate in our path, we need to seize them as opportunities to work even more deliberately in sisterly solidarity and cooperation. This is, of course, difficult because conquest ideology likes to divide and conquer. It takes concentrated focus, commitment, and the conviction that feminist work matters unquestionably to carry on. My hope is that this volume will contribute toward this effort. I am truly honored to be part of this ongoing intellectual development and grateful to all of us for working toward a feminist defined future in biblical studies and beyond.

Susanne Scholz

ABBREVIATIONS

AB	Anchor Bible
ABD	David Noel Freedman (ed.), *The Anchor Bible Dictionary* (New York: Doubleday, 1992)
AOAT	Alter Orient und Altes Testament
Bib	*Biblica*
BibInt	*Biblical Interpretation*
BR	*Biblical Research*
BRev	*Bible Review*
CBQ	*Catholic Biblical Quarterlyy*
CBR	*Currents in Biblical Research*
ETR	*Evangelical Theological Review*
FCB	Feminist Companion to the Bible
FemTh	*Feminist Theology*
GCT	Gender, Culture, Theory
HBT	*Horizons in Biblical Theology*
HeyJ	*Heythrop Journal*
HTR	*Harvard Theological Review*
Int	*Interpretation*
JAAR	*Journal of the American Academy of Religion*
JBL	*Journal of Biblical Literature*
JBQ	*Jewish Bible Quarterly*
JBTh	*Jahrbuch für biblische Theologie*
JFSR	*Journal of Feminist Studies in Religion*
JHS	*Journal of Hellenic Studies*
JSOT	*Journal for the Study of the Old Testament*
JSOTSup	Journal for the Study of the Old Testament: Supplement Series
LHBOTS	Library of the Hebrew Bible/Old Testament Studies
NRSV	New Revised Standard Version
OBO	Orbis biblicus et orientalis
OBT	Overtures to Biblical Theology
OTE	*Old Testament Essays*
OTL	Old Testament Library
OTS	Oudtestamentische studiën
SBLDS	Society of Biblical Literature Dissertation Series
SBLSS	Society of Biblical Literature Semeia Studies
SBLSymS	Society of Biblical Literature Symposium Series
SJT	*Scottish Journal of Theology*

Abbreviations

SJOT	*Scandinavian Journal of the Old Testament*
TTod	*Theology Today*
VT	*Vetus Testamentum*
VTSup	Supplements to *Vetus Testamentum*
ZAW	*Zeitschrift für die alttestamentliche Wissenschaft*

ABOUT THE CONTRIBUTORS

Fiona C. Black is Associate Professor of Religious Studies at Mount Allison University in Sackville, New Brunswick, Canada. Using literary-, gender-, and cultural-critical approaches, she researches in the areas of Hebrew Bible poetry, reception history, and Caribbean hermeneutics. She has published *The Recycled Bible: Autobiography, Culture, and the Space Between* (2006), *The Artifice of Love: Grotesque Bodies and the Song of Songs* (2009) and numerous articles on the Song of Songs and Psalms. She is currently working on a reception history commentary on the Song of Songs.

Amelia Devin Freedman is Adjunct Lecturer in Religious and Theological Studies at Merrimack College in North Andover, Massachusetts. Her scholarly interests include biblical narrative, feminist hermeneutics, and the Bible in contemporary culture. She is the author of *God as an Absent Character in Biblical Hebrew Narrative: A Literary-Theoretical Study* (2005).

Sandie Gravett is Professor of Religious Studies at Appalachian State University in Boone, North Carolina. Her research focuses on the expression of religious themes and images in film and literature, the teaching of religious studies, and the interpretation of the Bible in contemporary culture. Among her publications are *From Twilight to Breaking Dawn: Religious Themes in the Twilight Saga* (2010), *An Introduction to the Hebrew Bible: A Thematic Approach* (co-written, 2008), 'Reading Rape in the Hebrew Bible: A Consideration of Language' (2005), and 'Marla, Freud, Religion and Manhood: An Interpretation of David Fincher's *Fight Club*' (2002).

Susan E. Haddox is Associate Professor of Philosophy and Religious Studies at University of Mount Union in Alliance, Ohio. Her research focuses on gender issues in the biblical texts, with particular emphasis on masculinity studies. Her publications include *Metaphor and Masculinity in Hosea* (2011), 'The Lord is with You, You Mighty Warrior: The Question of Gideon's Masculinity' (2010), 'Favoured Sons and Subordinate Masculinities' (2010), and '(E)masculinity in Hosea's Political Rhetoric' (2006).

Julie Kelso is Assistant Professor of Philosophy and Literature at Bond University and Honorary Research Adviser (Women's Studies) in the School of English, Media Studies, and Art History at the University of Queensland. Her publications include *O Mother Where Art Thou: An Irigarayan Reading of the Book of Chronicles* (2007), three co-edited collections, along with numerous essays in feminist philosophy, biblical and literary studies. She is co-managing editor (with Roland Boer) of the journal *The Bible and Critical Theory*.

Helen Leneman obtained her Ph.D. in Biblical Studies from the University of Amsterdam, under the direction of Athalya Brenner. As well as being a biblical scholar, she is a professional singer and pianist. She combines her expertise in music with her research on the Bible. Among her publications are 'Moses and the Exodus in Italian Opera' (2012); *Love, Lust and Lunacy: The Stories of Saul and David in Music* (2010); 'More than the Love of Men: Ruth and Naomi's story in Music' (2010); 'From Scroll to Stage: The Story of Ruth in Cantillation and Opera' (2008); *The Performed Bible: The Story of Ruth in Opera and Oratorio* (2007); 'Re-visioning a Biblical Story through Libretto and Music: *Debora e Jaele* by Ildebrando Pizzetti' (2007).

Lai Ling Elizabeth Ngan is Associate Professor of Christian Scriptures at George W. Truett Theological Seminary at Baylor University in Waco, Texas. Her research focuses on Asian American Feminist Biblical Hermeneutics in the Hebrew Bible, Contextual Reading of Biblical Women's Stories through Immigrant Experiences, and Social Justice as Proclamation and Praxis. Among her publications are 'Until Everyone Has a Place under the Sun' (2009); 'Bitter Melon, Bitter Delight: Reading Jeremiah Reading Me' (2007); 'Neither Here nor There: Boundary and Identity in the Hagar Story' (2006).

Carleen Mandolfo is Associate Professor of Religious Studies at Colby College in Maine. Her research focuses on feminist hermeneutics, dialogic biblical theology, and Lament literature of the Hebrew Bible. She has authored or edited several articles, monographs, and anthologies in these areas, including *Lamentations in Ancient and Contemporary Cultural Contexts* (edited, 2008); *Daughter Zion Talks Back to the Prophets: A Dialogic Theology of the Book of Lamentations* (2007); and *God in the Dock: Dialogic Tension in the Psalms of Lament* (2002).

Madipoane Masenya (ngwan'a Mphahlele) is Professor at the University of South Africa. Her scholarly research focuses on the Old Testament and contextual concerns affecting Africa, wisdom literature, and womanist/

feminist/mujerista hermeneutics. Among her publications are 'Is Ruth the *'ēšet ḥayil* for Real? An Exploration of Womanhood from African Proverbs to the Threshing Floor (Ruth 3:1-13)' (2010); 'Women, Africana Reality, and the Bible' (2010); *How Worthy Is the Woman of Worth? Rereading Proverbs 31:10-31 in African-South Africa* (2004); *African Women, HIV/AIDS and Faith Communities* (co-edited, 2003).

Julie Faith Parker earned her doctorate in Hebrew Bible at Yale University and is a Visiting Professor at Andover Newton Theological School in Newton Centre, Massachusetts. Her research focuses on Feminist Interpretation, Ancient Near Eastern Languages and Cultures, and Childist Interpretation. Among her publications are *Valuable and Vulnerable: Children in the Hebrew Bible, especially the Elisha Cycle* (2013); 'Blaming Eve Alone: Translation, Omission and Implications of *'immah* in Genesis 3:6b' (2013); 'You Are a Bible Child: Exploring the Lives of Children and Mothers through the Elisha Cycle' (2009); and 'Women Warriors and Devoted Daughters: The Powerful Young Woman in Ugaritic Narrative Poetry' (2008).

Susanne Scholz is Associate Professor of Old Testament at Perkins School of Theology at Southern Methodist University in Dallas, Texas. Her research focuses on Feminist Biblical Hermeneutics, Epistemologies and Sociologies of Biblical Interpretation, and Cultural and Literary Methodologies. Among her publications are *God Loves Diversity and Justice: Progressive Scholars Speak about Faith, Politics, and the World* (editor, 2013); S*acred Witness: Rape in the Hebrew Bible* (2010); *Introducing the Women's Hebrew Bible* (2007); *Biblical Studies Alternatively: An Introductory Reader* (editor, 2003); *Zwischen-Räume: Deutsche feministische Theologinnen im Ausland* (co-editor, 2000); *Rape Plots: A Feminist Cultural Study of Genesis 34* (2000).

Yael Shemesh is a senior lecturer in Bible at Bar-Ilan University in Ramat-Gan, Israel. Her research focuses on the poetics of biblical narrative, prophetic stories, feminist interpretation of the Bible, and animal ethics. Among her publications are: 'Jephthah: Victimizer and Victim: A Comparison of Jephthah and Characters in Genesis' (2011); 'And Many Beasts (Jonah 4:11): The Function and Status of Animals in the Book of Jonah' (2010); 'A Gender Perspective on the Daughters of Zelophehad: Bible, Talmudic Midrash, and Modern Feminist Midrash' (2007); 'Rape Is Rape Is Rape: The Story of Dinah and Shechem (Genesis 34)' (2007).

Beverly J. Stratton is Professor of Religion at Augsburg College in Minneapolis, Minnesota, where she recently directed the first-year transition program. Her current interests include experiential education, interfaith understanding, wellness in the workplace, positive psychology, the life and ministry of Oscar Romero, and learning through hybrid courses. Among her publications are 'The Word on Sex: Biblical Interpretation on the Web and Constructed Realities' (2002), 'Ideology' (2000), 'God Reviewed: Some Feminist Perspectives on God in the Bible' (1998), 'Here We Stand: Lutheran and Feminist Issues in Biblical Interpretation' (1997), and *Out of Eden: Reading, Rhetoric, and Ideology in Genesis 2–3* (1995).

David M. Valeta is Instructor in Religious Studies at the University of Colorado, Boulder. His research focuses on the book of Daniel, Apocalyptic Literature, Resistance against Imperialism in the Ancient World, and Humor and Satire in Religious Traditions. Among his publications are 'Court Tales' (2012); 'Daniel: Piety, Politics and Perseverance' (2010); *Lions and Ovens and Visions: A Satirical Reading of Daniel 1–6* (2008); 'Recent Research in Daniel 1–6' (2008); 'Polyglossia and Parody: Language in Daniel 1–6' (2007); 'The Satirical Nature of the Book of Daniel' (2003).

INTRODUCTION:
THE PAST, THE PRESENT, AND THE FUTURE OF FEMINIST HEBREW BIBLE INTERPRETATION

Susanne Scholz

This volume, presenting fourteen essays that examine feminist scholarship on the Hebrew Bible, pursues what Esther Fuchs calls the centripetal approach of feminist biblical studies.[1] It presupposes feminist biblical studies as a coherent academic field and works within disciplinary boundaries. It gathers, reviews, and evaluates the past, present, and future of the field. Hence, the contributions of this book clarify the foundations of the field, they establish genealogies of knowledge and an evolutionary trajectory, and they credit and acknowledge theoretical points of origination. Conceptualized as a retrospective on feminist interpretations, this book synthesizes, organizes, and classifies selectively though representatively what feminist scholars have done so far and it ponders what they might want to do next when they read the Hebrew Bible. As Fuchs states eloquently, the goal of the centripetal approach is to contribute to 'laying the foundations of a genuinely autonomous field of [feminist biblical] studies' and 'to reshape the future of Biblical Studies as a whole'.[2]

Of course, Fuchs rightly asserts that both the centripetal and the centrifugal approaches of analysis are necessary to reach this goal. Yet this book focuses on the former only, and so it does not deconstruct the field as such. It also does not look for heterogeneity and plurality, and it does not aim to move the feminist hermeneutical conversation toward an integrated conversation with other biblical academic discourses, such as queer, masculinity, or postcolonial studies. The other two volumes in this series will explore the relationship between feminist biblical hermeneutics and social location as well as methodologies, and will pursue these issues with more vigor. Thus, together the three volumes will contribute toward the overall development of feminist biblical studies as an autonomous field and challenge biblical studies to make the work of feminist biblical hermeneutics more central than

---

1. Esther Fuchs, 'Biblical Feminisms: Knowledge, Theory and Politics in the Study of Women in the Hebrew Bible', *BibInt* 16 (2008), pp. 205-26 (207).
2. Fuchs, 'Biblical Feminisms', p. 224.

it currently is. Thus the present volume, pursuing the centripetal approach, ought to be viewed as a *Bestandsaufnahme*. It describes, discusses, and assesses the impressive record of feminist Hebrew Bible interpretation of the past forty years or so.

A Success Story

It is amazing to realize that the field of feminist biblical studies has such a short history. Although there were antecedents, none of them made in-roads into academia as those accomplished since the 1970s. The success story of feminist biblical studies can certainly not only be attributed to the persistence of individual scholars and their commitments to feminist biblical hermeneutics. For sure, it must be related to the grassroots-based and globally evolving movements of feminism that had sprung up nurturing 'women's liberation' in various ways, forms, and venues,[3] and several decades later feminist biblical scholarship abounds. The same cannot necessarily be said about employment opportunities in colleges, universities, and seminaries. It is the rare teaching and research position that invites feminist Bible scholars to apply. Furthermore, today's biblical studies curriculum is not exactly informed by feminist perspectives and research, and instead an add-on approach often prevails. It should also come as no surprise that most students, entering our academic Bible classrooms, have not usually heard of feminist biblical studies. After about forty years institutional, disciplinary, and curricular deserts surround us still, and we cannot take for granted the accomplishments of feminist scholarship anywhere.

Thus, without a doubt, the feminist movement of the 1960s and 1970s provided the nurturing background for the rise of feminist biblical studies. Several feminist Bible scholars of the pioneering generation have reminisced about the impact of the larger social movements on the development of feminist biblical exegesis. Kathleen M. O'Connor, professor of Old Testament at Columbia Theological Seminary, explains in 2006: 'Feminist ideas broke in upon us all as a troubling disruption of the way things were and as an exhilarating revelation of how they might be... They stirred up vital energy to work for the well-being of future generations, and ultimately for the earth itself.'[4] Similarly, Phyllis Bird, professor emerita of Old Testament

---

3. For a powerful description of this connection, see Beverly Wilding Harrison, 'Feminist Thea(o)logies at the Millennium: "Messy" Continued Resistance or Surrender to Post-Modern Academic Culture?', in Margaret A. Farley and Seren Jones (eds.), *Liberating Eschatology: Essays in Honor of Letty M. Russell* (Louisville, KY: Westminster/John Knox Press, 1999), pp. 156-71.

4. Kathleen M. O'Connor, 'The Feminist Movement Meets the Old Testament: One Woman's Perspective', in Linda Day and Carolyn Pressler (eds.), *Engaging the Bible in a*

at Garrett-Evangelical Theological Seminary, acknowledges the far-reaching effects of the 1960s and 1970s on feminist biblical work when she explains:

> The women's movement of the seventies and eighties has affected us all, male and female. We have been led in directions we never planned to go, and we have arrived at places we could not have imagined when we began our journeys... It was an exciting time of discovery as we explored a largely unknown past, attempting to disentangle it from an interpretive legacy of narrow and oppressive stereotypes.[5]

And New Testament professor at the Harvard Divinity School, Elisabeth Schüssler Fiorenza, connects comprehensively the social justice movements of the Civil Rights Era and the emergence of feminist scholarship when she explains:

> The resurgence of the women's movement in the 1960s not only revived women's political struggle for civil rights and equal access to academic institutions but also brought forth feminist studies as a new intellectual discipline. In all areas of scientific and intellectual knowledge there now exist courses and research projects that seek to expand our knowledge of women's cultural and historical contributions as well as to challenge the silence about us in historiography, literature, sociology, and all the human sciences. Such feminist scholarship is compensatory as well as revolutionary. It has inaugurated a scientific revolution that engenders a scholarly paradigm shift from an androcentric—male-centered—world view and perspective to an inclusive feminist comprehension of the world, human life, and history.[6]

Back in the Day...

The confluence of the Civil Rights and feminist movements of the 1960s in the United States, then, helped in bringing forth feminist biblical studies.[7] Although it began in the United States, it has since spun into many regions in the world.[8] Yet it took courageous young women scholars to organize

---

Gendered World: An Introduction to Feminist Biblical Interpretation in Honor of Katharine Doob Sakenfeld (Louisville, KY: Westminster/John Knox Press, 2006), pp. 3-24 (3).

5. Phyllis A. Bird, 'Preface', in *Missing Persons and Mistaken Identities: Women and Gender in Ancient Israel* (Minneapolis: Fortress Press, 1997), pp. 1-10 (3, 4).

6. Elisabeth Schüssler Fiorenza, *Bread Not Stone: The Challenge of Feminist Biblical Interpretation* (Boston: Beacon Press, 1984), p. 2.

7. See also the influential works of Mary Daly, *The Church and the Second Sex* (New York: Knopf, 1968); Daly, *Beyond God the Father: Toward a Philosophy of Women's Liberation* (Boston: Beacon Press, 1973).

8. See, e.g., Kyung Sook Lee and Kyung Mi Park (eds.), *Korean Feminists in Conversation with the Bible, Church and Society* (Sheffield: Sheffield Phoenix Press, 2011); Lung Kwong Lo (ed.), *Crossing Textual Boundaries: A Festschrift in Honor of Professor Archie Chi Chung Lee for his Sixtieth Birthday* (Hong Kong: The Divinity

themselves during the 1971 Annual Meeting of two major professional societies, the American Academy of Religion (AAR) and the Society for Biblical Literature (SBL). Up to this time very few women had been admitted into the ranks of biblical scholarship, and those who had become professors labored on the margins of scholarly discourse, as a cursory look at the membership roster of the Society of Biblical Literature illustrates.[9] As published notes on the 1971 gathering indicate, the goal of the women scholars was to establish 'a women's caucus in the field and to demand that program time be allotted to papers and panels on women and religion'.[10] Rita Gross, a professor of comparative religion, remembers:

> That meeting, which occurred in November in Atlanta, was probably the single most generative event of the feminist transformation of religious studies. Before the meeting, isolated, relatively young and unestablished scholars struggled to define what it meant to study women and religion and to demonstrate why it was so important to do so. After the meeting, a strong network of like-minded individuals had been established, and we had begun to make our presence and our agenda known to the AAR and the SBL.[11]

At that very meeting the AAR/SBL Women's Caucus was founded and two chairs were elected: Carol Christ, who become renowned for her work on goddess religions, and Elisabeth Schüssler Fiorenza, who in 1987 became the first woman president of the Society of Biblical Literature.[12]

School of Chung Chi College, 2010); Yeong Mee Lee and Yoon Jong Yoo (eds.), *Mapping and Engaging the Bible in Asian Cultures: Congress of the Society of Asian Biblical Studies 2008 Seoul Conference* (Korea: Christian Literature Society of Korea, 2009); Gerald O. West and Musa W. Dube (eds.), *The Bible in Africa: Transactions, Trajectories and Trends* (Boston/Leiden: Brill Academic Publishers, 2001); Musa W. Dube (ed.), *Other Ways of Reading: African Women and the Bible* (Atlanta: Society of Biblical Literature; Geneva: WCC Publications, 2001).

9.   See Dorothy C. Bass, 'Women's Studies and Biblical Studies', *JSOT* 22 (1982), pp. 6-12 (9): 'Similar growth between 1910 and 1920 brought women's membership to twenty-four in a total of 231, better than ten per cent... After 1920, however, the figures began to slip. In 1930, women were at approximately eight per cent; in 1940, about six per cent; and in 1950, five per cent. Figures are missing for 1960, but by 1970 women were only three and one-half per cent of SBL members.'

10.   Rita Gross, *Feminism and Religion: An Introduction* (Boston: Beacon Press, 1996), p. 46.

11.   Gross, *Feminism and* Religion, p. 47.

12.   Today, only four additional women scholars have served as SBL presidents: Phyllis Trible in 1994, Adele Berlin in 2000, Carolyn Osiek in 2005, and Katherine Doob Sakenfeld in 2007. Patrick Gray calls the SBL 'an exclusive fraternity' and finds this 'not a wholly inappropriate term' despite the service of several women presidents since its founding in 1880; see Patrick Gray, 'Presidential Addresses of the Society of Biblical Literature: A Quasquicentennial Review', *JBL* 125 (2006), pp. 167-77 (167).

The creation of a feminist infrastructure at the scholarly level helped to gather momentum on the feminist hermeneutical level. In 1973, Phyllis Trible published an article entitled 'Depatriarchalizing in Biblical Interpretation'[13] in which she acknowledges a 'terrible dilemma'[14] posed by the feminist movement: to choose between 'the God of the fathers or the God of sisterhood'.[15] Trible considers this choice to be a false dichotomy. To her, the Bible is not irredeemably patriarchal,[16] and so she asserts: 'The Women's Movement errs when it dismisses the Bible as inconsequential or condemns it as enslaving. In rejecting Scripture women ironically accept male chauvinistic interpretations and thereby capitulate to the very view they are protesting.'[17] Instead, in her view, 'the Hebrew Scriptures and Women's Liberation do meet and...their encounter need not be hostile'.[18] She also warned that feminist Bible readers are 'unfaithful readers' if they do not apply 'the depatriarchalizing principle and recover it in those texts and themes where it is present, and...accent it in our translation'.[19] Otherwise, she warns, they 'neglect biblical passages which break with patriarchy'[20] and permit 'interpretations to freeze in a patriarchal box of our own construction'.[21]

Other feminist scholars also produced pioneering work. In 1974, Rosemary Radford Ruether, at the time professor at Garrett-Evangelical Seminary, edited a highly influential anthology entitled *Religion and Sexism: Images of Women in the Jewish and Christian Traditions*.[22] The volume includes one article on the Hebrew Bible by Phyllis Bird and another on the New Testament by Constance F. Parvey.[23] Bird presents a reading of Genesis 1–3

13. Phyllis Trible, 'Depatriarchalizing in Biblical Interpretation', *JAAR* 41 (March 1973), pp. 30-48.

14. Trible, 'Depatriarchalizing', p. 30.

15. Trible, 'Depatriarchalizing', p. 31.

16. Trible, 'Depatriarchalizing', p. 31.

17. Trible, 'Depatriarchalizing', p. 31.

18. Trible, 'Depatriarchalizing', p. 47.

19. Trible's proposal created important inner-feminist biblical critique; see, e.g., Nancy Fuchs-Kreimer, 'Feminism and Scripture Interpretation: A Contemporary Jewish Critique', *Journal of Ecumenical Studies* 20 (1988), pp. 539-41; Elisabeth Schüssler Fiorenza, *But She Said: Feminist Practices of Biblical Interpretation* (Boston: Beacon Press, 1992), pp. 21-24.

20. Trible, 'Depatriarchalizing', p. 48.

21. Trible, 'Depatriarchalizing', p. 48.

22. Rosemary Radford Ruether (ed.), *Religion and Sexism: Images of Women in the Jewish and Christian Traditions* (New York: Simon & Schuster, 1974).

23. Phyllis Bird, 'Images of the Women in the Old Testament', and Constance F. Parvey, 'The Theology and Leadership of Women in the New Testament', in Ruether (ed.), *Religion and Sexism*, pp. 41-88 and 117-49, respectively. For yet another influential early feminist interpretation, see Phyllis Trible, 'Eve and Adam: Genesis 2–3 Reread', *Andover Newton Quarterly* (March 1973), pp. 251-58.

that assesses the biblical creation narratives from a feminist perspective grounded in historical criticism. According to Bird, the first story portrays humanity—female and male—with its biological functions as divinely created in the image of God. The second narrative stresses psychosocial rather than biological functions of women and men in ancient Israelite society. Bird's interpretation highlights gender with the aim of challenging essentialized meanings attributed to the biblical creation texts in Western society.

In her article Constance F. Parvey examines 'how the early Church embodied theologically and socially different attitudes toward women as a consequence of Jesus' coming'.[24] She asserts that '[i]n contrast to Judaism, the Greco-Roman religions were more open to the participation of women'.[25] Parvey also suggests that the Apostle Paul made 'a fundamental break-through in new images for women'[26] when he allowed 'a primary place for the participation of women'.[27] She finds a similar attitude in the gospel of Luke which, in her view, prescribed a 'dramatic new role for women'.[28] Thus, to her, early Christian attitudes toward women stood in line with contemporary feminist sensibilities but contrasted with Jewish practices at the time.

We should note that feminist New Testament scholars criticize this kind of historical analysis for its anti-Jewish stereotypes.[29] In 1983, Elisabeth Schüssler Fiorenza urges feminist Christian historians to identify egalitarian impulses within first-century Judaism to make the Jesus movement as 'the discipleship of equals...historically plausible'.[30] Schüssler Fiorenza maintains that '[w]omen as the *ekklēsia* of God have a continuous history that can claim women in Judaism, as well as in the Jesus and the early Christian movements, as its roots and beginnings. This history of women as the people of God must be exposed as a history of oppression as well as a history of conversion and liberation.'[31] The fact that feminist scholars advise not to reconstruct women's lives in the first century with a competitive model—as if the emerging Christian movement stood above Judaism—recognizes the strength of Judaism. The argument also maintains that an inclusive paradigm

    24. Parvey, 'Theology and Leadership', pp. 117-18.
    25. Parvey, 'Theology and Leadership', p. 121.
    26. Parvey, 'Theology and Leadership', p. 128.
    27. Parvey, 'Theology and Leadership', p. 132.
    28. Parvey, 'Theology and Leadership', p. 137.
    29. See, e.g., Judith Plaskow, 'Christian Feminism and Anti-Judaism', *Cross Currents* 28 (1978), pp. 306-309; Bernadette Brooten, 'Jüdinnen zur Zeit Jesu: Ein Plädoyer für Differenzierung', *Theologische Quartalschrift* 161.4 (1981), pp. 280-85.
    30. Elisabeth Schüssler Fiorenza, *In Memory of Her: A Feminist Theological Reconstruction of Christian Origins* (New York: Crossroad, 1983), p. 107.
    31. Schüssler Fiorenza, *In Memory of Her*, p. 350.

is better suited to describe the complex interactions of first-century women in society and religion than a Christian supersessionist model.[32] At the end of the 1970s, then, the feminist study of biblical literature in North America had burst onto the scholarly scene, tackling old and new controversies. Although there still exist many biblical scholars, classrooms, and institutions ignoring this development, this volume systematizes the countless publications, arguments, and insights as they have emerged from one of the most important scholarly innovations produced within biblical studies during the past forty years.

Surveying, Assessing, and Creating Visibility

It is interesting to note that some biblical books have received more extensive feminist treatment than others. The resulting imbalance has contributed to understanding the directions, interests, and concerns in feminist exegesis so far. For instance, biblical books filled with narratives on women have fared much better than terse poetry without any female characters or images. As a result, the book of Judges has received much more feminist attention than Qohelet or Chronicles. Other examples could be easily added. The book of Joshua is another case that has attracted only timid feminist engagement. Yet even when little feminist scholarship exists for certain biblical books, this exegetical situation does not mean that contributors to this volume have nothing to say about the particular biblical texts under consideration. On the contrary, a few feminist publications are always available, inviting reflection on possible reasons for the feminist omission. Thus, even when feminist engagement has been sparse in one area, and certainly when it has been plentiful in others, all essays gathered here present substantial yet easily digestible reviews on trends, preferences, and perspectives in feminist interpretation of the Hebrew Bible.

A note of caution: The Apocrypha, except for Susannah and Judith, are not included in this survey mainly for space reasons, general disciplinary marginalization in Hebrew Bible studies, and relative neglect in feminist exegesis. It also needs to be said that several essays discuss more than one biblical book. This approach has enabled a chapter-length analysis of the existing feminist literature on the biblical canon. For instance, the essays on the legal texts in Exodus to Deuteronomy, the major and minor prophets, and the books of Ezra, Nehemiah, and Chronicles make important links between the selected biblical books that a different organizational structure might not have facilitated so readily.

32. Supersessionism comes from the verb 'supersede' and refers to the Christian theological notion that Christianity (the 'Church') replaced Judaism ('Israel').

Each essay, then, provides a basic understanding of critical issues and questions raised by the existing feminist work and each chapter also offers suggestions for future feminist engagement. The contributions demonstrate that feminist readings on the Hebrew Bible are not monolithic and isolated instances of biblical exegesis but embedded in a wide range of feminist approaches, hermeneutics, and methods. The essays examine the scholarly discussions, organizing them by biblical books or by topics. Although each essay cannot reasonably deal with every feminist exegetical publication produced during the past few decades, each includes important, illustrative, and well-known and lesser-known scholarship so that the review is relevant, substantive, and comprehensible. Importantly, all contributions conceptualize the adjective 'feminist' in a broad sense to include queer readings as well as postcolonial and ethnic perspectives, although not every essay includes such work depending on the existing feminist discussion on the biblical book under consideration.

What the volume as a whole makes overwhelmingly evident is the fact that, so far, most feminist interpretations focus on female characters and imagery. Clearly, then, feminist exegesis will greatly benefit from the ongoing broadening efforts already under way so that intersectional studies that relate 'women' and gender to other socio-political categories of analysis will soon be second nature to feminist exegesis. The analysis of the feminist works on each biblical book makes another matter obvious. Again, Esther Fuchs says it best when she urges for more theoretical reflection in feminist biblical work. She summons feminist Bible scholars to build up the field's theoretical sophistication and conceptual analysis of the knowledge feminist biblical scholarship produces. The discussions gathered in this volume prove her right, as the general lack of theory in feminist exegesis stands in sharp contrast to, for instance, women's and gender studies.[33] Hence, most feminist exegesis does not usually ask meta-level questions. For the most part, feminist interpreters are content to reconstruct their versions of the historical realities behind the text or they explore the literary meanings of the text itself, and only sometimes do they regard the text as a cultural or political/ideological object of inquiry into the construction of 'women' today. In general, then, feminist exegetes simply present their interpretations, whether they are historical, literary, cultural, or a mixture of these approaches, without self-reflective and meta-level interrogations into the research procedures and implied epistemological and political research procedures. The call for theoretical reflection by other feminist scholars, such as Elizabeth Schüssler Fiorenza, go relatively unheard when feminist exegetes

---

33. Fuchs, 'Biblical Feminisms', p. 206.

deal with particular biblical texts.[34] Thus, rarely do feminist Bible scholars reflect on why we do what we do and how we do it. Hence, none of the studies included in this volume are able to refer to a particular biblical book, be it Genesis, Jeremiah, or Job, and answer the questions Fuchs is raising: 'What is a feminist approach to the Bible? What is the difference that a feminist approach makes? What are the major theoretical debates in the field? Is there more than one approach, and if so what is the relationship between the various approaches?'[35]

About Miracles, Integrity, and a Vibrant Future

It is obvious, then, that the field of feminist Hebrew Bible studies has not yet reached this theoretical-feminist paradise. In fact, the field has barely moved out of its 'foundational' phase, which consists of a text-focused approach limited by institutional location and the confining politics of epistemology, methodology, and hermeneutics.[36] In addition, feminist Bible exegesis is 'still marginal within the field at large'.[37] Unsurprisingly, then, we learn from the discussions in this book that feminists are still largely aiming to establish an often singularly defined biblical meaning, to historicize women's lives in ancient Israel, and to redeem biblical texts from the androcentric histories of interpretation. Importantly, we learn that there is still little dialog among the various feminist interpretations. For instance, little dialogical effort is made in negotiating the various historical reconstructions about ancient Israelite women's lives. The same is true for literary-symbolic interpretations on the so-called marriage metaphor. The various proposals stand side by side awaiting further evaluative discussion in feminist biblical studies. There are also few cross-cultural conversations going on, for instance, regarding the oppositional feminist readings of the book of Ruth. The essays of this volume indicate further that gender-essentializing interpretations continue to be produced in considerable numbers and intersectional interpretations on gender, sexuality, race, class, or geopolitics are still sparse.

34. See, e.g., Elisabeth Schüssler Fiorenza, *The Power of the Word: Scripture and the Rhetoric of Empire* (Minneapolis: Augsburg Fortress, 2007); *Democratizing Biblical Studies: Toward an Emancipatory Educational Space* (Louisville, KY: Westminster/John Knox Press, 2009). See also, e.g., Stephen D. Moore and Yvonne Sherwood, *The Invention of the Biblical Scholar: A Critical Manifesto* (Minneapolis: Fortress Press, 2011).

35. Fuchs, 'Biblical Feminisms', p. 206.

36. Some work does exist; see most recently, e.g., Deryn Guest, *Beyond Feminist Biblical Studies* (Sheffield: Sheffield Phoenix Press, 2012). However, in fairness it must be noted that such work does not usually connect the theoretical deliberations to specific biblical texts, and so they cannot be taken into account in this volume, which examines feminist biblical interpretations on particular biblical books.

37. Fuchs, 'Biblical Feminisms', p. 221.

This last comment is, of course, not meant as criticism but merely as an observation about the state of much of feminist biblical work today. As Deryn Guest puts it: 'I am calling upon feminist biblical scholars to tool up and become even more expansively theory-rich, able to bring the critical studies of masculinities, queer studies, trans studies, intersex studies, and lesbian and gay studies into negotiation with feminist theory without neces-sarily privileging what have been, to date, stalwart feminist positions'.[38] Without a doubt, we are still at the very beginning when it comes to feminist scholarship on the Hebrew Bible. Very few endowed research chairs for feminist biblical exegesis currently exist, and sometimes it seems that institutional support is progressively decreasing rather than increasing. Feminists do not usually hold institutional power whether in biblical studies or anywhere else in contemporary colleges and universities. In fact, the humanities as a whole are under considerable attack by various forces of corporate power and educational elites.[39] These are some of the reasons why feminist Bible scholars cannot always do what feminist Bible theorist, Esther Fuchs, advises us to do: 'We should rather strive to maintain the integrity of our courses as apparently marginal points of entry into the very heart of Biblical Studies and the theories that currently shape it'.[40] More often than not, we need to compromise to keep our teaching positions or to get our work published, so it seems. Still, it is a miracle what feminist biblical scholars have accomplished in only forty years. This volume contributes to the effort of making visible their work, exploring the range and depth of feminist exegetical scholarship thus far, and recapturing the early optimistic spirit in feminist work that regarded biblical interpretations as part of the larger justice movements in the world.

38. Deryn Guest, *Beyond Feminist Biblical Studies* (Sheffield: Sheffield Phoenix Press, 2012), p. 150.

39. For an exploration of this topic, see, e.g., Susanne Scholz, 'Occupy Academic Bible Teaching: The Architecture of Educational Power and the Biblical Studies Curricu-lum', in Jane S. Webster and Glenn S. Holland (eds.), *Teaching the Bible in the Liberal Arts Context* (Sheffield: Sheffield Phoenix Press, 2012), pp. 28-43.

40. Fuchs, 'Biblical Feminisms', p. 224.

1

GENEALOGIES OF FEMINIST BIBLICAL STUDIES:
AN INTERVIEW REPORT FROM THE 1970S' GENERATION[*]

Helen Leneman

Feminist biblical scholarship emerged in the late twentieth century with strong roots in the Second Women's movement, itself an outgrowth of the Civil Rights movement. It has to be considered a parallel development to the First Women's movement which originated in the abolitionist and suffrage movements during the nineteenth century. The Second Feminist movement began in the United States with the publication of Betty Friedan's ground-breaking *The Feminine Mystique* in 1963.[1] Biblical scholars began to absorb ideas from this feminist movement in the 1970s, starting with Rosemary Radford Ruether's influential anthology *Religion and Sexism* in 1974.[2] The volume included several essays on women in the Bible. Yet the roots of feminist biblical interpretation are even older and go back to the European Enlightenment, which influenced the nineteenth-century women's suffrage movement in the United States and also overlapped with the emancipation struggles of slaves.[3] The SBL (Society of Biblical Literature), the 'establishment' of biblical scholarship, only allowed the admission of women 15 years after the founding of the society in 1880. Even when women joined and became more active, in the first half of the twentieth century they did not address gender issues. These women may have been active in women's causes, but in their role as biblical scholars they 'dealt with more "acceptable" topics'.[4]

---

* The interviews discussed in this essay took place in 2006 and 2007.
1. Betty Frieden, *The Feminist Mystique* (New York: W.W. Norton, 1963).
2. Rosemary Radford Ruether (ed.), *Religion and Sexism* (New York: Simon & Schuster, 1974).
3. Alice Ogden Bellis, 'Feminist Biblical Scholarship', in Carol Meyers (ed.), *Women in Scripture* (Grand Rapids, MI: Eerdmans, 2001), pp. 24-32 (24).
4. Bellis, 'Feminist Biblical Scholarship', p. 25.

The following presents selections from interviews with several feminist Hebrew Bible scholars, all of whom were influenced by the Second Women's movement and its writings. Some of them discovered their feminist consciousness after entering the field of biblical studies. Others became interested in biblical scholarship because of their feminism. Hence, this chapter does not discuss feminist theory or ideas but it explores what made these scholars pioneers in feminist biblical studies. At the time, there were no feminist biblical scholars who served as role models, and so how did a handful of women scholars become the first role models for themselves? How and why does anyone become a 'first'? There are some commonalities in the stories presented here, some intersecting lines, but for the most part these women arrived at a similar place despite different paths. I included scholars who began exploring feminist approaches to the Hebrew Bible, formally or informally, during the 1970s or early 1980s. These scholars continued working in the field at least into the late 1990s.

It is worth noting that there have been two 'waves' of feminist biblical studies. The feminist scholars interviewed here represent the first wave, which began in the 1970s and laid the groundwork for later studies. They are: Phyllis Bird, Esther Fuchs, Carol Meyers, and Katherine Doob Sakenfeld. Phyllis Trible, an important member of this wave, was not available for the interview.[5] The scholars of the second wave, characteristic of the 1980s and into the early 1990s, are: Mieke Bal, Athalya Brenner, Claudia Camp, Toni Craven, Danna Fewell, and Carole Fontaine. Cheryl Exum, a key member of this wave, was unavailable. I am grateful to all of these scholars for generously giving of their time to share stories. We corresponded either in writing or in personal interviews. I regret that much of what they said or wrote is not included, primarily due to space limitations. I apologize for leaving out any scholars who should have been included, but for one reason or another are not.

To begin, I asked a broad introductory question: What was it like to be a 'pioneer' and to write about a subject that no one had yet explored? Phyllis Bird describes it this way:

> My generation—the first generation of female/feminist biblical scholars—invented and discovered feminist biblical scholarship as we entered into the profession. We were educating ourselves as we explored the meaning of feminism in our own lives, work environments, and disciplines. We learned along with our students, spouses of male colleagues, and women in other disciplines what feminism implied—out of solidarity with academic and non-academic feminists and out of pain at the insensitivity, resistance, and incomprehension of male friends and colleagues.

---

5. For a brief discussion of her life and work as a feminist scholar, see Susanne Scholz, *Introducing the Women's Hebrew Bible* (London: T. & T. Clark, 2007), pp. 34-40.

There was no 'feminist interpretation' out there to react to. A first move, especially by lay women, was an attempt to find foremothers—and one of the reasons that some of us began exploring the realm of women in scripture was the recognition that the work of the foremothers [like Deen's *All of the Women of the Bible*] needed to be updated and corrected using the tools of modern biblical scholarship. So we were learning and creating at the same time.

Katherine Doob Sakenfeld relates the following anecdote:

My senior year in seminary, guys would say I couldn't be in the PhD program because I wasn't strong enough to carry all the books, and on the path I'd have to walk there was always a puddle and my legs weren't long enough to jump over it. The guys were teasing but it didn't even occur to me that it might not be funny.

In a metaphoric sense, then, Bird and Sakenfeld discovered that they had the necessary strength to carry their books and complete their studies, and to jump over any puddle—or other hurdle—that was in their way. They may have gotten their feet wet, but they all reached the other side. In this chapter, they relate their journeys.

The Interviews: Perspectives and Insights from Feminist Hebrew Bible Scholars

When I contacted the selected feminist Hebrew Bible scholars, I asked two sets of questions that structure the following analysis. The first set of questions centers on the biographical and scholarly connections; the second set of questions focuses on the developments of feminist Hebrew Bible studies. I asked each scholar these questions: First, was there one transforming experience in your life that led you to explore this area of study, or did you become a feminist Bible scholar because of a series of circumstances? Second, what changes in the field have you seen since you started? Have you changed your position or methods over the years? How and why?

Question 1: Connections between Biography and Scholarship
The respondents had lots to say about the connection between biography and scholarship. Both first-wave and second-wave scholars differentiated between early life experiences and later teaching and writing opportunities to explain how they became interested in feminist Hebrew Bible work.

Feminist Hebrew Bible Scholars of the First Wave: Early Life Experiences. In answering the first question on the biographical connections to their interest in biblical studies, Phyllis Bird elaborates on the profound influence of her religious upbringing on all her later work:

I come from a family that is deeply religious, socialist, and pacifist who were deeply concerned with injustice. My history and experience are rather unusual for women in the field of Hebrew Bible. But it is important to stress that my feminism is a direct and necessary expression of the kind of Protestant Christian faith in which I was raised and which I claim. My feminism, in other words, is religiously motivated.

My parents did not give us Bible story books. My dad taught adult Bible class, but my parents were pacifists and didn't think David and his ilk were proper models. So I only came to the Bible as an adult, as something for adult readers. My father (as well as my mother, but especially my father as an intellectual) was a feminist before I was. He was intellectually committed to the full equality of women and always insisted that there should be no barriers to women's exercising their full God-given potential.

Katherine Doob Sakenfeld explains that her early interest in the Hebrew Bible was sparked by taking a Bible course in college:

In my first year in college, a Hebrew Bible course was required. My professor told the story of Micaiah ben Imlach (1 Kings 22), where Ahab and Jehoshaphat are together and the 400 prophets tell him to go ahead. The whole drama of the scene hooked me on Hebrew Bible. There are no women in the story, but it was one of the defining moments that made me think, 'Wow! I could spend a lot of time studying this part of the Bible'. It was not so much the material as the way this professor brought it to life.

The story is different for Esther Fuchs. Growing up in Israel, she rebelled against her secular upbringing by exploring Orthodoxy. Her disappointment in that movement dovetailed with a burgeoning feminist movement in Israel. It led her to embrace feminism and question many of her previous assumptions. Initially, Fuchs did not bring these new insights into biblical studies:

When I reached puberty I joined a religious nationalist youth group and began to follow some Orthodox rules of behavior, flouting the secular education I received. When I began studies at the Hebrew University, I also joined an Orthodox college for girls. I went there to understand traditional Judaism more deeply, but while the tools and interpretive skills I received there were invaluable (particularly in the area of biblical and Talmudic texts), I was disappointed with the repressive discipline and pressure to find a 'good match' and get married.

In the early 1970s, there were very few religious institutions that accommodated women who sought higher education in Jewish Studies, and I began to feel rather alienated in the environment that I initially sought out as a spiritual and intellectual home. My disappointment with this environment led me to begin reading feminist texts. A transformative event may have been the Yom Kippur War, which gave rise to a fledgling feminist movement in Israel. This movement questioned Jewish traditionalism, the conventions of 'familism' and the pressure to be married and reproduce. These criticisms made sense to me as a student activist at the Hebrew University. The discovery of feminism led me to question as well the religious right, the settlers' movement and the policy of occupation. You might say that I became radicalized during that period.

The situation for Carol Meyers was different again. She began her teaching career in the early years of the women's liberation movement, and eventually her interest in the Bible merged with the feminist approach as it became steadily more popular. So for her, it was a matter of being in the right place at the right time:

> Actually, there was no initial transformative experience. That is, it wasn't my idea to enter this field. The reality is that my move into feminist biblical study came from without, from the circumstances in my university in the mid-1970s when I began to teach at Duke. The social movement of the 1960s and 1970s, then called the women's liberation movement, was becoming manifest on many campuses. Faculty and students on many campuses, in response to the women's liberation movement and its call for change, began to develop courses that they hoped would generate new information about women and their role in cultures around the world—information deemed necessary for the desired social transformation, information that would fill the enormous gaps in our knowledge about women's lives, talents, potentials. The new knowledge would help to critique the systems that had limited women's choices.

Feminist Scholars of the Second Wave: Early Life Experiences. The connections between life and scholarly interest do not look much different for second-wave scholars. A strong correlation exists for Mieke Bal whose early experiences with biblical stories shaped her later feminist focus. She recounts how she developed a life-long fascination with the story of Joseph and Potiphar's wife through tales she heard as a child in the Netherlands:

> It was a winter afternoon in primary school, perhaps third or fourth grade. I attended a Catholic girls-only school in a predominantly Protestant village near Haarlem in the Netherlands. In the afternoon, when concentration is hard to muster, the classroom was hot, and many girls had trouble keeping their eyes open. Not me. Given my life-long obsession with narrative, it comes as no surprise to me, decades later, that I was an eager listener to the stories the schoolmistress used to recount. I think she told at least one story every few hours, often after the break or at the end of the day. At such sleep-inducing times of the day she dished up an incredible number of stories, the sole common feature of which was their baggage of moral lessons. We never read the Bible. Nevertheless, I think it was a form of religious education, with religion and ideology not very clearly distinguished. With my rather vivid imagination I tended to bring the stories to bear on my own life all the time.
>
> With the story of Potiphar's wife's wicked attempt at Joseph's virtue, this proved to be a bit difficult. Neither I nor, I expect, my classmates, had any education on matters sexual at the age of eight or nine. I even remember wondering what it was exactly that the woman wanted Joseph to do. But whatever it was, he didn't want to do it. And I understood that she insisted and

he fled. She, I never doubted that, was wicked. The heart of the story, of course, was her lie. This was what the teacher was trying to convey. Potiphar's wife lied, and as a result, he went to prison. The horror was obvious, translated into absolute silence while the teacher lowered her voice to a near-whisper, and somehow, I went home with the notion that women can be dangerous to men.

This was a point worth making. More often than not, stories about danger targeted men, cautionary tales of terror, concerned strangers offering candy only in order to abduct children, or bad men hidden in dark corners. Now, I learned, women could be dangerous as well. But strangely, in ways I did not understand, they were dangerous especially or exclusively to men.

These are my first memories of the story of Joseph and Potiphar's wife. I don't recall the precise story, but I know it was about a woman in whose house Joseph was working. He was in good standing; his master appreciated him a lot, and so did, in fact, his mistress. She wanted something from him that he didn't want to give her, and he was right in his refusal. I don't remember what I thought it was she wanted. She then trapped him, deceived her husband and Joseph went to jail. Luckily, and as a reward for his steadfastness, he went up from there like a comet because he was so good at explaining dreams. I tell this tale of getting to know the story, not to make this essay unnecessarily personal, but because I want to understand how books and lives hang together. By training, I am a literary scholar, and I love texts.

Then again, Danna Fewell had very different early encounters with the Bible. She grew up in the deep South of the United States and at an early age she began questioning the fundamentalist view of the Bible prevalent in that region of the country. She remembers:

Part and parcel of southern culture, religious billboards were as prevalent as traffic signs when I was growing up, and often just as directive. And some-times even the traffic signs themselves were enhanced with prophetic graffiti from some of the more evangelically inclined: STOP in the name of Jesus. YIELD to God's love. DO NOT ENTER this road leads to hell. Learning how to drive when I was sixteen was literally a religious experience. It was nothing to see road-side farm stands touting things like 'Jesus and Fresh Peaches Coming Soon'—probably an apt metaphor for the connection between our homegrown tomatoes and our homegrown religion. For anyone traveling on the highways, byways, or back roads, this was a good way to get a daily dose of devotion without ever having to open a Bible or darken the doors of a church.

When I was in the fourth grade, I had gotten in trouble at school for skipping choir rehearsal to play kiss chase outside with the boys. If that weren't bad enough, I lied to my mother about it. Now, *this* brought down divine wrath sure enough, and when the smoke from the fire and brimstone had cleared, I was told, 'You had better go read your Bible, young lady'. So I contritely retrieved the Bible my grandmother had given me when I was baptized, and I retired to a corner of the living room to serve my penance. There was just one problem. I didn't know where to start. So I started at the beginning.

I read. And I read. And I read. Do you know how far you have to read before you encounter anything that remotely suggests you shouldn't lie to your mother? I read story after story of all kinds of folks deceiving each other—Abraham lying about his wife being his sister, Jacob lying about being Esau, even God telling Moses to lie to Pharaoh—and they all seemed to get away with it just fine. I thought to myself, 'My mother doesn't know what's in this book. Or else she wouldn't want me to read it.' After a few more chapters I thought, 'Hmm, I don't think my Sunday school teacher knows what's in this book'. By the time I was half-way through, I was pretty convinced that my minister had never read it either, and that, for all I knew, I might be the only one in my church who had ever read this book at all. It was a moment of great liberation in which I, a sinning nine-year-old, had just taken one step back from the verge of eternal damnation with this major discovery: The Bible was anything but a book of instructions.

In addition to this precocious understanding of the Bible's limitations, Fewell experienced 'a pre-feminist rebellion' at the age of seventeen. She explains:

> The local church marquee read '*Great men criticize themselves*'. This mes-sage stayed up for months on end. What did great women do? I wondered. Did this church even know that great women existed? The sign became a source of increasing irritation as it stood there week after week, month after month excluding half the human race. *Great men criticize themselves*. Not half as much as I criticized that sign. Finally, one night the sign got altered mysteriously to read '*Great men circumcise themselves*'. I have no idea *how* such a spiteful thing could have happened... Unfortunately, religious readers in the South have rarely been close readers. The sign, with its scribal emenda-tion, stayed up for another several months without anyone ever noticing the difference.

Bal's and Fewell's experiences are not necessarily 'transforming', but they were surely influential ones. In my view, more truly transformative experiences tend to come later in life. This was the case for Toni Craven, who left her novitiate after being inspired to study Hebrew Bible by Phyllis Trible's teaching. She writes:

> A wonderful set of 'accidents' transformed the direction of my life. In 1970, I entered the Society of the Sacred Heart, a Roman Catholic community of women. In 1971, I began my year of novitiate in Boston (Newton Centre, actually), and as part of the requirements of that year, took two courses at Andover Newton Theological School, which I selected because it was within walking distance (so much for rigor in choice of programs!). I registered for 'Introduction to the Old Testament,' because I had always wanted to know something more about this literature. As it happened, Phyllis Trible came to ANTS that very year, and it was she who opened this amazing literature to me. Study with her was literally life changing for me.

In 1972, I left the Society of the Sacred Heart, enormously grateful to the Sisters for my novitiate in Boston and entirely clear that community life was not for me. I had found what I wanted in study of the Hebrew Bible. And when I finished my Master of Arts at ANTS, I continued my studies in Hebrew Bible at Vanderbilt University. It was Phyllis Trible who transformed my life, and from her I received a great gift, which has been and continues to be most precious. I found a teacher whose mentoring made a difference and an area of study that brought together my interests in artistry, faith, and literary study.

Hence, feminist Bible scholars of the second wave were already privileged with having feminist teachers. For some, they played a major role in moving toward the field. Danna Fewell also mentions Phyllis Trible as an important early influence for her work, stating:

In graduate school I was, like many others of my generation, affected profoundly by the work of Phyllis Trible. Not only did she model a meticulously close way of reading the text, she asked feminist questions that had not been typically allowed—or even imagined—in religious contexts or academic classrooms.

Yet for most interviewees, the interest in feminist studies grew out of a series of events, rather than one single transformative moment. The next set of responses relates to events that included first teaching assignments and writing requests. For some feminist Hebrew Bible scholars, teachers, teaching, and writing made it all come together.

Feminist Scholars of the First Wave: Teaching and Writing Opportunities. The transformative experience for Phyllis Bird was when Rosemary Radford Ruether invited her to write an essay on the image of woman in the Hebrew Bible for the influential anthology *Religion and Sexism* published in 1974. Bird explains:

I got into this because I happened to be in the right place at the right time when Rosemary Ruether wanted to produce a book to be used in Women's Studies programs in colleges. Feminism was then taking hold in the academy and she wanted something comprehensible. I had just finished my dissertation and was in my first year of teaching. She suggested I do a chapter on women in the Hebrew Bible. I thought that would be fun, as I didn't know a thing about it! I thought 'I can do this because it's going to be in a book for feminist studies and my colleagues will never see it'. When I told my thesis advisor I had agreed to do this, he warned me not to get distracted by 'women's lib'. The year the book came out, I went to the SBL meeting, and at the reception a colleague from another seminary said 'Thank you so much for that chapter!' So my self-assurance that it would not be seen by other scholars was gone.

I then developed this idea of reading through the whole Hebrew Bible, making notes about all the women. I did this with a small group. There were no books, no references, at that point. We met every week in my little apartment. (I read some of the earlier women, such as Edith Deen and others, but they were very moralistic and not scholars.) This was a fascinating venture.

Unlike most of my male colleagues, and many of my female colleagues, who knew in their undergraduate days that they wanted to be Hebrew Bible scholars (or at least teach Hebrew Bible), I didn't know that the field even existed until I was in graduate school in an entirely different field, and even then it never occurred to me to imagine myself in the field or in the role of a professor.

I became the first woman on the faculty at Perkins. That was a time when women students who were preparing to be pastors were having a hard time at interviews, when inappropriate questions were asked. I got to know the few women who did any kind of women's studies. Of course, I was conscious of making history, as the first woman. The first thing I did was to add WO to the MEN's sign. I think I was well accepted by my male colleagues but they had no consciousness. You couldn't avoid a certain feminist consciousness when you were the first woman.

Katherine Doob Sakenfeld encountered a similar situation. She also entered the field when there were as yet no role models. She was the first woman ever hired by a Presbyterian seminary for a faculty position. She talks of those early years on the faculty:

I had always wanted to take on a teaching vocation in the service of the church and my Christian faith. It was an important part of my upbringing and identity. As things turned out, I accepted an offer to teach at Princeton Theological seminary in 1970. I was ordained as a Presbyterian for the purpose of teaching in one of its Seminaries. I had never met an ordained woman in any denomination at that point. (I was apparently number 144, but I'd never heard of the others.)

I had never imagined teaching in a seminary. My dream had been to teach in a small liberal arts college like the one I'd come from. I didn't even want to go to the interview at Princeton. Seminaries (I thought) are places where men learn to be ministers; they don't need women there. I was truly a product of the assumptions of the culture, and was so unreflective. I had never heard of feminism. Friedan's book wasn't published until I was in my doctoral studies. Eventually I did choose Princeton.

I remember that aha-experience. Frieda Gardner was another woman on the faculty, in Christian education. We became best friends and started the first women's studies group. We started having informal meetings with the maybe 15 women students (in a student body numbering about 400). We'd sit in a corner of the room and share experiences of women who hadn't been able to have opportunities because they were women. It reminded me of when I was a seminary student 10 years earlier and was up for a position to lead their children's ministries. The lay committee refused to even interview me because I was a woman. This kind of attitude has been an issue for me not so much in the academy as in the churches. Because I'm rather a timid person I look back on this and say the hand of God must have been upon me because I never realized at the time I was doing something unusual.

Teaching also proved decisive for Esther Fuchs, who moved from Israel to the United States at the height of the emerging Second Feminist movement. It had a powerful influence on her development as a feminist Hebrew Bible scholar. She explains:

The opportunity of a doctoral scholarship from Brandeis University in 1975 was tough to resist, and besides I needed a break from politics and religious conflict. This is why I decided to embark on literature, an area that explored the imagination—or so I thought at the time—rather than society and the nation. The late 1970s was the time of the emergence of radical feminism in the American Women's Movement and the ripple effects could not be missed in the academe. Adrienne Rich's *Of Woman Born* increased my resolution to not give in easily to conventional expectations regarding marriage and reproduction, not only in Judaism, and in my own country, but in the West in general.

At Brandeis I discovered that the Israeli literary canon, in contrast to the American one, was dominated by male authors, as was the field in general. Again, this was in the mid and late 1970s, before the dramatic efflorescence of work by women that would transform the scene in the late 1980s. It was unthinkable at the time for me to do a dissertation on a woman author, or to examine literature from a 'woman's' point of view. It would take years for this practice to become normative, and I like to think that my work had something to do with this change. My dissertation, however, because of the dominance of the androcentric canon, was on the Israeli Nobel Prize Laureate S.Y. Agnon.

Fuchs found her voice only after completing her PhD. When she was able to decide on her research focus unencumbered by any male mentors, she began working in feminist studies. She writes:

As soon as I released myself from the academic hold of my advisors, professors, and mentors, I began to seriously explore feminist literary methods and theories. I intensified my search for a feminist approach to Hebrew literature, and soon became aware of a connection between biblical gender representations and the representations I found in Hebrew literature. After I moved to the University of Texas as an assistant professor in 1979, I began to give papers and publish on the politics of gender representation in biblical literature, which I referred to as 'sexual politics' in the biblical narrative. The transformative event was my radicalization as a feminist scholar at the University of Texas, where I decided to focus on feminism as my main approach to my professional pursuits and my research.

But even in biblical studies, there were few models of feminist scholarship. What I found instead were books in theology, such as Mary Daly's *Beyond God the Father* and Phyllis Trible's *God and the Rhetoric of Sexuality*. Much as I agreed with both of these books, I had to forge my own way between them.

After I moved to the University of Arizona as Associate Professor in 1985 I began to teach courses which I literally had to invent, on 'Women in Judaism', 'Israeli Women', and 'Feminist Approaches to the Bible'. I see the classroom as an arena for political activism, not in the sense of indoctrination or following a left wing feminist line, but in the sense of bringing political questions to the fore and making students aware of the political investments of any and all scholarly pursuits as well as literary texts, including the Bible.

Carol Meyers, too, found her voice after completing her PhD. Today, she believes this was partly a response to the growing interest in feminism at her university. She remembers:

In the mid-1970s, when I had finished my doctorate and was beginning to teach in Duke's Religion Department, many departments across campus were beginning to create their own courses in response to the larger feminist challenges. Occasional courses dealing with gender, with women in particular, were already offered at Duke. (For example, a prominent historian, Anne F. Scott, had long been teaching a history course on women in the American South.) But I was the only woman in my department at that time, in which there were around twenty men. I had been hired mainly to teach the introductory Hebrew Bible course (then called Introduction to the Old Testament).

One day the chair called me into his office and said that I should also offer another course, one of my own choosing. He asked me what I would be interested in teaching and then, before I could open my mouth, he put words in my mouth, saying that I should teach something to do with women. I understood his suggestion as a move to show that the Religion Department was keeping up with the times and trends in academia, and I cringed at the notion that only women could teach about women; but as a new, non-tenured member of the department, I felt that I couldn't object to his suggestion. And, as a feminist, I truly believed that courses like the one he proposed were long overdue.

But was I prepared to teach a course dealing with women? Well, I'm not sure that I could have been prepared specifically for this endeavor. I had had no training at all in women's studies—which didn't exist when I was in college. And in biblical studies, there was as yet virtually no scholarship on this topic, no secondary literature to which I could turn. And as for the primary sources—the Bible and relevant ancient Near Eastern texts—I felt that my graduate training in Hebrew Bible would enable me to muddle my way through a gender-related course in biblical studies.

I named the course 'Women in Biblical Tradition' and offered it as a seminar for the first year or two. I would say that the experience of teaching that course was transformative for me. The analysis of familiar texts in a new way and the spirited discussions with the students in the course led me to see that there was much work to be done. Feminist biblical scholarship was a wide-open field, and I wanted to contribute what I could. As a result of teaching that course, my research interests turned in feminist directions.

Two other experiences in the 1970s were also transformative and helped form the intellectual form that my work in feminist biblical studies would take. One was the *eureka* moment when I read Phyllis Trible's *JAAR* article on 'Depatriarchalizing in Biblical Interpretation'. I was intrigued by the idea that traditional translations and interpretations of biblical texts dealing with gender need to be re-examined and often challenged.

The second experience came when I was invited to give a lecture at the University of Michigan in the spring of 1978. This was the first time I had received such an invitation. David Noel Freedman called to extend the invitation and suggested that I talk about something that I was currently working on. I blurted out that I was teaching a new course on Women in Biblical Tradition and that perhaps I could generate something from that. He said it was a splendid idea, and then the reality set in. The thought of preparing a lecture to give with a leading scholar as my host was daunting enough. The realization that George Mendenhall too would be in the audience added to my anxiety.

As I shaped my lecture for Michigan, I found myself investigating the social location of biblical texts dealing with women; I was looking for the social reality of Israelite women as it impinged upon or illuminated biblical texts. I titled my lecture 'Women in the Bible: The Real and the Ideal' and was pleased that it was well received. This experience launched me into feminist biblical study. And the social science orientation underlying that article would become the intellectual cornerstone of most of my subsequent work in this area and in other aspects of biblical study.

However, it wasn't until the early 1980s, when I spent a year at Oxford University, attending several graduate seminars in social anthropology and immersing myself in the burgeoning scholarship on anthropology and gender, that I would acquire more of the intellectual tools needed to engage social science methods more effectively in my work. *Discovering Eve* was the initial result.

In a nutshell, these pioneering women scholars share several common experiences. Three of them faced being either the first or the only woman on the faculty into which they were hired. Many of them discovered feminist perspectives *after* they had completed their doctoral work. Their early feminist work emerged in response to an invitation to write, lecture, or teach from a feminist perspective. And they all had a sense that they participated in creating something new and there was no role model to guide them.

Feminist Scholars of the Second Wave: Teaching and Writing Opportunities. Scholars of the second wave had some role models, yet for the most part they came to feminism through personal experiences. One of them is Claudia Camp, who entered feminist biblical scholarship almost 'accidentally'. She did not initially apply her feminist views to her biblical studies. She explains:

> I became a feminist by osmosis rather than transforming experience, during the time I was at Harvard Divinity School working on my M.Div. (1975–77). This was at first a political identification that did not show up in my academic work, and it was in a sense a fairly simple-minded one. At that time and in

that place, it was taken for granted among my peers that one would be in favor of equal rights for women, and the name for that was 'feminism'; ergo, I regarded myself as a feminist. I'd read Phyllis Trible's early essay on Eve and Adam, and I was familiar with Mary Daly's more radical thought, but I was unaware of the degree to which they represented different real-life positions on religious identification for scholars of religion—perhaps because I didn't have a clear-cut religious identity myself. (My heritage was something of a Christian mutt, but I was really enamored of the Hebrew Bible. I knew I couldn't call myself Jewish, but I sometimes said if I could be called anything it would be 'Yahweh-worshiper'.)

I wasn't sure I wanted to work in wisdom literature when I pursued my PhD at Duke, and I didn't know anything about Proverbs. A number of factors dovetailed to result in my dissertation on personified Wisdom. Roland Murphy was the obvious choice for an advisor, but Carol Meyers was also there, doing her early work on Genesis 2–3 from the perspective of an archeologist and social-historian. The suggestion of a connection between women and wisdom came from an odder source, though, when the Semiticist Orval Wintermute mentioned to me one day that he'd been teaching II Samuel to his adult Sunday school class, and they'd been asking questions about the wise women (chapters 14 and 20). I did some literary critical work on typologies of female characters in literature, along with some early Second Temple material, for my dissertation on wisdom and the feminine in Proverbs. It manifested both my interest in a multidisciplinary approach to biblical studies and my growing commitment to woman-oriented issues and interpretation in particular.

The situation was different for Athalya Brenner. Already a feminist, she wanted to write an introductory text on women in the Hebrew Bible after the completion of her PhD in Israel. She never imagined that the publication of this book would remove her to the margins of the field. But from that marginal location, Brenner created a niche for herself from where she produced the numerous volumes of the *Feminist Companion*. She recalls:

> After I got my PhD at the University of Haifa, I wrote *The Israelite Woman* which was published in 1985. There was a strong grass-roots feminist movement in Haifa at that time, started mostly by American immigrants. Some of my family members and friends were active in that movement. From experience I knew there had not been much written on women in the Hebrew Bible and I wanted to write an introductory text. I was not at that time theoretically a feminist, only in my real life and in what I was doing and how I was living. There was a quiet knowledge that women in the Bible felt different than men, and it had to be pointed out. I wanted to fill in this gap. In my innocence (this is how non-feminist I was) I thought everyone, even my institution, would welcome it. I didn't believe for a minute that it wasn't scientific, academic, and important. I was up for tenure, and until then I was a bright-eyed star. It was a very tame book, but as soon as it came out my committee decided it was *not* scientific or academic enough. I could not get tenure, which effectively meant I was thrown out of the system.

I became an adjunct, and had a series of jobs for the next eleven years, which was a real formative experience for me. After the first shock—which lasted about two years—anger set in and I just knew I was going to do feminist studies. I was angry enough to get out of my depression. I'd done a Hebrew book (a commentary on *Ruth*) and was beginning to think about the *Feminist Companion*, because I thought there was a real need.

Brenner remembers how she came to develop and edit her series, *A Feminist Companion*, stating:

I thought unless other people knew what others were doing, this feminist approach would continue to be considered not scientific or important. So, for the next twelve years from 1989 to 2001, most of my resources went into that project, the *Feminist Companion* series. I didn't become more feminist over those years; what I became was angrier. In that sense it was transformative.

In 1992, I was in Utrecht for a six-month visiting professorship. This is where I met Fokkelien [van Dijk-Hemmes] and she had a lot of influence on me. The first volume in the *Feminist Companion* series [Song of Songs] appeared in 1993, followed quickly by two others. To find contributors, I read extensively, somehow unearthed addresses, through SBL and publishers. People didn't have email then, so I wrote letters. Not everyone would respond at first (an understatement). But after the first two volumes appeared, everyone responded. A total of 19 volumes came out in less than four years.

My idea was not to displace or replace other methods of study, but to have as many viewpoints as possible from as many places as possible, to not be uniform. I wanted a multi-vocal series. The series fulfilled a function, it was useful. People bought the books.

Initially, Carole Fontaine did not want to study women's texts. She found her feminist consciousness after graduation when she became politicized and began identifying herself as a feminist. She remembers:

I had special experiences which made me realize that whether I liked it or not, I was going to be classed as 'woman', no matter what my academic credentials and accomplishments might be. During graduate school, I never paid any particular attention either to women's texts, feminist theology, or gender issues. In Semitic studies, one has no time for 'frills' of hermeneutics or theory; one simply masters languages as needed and reads texts. If I thought about it at all, I thought about gender in the Bible in the context of the ancient Near East: Woman Wisdom looked like a goddess to me, and that was interesting, but I never sought to make any theological hay out of that insight. In general, I considered women's texts and issues to be under-represented in the textual and archeological record, and as such, more difficult topics to study, should one care to.

When I began to teach, I quickly discovered that, in fact, gender *did* matter—apparently more than anything else. Hired fresh from graduate school to replace feminist giant Phyllis Trible, interviewers made quite sure that I had no feminist leanings to speak of, and hence, would not be trouble as they could 'mold' me. For some time, I simply walked around shocked at the reports of my women students' experiences in congregations for field education, with ordaining bodies, with various classes so clearly designed to socialize young males, but wholly inappropriate for the women students. In particular, I was trotted out to preach on Inclusive Language at the church of the Chair of our Board of Trustees, and not having tenure or a reason to fear, I assented. Armed with my pristine degree and Hebrew Bible ('Sing a new song!'), trussed up in academic wear for the pulpit, I was dumbfounded when the Trustee, loudly and publicly, stomped out of the sanctuary before I had even opened my mouth!

Obviously, it could not be anything I had said, for I had not yet spoken. It must be something else, I thought.

At this point, I became a 'feminist sympathizer'. I still had trouble with neo-pagan reconstructions of Near Eastern history; the text-less-ness of women's quest for their own past; and I had a series of methodological quibbles to solve, but I was at least convinced finally that gender mattered. I still naively assumed that any problems other women in the professions might have had were personal rather than structural. This or that candidate must not have been as well-trained as the males, or had a fractious, grating personality, or whatever. My experiences teaching and preaching brought me to the clear-eyed recognition that the problem was structural, existing at perhaps the deepest levels of text and tradition, and that I had no immediate guides for how this difficulty might be overcome.

But, indelibly Woman, I did what I had to. I became a feminist. The simple change of self-designation from 'idiot who got a degree in Biblical Studies without ever realizing what that meant for a woman' to 'member of the feminist resistance' changed everything.

Other scholars, too, came to feminism through later personal experiences. Mieke Bal attributes her scholarly interest in biblical literature partially to her childhood exposure to biblical stories (see above). But it was an invitation by a friend, Fokkelien van Dijk-Hemmes, which sparked her commitment to feminist studies. She recalls:

Much later in life, I had another experience with biblical stories that actually compelled me to continue working on them. I was invited by my friend the late Fokkelien van Dijk-Hemmes and her friend Grietje van Ginneken to join a small group of feminists studying the Bible. Fokkelien and Grietje were certified biblical scholars, while I was a literary theorist. They invited me to help them with my theoretical knowledge. Preparing for the first meeting, I read the story of Samson and Delilah. I was about to write 'I reread' but no, only then did I realize I had never read it before, only had it told to me in the same way as the Joseph story: by a schoolmistress in an all-girls school, warning us about dangerous women. Now, because I am a woman, I read this and other biblical narratives from the (missing) point of view of women.

I had my own theory of narrative, which had been rather successful, and so I confidently started to analyze the text. It was an eerie sensation that the theory didn't quite 'fit', and that made me change my view of theory. The story's resistance to the theory hooked me on biblical stories, which have had such profound cultural impact. What hooked me was the succinctness combined with the complexity of the biblical stories.

Interestingly, connections to her childhood Bible readings gave Danna Fewell the confidence to trust her own feminist voice later on. She writes:

> I think my emerging feminist stance was tied to this realization that, when I read for myself, rather than have someone tell me what a text says or what I should think about it, I often come to very different conclusions about what that text might be saying. It's the basic issue of finding in one's experience the authority for critical interpretation. I discovered this as a child, and because of that, I never wanted to do anything other than teach biblical studies. I thought everyone should have the right, the space, to read and think about the Bible for themselves.

Again, important similarities appear from the accounts of these second-wave scholars. Several cite the influence of Phyllis Trible's teaching or writing. The two scholars working in the Netherlands mention the strong influence of Fokkelien van Djik-Hemmes. Brenner, like Meyers and Fuchs of the first wave, found her voice only after completing her PhD, while Camp incorporated feminist perspectives into her doctoral dissertation. Fontaine and Fewell learned that reading for themselves required a feminist stance. Several scholars gradually realized that women were treated differently and only a feminist analysis could counteract the experienced discrimination in society and its institutions. The extent to which all of them incorporated feminist hermeneutics in their academic work varies greatly.

Question 2: About the Developments in the Field of Feminist Biblical Studies
Most interviewees used this question as an opportunity to reflect on their own work, on the field in general, and on possible future directions. They commented on the increased diversity and greater number of women in the field of feminist biblical scholarship. Again, I organized the answers according to first-wave and second-wave scholars.

Feminist Scholars of the First Wave. Phyllis Bird reflects on the definition of feminism itself, and how the movement has changed in the past thirty years. She explains:

> Feminism was a social movement. I don't think it's a position, it's a movement for full equality. It means different things to different women, and to different women in different cultures. Feminism is culturally determined, it doesn't have a single context. Even now, women are in different places. That's why I promote readings from different cultures. As someone deeply involved in justice and social equality, feminism has particular meaning for me. My understanding of my Christian faith requires that I be a feminist.
> Feminism is a modern movement and it's an anachronism to think you'll find it in the Bible. You have to train yourself to recognize that when you're

reading the Hebrew Bible, you're seeing through men's eyes. Social context is everything—it determines what things are seen and which are not, how gender roles are described. Nothing escapes culture. Theology is not timeless and absolute, that's why Bible must be contextualized and cannot be used as a moral guide.

The problem for me is that feminist biblical scholarship has become ghetto-ized: feminists talk to feminists and other people don't have to bother with it. I write feminist interpretations in non-feminist publications whenever I can. Feminists have to write their ideas in works dealing with more general issues. I see this as a weakness of the movement, that they don't deal with this problem.

Katherine Doob Sakenfeld comments on the increased number of scholars in the field and the changes in the course offerings thirty and even twenty years ago in contrast to today:

In terms of general changes: there are so many people in the field now that I've started thinking, I'll look at a text with *no* women and study it, though not necessarily without a feminist slant. It's great that the field is so full now, looking over every jot and tittle of these texts about women.

There's also the increase of women faculty members. Just in my own school, we've gone from 15 out of 450 students when I started, to almost 50% women, a huge difference. There are also 14 of us on the faculty—maybe 35% or more.

In around 1975 we developed a course 'Teaching the Bible as Liberating Word'. That has morphed many times. Now I teach another version of it 'Women in the Old Testament: Cultural and Ecclesial Diversity'. The difference is the trajectory of how the field has changed and I myself have changed. The global sense and the interlocking of women's issues with those of race, class and global colonialism are the big places that have changed and have changed the kind of things that I look at and bring up with my students. I'm very excited about exposing my students to ecclesial and cultural diversity.

I'm still struggling with the part of how that makes a difference for us, other than simple cultural voyeurism. Look how interesting this is... The challenge in preparing church leaders is, how does that lens cause me to look at my own world differently? How does it make me more genuinely challenged, rather than just seeing it as a curiosity? How can it help me become open in a more genuine way to someone of a different cultural even religious tradition? How can I encounter such a person appropriately as an 'other' without 'othering' that person or othering them by subsuming them under my paradigm—consciously or unconsciously.

Another place I'm doing things differently: I cannot demonstrate that the Bible has answers to any one question. In grad school we were still in historical critical positivistic model. If you studied long and hard enough, you'd get the answer. That idea is just gone. In Christian tradition in general, you introduce all those categories, texts, interpretations, ways to deal with texts damaging to women, in order to create complexity for people who think they already know the answer and the Bible only has one thing to say. My goal is transforming what's going on in the church and society in general so men who think it's ok to beat up their wives, will be challenged. Or ministers who think women should stay with their husbands no matter what, will have to question that. Since I'm training people for the church, this is my goal.

Esther Fuchs has yet a different set of concerns when she reflects on the wide range of approaches used within feminist biblical scholarship. In fact, she has coined the term 'feminisms'. She is also interested in developing new pedagogical tools to carry the work of the first two waves of feminist biblical scholarship into coming generations. She writes:

The changes I have seen in the field are both a source of delight and concern. First, when I began to write on the Bible from a feminist perspective in the early 1980s there were few if any feminist scholars with whom I could enter into any sort of meaningful dialogue or debate. In my opinion the earlier debate between academic feminism and theological feminism continues today between postmodern and traditional feminist scholarship. This is why, in a recent panel I organized at the SBL, I suggested that we understand our theoretical differences as a source of empowerment, and that we consider the term 'feminisms' as the best description for the various theories that currently drive the field.

What has been developing then since the late 1990s is a tendency to follow rather than lead breaking trends in biblical studies. 'Gender' has become a sub-category in 'larger' critical ventures, instead of a category that is capable of including other analytic theories. I hope we return to a serious study of what biblical feminism, or feminisms, are all about, set goals and understand not only our differences but our common agenda, both theoretical and political. In other words, even as we acknowledge difference as a positive development in feminist biblical studies, we ought to keep our eye on the ball, on the feminist question *cui bono*, whose interests are being served by our efforts.

I changed both in the sense that I became more theoretical and at the same time more pragmatic in my focus on feminist biblical studies. This was a kind of evolution, from an interest in specific texts, in reading the text 'as a woman' which I code as a feminist slant, to a more theoretical interest in feminist theory and scholarship. I am now interested in tracing the evolution of the field of biblical feminist studies, its important accomplishments, and the equally numerous challenges it has yet to face.

I also developed an interest in the practical side of our shared venture—in questions of pedagogy. How do we translate our work into the classroom?

Carol Meyers, too, remarks on the increased numbers of women on faculties, as well as on the changes in her thinking about biblical women in ancient Israel.

Just in sheer numbers on the faculty, there are now three women and eleven men, contrasted to one versus twenty when I started. So clearly, one of the ways the field has changed is that it has grown! There were relatively few of us doing feminist biblical scholarship in the 1970s; now scores of women and men are working directly or tangentially in this field. At the same time, methodologies have become ever more sophisticated, following general developments in biblical studies; at the same time, I lament the fact that relatively few scholars turn to archaeological data and social sciences models.

One definite sign of progress is that papers dealing with women or gender have become more mainstreamed at SBL meetings; they are no longer relegated to units like Women in the Biblical World, which still exists and rightly so, but are also integrated into many other relevant sessions.

My own work has certainly changed, and the answers to the how and why are intermingled. I no longer begin with a particular text and try to contextualize, attempting to discover the social world that it reflects or to which it is speaking, or both. Rather, I am much more interested in what we can discover about the lives of real Israelite women in the biblical period, not those appearing in a literary production. Looking at the textual record of that world, despite our best efforts at contextualizing, is not sufficient because of the sometimes insuperable problems resulting from the oft-mentioned androcentric perspective of the Bible—a perspective that dominates the narrative presentation of women, the legal materials relating to gendered existence, and the metaphoric female images of biblical poetry. But even more, I am referring to the enormous gaps, to the textual silences, that are the result of the Bible's androcentrism and also its concern with issues of Israel's national and corporate existence. The nitty-gritty of daily life as ordinary women in agricultural households would have experienced it is thus virtually invisible.

The social 'history' of women in the biblical period, as for many pre-modern cultures, is fundamentally a-textual—for women's culture tends to be transmitted by non-epigraphic means—and must be approached the way one would set out to study prehistoric peoples for which written sources are non-existent. I am committed to beginning not with the Bible but with the material evidence of women's social, economic, and even religious lives in order to reconstruct the dynamics of their daily existence.

I still think of myself as a biblical scholar involved in feminist biblical study. But in fact I am probably more of an anthropologist, or perhaps an ethnohistorian, in my commitment to interdisciplinarity. I long ago recognized the disjunction between biblical presentations of women and the social reality of their lives; and now I feel I am much better equipped to investigate that social reality.

Feminist Scholars of the Second Wave. Similar concerns, observations, and outlook characterize the second wave of feminist Hebrew Bible scholars. Claudia Camp acknowledges how changes in the discipline led to modifications in her methodology and approach. She, like some of the other scholars, also wonders about the next step and who is the audience for feminist work:

> The field has of course changed over the years, as has feminism itself, and I along with them. Like many scholars in all disciplines early on, my first efforts were simply to the recovery of information about women, which was enabled both by feminism's focus on women and female characters and by newer (at

least newer to biblical studies!) interpretive methods that allowed us to make more of the limited available data. Carol Meyers' work that nuanced gender power relationships within patriarchy combined with Gottwald's reconstruction of ancient peasant society allowed me to think about the 2 Samuel wise women as possible role models rather than one-off oddities.

Feminism also made female Wisdom in Proverbs an obvious—and remarkably understudied—focal point, but also offered a new critical question: what was her role in a patriarchal society and a patriarchal literature? Though previous work had been done on the figure, none had been able to ask the question of gender-related power. Dealing with Proverbs also forced me to think in literary terms as well as social-historical ones in a way that 2 Samuel (as I understood it then) did not. While the wise women seemed, at least, to be 'real' women, personified Wisdom is neither more nor less than the product of someone's literary imagination. I assumed that the figure had something to tell us about real women, but what exactly that was had to be addressed more indirectly. My attempt to address this question led to the use of literary typologies of female characters, as well as to consideration of the post-exilic social, political, and theological environment, as ways of contextualizing female Wisdom within the canon and society.

When I first wrote about female Wisdom, I was in love with her. Though I recognized that she was the product of male authors, I believed that she transcended their patriarchal interests, and that indeed she reflected a cultural moment (a new 'pioneer period' following the exile) when women were unusually highly valued, even if it was within a patriarchal system. I now think that my reconstruction of such a gender-equal 'golden age' was a product of wishful thinking. I think we see much more clearly now how even 'positive' depictions of women in the Bible often served the purposes of male power.

My Strange Woman/strange women work has involved using, and I hope contributing to, some newer developments in the field and in feminist research. For example, while I always considered so-called wisdom literature to be a more integral part of the canon than did many scholars at the time, I now work with a more sociologically rigorous understanding of scribal work as the source of almost all biblical literature, a perspective that incorporates more particular class and gender considerations. I see the analysis of gender not in isolation but as part and parcel of other specific social-cultural dynamics, as an important recent move in feminist biblical studies.

I wonder how feminist biblical critics can make more of a difference in the world with our work. Who are we talking to? In my more theoretically naïve younger days, I guess I assumed an audience of biblically identified folks who would be empowered to take more responsibility for their readings, and thus for the world. As my own relationship to a religious community has grown more tenuous, so has my sense of the worth of what I do outside the intellectual community. I don't devalue the latter, yet I do seek as well a way to transform that into a more engaged scholarship.

Similarly to Esther Fuchs, Toni Craven gives much importance to teaching and learning:

There have been, of course, many changes in my field since I started. Experiences with appreciation of teaching and learning and appreciation of diversity are at the top of my list of most significant changes.

In the last ten years, The Wabash Center for Teaching and Learning, University Learning Centers, and the Association of Theological Schools in the United States and Canada (ATS) have fostered greater interest in the art and practice of teaching and learning.

I think our world—as well as my field—is still in the late modernist period, progressing from time to time—or from bold colleague to bold colleague— along with the deep changes that are altering our work. All this came clear to me when I tried to describe Judith studies across the last hundred years for an article in *Currents in Biblical Research* ('The Book of Judith in the Context of Twentieth-Century Studies of the Apocryphal/Deuterocanonical Books', *Currents in Biblical Research* 1.2 [April 2003], pp. 187-230).

By the 1980s, the field was changed—not changing—in many ways. A relatively few authoritative readings were replaced by a proliferation of studies. Sorting these numerous and diverse studies on Judith opened my eyes to the eclipse of ordered progression in biblical studies as a whole. Women, culturally diverse interpreters, and readings from plural social locations are in the field to stay. Biblical criticism simply isn't what it used to be at the start of the twentieth century. Its trajectories have flown off into multiple directions, forcing us to redefine our 'interpretive circle'. Females and males representing a broad spectrum of ecumenical, interfaith, and secular perspectives, with a variety of epistemological and ideological concerns, now share a circle-like figure. But the boundaries of this circle are irregular, rich, and open, as I see it.

Danna Fewell sees changes in the kinds of questions feminist scholars ask of the text, and in attitudes to gender. She also reflects on how the work of feminist scholarship can make a difference:

The questions in feminist biblical study have changed over the years: from 'where and who are the women of the Bible' to 'in whose interests have the characters of biblical women been constructed'.

I don't see myself as a scholar that is constantly touting and taunting the Bible's patriarchal values. The patriarchal nature of the Bible is a given. But I don't see myself as a simplistic apologist for the Bible either. I see myself as advocating a different kind of reading that acknowledges the Bible's problems and challenges but also recognizes the power of the Bible to create a particular kind of space for ethical and theological reflection on human behaviors and social systems that are still profoundly relevant.

Gender continues to be an interpretive lens for me, but it is not an issue in and of itself. It's a lens that can help us get a handle on a more complicated textual world, and the ways in which the biblical world continues to invade our own, for good and for ill. In the final analysis, the question that drives me is, what difference does our (feminist, religious, political, ethical, theological, you fill in the blank) reading make?

Similarly, Athalya Brenner comments on the new diversity in the field, as well as its greater incorporation into the mainstream. She states:

The field is more diverse now than in the 1980s or even 1990s. Early on, the main criteria was reading as a woman against the grain with a hermeneutics of suspicion. Now it's different. There are many different methodologies, but they all have feminist views super-imposed. This has evolved in stages.

I also think feminist scholarship is much more incorporated now than it was. Of course, it depends on whether you're talking about seminaries or the academy. There are Women's Studies, Gender Studies, etc. into which feminism can be incorporated and/or integrated.

For me feminism is not a methodology, it's an approach or a life style or a way of being. Feminism itself has become more appreciated, if not mainstream.

The Journey Continues: Concluding Comment

The next logical step for the field of feminist biblical studies is to carry on into the next 'waves'. Fuchs makes this important point when she suggests the following:

> Why and how is our work important within the academic context of the university? What is it that we as feminist scholars of the Hebrew Bible hope to achieve and to leave as our legacy for our students?

And Toni Craven leaves the future open when she states:

> I think we all sense that it's time for a new story that we will tell together. How it will turn out remains to be seen and gives me heart to keep at the tasks of biblical criticism and teaching/learning.

It is my hope and belief that familiarity with the genealogies of the ground breaking feminist scholars will inspire the next generation to carry on the work. Feminism has been called a methodology, but feminism is also an approach, a way of being (Brenner) and a movement for full equality (Bird). We are still on the path toward the realization of the ideal for equality and fullness, whether we are part of the first, second, third, or any future waves of feminist Hebrew Bible studies.

2

EVE'S DAUGHTERS LIBERATED?
THE BOOK OF GENESIS IN FEMINIST EXEGESIS

Susanne Scholz

The scholarly feminist discussion on Genesis is so vast that it is impossible to analyze all of it in one chapter. For instance, so many detailed and extensive feminist interpretations on the Eve and Adam story in Gen. 2.4a–3.24 exist that a whole book could be written about them. Similarly, most of the female characters in Genesis are the subject of entire books, and countless journal articles present complex and even contradictory portrayals of the many female Genesis characters. Thus, this essay does not aim for comprehensiveness but presents feminist exegesis on Genesis selectively to illustrate the history of the feminist conversation on this popular biblical book and to introduce pertinent feminist positions, viewpoints, and insights.

Four sections organize the analysis. A first section describes how feminist scholars approached Genesis 1–3 in light of Mary Daly's provocative views on the androcentric history of Genesis interpretations. A second section examines feminist interpretations on prominent Genesis women, such as Hagar, Lots' daughters, and Dinah. A third section discusses how feminist biblical scholars engage the quest for the goddess, as it was articulated in the 1970s and 1980s. A fourth section examines feminist biblical proposals to read Genesis as literature in which the Israelite matriarchs take center stage. A conclusion rehearses the main points and looks into future possibilities for feminist studies on Genesis.

The Case of Eve's Story

In 1973, Mary Daly explains that Genesis 2–3 has doubly justified 'the problem of sexual oppression in society': woman is inferior because she has her origin in man, and she has caused 'his downfall and miseries'.[1] The story

---

1. Mary Daly, *Beyond God the Father: Toward a Philosophy of Women's Liberation* (Boston: Beacon Press, 1973), p. 46.

expresses the 'original sin' of patriarchal religion,[2] which defines women as 'the primordial scapegoats' for the distance between the divinity and humanity. Accordingly, classic Christian doctrine proclaims that Eve brought sin into the world,[3] a viewpoint already fully developed in second-century CE theology. For instance, in a famous statement Tertullian refers to the first woman as evidence for women's biological and social inferiority to men, declaring:

> Do you not believe that you are [each] an Eve?... You are the one who opened the door to the Devil, you are the one who first plucked the fruit of the forbidden tree, you are the first who deserted the divine law; you are the one who persuaded him whom the Devil was not strong enough to attack.[4]

Daly maintains that Tertullian's reading is not unique. Countless other church theologians validate women's secondary socio-political, economic, and religious status with references to the biblical tale and the first woman. For instance, Augustine exclaims: 'It is not by her nature but rather by her sin that woman deserved to have her husband for a master. But if this order is not maintained, nature will be corrupted still more, and sin will be increased.'[5] Things became even worse in the European Middle Ages. The *Malleus malificarum* by H. Kramer and J. Sprenger (1486 CE) depicts Eve as the first temptress and women as more superstitious and credulous, as more impressionable and wicked than men.[6] The rabbinic literature, too, blames Eve for having brought death to humanity, but the Jewish minority status throughout Western history made this view less harmful.[7]

Throughout the Western centuries, proto-feminist and feminist interpreters tried their best, within the limitations of their times, to fight off

2. Daly, *Beyond God the Father*, p. 47.

3. For an early (1979) discussion of this problem, see Fokkelien van Dijk-Hemmes, 'For Adam Was Created First, and Then Eve...', in J. Bekkenkamp and F. Dröes (eds.), *The Double Voice of her Desire: Texts by Dijk-Hemmes* (trans. David E. Orton; Leiden: deo Publishing, 2004), pp. 31-44.

4. Tertullian, 'The Apparel of Women', in *Disciplinary, Moral and Ascetical Works* (trans. Rudoph Arbesmann *et al.*; New York: Fathers of the Church, 1959), pp. 117-18.

5. Augustine, 'The Literal Meaning of Genesis', in Kristen E. Kvam, Linda S. Schearing, and Valerie H. Ziegler (eds.), *Eve and Adam: Jewish, Christian, and Muslim Readings* (Bloomington/Indianapolis: Indiana University Press, 1999), pp. 148-55 (150-51).

6. H. Kramer and J. Sprenger, *Malleus malificarum* (1486 CE) (trans. Montague Summers; repr. from 1928 edn; New York: Dover Publications, 1971), pp. 43-47. For a comprehensive collection of relevant interpretations through the ages, see Kvam, Schearing, and Ziegler (eds.), *Eve and Adam*.

7. For details, see, e.g., Tamara Cohn Eskenazi and Andrea L. Weiss (eds.), *The Torah: A Women's Commentary* (New York: URJ Press and Women of Reform Judaism, 2008).

misogynist readings of Genesis 1–3 and to offer alternative interpretations. Among them is fourteenth-century writer Christine de Pizan who defends women's equality on the basis of Genesis 1–2. She maintains that woman, like man, is not only created in God's image (Gen. 1.28) but also made with far superior material than man, as the first woman is not merely taken from soil, like man, but from human flesh. Pizan also emphasizes that the location of woman's creation is far better than man's; woman is created in paradise and, as a result, her noble nature is guaranteed by God. But most importantly, the first woman is God's masterpiece because she is made last; she is the culmination of divine creation. Six centuries prior to the Women's Liberation Movement of the 1970s, de Pizan contests the androcentric meaning of Genesis 2–3. Yet her extraordinary exegesis is quickly forgotten and disappears from the memory of biblical hermeneutics.[8]

Unsurprisingly, then, this and other counter-traditions did not make it into the mainstream of societies shaped by biblical traditions and religions.[9] When women such as Elizabeth Cady Stanton or Sojourner Truth fight for women's civil rights during the nineteenth-century women's movement, they mention the Bible but they do not know of the women's works that came before them.[10] Importantly, their works too are soon forgotten. Since the 1920s to the 1950s were a period of stalled progress for women's rights, earlier counter-traditions to the androcentric mainstream disappear from public consciousness. Although books on women and the Bible are popular in that period, they reinforce religiously and socio-politically conservative views and values, lacking the intellectual fervor and political zeal of the earlier period. Writers depict biblical women as mothers, caretakers, daughters, sisters, and wives, and they refrain from interpreting the first woman's

8.   See Christine de Pizan, *The Book of the City of Women* (trans. with an introduction and notes by Rosalind Brown-Grant; London: Penguin Books, 1999). For a description of other Christian medieval women, see Elisabeth Gössmann, 'History of Biblical Interpretation by European Women', in Elisabeth Schüssler Fiorenza (ed.), *Searching the Scripture: A Feminist Introduction* (New York: Crossroad, 1993), pp. 27-40 (29-32). For a nineteenth-century Jewish woman interpreter, see Grace Aguilar, *The Women of Israel or Characters and Sketches from the Holy Scriptures and Jewish History Illustrative of the Past History, Present Day, and Future Destiny of the Hebrew Females, as Based on the Word of God* (London: Routledge, 1845). See also Christiana de Groot and Marion Ann Taylor (eds.), *Recovering Nineteenth-Century Women Interpreters of the Bible* (Atlanta, GA: Society of Biblical Literature, 2007).

9.   See Ilana Pardes, 'Creation according to Eve', in Pardes, *Countertraditions in the Bible: A Feminist Approach* (Cambridge, MA: Harvard University Press, 2004), pp. 13-38.

10.   For a description of women interpreters' positions into the twentieth century, see Susanne Scholz, 'From the "Woman's Bible" to the "Women's Bible": The History of Feminist Approaches to the Hebrew Bible', in Scholz, *Introducing the Women's Hebrew Bible* (London: T. & T. Clark, 2007), pp. 12-32.

tale. When Eve is mentioned, she turns into a good wife and mother. For instance, in 1955, Edith Deen publishes a popular book, entitled *All of the Women of the Bible*, in which she writes about the first woman: 'Eve fell far short of the ideal in womanhood' but 'rose to the dream of her destiny as a wife and mother' and 'despite her later transgressions, Eve still stands forth as a revelation of the Father, and as one who can rise above her transgressions'.[11] To Deen, the first woman in the Bible is redeemed by becoming a wife and mother, a rather patriarchal view. The dire hermeneutical situation changes only with the emergence of the Second Women's Movement in the 1970s when fully credentialed feminist Bible scholars read Genesis.

They read biblical literature with feminist convictions in mind as defined by feminism.[12] In 1973, biblical scholar, Phyllis Trible, pioneers such an interpretation in an article, entitled 'Eve and Adam: Genesis 2–3 Reread'.[13] She employs a feminist-literary hermeneutic 'to recover old treasures and

11. Edith Deen, *All of the Women of the Bible* (Edison, NJ: Castle Books, 1955), pp. 6, 7.

12. For a sociological survey analysis of contemporary feminist interpretations on Gen. 1–3, see Susanne Scholz, 'A "Third-Kind" of Feminist Reading: Toward a Sociology of Feminist Biblical Hermeneutics', *CBR* 9.4 (2010), pp. 1-22. For feminist interpretations on Gen. 2–3, see, e.g., Walter Brueggeman, 'Of the Same Flesh and Bone (Gn 2, 23a)', *CBQ* 32 (1970), pp. 532-42; Adrien Janis Bledstein, 'The Genesis of Humans: The Garden of Eden Revisited', *Judaism* 26 (1977), pp. 187-200; Frank Crüsemann and H. Thyen, *Als Mann und Frau geschaffen* (Gelnhausen/Berlin: Burckhardhaus, 1978); Alice Ogden Bellis, *Helpmates, Harlots, and Heroes: Women's Stories in the Hebrew Bible* (Louisville, KY: Westminster/John Knox Press, 1994); Helen Schüngel-Straumann, *Die Frau am Anfang: Eva und die Folgen* (Freiburg i. Br.: Herder, 1989); Helen Schüngel-Straumann, 'On the Creation of Man and Woman in Genesis 1–3: The History and Reception of the Texts Reconsidered', in Athalya Brenner (ed.), *Feminist Companion to Genesis* (FCB, 2; Sheffield: Sheffield Academic Press, 1993), pp. 53-76; Ann Gardner, 'Gen. 2.4b–3.24: A Mythological Paradigm of Sexual Equality or of the Religious History of Pre-Exilic Israel?', *SJT* 43 (1990), pp. 1-18; Mary Phil Korsak, *At the Start...Genesis Made New: A Translation of the Hebrew Text* (Louvain: European Association for the Promotion of Poetry, 1992); Azila Talit Reisenberger, 'The Creation of Adam as Hermaphrodite and its Implications for Feminist Theology', *Judaism* 42 (1993), pp. 447-52; Mary Phil Korsak, 'Eve, Malignant or Maligned?', *Cross Currents* 44 (1994–95), pp. 453-62; Ilona Rashkow, *The Phallacy of Genesis: A Feminist-Psychoanalytic Approach* (Louisville, KY: Westminster/John Knox Press, 1993); Danna Nolan Fewell and David M. Gunn, *Gender, Power and Promise: The Subject of the Bible's First Story* (Nashville, TN: Abingdon Press, 1993); L. Juliana M. Claassens, 'And the Moon Spoke Up: Genesis 1 and Feminist Theology', *Review and Expositor* 103.2 (2006), pp. 325-42; Deborah W. Rooke, 'Feminist Criticism of the Old Testament: Why Bother?', *FemTh* 15 (2007), pp. 160-74.

13. Phyllis Trible, 'Eve and Adam: Genesis 2–3 Reread', *Andover Newton Quarterly* (March 1973), pp. 251-58; Trible, 'Genesis 2–3 Reread', in Carol Christ and Judith Plaskow (eds.), *Womanspirit Rising: A Feminist Reader on Religion* (New York: Harper & Row, 1975), pp. 74-83.

discover new ones in the household of faith'.[14] Her interpretation responds to Daly who rejects the Bible as utterly androcentric literature and as a detriment to women's rights. Trible does not accept this judgment and sets out 'to examine interactions between the Hebrew Scriptures and the Women's Liberation Movement'.[15] Asserting that careful exegesis leads to more nuanced appreciation than Daly recognizes, Trible shows that the noun *ha-adam* holds four possible meanings: it may generically refer to humanity, specify the male gender, serve as a proper name for the first name, or depict the sexually undifferentiated earth creature that is not yet female or male. The linguistic observation is significant because it enables Trible to offer an interpretation that regards the first human creature as not yet gender differentiated. It assumes the simultaneous creation of woman and man.

Trible also takes advantage of other exegetical strategies to develop a feminist meaning of the narrative. She notes that the noun 'helper' in Gen. 2.18 characterizes the deity in other biblical passages (e.g. Ps. 121.2), depicting a mutually beneficial and not a hierarchical relationship between the parties. Trible applies this egalitarian meaning of the woman to Genesis 2 so that the woman turns into a helper equal to the man. Similarly, Trible makes a case for the intellectual, exegetical, and ethical capacities of the woman when the woman considers the fruit in Gen. 3.1-7. Even the divine punishment in Gen. 3.11-24 loses its disastrous consequences for women in this feminist reading. Trible clarifies that God curses only the serpent and the ground but not the human couple, who are judged for 'shared disobedience'.[16] Since the divine judgments are not prescriptive—how things should be, but prescriptive—how things are, Trible stresses that Gen. 3.16 'is not license for male supremacy, but rather a condemnation of that very pattern'.[17] In other words, Trible reads the ending of the Eve and Adam story as a theological mirror that critiques androcentric society.

Another early feminist interpretation, this one grounded in historical criticism, comes from Phyllis A. Bird.[18] She emphasizes the difference

---

14. Phyllis Trible, *God and the Rhetoric of Sexuality* (Philadelphia: Fortress Press, 1978), p. xvi.

15. Phyllis Trible, 'Depatriarchalizing in Biblical Interpretation', *JAAR* 41 (1973), pp. 30-48 (30).

16. Trible, 'Eve and Adam', p. 257.

17. Trible, 'Eve and Adam', p. 257.

18. Phyllis A. Bird, 'Images of Women in the Old Testament', in Rosemary R. Ruether (ed.), *Religion and Sexism: Images of Woman in the Jewish and Christian Traditions* (New York: Simon & Schuster, 1974), pp. 44-88. The article was later republished in *Missing Persons and Mistaken Identities: Women and Gender in Ancient Israel* (Minneapolis: Fortress Press, 1997), 13-51. See also Bird's other publications on Gen. 1–3: '"Male and Female He Created Them": Gen. 1:27b in the Context of the Priestly Account of Creation', *HTR* 74 (1981), pp. 129-59; 'Genesis 1–3 as a Source for a

between the Priestly account in Gen. 1.1–2.4a and the Yahwistic account in Gen. 2.4b–3.24. Whereas the Priestly account locates gender distinctions in biology and regards both genders as divinely created in the image of God, the Yahwist account sees the origins of gender culture.[19] In that part of the narrative, gender differences are described as being part of psychosocial realities that do not require dominance or subordination. Thus, so Bird, the Yahwist account depicts the human couple in Genesis 2 as equal to each other, whereas the developments of Genesis 3 turn the gender differences into a gender hierarchical relationship.[20] Bird, however, also acknowledges that both the Priestly and the Yahwist versions are 'androcentric in form and perspective'.[21] For instance, in Genesis 2 the man stands in the center, as he needs a companion and a helper, and the creation of woman meets his need. Nevertheless, Bird insists that the narrative does not make a 'statement of dominance or subordination in the relationship of the sexes',[22] as this dynamic changes only in Genesis 3 depicting the male as the master of the woman.

Yet another early feminist analysis comes from Carol L. Meyers. Grounded in archaeology, this feminist interpreter regards the Genesis story as a reflection of the Iron Age I era during which Israelites lived in rural, small, and decentralized communities in the highlands of central Palestine. Organized in family households, women and men held equal status, responsibilities, and economic rights.[23] Since they lived under harsh conditions,

Contemporary Theology of Sexuality', *Ex auditu* 3 (1987), pp. 31-44; 'The Harlot as Heroine: Narrative Art and Social Presupposition in Three Old Testament Texts', *Semeia* 46 (1989), pp. 119-39; 'Bone of My Bone and Flesh of My Flesh', *Theology Today* 50 (1993), pp. 521-34; 'Genesis 3 in Modern Biblical Scholarship', in Bird, *Missing Persons and Mistaken Identities*, pp. 174-93 (originally published in German in *JBTh* 9 [1994], pp. 3-24). Many of the articles are re-published in *Missing Persons and Mistaken Identities*.

19.   For a clear statement of the nature–culture divide in the Genesis texts, see Bird, 'Genesis 1–3 as a Source for a Contemporary Theology of Sexuality'.

20.   For a discussion of this idea from a queer hermeneutics, see Michael Carden, 'Genesis/Bereshit', in Deryn Guest *et al.* (eds.), *The Queer Bible Commentary* (London: SCM Press, 2006), pp. 26-30.

21.   Bird, 'Genesis 1–3 as a Source for a Contemporary Theology of Sexuality', p. 165.

22.   Bird, 'Genesis 1–3 as a Source for a Contemporary Theology of Sexuality', p. 165.

23.   Carol Meyers, *Discovering Eve: Ancient Israelite Women in Context* (New York: Oxford University Press, 1988). For a different historical assessment of Israelite women's lives, see, e.g., Silvia Schroer, 'Diachronic Sections', in Luise Schottroff, Silvia Schroer and Marie-Theres Wacker (eds.), *Feminist Interpretation: The Bible in Women's Perspective* (Minneapolis: Fortress Press, 1998), pp. 102-44. Many if not most of Meyers's historical descriptions seem dated due to scholarly advances in Israelite historiography

both women and men were equals because everybody was equally necessary for survival. When this socio-historical reality is applied to the narrative, the first couple represents 'every woman and every man'.[24] Hence, for Meyers, the story describes the social problems with which women and men were confronted on a daily basis. For instance, life demanded 'an intensification of female labor and fecundity',[25] and so 'women increased their procreative role and also made large contributions to the subsistence sphere'.[26] Meyers emphasizes that only a later editorial strata distorts this early depiction of women's and men's struggles for survival. The later editions were made by elite men who lived during the Israelite monarchy. They inserted their religious, political, and social interests into the story, endorsed hierarchical structures between woman and man, and eliminated the egalitarian characteristics of the original tale. After their work was done, Genesis 2–3 promoted the socio-political and economic views of the Israelite king.

Thus, so Meyers, the final version does not reliably depict early Israelite life although the process of subordinating 'Eve' or 'Everywoman' to 'Adam' or 'Everyman' remained incomplete during the biblical era. Meyers explains that androcentrism began to dominate interpretations of Genesis 2–3 only when Greco-Roman culture introduced dualistic thinking to 'the Semitic world'. Then, '[t]he misogynist expansions of the Eden story in early Christian and Jewish literature begin to emerge' and 'a new concept of Eve [was] associated with sin, death, and suffering…[and] superimposed…on the assertive and productive figure of the Eden narrative that we can hardly see the original woman of Genesis 2–3'.[27] Yet this editorial process can only be uncovered when historians use archaeological, anthropological, and literary data to 'rediscover and reclaim the pristine Eve'.[28] Only then, so Meyers,

especially since the 1990s; see, e.g., Philip R. Davies, *In Search of 'Ancient Israel'* (JSOTSup, 148; Sheffield: Sheffield Academic Press, 1995); Philips V. Long (ed.), *Israel's Past in Present Research: Essays on Ancient Israelite Historiography* (Winona Lake, IN: Eisenbrauns, 1999); Mario Liverani, *Israel's History and the History of Israel* (trans. Chiara Pari and Philip R. Davies; London: Equinox, 2006).

24. Meyers, *Discovering Eve*, p. 80.

25. Meyers, *Discovering Eve*, p. 120.

26. Carol Meyers, 'Gender Roles and Genesis 3:16', in Brenner (ed.), *A Feminist Companion to Genesis*, pp. 118-41 (140).

27. Meyers, *Discovering Eve*, p. 196. For a similar view, see also Gary A. Anderson, *The Genesis of Perfection: Adam and Eve in Jewish and Christian Imagination* (Louisville, KY: Westminster/John Knox Press, 2002).

28. Meyers, *Discovering Eve*, p. 196. See also Roland Boer's comparison of Meyers's work with a recent study on Gen. 2–3 by Mark Brett, *Genesis: Procreation and the Politics of Identity* (London: Routledge, 2000); he proposes that Gen. 2–3 be viewed as a 'fantasy' and not as a reference to 'social reality' of any kind; see Roland Boer, 'The Fantasy of Genesis 1–3', *BibInt* 14 (2006), pp. 309-31.

does the biblical story's egalitarian impetus become available again despite the manifold distortions inherent in the final form of the story.

The initial and influential feminist interpretations of Eve's story have been augmented ever since. They have also been deconstructed and critiqued.[29] Among them is the reading of Mieke Bal who evaluates both feminist and androcentric readings as 'equally false'.[30] She emphasizes that the Genesis story is not 'a feminist, feminine, or female-oriented text'[31] because an androcentric text, such as Genesis 1–3, relies on both negative and positive gender markers. Bal explains that the markers serve 'to limit repression to acceptable, viable proportions', making the domination bearable to both the dominators and the dominated.[32] This technique ensures that both women and men believe in the androcentric position, as it consists of both women-friendly and women-hating elements. Bal also observes that, unfortunately, both androcentric and feminist interpretations have streamlined the Bible's heterogeneous ideology by committing the 'retrospective fallacy'. This

29.   Often these interpretations are also classified as 'feminist', but my analysis suggests to regard them as 'deconstructionist responses' to feminist interpretations; see, e.g., David Jobling, 'The Myth Semantics of Gen. 2:4b–3:24', *Semeia* 18 (1980), pp. 41-49; Jobling, 'Myth and its Limits in Gen. 2:4b–3:24', in Jobling, *The Sense of Biblical Narrative*. II. *Structural Analysis in the Hebrew Bible* (Sheffield: JSOT Press, 1986), pp. 17-43; Pamela Milne, 'Eve and Adam: Is a Feminist Reading Possible?', *BR* 4 (1988), pp. 12-21, 39; also published in Brenner (ed.), *A Feminist Companion to Genesis*, pp. 146-72; Ellen van Wolde, *A Semiotic Analysis of Genesis 2–3: A Semiotic Theory and Method of Analysis Applied to the Story of the Garden of Eden* (Studia semitica neerlandica; Assen: Van Gorcum, 1989); David J.A. Clines, *What Does Eve Do to Help? And Other Readerly Questions in the Old Testament* (JSOTSup, 94; Sheffield: JSOT Press, 1990); Lyn M. Bechtel, 'Rethinking the Interpretation of Genesis 2:4b–3:24', in Brenner (ed.), *A Feminist Companion to Genesis*, pp. 77-117; David McLain Carr, 'The Politics of Textual Subversion: A Diachronic Perspective on the Garden of Eden Story', *JBL* 112 (1993), pp. 577-95; Eileen M. Schuller, 'Feminism and Biblical Hermeneutics: Genesis 1–3 as a Test Case', in Morny Joy and Eva K. Neumaier-Dargyay (eds.), *Gender, Genre and Religion: Feminist Reflections* (Waterloo, ON: Wilfrid Laurier University Press, 1995), pp. 31-46; John Goldingay, 'Postmodernizing Eve and Adam (Can I Have My Apricot as Well as Eating It?)', in Philip R. Davies and David J.A. Clines (eds.), *World of Genesis: Persons, Places, Perspectives* (JSOTSup, 257; Sheffield: Sheffield Academic Press, 1998), pp. 50-59; Deborah Sawyer, *God, Gender and the Bible* (London: Routledge, 2002); David McLain Carr, *The Erotic World: Sexuality, Spirituality, and the Bible* (Oxford: Oxford University Press, 2003).

30.   Mieke Bal, 'Sexuality, Sin, and Sorrow: The Emergence of the Female Character', in Bal, *Lethal Love: Feminist Literary Readings of Biblical Love Stories* (Bloomington: Indiana University Press, 1987), pp. 104-32 (110); first published in *Poetics Today* 6.1–2 (1985), pp. 21-42.

31.   Bal, 'Sexuality, Sin, and Sorrow', p. 110.

32.   Bal, 'Sexuality, Sin, and Sorrow', p. 110.

strategy consists of projecting a character's fully developed identity, as it appears at the end, to the beginning of the story. As a result, feminist and androcentric interpreters skew the meaning of Genesis 2–3. They assume that the final character of Eve is the same at the beginning and at the end of the story. They ignore her developmental stages and miss the 'semiotic chronology' in which 'Eve' appears only in Genesis 3.[33] They forget that '[w]hat existed before was an earth creature, then a woman, next an actant, then a mother, and finally, a being named "Eve"'.[34] Yet when one avoids the retrospective fallacy, it becomes clear, so Bal, that Genesis 2–3 contains two stories. An early version presents a 'myth of creation' and a later version presents a 'myth of Eve'. Feminist and androcentric readers collapse both into one narrative and supply the lacking features from the end to the beginning of the story, missing the gradual development of the characters and the textual ideology. The results are distorted interpretations that eliminate the heterogeneous ideology of the text.[35]

Some deconstructionists on Genesis 1–3 expose limitations of the earlier feminist interpretations. One of them is Gale Yee who correlates a gender analysis with the social category of class.[36] Yee maintains that, in general, biblical texts do not reflect the social conditions and gender relations in ancient Israelite society. Rather, they contain representations of gender that mirror the complex ideological interchange between the original writers and their socio-historical contexts. The writers were mostly of upper class and elite male background. They promoted different gender ideologies during different centuries in ancient Israel and all of them articulated 'issues of power and its asymmetry in class and colonial relations', and 'replicated the material and ideological disparities found in male–female relations in ancient Israel'.[37]

During the early stages of its history, Israel transformed its economic structure from a familial mode of production typical of the tribal period to the native-tributary mode of production typical of the pre-exilic monarchy. At this time, Genesis 2–3 served as a response to socioeconomic contradictions that emerged when Israelite society was shaped both by 'a loose confederation of family groups, lineages, and tribes' and 'a hierarchical,

33. Bal, 'Sexuality, Sin, and Sorrow', p. 107.

34. Bal, 'Sexuality, Sin, and Sorrow', pp. 107-8.

35. For another deconstruction of feminist readings, see Susan S. Lanser, '(Feminist) Criticism in the Garden: Inferring Genesis 2–3', *Semeia* 41 (1988), pp. 67-84.

36. Gale Yee, *Poor Banished Children of Eve: Woman as Evil in the Hebrew Bible* (Minneapolis: Fortress Press, 2005), esp. Chapter 2 'Eve in Genesis: The Mother of All Living and We her Children', pp. 59-79. For a similar position, see Boer, 'The Fantasy of Genesis 1–3'.

37. Yee, *Poor Banished Children of Eve*, p. 164.

socially stratified, and centralized territorial state governed by a dynastic monarchy'.[38] The original authors, who supported the monarchy, constructed a hierarchical gender ideology that tried to change, to accommodate, and to solidify the socioeconomic conditions of the monarchy. Their goal was to legitimize the increased subordination of the wife to her husband as a way to control the population in general.[39] Yee's historical reading of Genesis, then, does not detect feminist potential in the creation story but an elaborate discriminatory gender hierarchy.

In short, feminist-deconstructionist interpreters affirm the androcentrism in the biblical text and in Israelite history. They do not attempt to make contemporary references. They characterize the Genesis tales as textual artifacts of a past with far different views on gender from today. Yet, in their effort to separate the meaning of Genesis 2–3 from contemporary ideas, deconstructionist feminist interpreters come closer to making Daly's rejectionary stance acceptable than those feminist exegetes who insist on the feminist potential of the Bible. Daly proclaims that 'the symbols of patriarchal religion deserved to "die"' so that women can be free of the oppressive past and enter something 'like a new creation'.[40] Since deconstructionist feminist scholars work in the field of biblical studies, their apparent agreement with Daly's allocation of Genesis 1–3 as an androcentric elite relic of the past has not resulted in their move away from the academic field of biblical studies. Rather, they limit their task to pointing out the historical-critical dynamics in ancient Israel that produced the Hebrew Bible in general and the book of Genesis in particular.

Other Prominent Women in the Genesis Narratives

While feminist discussions on Eve's story catapulted feminist biblical studies onto the scene, soon other female characters in Genesis received considerable attention. Foremost among them are Sarah, Hagar, Leah, and Rachel with passing references to Bilhah and Zilpah, Dinah, Tamar, and Ms Potiphar. For the most part, the hermeneutical pattern is similar to feminist interpretations on Eve. Historical, literary, and cultural explorations of the selected female character bring the women's stories to light, identify gender-related conventions as related to their stories in ancient Near Eastern and Israelite settings, and expose androcentric interpretations throughout the centuries.

---

38. Yee, *Poor Banished Children of Eve*, p. 63.
39. Yee, *Poor Banished Children of Eve*, p. 67.
40. Daly, *Beyond God the Father*, p. 68.

Thus, for instance, the pattern appears in feminist approaches to Hagar's story. While Phyllis Trible applies the literary methodology of rhetorical criticism to recover Hagar from the androcentric shadows of Genesis, insisting that Hagar's tale is a preeminent 'text of terror', Jo Ann Hackett offers a historical-literary reading that correlates Genesis 16 and 21 to myths from Mesopotamia and Ugarit.[41] Hackett maintains that the biblical narrative is a variation of the Gilgamesh and Aqhat texts that present a less powerful person as the protagonist and hero, an observation standing in contrast to the countless Genesis commentaries that ignore Hagar and regard Abraham as the central character. Both approaches have in common that they emphasize Hagar's significance in the biblical text. Trible suggests that Hagar requires attention as she is one of the first biblical women 'to experience use, abuse, and rejection'.[42] For Trible, Hagar is 'a pivotal figure in biblical theology' because '[s]he is the first person in scripture whom a divine messenger visits and the only person who dares to name the deity'.[43] Hackett centers her literary-historical reading on Hagar but with a different methodological goal. Hackett highlights Hagar because the biblical narrator made this female character even more powerless than the equivalent characters in the ancient Near Eastern myths. It indicates to Hackett that the narrator was 'sensitive not just to power relationships, but also to gender relationships'. The narrator was 'not above making a female, a particularly powerless one at that, the hero of the story'.[44]

Cultural-theological feminist interpretations have also emerged. An influential womanist reading comes from Delores Williams who locates the tale of Hagar within the reading traditions of the African-American community. This tradition, so Williams, 'emphasized female activity and de-emphasized male authority. It lifted up from the Bible the story of a female slave of African descent who was forced to be a surrogate mother, reproducing a child by her slave master because the slave master's wife was barren.'[45] African-American Christians identify with Hagar because Hagar was from Africa, enslaved, raped, and violently abandoned. To Williams, Hagar's story is a foundational biblical text for a theology based on black women's experiences, as for both Hagar and African American women issues of

---

41. Phyllis Trible, 'Hagar: The Desolation of Rejection', in Trible, *Texts of Terror: Literary-Feminist Readings of Biblical Narratives* (Philadelphia: Fortress Press, 1984), pp. 9-35; Jo Ann Hackett, 'Rehabilitating Hagar: Fragments of an Epic Pattern', in Peggy L. Day (ed.), *Gender and Difference in Ancient Israel* (Minneapolis: Fortress Press, 1989), pp. 12-27.

42. Trible, 'Hagar', p. 9.

43. Trible, 'Hagar', p. 28.

44. Hackett, 'Rehabilitating Hagar', pp. 24-25.

45. Delores S. Williams, *Sisters in the Wilderness: The Challenge of Womanist God-Talk* (Maryknoll, NY: Orbis Books, 1993), p. 2.

survival, surrogacy, economic realities, and God are central. Williams also observes that both Hagar and African American women resist oppression and thus survive on their own with their children in tow. They are strong women who trust each other and God, even when God makes an untrustworthy command (Gen. 16.9). Yet ultimately, Hagar's child survives, as does she when she returns to her masters although, eventually, she and her son find freedom in the wilderness.

Other womanist interpreters advance similar ideas. Renita Weems reads Hagar's story from the perspective of African American women, for whom it 'is a haunting one' because to them it is 'peculiarly familiar'.[46] As stories of ethnic-racial prejudice and power differential, Genesis 16 and 21 depict the struggles 'between an African woman and a Hebrew woman, a woman of color and a white woman, a Third World woman and a First World woman'.[47] Weems notes that Hagar's story 'encompasses more than ethnic prejudice'. It accounts for the interlocking structures of domination of ethnicity, race, class, and gender.

Yet some feminist interpreters focus on gender alone. For instance, Sharon Pace Jeansonne offers a literary retelling that views the story of Hagar as 'a portrayal of a woman who has little control over her destiny and therefore is required to do the bidding of her mistress'.[48] Feminist exegetes also refer to the extensive history of interpretation when they investigate Genesis 16 and 21. Katheryn Pfisterer Darr, presenting a feminist-literary retelling of Hagar's story, includes both the androcentric and feminist Christian and Jewish histories of interpretations. She cautions to stress the conflict between Hagar and Sarah because this emphasis merely enhances 'the patriarchal objectives of the narrator'.[49]

46. Renita Weems, 'A Mistress, a Maid, and No Mercy (Hagar and Sarah)', in Weems, *Just a Sister Away: Understanding the Timeless Connection between Women of Today and Women in the Bible* (New York: Time Warner Book Group, 1988, 2005), pp. 1-21 (1).

47. Weems, 'A Mistress, a Maid, and No Mercy (Hagar and Sarah)', pp. 1-2. See also Jessica Grimes, 'Reinterpreting Hagar's Story', *lectio difficilior: European Electronic Journal for Feminist Exegesis* 1 (2004): http://www.lectio.unibe.ch/04_1/Grimes.Hagar. htm; Susanne Scholz, 'Gender, Class, and Androcentric Compliance in the Rape of Enslaved Women in the Hebrew Bible', *lectio difficilior: European Electronic Journal for Feminist Exegesis* 1 (2004): http://www.lectio.unibe.ch/04_1/Scholz.Enslaved.htm.

48. Sharon Pace Jeansonne, 'Hagar: Powerless Foreigner', in Jeansonne, *The Women of Genesis: From Sarah to Potiphar's Wife* (Minneapolis: Fortress Press, 1990), pp. 43-52 (43).

49. Katheryn Pfisterer Darr, 'More than a Possession: Critical, Rabbinical, and Feminist Perspectives on Hagar', in Darr, *Far More Precious than Jewels: Perspectives on Biblical Women* (Louisville, KY: Westminster/John Knox Press, 1991), pp. 132-63 (156).

Another Genesis tale has fascinated feminist readers. It is the story of Sodom and Gomorrah and the fate of the daughters of Lot in Genesis 19. Traditionally, this narrative has played a significant role in the endless debates on the Bible's stance on homosexuality,[50] but feminist readers do not usually focus on this issue. Their concern pertains to the treatment of the women. They note that Lot's invitations to the town mob to sexually violate the women, as well as the father–daughter incest toward the end of the biblical chapter, turn Genesis 19 into a terrifying story, whether it is interpreted with historical, literary, or ethical-cultural methodologies.

Katherine B. Low states unambiguously that '[i]n essence, Lot violates his daughters', and she offers a retelling of Genesis 19 based on feminist-psychoanalytical scholarship that sides with the women.[51] She shows that Lot's control of his daughters' sexuality in Sodom ought to be regarded as sexual abuse. It makes the daughters confused about kinship so that they initiate incest with their father in Gen. 19.30-38. Some feminist exegetes deconstruct the daughters' initiative and classify it as a reflection of 'the unconscious desire of Lot'[52] and patriarchy. J. Cheryl Exum takes this position when she explains:

> Leaving aside its other, perhaps more intentional functions, let us concentrate on Genesis 19 as a literary production that allows the collective male narrative unconscious to engage in its forbidden fantasies. The forbidden fantasy is the Father's wish (that is, the desire of the spokesperson for the collective cultural unconscious) to have sex with his daughters... But because the desire is unacceptable, because he would recoil from it in horror if he acknowledged it, it appears in a distorted form. He displaces his desire onto his daughters. Unable to face the fact that he desires them sexually, he imagines instead their desire for him and their desire to have his child. It is important to keep in mind that the daughters are also creations of the collective androcentric unconscious that desires the incestuous relations. The fantasy—and the story—is not about the daughters, except in so far as they are the object of the Father's incestuous desire.[53]

---

50. For an analysis of the contemporary online culture in this debate, see, e.g., Susanne Scholz, 'Sodom and Gomorrah (Gen. 19:1-29) on the Internet', in Scholz (ed.), *Biblical Studies Alternatively: An Introductory Reader* (Upper Saddle River, NJ: Prentice–Hall, 2003), pp. 137-53.

51. Katherine B. Low, 'The Sexual Abuse of Lot's Daughters: Reconceptualized Kinship for the Sake of Our Daughters', *JFSR* 26.2 (2010), pp. 37-54 (40).

52. Ilona N. Rashkow, *Taboo or Not Taboo: Sexuality and Family in the Hebrew Bible* (Minneapolis: Fortress Press, 2000), p. 111.

53. J. Cheryl Exum, 'Desire Distorted and Exhibited: Lot and his Daughters in Psychoanalysis, Painting, and Film', in Saul M. Olyan and Robert C. Culley (eds.), *'A Wise and Discerning Mind': Essays in Honor of Burke O. Long* (Providence, RI: Brown University Press, 2000), pp. 83-108 (89).

Other feminist interpreters offer similarly critical views, reminding readers of the correlations between misogyny, sexual violence, and homophobia. Elke Seifert, for instance, classifies Genesis 19 as an example of the prevalence of father–daughter incest in patriarchal societies.[54] Mai-Anh Le Tran highlights Lot's wife in an interpretation that exposes the 'narrative encoding of ideologies of subordination and domination through gender and racial representation'.[55] Holly Toensing emphasizes the presence of women to show that 'the sexual orientation of the men and women of Sodom and Gomorrah is heterosexual rather than homosexual'.[56] Finally, Michael Carden does not mince words regarding the failure of Christian interpreters who confuse rape 'with consensual homoeroticism and same-sex love' in Genesis 19 but also 'exonerate Lot for offering his daughters to the mob in place of the angels'.[57] Thus a feminist hermeneutical solution to this text of terror seems not in sight, but the plethora of feminist approaches illustrates the ongoing feminist need to read this biblical text carefully in a world filled with sexual abuse, incest, misogyny, and homophobia.

Two recent feminist readings attempt to break through the negative assessment of Genesis 19, seeing feminist potential in the story. One comes from Melissa Jackson who characterizes the narrative as a comedy. She depicts Lot's daughters as tricksters who advance comedic relief for the absurdities of patriarchy within the story and in the world. Thus, so Jackson, Genesis 19 does not depict the oppression of women in ancient Israel but an alternative reality in which 'patriarchy was not the status quo, men were seen as fools for behaving as if they were in total control, and women were

54. Elke Seifert, 'Lot und seine Töchter: Eine Hermeneutik des Verdachts', in Hedwig Jahnow *et al.* (eds.), *Feministische Hermeneutik und Erstes Testament* (Stuttgart: Kohlhammer, 1994), pp. 48-66. See also Carol Smith, 'Challenged by the Text: Interpreting Two Stories of Incest in the Hebrew Bible', in Athalya Brenner and Carole Fontaine (eds.), *A Feminist Companion to Reading the Bible* (FCB, 11; Sheffield: Sheffield Academic Press, 1997), pp. 114-35; Anne Michele Tapp, 'An Ideology of Expendability: Virgin Daughter Sacrifice in Genesis 19:1-11, Judges 11:30-39 and 19:22-26', in Mieke Bal (ed.), *Anti-Covenant: Counter-Reading Women's Lives in the Hebrew Bible* (Sheffield: Almond Press, 1989), pp. 157-74.

55. Mai-Anh Le Tran, 'Lot's Wife, Ruth, and Tô Thi: Gender and Racial Representation in a Theological Feast of Stories', in Mary F. Foskett and Jeffrey Kah-Jin Kuan (eds.), *Ways of Being, Ways of Reading: Asian American Biblical Interpretation* (Saint Louis, MI: Chalice Press, 2006), pp. 123-36 (125).

56. Holly Joan Toensing, 'Women of Sodom and Gomorrah: Collateral Damage in the War against Homosexuality?', *Journal of Feminist Studies in Religion* 21.2 (2005), pp. 61-74 (62).

57. Carden, 'Genesis/Bereshit', p. 37. See also Carden, *Sodomy: A History of a Christian Biblical Myth* (London: Equinox, 2004); Edward Noort and Eibert J.C. Tigchelaar, *Sodom's Sin: Genesis 18–19 and its Interpretation* (Leiden/Boston: E.J. Brill, 2004).

valued for motherhood and also for their intelligence, courage, inventive-ness, creativity'.[58] In fact, so Jackson, the writers of this and other biblical trickster tales ought to be regarded as 'the first feminist theologians',[59] a remarkable conclusion. Another feminist scholar also presents an optimistic reading of Genesis 19. Thalia Gur-Klein, investigating the practice of sexual hospitality in biblical literature, proposes to read texts such as Genesis 19 as remnant memories of an alternative sexuality based on a less strict procrea-tion code than the one stipulated by patriarchal laws and customs in the ancient Near East.[60]

Finally, yet another Genesis story has produced a considerable amount of feminist engagement. It is the story of Dinah in Genesis 34 which was largely ignored in the Jewish and Christian androcentric history of interpretation. As it turns out, this narrative compels readers, perhaps more than other stories in Genesis, to confront complex hermeneutical, theological, and socio-political issues.[61] Consequently, feminist scholars sharply contest each other's views on Genesis 34. While some argue that the story is about Dinah, others maintain it is about her brothers. They disagree whether the narrative is about rape, love, marriage, or family honor.[62] They contest whether linguistic, literary, anthropological, or contemporary feminist standards ought to provide the methodological and hermeneutical standards in the process of reading the story.[63] They differ in their assessment of

58. Melissa Jackson, 'Lot's Daughters and Tamar as Tricksters and the Patriarchal Narratives as Feminist Theology', *JSOT* 98 (2002), pp. 29-46 (46).

59. Jackson, 'Lot's Daughters', p. 46.

60. Thalia Gur-Klein, 'Sexual Hospitality in the Hebrew Bible?', *lectio difficilior: European Electronic Journal for Feminist Exegesis* 2 (2003): http://www.lectio.unibe.ch/03_2/gur.htm.

61. For detailed support of this statement, see Susanne Scholz, 'Was It Really Rape in Genesis 34: Biblical Scholarship as a Reflection of Cultural Assumptions', in Harold C. Washington, Susan Locham, and Pamela Thimmes (eds.), *Escaping Eden: New Perspectives on the Bible* (The Biblical Seminar, 65; Sheffield: Sheffield Academic Press, 1998), pp. 182-98. See also Mary Anna Bader, *Tracing the Evidence: Dinah in Post-Hebrew Bible Literature* (New York: Peter Lang, 2008).

62. See, e.g., Mignon R. Jacobs, 'Love, Honor, and Violence: Socioconceptual Matrix in Genesis 34', in Cheryl Kirk-Duggan (ed.), *Pregnant Passion: Gender, Sex, and Violence in the Bible* (Atlanta, GA: Society of Biblical Literature, 2003), pp. 11-35.

63. See, e.g., Adele Berlin, 'Literary Approaches to Biblical Literature: General Observations and a Case Study of Genesis 34', in Frederick E. Greenspahn (ed.), *Hebrew Bible: New Insights and Scholarship* (New York: New York University Press, 2008), pp. 45-75; Frank M. Yamada, *Configurations of Rape in the Hebrew Bible: A Literary Analysis of Three Rape Narratives* (New York: Peter Lang, 2008); Todd C. Penner and Lilian Cates, 'Textually Violating Dinah: Literary Readings, Colonizing Inter-pretations, and the Pleasure of the Text', *Bible & Critical Theory* 3.3 (2007): http://bibleandcriticaltheory.org/index.php/bct/article/viewFile/156/140.

Dinah's silence,[64] and they debate whether to side with Dinah or Shechem, the rapist.[65]

The feminist debate has been so heated that even evangelical, non-feminist critics have entered the controversy. For instance, Robin A. Parry traces what he characterizes as 'contrasting feminist attempts to read Genesis 34 *with* the text but *against* androcentric interpreters'.[66] He is astonished about the position of Danna Nolan Fewell and David Gunn who acknowledge Dinah's rape but favor the marriage proposal by the rapist. Fewell and Gunn explain that the marriage with the rapist would have provided Dinah with a realistic solution in a patriarchal society while her brothers quashed her option for an adequate future.[67] Interestingly, some interpreters, such as Ellen Van Wolde, approach the text with linguistic-semantic convictions and do not even find a rape in Genesis 34. Van Wolde asserts that the verb *'innah* does not connote 'to rape' but 'to debase' a woman from a social-juridical point of view. She explains: ' *'innâ* in Gen. xxxiv 2 does not describe Shechem's rape or sexual abuse of Dinah, but evaluates Shechem's previously described actions ("take" and "sleep with") as a debasement of Dinah from a social-juridical point of view'.[68]

However, other feminist exegetes criticize interpretations that give Shechem the benefit of the doubt or affirm kyriarchical-androcentric views. In my own work, I maintain firmly that feminist readings need to side with Dinah and end the common practice of obfuscating the rape and highlighting the rapist's presumed love. I assert: 'When rape is accentuated, love talk is

---

64. Julie Kelso, 'Reading the Silence of Women in Genesis 34', in Roland Boer and Edgar W. Conrad (eds.), *Redirected Travel: Alternative Journeys and Places in Biblical Studies* (London: T. & T. Clark, 2003), pp. 85-109; Caroline Blyth, 'Terrible Silence, Eternal Silence: A Feminist Re-reading of Dinah's Voicelessness in Genesis 34', *BibInt* 17 (2009), pp. 483-506.

65. Susanne Scholz, 'Through Whose Eyes? A "Right" Reading of Genesis 34', in Athalya Brenner (ed.), *Genesis: A Feminist Companion to the Bible* (FCB, 2nd Series, 1; Sheffield: Sheffield Academic Press, 1998), pp. 150-71.

66. Robin A. Parry, 'Feminist Hermeneutics and Evangelical Concerns: The Rape of Dina as a Case Study', in Andrew Sloane (ed.), *Tamar's Tear's: Evangelical Engagements with Feminist Old Testament Hermeneutics* (Eugene, OR: Pickwick Publications, 2012), pp. 36-64 (37, original italics).

67. Danna Nolan Fewell and David Gunn, 'Tipping the Balance: Sternberg's Reader and the Rape of Dinah', *JBL* 110 (1991), pp. 193-211.

68. Ellen J. Wolde, 'Does *'innâ* Denote Rape? A Semantic Analysis of a Controversial Word', *VT* 52 (2002), pp. 528-44. See also Lyn M. Bechtel, 'What if Dinah Is Not Raped? (Genesis 34)', *JSOT* 62 (1994), pp. 19-36. For the opposite argument, see Yael Shemesh, 'Rape Is Rape: The Story of Dinah and Shechem (Genesis 34)', *ZAW* 119 (2007), pp. 2-21.

not involved'.[69] Similarly, Carolyn Blyth maintains that the marriage offer in Gen. 34.4 does not make the rapist a sympathetic figure. She reminds readers that 'sexual violence is an appalling and inexcusable crime, which can never be absolved merely by a declaration of desire by the perpetrator for his victim'. She thus notes: 'It would be an admirable achievement were every biblical interpreter commencing a study of Genesis 34 to bear this fact in mind'.[70]

There are many other female Genesis characters and all of them have received extensive feminist treatment.[71] Gone are the days when it was possible to relegate the women of Genesis into the shadows of their male counterparts. Only Keturah in Gen. 25.1 (1 Chron. 1.32) has not yet received much feminist discourse although she is important in the Bahá'í Faith.

Feminist Biblical Responses to the Goddess Quest

Besides the detailed and comprehensive efforts of rereading female characters and their stories in Genesis, feminist exegetes also produced works on particular topics. Among them are feminist explorations that connect Genesis with the 1970s' and 1980s' quest for recovering pre-biblical goddess worship and matriarchal societies in ancient Near Eastern cultures. The debate about the feminist value of goddess religiosity begins with the general observation about the lack of goddess worship in the Bible. Peggy L. Day states it well when she writes that '[t]he concept of female divinity is a familiar one in many of the world's religions, past and present' but it is 'noticeably absent' in the Jewish and Christian traditions and practices.[72] When feminists study the Hebrew Bible with the goddess question in mind, the absence of female deities makes them wonder if the patriarchal bias in ancient Israel led to the suppression of the goddess. Since the biblical God is heavily referenced with male terminology, feminist interpreters wonder whether the characterization of a male God was a major factor in women's societal oppression. In the 1970s and early 1980s, books on the liberating potential of pre-patriarchal goddess worship proliferated, all rejecting the androcentric God and religion of the Hebrew Bible. For instance, Merlin

69. Scholz, 'Through Whose Eyes?', p. 171. See also Susanne Scholz, *Rape Plots: A Feminist Interpretation of Genesis 34* (New York: Peter Lang, 2000).

70. Caroline Blyth, 'Redeemed by his Love? The Characterization of Shechem in Genesis 34', *JSOT* 33 (2008), pp. 3-18 (18).

71. The references to feminist exegesis on Sarah, Rebekah, Rachel, Leah, Bilhah, Zilpah, Tamar, and Ms Potiphar are too extensive to list comprehensively, but any bibliographical search will quickly display numerous feminist articles and books.

72. Peggy L. Day, 'Hebrew Bible Goddesses and Modern Feminist Scholarship', *Religion Compass* 6.6 (2012), pp. 298-308 (298).

Stone imagines women gaining power in their lives and in the world when they reconnect to the feminine powers of ancient goddesses.[73] The idea of Stone's and similar publications is that the biblical tradition legitimated the patriarchal oppression of women and successfully replaced matriarchal societies and their goddesses. Contemporary goddess books thus advise women to reclaim women-friendly goddess traditions and to leave biblical patriarchy and religion behind.[74]

Several goddess historians are very explicit in locating the effects of women's secondary status in Western society in the Hebrew Bible. A highly influential and well-articulated example for the impact of goddess research on feminist biblical scholarship is the work of Gerda Weiler, although her books are not translated into English.[75] Weiler maintains that the worship of the goddess was systematically suppressed and eventually expunged from the religious imagination in ancient Israel. She writes: 'Under the pressures of developing a patriarchal worldview strictly male defined characteristics become increasingly defined as the exclusive values for society. The "Female"—in contrast to the wholistic concept of matriarchy—turns into the split-off shadow, those human characteristics with which the Male did not want to identify.'[76] Weiler's insistence that the Hebrew Bible is the cause of women's oppression provoked serious and persistent critique in the German context of the 1980s. Critics characterized her argumentation as anti-Jewish because it regards the literary-historical origins of Judaism as the reason for the emergence of patriarchy.[77]

73.   Merlin Stone, *When God Was a Woman* (New York: Harcourt Brace Jovanovich, 1978).

74.   For other examples of this kind of argument, see Monica Sjoo and Barbara Mor, *The Great Cosmic Mother: Rediscovering the Religion of the Earth* (New York: HarperOne, 2nd edn, 1987); Heide Göttner-Abendroth, *Matriarchal Mythology in Former Times and Today* (Freedom, CA: Crossing Press, 1987).

75.   Gerda Weiler, *Ich verwerfe im Lande die Kriege: Das verborgene Matriarchiat im Alten Testament* (Munich: Frauenoffensive, 1983); *Das Matriarchat im alten Israel* (Stuttgart: Kohlhammer, 1989); *Ich brauche die Göttin: Zur Kulturgeschichte eines Symbols* (Königstein/Taunus: Helmver Verlag, 1997).

76.   Weiler, *Ich verwerfe im Lande die Kriege*, p. 347. All translations from the original German are mine.

77.   See, e.g., Katharina von Kellenbach, *Anti-Judaism in Feminist Religious Writings* (Oxford/New York: Oxford University Press, 1994); Manfred Hauke, *God or Goddess? Feminist Theology: What Is It? Where Does It Lead?* (trans. from the German original; San Francisco: Ignatius Press, 1995), esp. pp. 64-66; Leonore Siegele-Wenschkewitz (ed.), *Verdrängte Vergangenheit, die uns bedrängt* (Munich: Chr. Kaiser Verlag, 1988). For Weiler's response to the charge of anti-Judaism, see Weiler, *Das Matriarchat im alten Israel*, pp. 328-45.

Although Genesis stories do not play a key role in goddess studies, some references to Genesis appear here and there. For instance, Weiler explains: 'During that time people had a particular image about the original human, the "son of man", who was the "original male creature", while the woman was regarded as the incarnation of the creative powers of Nature'. In this sense, then, Weiler explains, the statement of the woman being a creature of 'God' who in the matriarchal belief system was regarded as a son constituted a complete reversal of what was believed to be true at the time. The matriarchal faith was turned upside down, regardless of whether the Yahwist imagines Eve as being created from a rib, or whether the Priestly source states simply: 'Also the woman is created'.[78] The biblical stories subordinate the woman to the male-identified God, and take away her nature-given divine powers. In the biblical tale, the woman loses her matriarchal primacy and turns into an accessory of the man.

In other words, in Weiler's study the Hebrew Bible is the original justification of women's subordinated status in patriarchy, certainly a highly problematic idea, and feminist theologians have protested against it, regarding it as an anti-Jewish interpretation by a post-Holocaust German feminist. For instance, Marie-Theres Wacker is adamant in her charge that Weiler's depiction of ancient Israelite suppression of the feminine is 'simply black and white and thus anti-Jewish'. She explains that Weiler places a pre-exilic matriarchal Israel in opposition to a patriarchal-monotheistic Judaism of the post-exilic time, a reductionist pattern that was already popular in classic Christian exegesis since the nineteenth century.[79] Yet the Christian-evangelical feminist, Virginia Ramey Mollenkott, offers a reconciliatory point of view. She appreciates that goddess scholars insist on the use of inclusive language for God, and remind everybody to keep 'a biblical balance between a "feminine" immanent God manifested in the depths of human experience and a "masculine" transcendent God who limits and holds us accountable'.[80]

Several feminist scholars offer additional solutions to bridging the seemingly irreconcilable gap between ancient Near Eastern goddess religions and the Hebrew Bible. The work of Savina J. Teubal must be mentioned here[81] even though it is not always accepted as mainstream even in feminist

---

78. Weiler, *Ich verwerfe im Lande die Kriege*, p. 116.

79. Marie-Theres Wacker, 'Matriarchale Bibelkritik—ein antijudaistisches Konzept?', in Siegele-Wenschkewitz (ed.), *Verdrängte Vergangenheit*. pp. 181-243 (201-202).

80. Virginia Ramey Mollenkott, 'An Evangelical Feminist Confronts the Goddess', *Christian Century* 99.32 (1982), p. 1046.

81. Savina J. Teubal, *Sarah the Priestess: The First Matriarch of Genesis* (Chicago/London: Swallow Press, 1984). See also her work on Hagar: Savina J. Teubal, *Hagar the Egyptian: The Lost Tradition of the Matriarchs* (San Francisco: Harper & Row, 1990).

biblical studies.[82] Teubal proposes to read the Genesis narratives with a focus on the women and to recover the supernatural themes embedded in the stories in which women play the main roles. For instance, Teubal observes that in ancient Near Eastern cultures 'the marriage of (royal or) semi-divine siblings was acceptable'.[83] When this custom is related to the sibling marriage between Sarah and Abraham, the Genesis narratives need to be regarded as a memory of the practice in early Israel. Thus, the biblical prohibitions on incestuous relationships and marriages emerge as later renditions of the earlier convention. Sarah's stories were changed to tone down semi-divine aspects and to eliminate the prominent status of Sarah and ancestor worship that may have resulted from early marriage practices between women and men of special status.

Based on Teubal's source critical and literary-historical speculations, the Genesis stories about Sarah turn into faded memory of matriarchal practices in early Israel. Originally, so Teubal, Sarah had been a priestess. There had been a 'Sarah tradition' and an 'Abraham tradition' that later 'were fused together into what is now our biblical text'.[84] Accordingly, 'Sarah is symbolic of woman's struggle against a male culture that finally prevailed and eventually subordinated women'.[85] Esther Fuchs comments on Teubal's work: '[Teubal's] controversial reconstruction of the historical Hagar and Sarah should certainly give scholars pause and offer suggestive techniques for further re-readings of ancient androcentric text'.[86]

The impetus of reclaiming biblical women characters as feminist resources in opposition to views that depict the Hebrew Bible as the cause of patriarchy and the elimination of the goddess is also the driving force behind the work of Tikva Frymer-Kensky.[87] She investigates how biblical texts compare to ancient Near Eastern ideas of polytheism and goddess worship to indicate the benefits of biblical monotheism to women.[88] For instance, Frymer-Kensky elaborates on the goddesses of Sumer to show that the existence of goddesses does not guarantee women's equality in society or

82. For instance, Susan Ackerman states that Teubal's 'method lags a generation behind current Genesis research', a devastating comment; see Susan Ackerman, 'Review of Savina J. Teubal, *Hagar the Egyptian: The Lost Tradition of the Matriarchs*', *Int* 46 (1992), p. 312.

83. Teubal, *Sarah the Priestess*, p. 16.

84. Teubal, *Sarah the Priestess*, p. 137.

85. Teubal, *Sarah the Priestess*, p. 136.

86. Esther Fuchs, 'Review of Savina J. Teubal, *Ancient Sisterhood: The Lost Traditions of Hagar and Sarah*', in *Women in Judaism: A Multidisciplinary Journal* 2 (Spring 2001), http://www.utoronto.ca/wjudaism/journal/vol2n2/documents/teubal.pdf.

87. Tikva Frymer-Kensky, *In the Wake of the Goddess: Culture, and the Biblical Transformation of Pagan Myth* (New York: Free Press, 1992).

88. Frymer-Kensky, *In the Wake of the Goddess*, p. 5.

matriarchal governance. The Sumerian pantheon was dominated by male gods while goddesses appeared on the margins. In fact, the gender distinctions of the Sumerian deities cemented human differences, so Frymer-Kensky, whereas in ancient Israel's characterization of God '[g]ender had disappeared from the divine'.[89] Thus, biblical texts depict the God of Israel with both male and female functions, making gender a non-issue for the deity. As the Genesis tales illustrate, procreation and gender are relegated to the human realm, characterizing human existence and not God. Frymer-Kensky states:

> In the Bible, the unfolding of human civilization is presented as part of the generations of humanity: as successive generations are born, they develop the elements of a civilized human existence. Adam and Eve begin as gatherers in the garden of Eden; forced out of this paradise, Adam turns to horticulture, laboring on the earth. Of the sons of Adam and Eve, Cain is a farmer, Abel a shepherd. This is noted in passing: there is no tale of how humans learned how to farm, how they domesticated animals. The implication is that these things just happened, that primeval humans discovered them on their own. In contrast, the Sumerians tell a number of tales about how people first learned agriculture, all of which concentrate on the beneficence of the gods... Later, the gods Ninazu and Ninmada went to the mountains to bring the barley down to Sumer.[90]

In other words, in Frymer-Kensky's analysis, ancient Near Eastern gender distinctions among the gods create gender equality neither within the pantheon nor among humans. The biblical tradition breaks with the ancient Near Eastern religious view in radical ways. The biblical God is regarded neither as female nor as male, but as uniquely interested in humanity and Israel. The absence of the goddess in Israel's monotheistic theology gives humans greater autonomy and a more direct and central position with God than they enjoy in ancient Near Eastern religions. Frymer-Kensky thus rejects the notion that 'the goddess can give women a sense of self-validation and, at the same time, lead to a more harmonious relationship with nature'.[91] Rather, the historical record indicates that a reliance on the goddess would lead to the very opposite, and thus only 'radical monotheism places the burden of the world in human hands'.[92] For Frymer-Kensky, biblical monotheism is preferred because it makes 'the unity of ultimate reality' in God 'immediate and accessible'.[93]

---

89. Frymer-Kensky, *In the Wake of the Goddess*, p. 6.
90. Frymer-Kensky, *In the Wake of the Goddess*, p. 111.
91. Frymer-Kensky, *In the Wake of the Goddess*, p. 219.
92. Frymer-Kensky, *In the Wake of the Goddess*, p. 219.
93. Frymer-Kensky, *In the Wake of the Goddess*, p. 219.

Frymer-Kensky's preference for the biblical God does not mean, however, that she dismisses other religious traditions. She recognizes that polytheistic religions, too, help people to connect to ultimate reality. She also acknowledges the imperfection of 'the biblical system'[94] because it 'faced an enormous task in its initial attempts to conceive and develop a new way to deal with issues once mediated by the presence of many gods and goddesses'. She states that it did 'not fully succeed in filling the gaps left in the wake of the goddesses'.[95] Yet she treasures that God's primary relationship is not with other gods, be they male or female, but with humanity. In this relationship, so Frymer-Kensky, gender plays a negligible role, and this is the contribution of biblical literature. To Frymer-Kensky, it stands far above the ancient Near Eastern mythology. Not everyone agrees with Frymer-Kensky's assessment, sometimes even characterizing her advocacy stance as 'jarring'.[96] However, she is clear about her goal. She wants to rescue the Hebrew Bible from the accusation of being the primary cause for women's oppression. Both Frymer-Kensky and Teubal reclaim the Hebrew Bible, including Genesis, as a worthy resource for feminist theological discourse. Their works challenge optimistic retrievals of goddess religiosity as automatically beneficial to women's status in society then and now.

A Woman-Centered Literary Structure in Genesis

The goddess debate is not the only topic feminist Bible scholars tackle. Another important area for studying Genesis with feminist hermeneutical approaches relates to the development of women-centered structural readings of the ancestor stories in Genesis. Prominent among such works is Irmtraud Fischer's proposal to read Genesis 12–36 as narratives about Israel's matriarchs. Fischer explains that her interpretation wants 'to give voice to the stories about the beginnings of the history of the relationship between Yhwh, the God of Sarah, Hagar, and Abraham, the God of Rebecca and Isaac, the God of Leah, Rachel, Zilpah, Bilhah, and Jacob, with God's people Israel'.[97] It stands in contrast to androcentric readings that focus on the 'patriarchs' as the protagonists in Genesis. Fischer explains that in the long history of Genesis interpretations '[s]cholarly publications, through

---

94. Frymer-Kensky, *In the Wake of the Goddess*, p. 219.
95. Frymer-Kensky, *In the Wake of the Goddess*, p. 219.
96. Jon Levenson, 'The Death of Goddess', *First Things* 27 (1992), pp. 50-53 (52).
97. Irmtraud Fischer, *Women Who Wrestled with God: Biblical Stories of Israel's Beginnings* (trans. Linda M. Maloney; Collegeville, MN: Liturgical Press, 2005), p. vii. See also her extensive and detailed study, entitled *Die Erzeltern Israels: Feministisch-theologische Studien zu Genesis 12–36* (Berlin/New York: W. de Gruyter, 1994).

their very choice of language, induce the notion that in these stories the "God of the fathers" deals only with representatives of the male sex and is exclusively *their* God'.[98]

Fischer exposes this androcentric bias and organizes Genesis 12–26 with the female characters at the center to reclaim Genesis as 'women texts'.[99] Her 'gender-fair' approach presents the 'family narratives' as *'political actions*, because the family *is*, in the form in which the national history is presented here, the *public, political sphere'*.[100] Accordingly, in Fischer's reading the narratives of Genesis 12–36 are not viewed as personal stories of a long-gone family but as a 'narrated and highly-analyzed theology of Israel'.[101] The result is a literary-chronological retelling that presents Genesis as a book populated consistently and unapologetically with women as the central agents, making it difficult to imagine that the Genesis narratives have ever been read in any other way.

Other feminist interpreters pursue similar strategies but they limit their work to less material in Genesis. For instance, Naomi Steinberg focuses on the 'Rebekah cycle' in Gen. 25.12–35.29 to show that 'men and women in ancient Israelite society performed as social actors in a much more complicated and interdependent fashion than has heretofore been suggested'.[102] Some feminist exegetes also combine an androcentric with a women-centered hermeneutic and analyze the existence and function of the Isaac–Rebekah cycle, or they debate the merits of female characters in the androcentrically defined 'Jacob cycle'.[103] There is also one dissertation that studies the rhetorical-literary structure of the Rebekah narratives.[104] None of these studies are as comprehensive as Fischer's, but all of them provide important historical, social scientific, and literary observations.

98. Fischer, *Women*, p. 1 (original italics).

99. Fischer, *Women*, p. 1.

100. Fischer, *Women*, p. 6 (original italics).

101. Fischer, *Women*, p. 6.

102. Naomi Steinberg, 'Gender Roles in the Rebekah Cycle', *Union Seminary Quarterly Review* 39.1 (1984), pp. 175-88 (175).

103. Jae Gu Kim, 'The Existence and Function of the Isaac–Rebekah Cycle (Genesis 23:1–25:18)', in Joyce Rilett Wood, John E. Harvey, and Mark Leuchter (eds.), *From Babel to Babylon: Essays on Biblical History and Literature in Honour of Brian Peckham* (New York: T. & T. Clark, 2006), pp. 38-47; Nelly Furman, "His Story versus her Story: Male Genealogy and Female Strategy in the Jacob Cycle', in Adela Yarbro Collins (ed.), *Feminist Perspectives on Biblical Scholarship* (Chico, CA: Scholars Press, 1985), pp. 107-16.

104. Yon Hee (Yani) Yoo, 'A Rhetorical Reading of the Rebekah Narratives in the Book of Genesis' (unpublished PhD thesis, Union Theological Seminary, 2001).

The Paradox of Mothers and Other Deceiving Women in Genesis

Research on the goddess discourse and attempts to highlight literary-historical prominence of female characters are not the only themes feminist scholars bring to bear in their studies of Genesis. Another theme relates to mothers and deceiving women. One of the first feminist interpreters to investigate the literary representation of biblical mothers is J. Cheryl Exum.[105] She acknowledges that mothers are not among the most important characters in the Bible, but their stories illustrate 'a striking paradox'.[106] Although women and especially mothers rarely play significant roles in biblical literature, when they appear they turn into full-fledged characters in their own right. Exum observes: 'Though frequently ignored in the larger story of Israel's journey toward the promise, the matriarchs act at strategic points that move the plot, and thus the promise, in the proper direction toward its fulfillment'.[107] She illustrates this paradox in exegetical discussions on the Hagar–Sarah stories in Genesis 16 and 21, the role of Rebekah in her sons' fate in Genesis 27, and the Leah–Rachel competition for sons in Genesis 29–30, as well as in other biblical books. Although all of these biblical women exhibit agency in various ways, Exum notes that 'the real source of the problem' is the patriarchal system, which remains, however, unrecognized in the tales.[108] Exum thus advises to appreciate the contributions of biblical women and at the same time to be suspicious of the androcentric perspective permeating the biblical text.

The need to expose the Bible's double-standard is also the primary goal of Esther Fuchs's work on the sexual politics in biblical narrative. Already in her early work of 1985, Fuchs interprets the female characters in Genesis and elsewhere as illustrations of the androcentric bias of the Bible. She shows that women such as Rebekah (Gen. 27.5-10), Rachel (Gen. 31.14, 19), Tamar (Gen. 38.24), Ms. Potiphar (Gen. 39.17-18), and even Lot's daughters (Gen. 19.31-32), as well as women elsewhere, such as Michal (1 Sam. 19.12-17) and Jael (Judg. 5.24-26), are depicted as deceptive in discriminatory ways. Either the text does not explain why a female character relies on deception, or the text presents the women negatively when their motivation does not benefit any man. In either case, so Fuchs, the characterizations of biblical women depends entirely on the value they bring to

---

105.   J. Cheryl Exum, '"Mother in Israel": A Familiar Figure Reconsidered', in Letty M. Russell (ed.), *Feminist Interpretation of the Bible* (Philadelphia: Westminster Press, 1985), pp. 73-85.

106.   Exum, 'Mother in Israel', p. 74.

107.   Exum, 'Mother in Israel', p. 76.

108.   Exum, 'Mother in Israel', p. 79.

men and male power. Thus Fuchs warns that '[t]he biblical text ignores the fact that if indeed prevalent, female deception of men stems from women's subordinate social status and from the fact that patriarchy debars them from direct action'.[109]

When Fuchs applies this insight to biblical mothers in particular, she does not get confused about their valorization in the stories. Working herself through the annunciation type-scene in the stories of Sarah, Rebekah, Rachel, and mothers outside of Genesis (Ms. Manoah, Hannah, the woman of Shunem), as well as through the temptation type-scene in the narratives of Lot's daughters, Tamar, and Ruth, Fuchs observes that not all mothers receive the same treatment. Some are accorded high national status while others receive impressive personal characterization. Divine approval and the significance of infertility ('barrenness') also play significant roles in their depictions, but regardless of details and distinctions biblical mothers are only important as long as they give birth to sons. Afterwards they disappear, as the genealogies in Gen. 4.17-26; 5.1-32; 10.1-32; 11.10-32; 22.20-24; 25.1-18 indicate. Fuchs writes:

> It seems to me that a much overlooked function of all-male biblical genealo-gies is to validate the idea that though mothers are admittedly important participants in giving birth, 'the fruit of their womb' belongs to the fathers.[110]

Hence, biblical motherhood is valued only and as long as it helps to cement androcentric authority, the father's authority, and to establish the security and prosperity of the sons. In other words, so Fuchs, '[t]he mother is a means to an end, she is necessary and therefore validated. But her validation functions ultimately as the validation of the patriarchal hierarchy.'[111]

Problematically, recent feminist approaches do not always remember Exum's and Fuchs's critical assessment of biblical motherhood. For instance, Leila Leah Bronner and Tammi J. Schneider write about selected biblical mothers, emphasizing their honor and power. For instance, Bronner explains: 'Some feminists assert that a biblical woman's function is to fulfill and sanction the demands of patriarchy. However, as a feminist and bibli-cal scholar I maintain that women as mothers are not merely constructed as male-dependent pawns within the biblical narrative. Though they are

109. Esther Fuchs, 'Who Is Hiding the Truth? Deceptive Women and Biblical Androcentrism', in Collins (ed.), *Feminist Perspectives on Biblical Scholarship*, pp. 137-44 (144).

110. Esther Fuchs, *Sexual Politics in the Biblical Narrative: Reading the Hebrew Bible as a Woman* (Sheffield: Sheffield Academic Press, 2000), p. 81. See also Esther Fuchs, 'The Literary Characterization of Mothers and Sexual Politics in the Hebrew Bible', *Semeia* 46 (1989), pp. 151-66.

111. Fuchs, *Sexual Politics*, p. 90.

confined to the parameters of a patriarchal system, they have room to operate within their own initiative.'[112]

Similarly, Schneider recognizes that the women in Genesis are marginal and their primary role is not as mothers. Schneider thus questions whether the women should be even characterized as mothers, as 'matriarchs', since it is not their primary function. She recognizes that '[t]he focus in Genesis is whether they can bear, who provides their fertility, and what circumstances allow them to become pregnant'. Only the women's physical ability to become pregnant is significant, not motherhood as such. This observation enables Schneider to ignore Exum's and Fuchs's critique of the Bible's androcentric attitude toward biblical mothers. Schneider merely observes that '[t]he female characters are complex' and cannot be reduced to being mothers. When she sums up the women's tales, she does not take into account the theoretical insights developed by the earlier feminist exegetes. Schneider writes:

> [T]he following points are now clear. Eve, first mother and first woman to lose a child, does not differ from other women in Genesis. Sarah is chosen by the Deity and frees Hagar. Hagar is brave and is allowed to play a major role in her son's life. Lot does not provide his wife the instructions to protect herself; his daughters try to repopulate the world. Rebekah protects her sons and the Deity's promise. Leah learns to be happy with what she has and honors the Deity. Rachel is proof that being loved for one's looks is fraught with problems. Everyone brings their own issues into Dinah's rape, neglecting her. And Tamar goes to extremes to do the right thing when Judah does not. The book of Genesis is filled with impressive women.[113]

It is as simple as that, or so it seems. Schneider's statement indicates that at least in this case the earlier feminist work is theoretically more sophisticated than the more recent feminist exegesis. It is unclear why more recently published feminist studies on Genesis do not build upon feminist interpretations, dismiss them, and claim to read the Bible as is. As a consequence, such studies become digestible even to conservative Bible readers. A focus on biblical women rather than an understanding on the androcentric structures of domination and obfuscation offers comfort that earlier and more radical feminist studies on mothers and deceiving women did not provide. The focus on motherhood illustrates that feminist biblical exegesis is (again) at an important hermeneutical and religious-political crossroad. The question

---

112.   Leila Leah Bronner, *Stories of Biblical Mothers* (Lanham, MD: University Press of America, 2004), p. ix.

113.   Tammi J. Schneider, *Mothers of Promise: Women in the Book of Genesis* (Grand Rapids, MI: Baker Academic Press, 2008). See also her *Sarah: Mother of Nations* (New York/London: Continuum, 2004).

is whether feminist biblical exegesis is a practice for dutiful daughters who want to please the fathers or whether it challenges the status quo of gender and the interlocking structures of domination.

Feminist Genesis Interpretations as Crowd Pleasers or as Challenges to Empire? Concluding Comments

Clearly, feminist scholarship on Genesis exists in abundance even when much of the work does not (yet) build upon feminist exegetical accomplishments, whether it is historical, literary, methodological, or hermeneutical in nature. In other words, the different strands of feminist biblical scholarship often stand in competition with each other, but this attitude might also be part of a field not exactly defined by collaboration and teamwork.[114] Nevertheless, feminist scholars produced an enormous amount of exegetical work on Genesis. Most of it is focused on female characters, relying on theories and hypotheses prevalent in Hebrew Bible studies in general and not usually reaching out to other fields such as women's and gender studies to further synthesize, criticize, and advance the area of feminist hermeneutics on Genesis. What is thus needed is feminist attention to the intersectionality of the multiple dimensions of social relationships and subject formations in Genesis and the histories of interpretation. Perhaps another way to tackle these issues would require feminist exegetes to come together and to dialog with each other, to more than ever take each other seriously as conversation partners. In an intellectual climate that does not foster feminist work—according to the motto 'one feminist Bible scholar is more than enough'—a move towards feminist Genesis scholars deliberately working together might strengthen our morale. It might also challenge those who want to essentialize 'women' and perhaps even 'womanhood' in their approaches to Genesis and beyond.

Another theoretical impetus is necessary to advance feminist Genesis scholarship beyond the status quo. It needs to open up intentionally to issues of gender, sexuality, masculinities, and heteronormativity. Deryn Guest makes a convincing case for feminist biblical studies in general, but her observations also pertain to feminist work on Genesis. She urges feminist Bible scholars to become lesbian exegetes even when they live as heterosexual people in the world. Adrienne Rich's notion of the lesbian continuum already argued for this kind of intellectual work twenty-five years ago. The idea suggests, for instance, that it does not suffice any more to highlight the great personalities of Sarah or Tamar. Instead, feminist work needs to link

114. For an exception to this common practice, see The Bible and Culture Collective, *The Postmodern Bible* (New Haven/London: Yale University Press, 1995).

Genesis interpretations with lesbian, queer, and masculinity theories and to analyze critically biblical texts, their interpretation histories, and their cultural appropriations in light of these theories. As Guest reminds feminist exegetes in general and feminist Genesis interpreters in particular:

> In biblical studies we are in the enviable position of being the experts on the very texts currently used to both uphold and challenge current religious/state politics on adoption, marriage, civil partnerships, who can serve as ministers, and so forth.[115]

This expanded and renewed view of the task and purpose of feminist biblical studies, including feminist Genesis interpretation, requires that feminist exegetes take themselves and each other even more seriously than they have so far. As the exegetical developments, especially on the mothers in Genesis but also in other areas of feminist Genesis exegesis, demonstrate, the motivation for feminist readings is on life support these days. It is so much easier to want to please and to let go and to move into research areas with less opposition. Sometimes these other areas are also more rewarded academically.

Hence, feminist Genesis scholars are at a crossroads and we have to ask ourselves where we want to go from here and with whom we want to read and why. Do we want to be crowd pleasers or challenge the empire? Elisabeth Schüssler Fiorenza's insistence that Bible scholars, including feminist Bible scholars, pursue the 'emancipatory-radical democratic paradigm' is important in this regard. She explains this paradigm in the following way:

> [I]t investigates the ways in which scriptural texts and icons exercise influence and power in cultural, social, and religious life. Its commitment to change structures of domination and practices of dehumanization compels it to explore how biblical texts function in specific social locations and religious contexts. Working within this paradigm, one investigates how Scripture is used to inculcate mind-sets and attitudes of submission and dependency as 'obedience' to the will of G*d, and examines the interpretive practices that condition people to accept and internalize violence and prejudice. One furthermore searches for visions of equality, freedom, and well-being for all of creation, which are historically unrealized possibilities inscribed in Scriptures.[116]

---

115.   Deryn Guest, *Beyond Feminist Biblical Studies* (Sheffield: Sheffield Phoenix Press, 2012), p. 163.

116.   Elisabeth Schüssler Fiorenza, *Democratizing Biblical Studies: Toward an Emancipatory Educational Space* (Louisville, KY: Westminster/John Knox Press, 2009), p. 81.

When we apply this description to the feminist study of Genesis, much work awaits us still. We need to analyze comprehensively and systematically how Genesis stories, concepts, and ideas have shaped the gendered and sexualized status quo in cultural, social, and religious life. It is urgent that we understand the function of Genesis in specific social locations and religious contexts. Texts in Genesis have to be examined coherently so that we understand how they and their histories of interpretation endorse attitudes and practices of submission and obedience. Furthermore, we need to examine the interpretative practices promoted in readings of Genesis to make gendered and sexual violence acceptable and to excuse all kinds of prejudices against the less powerful, the 'other'. Finally, feminist Genesis interpreters ought not to give up on 'visions of equality, freedom, and well-being' in their work. In short, much feminist work on Genesis has yet to be realized although much has already been accomplished. But without deliberate and conscious determination to broaden and to deepen the feminist exegetical status quo on the book of Genesis, feminist interpretations will become dull, boring, and predictable, and may even be regarded as passé. The same is certainly true for the field of biblical studies in general and perhaps of the study of sacred texts at large. Yet only when we hear the stories of Genesis without automatically assuming that they prescribe female oppression and submission to the 'Father', only then will it be time to perhaps forget about the feminist study of the first book of the Bible. Until then, much work has yet to be realized.

3

IMAGE, STATUS, AND REGULATION: THE FEMINIST INTERPRETATIVE HISTORY OF EXODUS TO DEUTERONOMY

Amelia Devin Freedman

Feminist exegetes took their time in addressing the books of Exodus, Leviticus, Numbers, and Deuteronomy, both the narrative and legal materials. The narratives of these books tell the story of the Israelites from their enslavement in Egypt to their impending arrival in the land of Canaan. In the legal materials, God, through Moses, delineates the behavior that God expects of the Israelites. Feminist scholars, broadly defined, have noticed many areas of interest in both the narrative and legal materials of Exodus to Deuteronomy. These areas of interest organize this chapter, which consists of six sections, as follows: first, feminist scholars have evaluated the Exodus motif; second, they have examined the literary images of women; third, they have reconstructed ancient Israelite women's historical roles; fourth, they have analyzed the legal codes for their assumptions about women's agency; fifth, they have dissected the legal material concerning menstruation, childbirth, and women's physical impurity; and sixth, they have assessed the laws about sexual intercourse.

Feminist Evaluations of the Exodus Motif

The first notable aspect of the narrative, from a feminist perspective, is the Exodus motif. In the book of Exodus, the children of Israel suffer under Egyptian oppression. They cry out to their God, who sends Moses to lead them out of slavery and into freedom. Traditional readings of the Exodus story have emphasized the movement from slavery to freedom and they understood this motif to be positive.[1] Feminist and gender-oriented readers, however, have read the Exodus motif in both approving and disapproving ways.

---

1. See, for example, Judy Fentress-Williams, 'Exodus', in Hugh R. Page *et al.* (eds.), *The Africana Bible: Reading Israel's Scriptures from Africa and the African Diaspora* (Minneapolis, MN: Fortress Press, 2009), pp. 80-88.

Rebecca Alpert takes an approving approach to the Exodus motif in her queer interpretation. She writes, 'The story of the Exodus from Egypt resonates deeply for translesbigay people, as it has for other oppressed communities'.[2] Specifically, she argues that the escape from oppression inherent in the motif speaks to many gay and transgendered people because mainstream society has forced them to live under the following painful conditions: 'It is acceptable for people to express hatred toward us in schoolyards, the media or political speeches…we do not have the rights that are commonly accorded to heterosexuals like marriage and adoption…we are denied the freedom to express affection for one another comfortably in public spaces'.[3] Alpert states that many gay and transgendered people who read the Exodus story put themselves in the place of the Israelites, since both groups have been 'oppressed simply because of who they were'.[4] Another connection such readers have to the Exodus motif, according to Alpert, is that 'the stories surrounding Moses' birth and life as a young man in Egypt reflect the experiences of gay people in the process of coming out: first hiding and then revealing identity'.[5] Alpert concluded, 'The theme of liberation that comes through in the Exodus story speaks to us [gay and transgendered people] as a model of a time when we can be truly free to express ourselves, and for which we are working and hoping'.[6] Thus, the Exodus motif inspires Alpert to have optimism for the future. Having used the motif as a lens through which to see the experience of gay and transgendered people, she is able to look forward to their liberation from societal prejudice and the suffering it has caused, both historically and in today's world.

By contrast, some contemporary readers have read the Exodus motif in a disapproving way. Suzanne Singer, a rabbi, is troubled by God's statement in Exod. 10.1 that God had hardened Pharaoh's heart.[7] While the hardening of Pharaoh's heart leads to the plague of the firstborn and the Israelites' escape from Egypt, she writes, "we [Jews] must never forget that this same night was a night of horror for the Egyptians'.[8] Moreover, Jews celebrate this 'night of horror' yearly in their Passover observances. Singer asserts:

---

2. Rebecca Alpert, 'Exodus', in Deryn Guest *et al.* (eds.), *The Queer Bible Commentary* (London: SCM Press, 2006), pp. 61-76 (62).

3. Alpert, 'Exodus', p. 63.

4. Alpert, 'Exodus', p. 63.

5. Alpert, 'Exodus', p. 63.

6. Alpert, 'Exodus', p. 63.

7. Suzanne Singer, 'Contemporary Reflection', in Tamara Cohn Eskenazi and Andrea L. Weiss (eds.), *The Torah: A Women's Commentary* (New York: URJ Press, 2008), pp. 374-75 (375).

8. Singer, 'Contemporary Reflection', p. 374.

'As we recall at our Seder table the wonders God performed for us, we must remember the price the Other paid for our liberation'.[9] Similarly, womanist scholar Cheryl Kirk-Duggan wonders, 'What about the Egyptians' plight who were Pharaoh's subjects? What was the justification for the premeditated, sacrificial murder of the Egyptian first born?'[10] Reading from a womanist perspective, Kirk-Duggan claims that womanist readers must 'challenge the necessity of...[the] horrific bloodshed'[11] that results from God's favoritism of Israel. Like Singer, she maintains that 'a reading that privileges a particular "chosen" group [i.e. Israel] cannot justify mass destruction of innocent people'.[12] Because 'Exodus is not liberatory for everyone within the text, or for those who may read it', she insists that womanist readers must be aware of 'the troubling way the reduction of these texts has produced an incomplete witness, thus making us complicit in the harm done to oppressed peoples'.[13] According to both Singer and Kirk-Duggan, readers must approach the Exodus motif with open eyes, attentive to the high human cost of the divinely authored liberation that it depicts.

Literary Images of Women in Feminist Interpretation

In keeping with the quest of early feminist biblical studies to recover the presence of women and female imagery, feminist scholars have focused on the literary characterization of women in the narratives of Exodus to Deuteronomy. Among the first feminist exegetes, Rita J. Burns wrote in her 1987 monograph on Miriam: 'My primary aim is to characterize the tradition's view of Miriam and not to establish historical facts about her'.[14] Although she concedes that Miriam probably was a historical person, this exegete's goal is 'to arrive at a characterization of the overall biblical portrait of Miriam'.[15] Burns thus pieces together a composite picture of Miriam by examining all the individual biblical narratives in which the character appears.[16] Similarly, Phyllis Trible produced a reading of the 'bits

---

9. Singer, 'Contemporary Reflection', p. 375.

10. Cheryl Kirk-Duggan, 'How Liberating Is the Exodus and for Whom? Deconstructing the Exodus Motifs in Scripture, Literature and Life', in Athalya Brenner and Gale A. Yee (eds.), *Exodus and Deuteronomy* (Minneapolis, MN: Augsburg, 2012), pp. 3-28 (3-4).

11. Kirk-Duggan, 'How Liberating Is the Exodus and for Whom?', p. 20.

12. Kirk-Duggan, 'How Liberating Is the Exodus and for Whom?', p. 20.

13. Kirk-Duggan, 'How Liberating Is the Exodus and for Whom?', pp. 27-28.

14. Rita J. Burns, *Has the Lord Indeed Spoken Only through Moses? A Study of the Biblical Portrait of Miriam* (SBLDS, 84; Atlanta, GA: Scholars Press, 1987), p. 6.

15. Burns, *Has the Lord Indeed Spoken Only through Moses*, pp. 6-7.

16. Burns, *Has the Lord Indeed Spoken Only through Moses*, p. 7.

and pieces' of Miriam's story in 1994.[17] Like Burns, Trible's method is 'to unearth the fragments, assemble them, ponder the gaps and then construct a text'.[18] By following these steps, Trible crafts 'a mosaic for Miriam'.[19] Feminist scholars have also uncovered the stories of the following female characters in the narrative: the Hebrew midwives, Shiphrah and Puah (Exod. 1);[20] Moses' unnamed mother (Exod. 2);[21] Moses' unnamed sister (Exod. 2);[22] the Pharaoh's unnamed daughter (Exod. 2);[23] the seven unnamed daughters of the priest of Midian (Exod. 2);[24] Zipporah (Exod. 4);[25] Miriam (Exod. 15; Num. 12);[26] and Mahlah, Noah, Hoglah, Milcah, and Tirzah, the daughters of Zelophehad (Num. 27; 36).[27]

As with the Exodus motif, feminist assessments of the literary images of women have been both affirming and critical. For instance, J. Cheryl Exum understands the women characters in Moses' story positively. She maintains that these characters play an essential narrative role in the book of Exodus. Specifically, they ensure that Moses survives as an infant so that, as an adult, he can save the people of Israel.[28] Exum summarizes the depiction of women in Moses' story as follows: 'women as defiers of oppression, women as givers of life, women as wise and resourceful in situations where

17. Phyllis Trible, 'Bringing Miriam out of the Shadows', in Athalya Brenner (ed.), *A Feminist Companion to Exodus to Deuteronomy* (FCB, 6; Sheffield: Sheffield Academic Press, 1994), pp. 166-86 (166).

18. Trible, 'Bringing Miriam out of the Shadows', p. 166.

19. Trible, 'Bringing Miriam out of the Shadows', p. 183.

20. See, for example, Dana Nolan Fewell and David M. Gunn, *Gender, Power, and Promise: The Subject of the Bible's First Story* (Nashville, TN: Abingdon Press, 1993).

21. See, for example, J. Cheryl Exum, '"Mother in Israel": A Familiar Figure Reconsidered', in Letty M. Russell (ed.), *Feminist Interpretation of Scripture* (Philadelphia: Westminster Press, 1985), pp. 73-85.

22. See, for example, An Asian Group Work, 'An Asian Feminist Perspective: The Exodus Story (Exodus I.8-22, 2.I-10', in R.S. Sugirtharajah (ed.), *Voices from the Margin: Interpreting the Bible in the Third World* (Maryknoll, NY: Orbis Books, 1991), pp. 267-79.

23. See, for example, Tikva Frymer-Kensky, 'Forgotten Heroines of the Exodus: The Exclusion of Women from Moses' Vision', *BR* 13 (1997), pp. 38-44.

24. See, for example, Jopie Siebert-Hommes, 'But If She Be a Daughter…She May Live! "Daughters" and "Sons" in Exodus 1–2', in Brenner (ed.), *A Feminist Companion to Exodus to Deuteronomy*, pp. 62-74.

25. See, for example, Rabbi Elyse Goldstein, *ReVisions: Seeing Torah through a Feminist Lens* (Woodstock, VT: Jewish Lights, 1998).

26. See, for example, Trible, 'Bringing Miriam Out of the Shadows'.

27. See, for example, Katharine Doob Sakenfeld, 'Feminist Biblical Interpretation', *TTod* 46 (1989), pp. 154-68.

28. J. Cheryl Exum, '"You Shall Let Every Daughter Live": A Study of Exodus 1.8–2.10', *Semeia* 28 (1993): 62–82 (81); repr. in Brenner (ed.), *A Feminist Companion to Exodus to Deuteronomy*, pp. 75-87.

a discerning mind and keen practical judgment are essential for a propitious outcome'.[29] The presence of these themes in Exodus 1–2, Exum suggests, means that future feminist scholars would do well to reexamine the entirety of the Exodus story and to reevaluate 'traditional assumptions' about women's roles in it.[30]

This initially positive portrayal of female characters in Exodus 1–2 had a powerful influence on early feminist work. Miriam, for example, becomes a feminist role model.[31] However, the initial enthusiasm soon turns into suspicion. Feminist interpreters then begin to view the women characters as patriarchal helpmates and tools of the androcentric narratives limiting women's roles to motherhood, child-rearing, and the support of the male figures. In 1994, Exum published a follow-up essay in which she reassesses the role of the female characters in Moses' story. In that essay, Exum states that she still finds the depiction of the female characters in Exodus 1–2 to be positive. Specifically, she notes that the female characters 'exhibit admirable qualities, such as heroism, fear of God (Exod. 1.17), compassion (Exod. 2.6), determination (Exod. 2.2-4), and cleverness, and they show that women can contribute significantly to the life of their people'.[32]

Yet Exum also recognizes several methodological flaws in her earlier essay. First, she explains that previously she accepted the gender ideology of the text without question, and 'because I used a literary method…I was able only to describe the view of women expressed in the text and not to critique it'.[33] She now wonders what 'those responsible for maintaining the social and symbolic order' would have gained from depicting female characters in a positive manner.[34] In her view, the reason is that the male biblical writers wanted to influence real women's attitudes and behavior. That is, according to Exum, the writers communicated the following message to women: 'Stay in your place in the domestic sphere; you can achieve important things there'.[35] The result of this message, Exum argues, would have been that women in ancient Israel would have accepted 'traditional female roles, and especially motherly activities, activities focused on children' willingly and happily.[36]

29.   Exum, '"You Shall Let Every Daughter Live"', p. 82.
30.   Exum, '"You Shall Let Every Daughter Live"', p. 82.
31.   See, for example, Judith Plaskow, *Standing Again at Sinai: Judaism from a Feminist Perspective* (New York: HarperCollins, 1991), p. 54, p. 247 n. 73.
32.   J. Cheryl Exum, 'Second Thoughts on Secondary Characters: Women in Exodus 1.8-2.10', in Brenner (ed.), *A Feminist Companion to Exodus to Deuteronomy*, pp. 75-87 (81).
33.   Exum, 'Second Thoughts', p. 77.
34.   Exum, 'Second Thoughts', p. 78.
35.   Exum, 'Second Thoughts', p. 81.
36.   Exum, 'Second Thoughts', p. 81.

Further, Exum acknowledges that, in her original essay, she does not examine 'the notable absence of women in the opening chapters in terms of gender politics'.[37] Not only do the female characters disappear from the story as it progresses, Exum asserts, male characters also usurp feminine power. Specifically, God and Moses 'are imaged as mother and midwives because male figures in these roles do not threaten the [patriarchal] status quo'.[38] Moreover, the one female character who reappears after Exodus 4, Miriam, is 'put in her place' by the narrative.[39] That is, Miriam is punished by God with a skin disease and expelled from the Israelite encampment when she and Aaron dare to question Moses' authority. Exum writes: 'While leaving Aaron unblemished and unpunished, Numbers 12 effectively humiliates and eliminates' Miriam.[40] In the closing of her second essay, Exum expresses her hope that explaining 'the distortion or absence or suppression of female presence after...Exodus 1 and 2 in terms of biblical gender politics' would advance the work of feminist biblical scholarship on the stories of the Exodus and the wilderness wanderings.[41] Exum's methodological approach exemplifies the increasingly negative response of feminist scholars to the ways in which biblical narratives depict female characters.

Historical Reconstructions of Ancient Israelite Women's Roles

Grounded in historical criticism, some feminist scholars have used the narratives of Exodus to Deuteronomy as a source for information about the lives of real ancient Israelite women. The earliest example of this approach dates from 1989, when Katharine Doob Sakenfeld examines the stories about the daughters of Zelophehad in Numbers 27 and 36 for what they could reveal about the lives of women in ancient Israel. She writes that these texts 'offer the possibility of at least four insights into the place of women in Judean culture of the postexilic period'.[42] She argues that these insights are as follows: (1) women were permitted to advocate for themselves in front of male authorities, and they did not need a male relative to represent them;[43] (2) women were permitted to inherit and to hold property, under certain circumstances;[44] (3) women who inherited from their fathers 'had to keep the property fairly closely within the family circle';[45] and (4) women were

37. Exum, 'Second Thoughts', p. 77.
38. Exum, 'Second Thoughts', p. 85.
39. Exum, 'Second Thoughts', p. 85.
40. Exum, 'Second Thoughts', p. 86.
41. Exum, 'Second Thoughts', p. 86.
42. Sakenfeld, 'Feminist Biblical Interpretation', p. 162.
43. Sakenfeld, 'Feminist Biblical Interpretation', p. 159.
44. Sakenfeld, 'Feminist Biblical Interpretation', p. 159.
45. Sakenfeld, 'Feminist Biblical Interpretation', p. 159.

expected to marry men from their own clans.[46] Thus, Sakenfeld maintains that ancient Israelite women had legal rights, but that their control over their property was limited by their male relatives.

Like Sakenfeld, Susan Ackerman is a scholar whose 'interest is the place of women within Israelite religion'.[47] In 2002, Ackerman used biblical narratives to establish historical facts about Miriam, Deborah, Huldah, and Noadiah, the only women accorded the title of 'prophet' (*nby'h*) in the Hebrew Bible.[48] She writes: 'It is my intent to explore the anomalous position of these four Israelite prophets within Israelite religion, asking in particular how *any* women could have come to be considered prophets given the overwhelmingly male character of the Bible's prophetic tradition'.[49] Ackerman shows that Miriam's identification as a prophet was possible only because her prophetic activity takes place during 'a liminal period of anti-structure' in Israelite history.[50] For Ackerman, then, Miriam is an 'anomaly', and her status as a prophet is 'exceptional rather than acceptable within Israelite religion'.[51]

In addition, Ackerman draws on a biblical narrative to establish information about Zipporah, Moses' wife. Ackerman describes Zipporah's actions in Exodus 4 as follows: 'Zipporah, in performing an actual circumcision of Gershom…[and] some sort of circumcision…of Moses; and in giving voice to a highly formalized and even formulaic pronouncement after all these acts, is characterized…as some kind of ritual specialist'.[52] In fact, Ackerman contends that Zipporah should be understood as occupying the role of a priest in Exodus 4.[53] As with Miriam, Ackerman insists that the 'liminal space and time in the life story of Israel' in which Zipporah lived provided her the opportunity to function in a traditionally male role.[54] Ackerman states that Miriam and Zipporah assumed leadership positions in ancient Israelite society because they lived under conditions which, cross-culturally, tend to afford women the ability '[to] achieve a more elevated status and [to] find opportunities for a greater exercise of power'.[55]

---

46. Sakenfeld, 'Feminist Biblical Interpretation', p. 160.
47. Susan Ackerman, 'Why Is Miriam Also among the Prophets? (And Is Zipporah among the Priests?)', *JBL* 121 (2002), pp. 47-80 (48).
48. Ackerman, 'Why Is Miriam Also among the Prophets?', p. 48.
49. Ackerman, 'Why Is Miriam Also among the Prophets?', p. 51.
50. Ackerman, 'Why Is Miriam Also among the Prophets?', p. 71.
51. Ackerman, 'Why Is Miriam Also among the Prophets?', pp. 50-51.
52. Ackerman, 'Why is Miriam Also among the Prophets?', p. 74.
53. Ackerman, 'Why is Miriam Also among the Prophets?', pp. 74-75.
54. Ackerman, 'Why is Miriam Also among the Prophets?', p. 75.
55. Ackerman, 'Why is Miriam Also among the Prophets?', p. 80.

Likewise, Wilda C. Gafney relies on historical criticism to answer the question of whether women functioned as prophets in ancient Israel. She assumes that the Hebrew Bible 'is a narrow, sectarian, and androcentric source...[and] simply do[es] not and cannot accurately reflect the religious experiences of all ancient Israelite women and men'.[56] She therefore examines comparative evidence from the ancient Near East, and evaluates the evidence for all named female prophets in the Hebrew Bible. She then turns to biblical references to unnamed women who held religious leadership roles, such as the women who follow Miriam with drums and dancing (Exod. 15)[57] and the *hatzvo'ot asher tzave'u* (Exod. 38.8), whose title she translated as 'women warriors'.[58] Gafney also suggests that biblical references to groups of prophets include 'hidden' female prophets, whose presence in the text is 'obscured' for readers by the use of the Hebrew male plural noun, *nevi'im*.[59] In addition, she investigates the textual information about named and unnamed female religious figures and reconstructs a list of attributes that characterize ancient Israelite prophets. Some of these attributes are as follows: 'intervening with Yhwh on behalf of human beings, performing musical compositions...[and] proclaiming the word of Yhwh'.[60] Since women appear in these roles throughout the canon, both literarily and historically, Gafney disagrees with Ackerman's characterization of Miriam as an 'anomaly'. Instead, she asserts that female prophets were 'a consistent expression of Israelite religious practice'.[61] Both Ackerman and Gafney, then, use the narrative material to reconstruct ancient Israelite women's leadership roles, although they disagree in their conclusions.

Feminist Analysis of Women's Legal Agency

Feminist exegetes have analyzed the legal texts of Exodus to Deuteronomy to uncover their assumptions about women's agency. To use Judith Romney Wegner's terminology, scholars have asked whether the legal materials found in these books define a woman as a 'person' or as 'chattel'. In her important study of women in the Mishnah, Wegner defines personhood as 'the complex of legal entitlements and obligations that largely define an individual's status in society'.[62] She views chattel, by contrast, as 'an entity

---

56. Wilda C. Gafney, *Daughters of Miriam: Women Prophets in Ancient Israel* (Minneapolis, MN: Fortress Press, 2008), p. 164.
57. Gafney, *Daughters of Miriam*, pp. 120-22.
58. Gafney, *Daughters of Miriam*, p. 153.
59. Gafney, *Daughters of Miriam*, pp. 160-64.
60. Gafney, *Daughters of Miriam*, p. 152.
61. Gafney, *Daughters of Miriam*, p. 15.
62. Judith Romney Wegner, *Chattel or Person? The Status of Women in the Mishnah* (New York: Oxford University Press, 1988), pp. 6-7.

lacking powers, rights, or duties under the law'.[63] Wegner maintains that the laws of the Hebrew Bible indicate that 'conflicting perceptions of woman as person and chattel existed already in biblical Israel'.[64]

Biblical scholars have agreed with Wegner's assessment of women's legal agency. In her study of the sexual laws in Leviticus and Deuteronomy, for example, Deborah L. Ellens analyzes this issue in terms of the concepts of marginalization, objectification, and focalization.[65] Ellens defines a woman as marginalized by a legal text when she 'is not addressed or is addressed implicitly'.[66] She considers a woman as 'objectified' by a legal text when she 'is placed in the object slot of the grammar of the language depicting the sex act'.[67] Finally, in reference to focalization, Ellens writes that 'where the authors' primary concern is to protect her sexuality as property, she is focalized as property. Where the author's primary concern is to protect an entity separate from her own body [such as the purity system dictated by the book of Leviticus], she is focalized as an agent'.[68] Ellens suggests that the focalization of women in the biblical corpora differs. While women in Deuteronomy are 'focalized as the sexual property of the man',[69] Ellens summarizes, they sometimes have agency in Leviticus.[70] By contrast, the marginalization and objectification of women in the laws of both Leviticus and Deuteronomy 'remain relatively constant'.[71] Thus, while feminist biblical scholars acknowledge that some legal texts treat women as full-fledged legal agents, they note that the majority of such texts marginalize and objectify women. To employ the words of Drorah O'Donnell Setel, feminist interpreters emphasize that the laws of Exodus to Deuteronomy display 'a mixed perspective on women'.[72]

Tikva Frymer-Kensky, for example, maintains that some biblical laws consider women legal agents equal to men. She writes that laws such as Deut. 5.14 'include women in the "you" [that is, the second person masculine being addressed by God]'.[73] She continues:

63.   Wegner, *Chattel or Person*, p. 7.

64.   Wegner, *Chattel or Person*, p. 13.

65.   Deborah L. Ellens, *Women in the Sex Texts of Leviticus and Deuteronomy: A Comparative Conceptual Analysis* (LHBOTS, 458; London: T. & T. Clark, 2008), p. 5.

66.   Ellens, *Women in the Sex Texts*, p. 7.

67.   Ellens, *Women in the Sex Texts*, p. 7.

68.   Ellens, *Women in the Sex Texts*, p. 7.

69.   Ellens, *Women in the Sex Texts*, p. 8.

70.   Ellens, *Women in the Sex Texts*, p. 291.

71.   Ellens, *Women in the Sex Texts*, p. 8.

72.   Drorah O'Donnell Setel, 'Exodus', in Newsom and Ringe (eds.), *The Women's Bible Commentary*, pp. 30-39 (34).

73.   Tikva Frymer-Kensky, 'Deuteronomy', in Newsom and Ringe (eds.), *The Women's Bible Commentary*, pp. 52-62 (54).

The inclusion of the daughter and the female slave shows that women are to stop work on the Sabbath...[since] if the wife worked, so would the daughter and the maidservant... [T]he omission of the phrase 'and your wife' shows that the 'you' that the law addresses includes both men and women, each treated as a separate moral agent.[74]

Similarly, Deborah Ellens argues that the laws about sexual intercourse with a menstruating woman (Lev. 15; 18; 20) assume that 'woman is an agent who must uphold the law'.[75]

By contrast, other feminist scholars maintain that many legal texts marginalize women. Setel, among others, points to Exod. 19.15 as a prime example of this phenomenon. She states that 'nowhere is the secondary status of women...more apparent' than in this verse.[76] Here, Moses instructs the people of Israel, who are awaiting the arrival of God on Mt Sinai, as follows: 'Prepare for the third day. Do not go near a woman.' In the words of Judith Plaskow: 'At the very moment that the Jewish people stands at Sinai ready to revive the covenant—not now the covenant with individual patriarchs but with the people as a whole—at the very moment when Israel stands trembling waiting for God's presence to descend on the mountain, Moses addresses the community only as men'.[77] For Plaskow, the 'invisibility' of women demonstrated in this text is not simply an historical artifact; rather, it continues to affect observant Jewish women into the present. Each time a Jewish woman hears this passage read in the liturgy, she is 'thrust aside anew, [relegated to] eavesdropping on a conversation among men and between men and God'.[78] For Setel and Plaskow, texts such as this one marginalize women.

Further, feminist scholars observe that sexuality is an area in which legal texts objectify women. While a woman is unmarried, the legal codes grant her father control over her sexuality. In Exod. 22.16-17, for example, a man who 'seduces a virgin who is not engaged to be married, and lies with her, he shall give the bride-price for her and make her his wife. But if her father refuses to give her to him, he shall pay an amount equal to the bride-price for virgins.' Frymer-Kensky finds it significant that 'the father is not obligated to give her [his daughter] to him [the man] in marriage. He can take the "virgin's brideprice" from the lover and then refuse to give her in marriage, thus demonstrating his control over his daughter.'[79] Elaine Adler

74. Frymer-Kensky, 'Deuteronomy', p. 54.
75. Ellens, *Women in the Sex Texts*, p. 291.
76. Setel, 'Exodus', p. 33.
77. Plaskow, *Standing Again at Sinai*, p. 25.
78. Plaskow, *Standing Again at Sinai*, pp. 25, 26.
79. Tikva Frymer-Kensky, 'Virginity in the Bible', in Victor H. Matthews, Bernard Levinson, and Tikva Frymer-Kensky (eds.), *Gender and Law in the Hebrew Bible and the Ancient Near East* (London: T. & T. Clark, 1998), pp. 79-96 (91).

Goodfriend agrees, asserting that the placement of this law 'after a series of laws regarding property loss…but before a series on the disruptions to the social order' demonstrates that the daughter's sexuality is understood as the property of her father.[80] Feminist exegetes also demonstrate that legal texts assume the transfer of the control of a woman's sexuality from her father to her husband upon marriage. According to Num. 5.11-31, for example, a husband has the right to expect his wife to be sexually faithful to him. If he suspects that she has not been faithful, or even if he simply is overtaken by 'a spirit of jealousy' (v. 14), he has the authority to bring her before the priest. The law continues: 'The priest shall bring her near and set her before the Lord' (v. 16), at which time the woman is subjected to a ritual which will reveal her guilt or innocence. Of this law, Danna Nolan Fewell and David M. Gunn observe:

> The woman has no recourse if she suspects her husband of 'behaving treacherously' against her. Implicit in this notion is that the wife has no right to question her husband's sexual behavior at all. He owns her sexuality, not vice versa. She is 'under her husband' in such things (if not all things).[81]

Whatever the outcome of the ritual described in Numbers 5, the text states carefully that 'the man shall be free of any iniquity, but the woman shall bear her iniquity' (v. 31). Sakenfeld notes: 'Not only may he [the husband] invoke this procedure on mere suspicion, he is not to be held accountable for his suspicions, even if his wife is vindicated'.[82] Feminist scholars thus expose the androcentric bias of the legal corpora. Biblical legislation assumes male control over women's sexuality in all phases of her life.

Moreover, feminists note that the biblical laws assume male control of women's reproductive capabilities. In Exod. 21.22, for example, a pregnant woman is injured accidentally and then miscarries. The law requires that those at fault for the accident to make monetary restitution. This restitution, however, is not made to the woman, but rather to her husband. Setel asserts that the monetary damages paid to the husband demonstrate 'the extent to which women's bodies were not just controlled but actually owned' by men.[83] Setel thus states explicitly that such laws imagine women's reproductive abilities to be male property.

In addition to the control of women's bodies and reproductive functions, feminist scholars maintain that biblical laws grant men control over women's religious activity. According to Num. 30.3-15, for example, men

---

80. Elaine Adler Goodfriend, '*Mishpatim,* Exodus 21:1–24:18: Rules for Life in a Covenant Community', in Eskenazi and Weiss (eds.), *The Torah: A Women's Commentary,* pp. 427-44 (437).

81. Fewell and Gunn, *Gender, Power, and Promise,* p. 110.

82. Sakenfeld, 'Numbers', p. 49.

83. Setel, 'Exodus', p. 34

have the authority to annul the vows made by their daughters and wives under certain circumstances. The nature of the vows in question is unclear. Sakenfeld suggests 'fasting, sexual abstinence, and some kind of economic payment' as the kind of vows that a male authority figure, whether father or husband, was able to annul.[84] These kinds of vows would have concerned men because they had the potential to impinge on male sexual and economic control over women.[85] Yet whatever their content, such laws 'presuppose that women were under the authority of their fathers before marriage...and under the authority of their husbands after marriage'.[86] From a feminist perspective, it is notable that biblical laws ensure that men control women in every aspect of their lives.

Such scholars also demonstrate that the legal material presents women as objects in need of male protection. In Deut. 21.10-14, for example, a man is permitted to marry an enemy woman but he is barred from mistreating her. Some feminist exegetes maintain that legal 'protection' such as this was not for the women's benefit, but actually served male interests. Harold C. Washington, for example, shows that the purpose of this law is to permit an Israelite man to marry the foreign woman he desires and to have sexual contact with her.[87] That is, the law's purpose was not to protect the captive woman. Instead, its purpose was to 'assure a[n Israelite] man's prerogative to abduct a woman through violence, keep her indefinitely if he wishes or discard her if she is deemed unsatisfactory'.[88]

Other laws, too, demonstrate to feminist scholars that legal claims to protect women served male interests. In the case of the law of levirate marriage, Deut. 25.5-10, a woman whose husband dies without having fathered children is allowed to marry her husband's brother for procreative purposes. Carolyn Pressler states that 'the overriding concern of Deut. 25.5-10 is the perpetuation of a "name" for the deceased man'.[89] For Pressler, this law is concerned about the first husband's lineage, rather than his widow's welfare. Similarly, other feminist scholars suggest that the texts on women's inheritance rights safeguard male interests. In Num. 27.1-11, the daughters of Zelophehad request that Moses permit them to inherit their dead father's

---

84. Sakenfeld, 'Numbers', p. 49.

85. Sakenfeld, 'Numbers', pp. 49-50.

86. Eryl W. Davies, *The Dissenting Reader: Feminist Approaches to the Hebrew Bible* (Farnham: Ashgate, 2003), p. 2.

87. Harold C. Washington, '"Lest He Die in Battle and Another Man Take Her": Violence and the Construction of Gender in the Laws of Deuteronomy 20–22', in Matthew, Levinson, and Frymer-Kensky (eds.), *Gender and Law*, pp. 208-12 (207).

88. Washington, '"Lest He Die in Battle"', p. 207.

89. Carolyn Pressler, *The View of Women Found in the Deuteronomic Family Laws* (BZAW, 216; Berlin: W. de Gruyter, 1993), p. 73.

property. Sakenfeld maintained that the biblical story reflects 'the concern of men who are anxious about the meaning of life and death in the face of the tragedy of only having fathered daughters'.[90] Thus, feminists insist that the issue in Numbers 27 does not pertain to the economic well-being of Zelophehad's daughters but to the remembrance of their father's name after his death.

Having established that most biblical laws marginalize and objectify women, feminist scholars have asked what underlying assumptions about female identity can be gleaned from these texts. Drawing on postmodern feminist legal theory,[91] Cheryl Anderson argues that biblical laws 'encode the female body with meaning'.[92] Specifically, she maintains that biblical laws 'create and enforce' several characteristics of female identity; these are that a woman 'submits to male authority…is meant for sex with men…and is meant for maternity'.[93] In Anderson's words, 'a result of the biblical laws' ability to shape behavior…is the ability to legitimate and therefore shape identity'.[94] Thus, according to Anderson, the laws regulating women's domestic and sexual behavior would also have had the effect of socializing ancient Israelite women to accept their own subjection to male authority as central to their identities as women. Overall, feminist interpretation has shown that the biblical law codes depict women as inherently submissive, sexual, and maternal.

Feminist Examination of Laws about Menstruation, Childbirth, and Women's Impurity

The Levitical laws, related to menstruation and childbirth, are of special interest to feminist interpreters. They have long noted that the book of Leviticus regards these normal, biological functions of a women's body as causing 'impurity' (*tum'ah*). Feminists have thus sought to identify the source of the legal texts' understanding of women's impurity. Some argue that the source was 'a spirit of egalitarianism' whereas others disagree and maintain that the laws are based on wholly negative male attitudes toward women's bodies.

---

90. Sakenfeld, 'Feminist Biblical Interpretation', p. 157.

91. See Mary Jo Frug, 'A Postmodern Feminist Manifesto (an Unfinished Draft)', in Dan Danielsen and Karen Engle (eds.), *After Identity: A Reader in Law and Culture* (New York: Routledge, 1995), pp. 7-23.

92. Cheryl B. Anderson, *Women, Ideology and Violence: Critical Theory and the Construction of Gender in the Book of the Covenant and the Deuteronomic Law* (London: T. & T. Clark, 2004), p. 69.

93. Anderson, *Women, Ideology and Violence*, p. 69.

94. Anderson, *Women, Ideology and Violence*, p. 73.

In her highly influential 1976 essay, Rachel Adler asserts that the Jewish family purity laws (*niddah*) are not based on negative attitudes toward women's sexual and reproductive functions,[95] but on the notion that throughout their lives both men and women move from death to life, from cultic impurity to cultic purity.[96] Thus, Adler argues: '*Niddah* is not a ritual which oppresses or denigrates women. Indeed *tumah/taharah* (purity) constitutes one of the few major Jewish symbolisms equally accessible to men and women'.[97] Building on Adler's early work, some feminist exegetes suggest that the laws about women's purity stem from a belief in the holiness of women's bodies and reproductive abilities. Kathleen O'Grady, for example, notes that 'an explanation that has been gaining currency in feminist circles is the view that menstruation regulations are not "prohibitive" but "celebratory" of women and their physiology'.[98] Likewise, Kristin De Troyer explains the differing periods of impurity for the mother of a girl and the mother of a boy in a way that assumes the latter to be more holy than the former. She maintains: 'Because of the life-giving capacity of a female grown-up "newborn" the mother is to be kept far away from the sanctuary. The mother who just gave birth to a baby girl is more dangerous to God than the one who gave birth to a baby boy. The mother not only gave life; she gave life to a child who one day may give life.'[99] Thus, these scholars state that the laws about women's physical purity are positive. They consider women as symbolically equal to men, and they assume that women's bodily holiness surpasses that of men.

Yet in 1993, Adler changes her earlier positive assessment of *niddah*. She writes that her 1976 essay was based on 'a denial that any special "women's meaning" distinguished menstrual impurity from impurities contacted by men'.[100] This denial, she realizes, led her to 'formulate a theology of purity that was blind to gender difference and silent about gender stigma'.[101] Moreover, she acknowledges having ignored the 'social facts' of living in an

95. Rachel Adler, '*Tumah* and *Taharah*: Ends and Beginnings', in Elizabeth Koltun (ed.), *The Jewish Woman: New Perspectives* (New York: Schocken Books, 1976), pp. 63-71.

96. Adler, '*Tumah* and *Taharah*', p. 65.

97. Adler, '*Tumah* and *Taharah*', p. 70.

98. Kathleen O'Grady, 'The Semantics of Taboo: Menstrual Prohibitions in the Hebrew Bible', in K. De Troyer *et al.* (eds.), *Wholly Woman, Holy Blood: A Feminist Critique of Purity and Impurity* (Studies in Antiquity and Christianity; London: T. & T. Clark, 2003), p. 14.

99. Kristin De Troyer, 'Blood: A Threat to Holiness or toward (Another) Holiness', in De Troyer *et al.* (eds.), *Wholly Woman, Holy Blood*, pp. 45-64 (55).

100. Rachel Adler, 'In Your Blood, Live: Re-visions of a Theology of Purity', *Tikkun* 8 (1993), pp. 157-64 (158).

101. Adler, 'In your Blood, Live', p. 158.

Orthodox Jewish community, in which menstruating women are socially and religiously excluded.[102] Adler summarizes the problems with her earlier article as follows: 'My theology claimed that impurity was universal. The social reality…was that impurity was feminine. My theology claimed that impurity was normal and morally neutral. Literary and anthropological evidence, as well as contemporary social reality, identify impurity as deviant and a source of stigma and exclusion.'[103] Yet now Adler realizes that the purity laws were never intended to establish gender neutrality but a social hierarchy 'in which the most impure people are women'.[104]

In keeping with Adler's 1993 essay, some feminist scholars concur that the purity laws in Leviticus are based on deeply negative male attitudes toward women's bodies. Wegner, for example, states that these laws are designed to control the uniquely female 'pollution-generating processes' of menstruation, childbirth, and sexual intercourse, which threaten the purity and holiness of both the land of Israel and its male inhabitants.[105] Ellens points to the use of the Hebrew term *dawah* in Lev. 15.33 referring to 'the infirmity' of menstruation. Ellens continues, 'the meaning of *dawah* is charged; it is connected with illness…it brands the woman's normal genital discharge as necessarily unhealthy and perhaps, therefore, dangerous, as compared with men's genital discharge'.[106] In general, feminist scholars agree that the purity laws in Leviticus denigrate women and the regular functioning of their bodies.

An analysis of the laws regulating sexual intercourse with a menstruating woman also supports this negative assessment of women's bodies in biblical laws. Rachel Havrelock, for instance, notes that sexual intercourse 'becomes an increasingly grave transgression in the sequence of Leviticus'.[107] In the textually earliest law (Lev. 15.24), it causes both the man and the woman to become impure, while the textually latest law (Lev. 20.18) leads to both of them being 'cut off from their people'.[108] Ellens thus argues that these laws betray a male anxiety about being 'contaminated' by a menstruating woman's physical impurity.[109] About the versions of the law appearing in Lev. 18.19 and 20.18, she writes that a menstruating woman is understood

102. Adler, 'In Your Blood, Live', p. 160.
103. Adler, 'In Your Blood, Live', p. 161.
104. Adler, 'In Your Blood, Live', p. 161.
105. Wegner, 'Leviticus', p. 38.
106. Deborah L. Ellens, 'Menstrual Impurity and Innovation in Leviticus 15', in De Troyer *et al.* (eds.), *Wholly Woman, Holy Blood*, pp. 29-44 (30).
107. Rachel Havrelock, '*Acharei Mot* (Leviticus 16:1–18:30), Boundaries of Rituals: The Sanctuary and the Body', in Eskenazi and Weiss (eds.), *The Torah: A Women's Commentary*, pp. 679-93 (691).
108. Havrelock, '*Acharei Mot*', p. 691.
109. Ellens, *Women in the Sex Texts*, p. 287.

to 'pose a special danger to the man…[who] must protect himself' from the impurity caused by contact with her.[110] Overall, feminist scholars see an androcentric perspective in the laws' negative assessment of women's reproductive functions.

Feminist Assessment of Laws about Sexual Activity

Having established that the laws of Exodus to Deuteronomy marginalize and objectify women and that they contain negative attitudes toward women's bodies and their reproductive functions, feminist scholars have further examined the laws on sexual intercourse. They have found that they include several androcentric and homophobic concerns.

First, feminist exegetes maintain that these laws exhibit male anxiety about preserving control over female sexuality.[111] The presentation of this control, Anderson notes, often involves prohibiting a man from having sexual contact with a woman who is under the legal control of another man.[112] Specifically, the laws bar a man from taking the following women as sexual partners: a woman related to him, either by blood or by marriage (see Lev. 18.7-18; 20.11-21; Deut. 27.14-16);[113] an unmarried virgin (see Exod. 22.15-16; Deut. 22.28-29);[114] and a woman married to another man (see Lev. 18.20; 20.11; Deut. 5.18; 22.22, 23-24).[115] Anderson observes that the laws define those women who are not controlled by other men as sexually available.[116] Among the women are those under a man's own control, namely his wife, his female slave (see Lev. 19.20-22),[117] and his female captive (see Lev. 19.20-22).[118] The law also considers prostitutes who are not under the

---

110. Ellens, *Women in the Sex Texts*, p. 287.

111. Wegner, 'Leviticus', p. 41.

112. Anderson, *Women, Ideology and Violence*, pp. 70-71.

113. See Athalya Brenner, 'On Incest', in Brenner (ed.), *A Feminist Companion to Exodus to Deuteronomy*, pp. 119-24.

114. Frymer-Kensky, 'Virginity in the Bible', pp. 91-93.

115. Ellens, *Women in the Sex Texts*, pp. 289, 298.

116. Anderson, *Women, Ideology and Violence*, p. 70.

117. Bernard S. Jackson, 'Gender Critical Observations on Tripartite Breeding Relationships in the Hebrew Bible', in Deborah W. Rooke (ed.), *A Question of Sex? Gender and Difference in the Hebrew Bible and Beyond* (Sheffield: Sheffield Phoenix Press, 2007), pp. 39-53 (41-44).

118. Jackson, 'Gender Critical Observations', pp. 44-46. On the omission of a man's daughter from the discussion of which women are sexually available and which are unavailable, see Geburgis Feld, "Leviticus: The ABC of Creation', in Luise Schottroff and Marie-Theres Wacker (eds.), *Feminist Biblical Interpretation: A Compendium of Critical Commentary on the Books of the Bible and Related Literature* (trans. Lisa E. Dahill *et al.*; Grand Rapids, MI: Eerdmans, 2012), pp. 51-67 (60).

control of any man as sexually available (see Deut. 22.20-21).[119] In addition, Ellens and many other feminist scholars observe that the laws define 'rape' as sexual intercourse that has not been authorized by the man who is rightfully in charge of the woman in question (see Deut. 22.25-27, 28-29).[120] That is, rape is understood as 'violence done to a man [by another man] by means of the sexual misuse of his betrothed wife-to-be or his unbetrothed daughter'.[121] Thus, feminist scholars observe that contemporary understandings of rape[122] are largely absent in biblical legislation; neither the woman's lack of consent[123] nor 'the injustice and suffering' she experiences are addressed.[124]

Feminist scholars also affirm that the legal material exhibits a heterosexist viewpoint. Laws describe homosexual contact between men as *to 'evah* ('an abomination'), and in Lev. 20.13 it is worthy of the death penalty.[125] It is unclear what kind of sexual contact between men is envisioned[126] because of a grammatical issue.[127] According to Havrelock, however, it is clear that the biblical laws define licit sexual activity solely as a man's 'penile penetration [of a woman] with the emission of semen'.[128] These texts do not show any awareness of homosexuality as an orientation[129] or of lesbianism, whether

119. Ellens, *Women in the Sex Texts*, p. 298.

120. Ellens, *Women in the Sex Texts*, p. 299.

121. Ellens, *Women in the Sex Texts*, p. 299.

122. Note that scholars disagree on which biblical laws address rape as understood in a modern context. Susanne Scholz, for example, categorizes the sexual contact with a captive woman (Deut. 21.10-14) as rape; see Scholz, '"Back Then It Was Legal": The Epistemological Imbalance in Readings of Biblical and Ancient Near Eastern Rape Legislation', *Journal of Religion and Abuse* 7.3 (2005), pp. 5-35 (7-9); also published in *The Bible and Critical Theory* 1.4 (2005), http://publications.epress.monash.edu/toc/bc/1/4.

123. Carolyn Pressler, 'Sexual Violence and Deuteronomic Law', in Brenner (ed.), *A Feminist Companion to Exodus to Deuteronomy*, pp. 102-12 (102-103).

124. Angelika Engelmann, 'Deuteronomy: Rights and Justice for Women in the Law', in Schottroff and Wacker (eds.), *Feminist Biblical Interpretation*, pp. 84-99 (92).

125. David Tabb Stewart, 'Leviticus', in Guest *et al.* (eds.), *The Queer Bible Commentary*, pp. 77-104 (96).

126. David Brodsky, 'Sex in the Talmud: How to Understand Leviticus 18–20, *Parashat Kedoshim* (Leviticus 19:1–20:27)', in Gregg Drinkwater, Joshua Lesser, and David Shneer (eds.), *Torah Queeries: Weekly Commentaries on the Hebrew Bible* (New York: New York University Press, 2009), pp. 157-69 (157). For a discussion of the possibilities as both rabbis and contemporary Jewish scholars have understood them, see Stewart, 'Leviticus', pp. 96-99.

127. For an explanation of the Hebrew *mishkebe-isha*, see Stewart, 'Leviticus', pp. 96-97.

128. S. Tamar Kamionkowski, '*K'doshim* (Leviticus 19:1–20:27): A Call to Holiness', in Eskenazi and Weiss (eds.), *The Torah: A Women's Commentary*, pp. 701-15 (713).

129. Brodsky, 'Sex in the Talmud', p. 157.

understood as an orientation or as a type of sexual behavior.[130] Thus, in their condemnation of homosexual male contact and their inattention to (or, perhaps, ignorance of[131]) lesbian sexual contact, biblical legislation contains considerable heterosexism.

'A Mixed Perspective on Women': A Conclusion

To employ the words of Drorah O'Donnell Setel once again, feminist interpreters conclude that the books of Exodus to Deuteronomy exhibit 'a mixed perspective on women'.[132] That is, they find both liberating and oppressive elements in the narrative and legal texts. They identify as liberating the following aspects in the narrative literature: the Exodus motif; various celebrations of female characters; and the suggestion that ancient Israelite women had legal rights. In reference to the legal corpora, feminist scholars note that some laws treat women as legal agents equal to men. Among the aspects of the narrative material that feminist scholars consider oppressive are the Exodus motif; the fact that the narrative uses female characters to induce women into accepting subordinate roles; and the demonstration that ancient Israelite men limit the exercise of women's legal rights and exclude them from leadership positions. In reference to the legal corpora, feminist scholars regard women as largely marginalized and objectified. They agree that androcentrism and heterosexism characterize laws on sexual activity. These laws display a male concern with preserving the sexual control of women, and a heterosexual concern with limiting sexual intercourse to that between a man and a woman. However, the diversity of scholarly opinion on the gender issues of the books of Exodus to Deuteronomy should hardly be surprising. Such multivocality, in the words of the editors of *The Torah: A Women's Commentary*, is 'not only a defining feature of the Jewish interpretive tradition, but also an explicit feminist endeavor'.[133]

130. Stewart, 'Leviticus', pp. 89-90.
131. Stewart, 'Leviticus,' pp. 89-90.
132. Setel, 'Exodus', p. 34.
133. Tamara Cohn Eskenazi and Andrea L. Weiss, 'Introduction: About This Book', in Eskenazi and Weiss (eds.), *The Torah: A Women's Commentary*, pp. xxxi-xxxv (xxxv).

4

CONSIDER, TAKE COUNSEL, AND SPEAK:
RE(MEMBERING) WOMEN IN THE BOOKS OF JOSHUA
AND JUDGES

Beverly J. Stratton

Feminist scholarship on Joshua and Judges over the past thirty years is vast. It ranges from recovering ignored women's stories[1] to reforming approaches to biblical interpretation.[2] Consequently, this review of feminist scholarship on Joshua and Judges does not attempt to be comprehensive but to highlight key contributions, to offer a sampling of feminist voices, and to suggest potential future directions.[3] Like most of the feminist scholarship on Joshua and Judges, this essay is organized primarily around the stories of named and unnamed women included in the biblical texts.[4] I begin with general

---

1. Phyllis Trible's early lifting up of two 'texts of terror' in Judg. 11 and 19 is a good example; see her *Texts of Terror: Literary-Feminist Readings of Biblical Narratives* (Philadelphia: Fortress Press, 1984).

2. Two early analyses of feminist biblical scholarship are Carolyn Osiek, 'The Feminist and the Bible: Hermeneutical Alternatives', in Adela Yarbro Collins (ed.), *Feminist Perspectives on Biblical Scholarship* (Chico, CA: Scholars Press, 1985), pp. 93-105, and Katharine Doob Sakenfeld, 'Feminist Uses of Biblical Materials', in Letty M. Russell (ed.), *Feminist Interpretation of the Bible* (Philadelphia: Westminster Press, 1985), pp. 55-64. For a recent and autobiographical review, including recommendations for future directions, see Elisabeth Schüssler Fiorenza, 'Reaffirming Feminist/Womanist Biblical Scholarship', *Encounter* 67 (2006), pp. 361-73.

3. Susan Niditch, *Judges* (OTL; Louisville, KY: Westminster/John Knox Press, 2008) provides an extensive bibliography of standard commentaries and monographs on Judges. See also Kenneth M. Craig, Jr, 'Judges in Recent Research', *CBR* 1 (2003), pp. 159-85. For a commentary geared for laity, see Carolyn Pressler, *Joshua, Judges, and Ruth* (Westminster Bible Companion; Louisville, KY: Westminster/John Knox Press, 2002). For a general bibliography on Joshua, see Richard D. Nelson, *Joshua: A Commentary* (OTL; Louisville, KY: Westminster/John Knox Press, 1997).

4. Mieke Bal's narratology would be the primary exception. Her early feminist scholarship on Judges draws its strength from addressing the book as a whole in relation to the role of the interpreter. Space constraints prevent a thorough analysis of her work in this essay. See her trilogy: *Lethal Love: Feminist Literary Readings of Biblical Love*

comments on Joshua scholarship, present the stories about women in both books—distilling, synthesizing, and presenting the questions and conclusions of various interpreters—and conclude with broader comments about feminist scholarship in relation to these two books.

Feminist Scholarship on the Book of Joshua

Compared to Judges, the book of Joshua has attracted relatively little attention from scholars of gender studies.[5] Its stories of conquest and land distribution hide the fates of people whose lives as colonizers, conquered, or assimilated have largely escaped notice, while until recently scholars have instead addressed matters of historical criticism or theological matters of redaction and covenant. Moreover, most of the few women mentioned in Joshua have similar or more detailed stories appear elsewhere in the canon, and feminist scholarship has focused on them there. The story of Mahlah, Noah, Hoglah, Milcah, and Tirzah, also known as the daughters of Zelophehad, is mentioned in Josh. 17.3-6 but also told in more detail in Num. 27.1-11 and 36.1-12.[6] The tale of Achsah, the bride awarded by Caleb to Othniel, who similarly negotiates for a worthy inheritance in Josh. 15.16-19, appears also in Judg. 1.12-15.[7]

Stories (Bloomington: Indiana University Press, 1987); *Murder and Difference: Genre, Gender, and Scholarship on Sisera's Death* (Bloomington/Indianapolis: Indiana University Press, 1988); and *Death and Dissymmetry: The Politics of Coherence in the Book of Judges* (Chicago: University of Chicago Press, 1988).

5. Masculinity studies scholar Ovidiu Creangă suggests that 'the biblical tradition sanctions Joshua because of homoerotic indiscretions' by feminizing him and leaving him 'single and childless in a culture predicated on heterosexual love and procreation'; see his 'Variations on the Theme of Masculinity: Joshua's Gender In/Stability in the Conquest Narrative (Josh. 1–12)', in Ovidiu Creangă (ed.), *Men and Masculinity in the Hebrew Bible and Beyond* (The Bible in the Modern World, 33; Sheffield: Sheffield Phoenix Press, 2010), pp. 83-109 (98, 100).

6. See Katharine Doob Sakenfeld, 'In the Wilderness, Awaiting the Land: The Daughters of Zelophehad and Feminist Interpretation', *Princeton Seminary Bulletin* 9 (1988), pp. 179-96; Sakenfeld, 'Zelophehad's Daughters', *Perspectives in Religious Studies* 15.4 (1988), pp. 37-47; Yael Shemesh, 'A Gender Perspective on the Daughters of Zelophehad: Bible, Talmudic Midrash, and Modern Feminist Midrash', *BibInt* 15 (2007), pp. 80-109; Josiah Derby, 'The Daughters of Zelophehad Revisited', *JBQ* 25 (1997), pp. 169-71; Zvi Ron, 'The Daughters of Zelophehad', *JBQ* 26 (1998), pp. 260-62; Heidi Neumark, 'Sisters Act', *Currents in Theology and Mission* 36.3 (2009), pp. 203-207; Delores Williams, 'A Theology of Advocacy for Women: Learning about Courage and Strength in Unity', *Church and Society* 91.2 (2000), pp. 4-8.

7. For space reasons, I leave discussion of the daughters of Zelophehad for this volume's essay on Numbers and discuss Achsah below in the chapter on Judges.

In her commentary, Carolyn Pressler notes the xenophobia in the Deuter-onomic History yet sees it tempered in Joshua. She observes: 'Israel enters with indigenous people into covenants that, although against Deuteronomic law, are upheld by Joshua and uncensored by the narrator'.[8] Touching on Joshua in her more general study of war in the Hebrew Bible, Susan Niditch warns: 'The particular violence of the Hebrew Scriptures has inspired vio-lence, has served as a model of and a model for persecution, subjugation, and extermination for millennia beyond its own reality'.[9] In her monograph, Lori L. Rowlett claims Joshua evinces 'a positive attempt to win the volun-tary loyalty of the people…[by] building their identity as a unified people endowed with a purpose'.[10] She argues:

> The text of Joshua is concerned with voluntary submission to a set of rules and norms; it is directed at Josiah's own people, not at real (ethnic) outsiders, but at insiders who pose a threat to the hierarchy being asserted. The message is that the punishment of Otherness is death and that insiders can easily become outsiders (Others) by failure to submit.[11]

While there have been some efforts to read Rahab's story, in particular, through postcolonial lenses (see below), postcolonial attention to the book of Joshua as a whole is largely an area for future work, as is further feminist exploration.

Scheming, Surviving, or Subverting? Rahab in Joshua 2 and 6

Perhaps surprisingly, the conquest story in Joshua begins with two young men visiting Rahab, a prostitute, who dwells in the walls of Jericho. Rationalizing commentators suggest that the men went to a brothel in order to secure good information about the town, but the text says nothing about the spies gaining any information from other men there. As Danna Nolan Fewell and David M. Gunn suggest, perhaps the young men were eager to exercise their independence from the stringent strictures of home by having sex with an outsider.[12]

Embarrassed that just after Joshua's hortatory oration in ch. 1 his chosen spies would so quickly thwart covenantal expectations, some traditional commentators elevate or even rehabilitate Rahab's status. She is not a

8.   Pressler, *Joshua, Judges, and Ruth*, p. 4.

9.   Susan Niditch, *War in the Hebrew Bible: A Study in the Ethics of Violence* (New York: Oxford University Press, 1993), p. 4.

10.   Lori L. Rowlett, *Joshua and the Rhetoric of Violence: A New Historicist Analysis* (JSOTSup, 226; Sheffield: Sheffield Academic Press, 1996), p. 13.

11.   Rowlett, *Joshua*, pp. 12-13.

12.   Danna Nolan Fewell and David M. Gunn, *Gender, Power and Promise: The Subject of the Bible's First Story* (Nashville, TN: Abingdon Press, 1993), p. 117.

madame, they protest, not a whore or brothel owner, but simply an 'inn-keeper'. Indeed, some rabbis even marry her off to Joshua himself, and she has children whose descendents include the prophet Jeremiah.[13] Most feminist scholars, like Phyllis Bird, recognize that the text requires Rahab precisely to *be* a harlot in order for the text to accomplish its purpose.[14]

In terms of both the text's tradition history and its rhetorical effects, queer theorist Erin Runions posits an earlier Canaanite tale in Josh. 2.1-8, 15-16, 22-23. Following the 'affective turn' in cultural studies, Runions argues that this underlying story subverts the eventual overpowering speech in 2.9-14 that the Israelite conqueror, in the form of the Deuteronomist, shoves down her throat.[15] By poking fun at the men in the story, the tale alters the affect from the disgust—that is so often 'stuck' to nonheteronormative Canaanite sexuality in biblical discourse—to laughter at the bumbling Israelite spies and the Keystone Cop-like pursuing royal soldiers.[16] The subverting tale plays on bawdy innuendo, using verbs frequently associated with sexual acts: the spies *entered* Rahab's house, as both the narrator (2.1) and Jericho's king's men note (2.3); Rahab admits they have *come* to her (2.4); and they *lie down* there (2.1,8).[17] There is additional talk about what *goes up* (2.8) or *down* (2.15) and the spirit of a man that will *not rise again* (2.11).[18] Appreciating the affect produced by the sexual banter, Runions concludes:

> Rahab the prostitute comically revalues the usual disciplinary responses to Canaanite sexuality. Her sexuality is not condemned. No longer disgusting and repulsive, but instead brilliant, assertive and funny, the racialized,

13. See, e.g., Pressler, *Joshua, Judges, and Ruth*, p. 24; Creangă, 'Variations on the Theme of Masculinity', p. 92; Lori L. Rowlett, 'Disney's Pocahontas and Joshua's Rahab in Postcolonial Perspective', in George Aichele (ed.), *Culture, Entertainment and the Bible* (JSOTSup, 309; Sheffield: Sheffield Academic Press, 2000), pp. 66-75 (72); Phyllis Silverman Kramer, 'Rahab: From Peshat to Pedagogy, or: The Many Faces of a Heroine', in Aichele (ed.), *Culture, Entertainment and the Bible*, pp. 156-72 (159); and Leila Leah Bronner, *Stories of Biblical Mothers: Maternal Power in the Hebrew Bible* (Lanham, MD: University Press of America, 2004), p. 90.

14. Phyllis Bird, 'The Harlot as Heroine: Narrative Art and Social Presupposition in Three Old Testament Texts', in Miri Amihai, George W. Coats, and Anne M. Solomon (eds.), *Narrative Research on the Hebrew Bible* (Semeia, 46; Atlanta, GA: Scholars Press, 1989), pp. 119-40 (130).

15. Erin Runions, 'From Disgust to Humor: Rahab's Queer Affect', *Postscripts* 4 (2008), pp. 41–69; on the 'affective turn' see p. 45 n. 3.

16. Runions, 'From Disgust to Humor', p. 62; see Frank Anthony Spina, 'Rahab and Achan: Role Reversals', in Spina, *The Faith of the Outsider: Exclusion and Inclusion in the Biblical Story* (Grand Rapids: Eerdmans, 2005), pp. 52-71 (57).

17. Numerous commentators remark on the double-entendres, the 'suggestive and teasing' or 'lewd and crude' language, e.g., Spina, 'Rahab and Achan', pp. 54-55.

18. Runions, 'From Disgust to Humor', p. 63, notes rabbinic sources that concur with her observations of sexual innuendo in the narrative.

nonheteronormative woman has the upper hand, which she demonstrates by turning military proceedings into futile silliness. Instead of being vomited from the land, Rahab drolly expulses the putative victors from her business and her city.[19]

So how should readers understand Rahab's speech in Josh. 2.9-11? When Rahab speaks of Yahweh's power, is she a survivor, just telling the spies what they want to hear?[20] Or does she genuinely respect Yahweh although she is the 'epitome of an outsider' (non-Israelite, woman, and prostitute)?[21] Rahab speaks like a reader of Deuteronomy,[22] so the story may have functioned metaphorically to call the exilic community to repentance, as Alice Ogden Bellis, quoting womanist scholar, Naomi Franklin, suggests: 'The message, although not explicit in the text, is that as Rahab was a harlot, so was Israel. Rahab turned and confessed Yhwh as the Almighty, so could Israel.'[23]

Yet it is precisely at this point, of Rahab sounding like the Deuteronomist, where postcolonial scholar, Musa Dube, suggests feminist readers should exercise greater suspicion and resistance. She warns us not 'to overlook that Rahab is a literary creation of the author of Joshua, the colonizer'.[24] Dube makes her case for how to read Rahab's submission later in the story:

> Through her actions, Rahab is portrayed as one who totally believes in the superiority of the colonizer... Rahab's voice is notably one with the colonizer. As a literary creation of the colonizer's pen, she is the mouthpiece of their agendas. The colonizer's ideal dream is that the colonized will proclaim the colonizer's superiority, pledge absolute loyalty, and surrender all their rights voluntarily... Rahab's story contains the somewhat hidden agenda of the colonizer.[25]

Zimbabwean postcolonial and feminist scholar, Dora Mbuwayesango, shares Dube's concerns. She sees the Joshua narratives as propagating a dangerous exclusive ideology of 'divine entitlement' and mission to the

---

19.   Runions, 'From Disgust to Humor', p. 64.

20.   Fewell and Gunn, *Gender, Power and Promise*, pp. 120-21.

21.   Danna Nolan Fewell, 'Joshua', in Carol A. Newsom and Sharon H. Ringe (eds.), *Women's Bible Commentary* (exp. edn with Apocrypha; Louisville, KY: Westminster/John Knox Press, 1998), pp. 67-77 (72).

22.   Fewell and Gunn, *Gender, Power and Promise*, p. 118.

23.   Alice Ogden Bellis, *Helpmates, Harlots, and Heroes: Women's Stories in the Hebrew Bible* (Louisville, KY: Westminster/John Knox Press, 1994), p. 114, citing Naomi Franklin, 'The Stranger within their Gates (How the Israelite Portrayed the Non-Israelite in Biblical Literature)' (unpublished PhD dissertation, Duke University, 1990), pp. 112-13.

24.   Musa W. Dube, *Postcolonial Feminist Interpretation of the Bible* (St Louis, MO: Chalice Press, 2000), p. 80.

25.   Dube, *Postcolonial*, p. 78.

postexilic returnees; by occupying the land as they return from exile 'they need to fulfill what Joshua had begun but had not quite completed'.[26]

Feminist readers thus pose multiple ways of reading the significance of Rahab's story. Danna Nolan Fewell observes:

> Rahab's faith and kindness raise serious questions about the obsession with holy war in the book of Joshua. How many Rahabs are killed in the attempt to conquer the land? How many people with vision and loyalty surpassing that of the Israelites are destroyed in the attempt to establish a pure and unadulterated nation?[27]

Rahab's story may suggest at the outset of this biblical narrative that conquest was a process, 'that there was an alternative to fighting the Israelites and that those whose heart was moved to fear of God did avoid destruction'.[28] It might also represent an alternative understanding of the 'ban' (*herem*), God's command in Exodus and Deuteronomy utterly to destroy foreign nations and all that belongs to them.[29] This tradition might have 'understood the *herem* to have applied only to those nations or kings who actively opposed Israel'.[30] On the other hand, read with the Deuteronomistic Historian, it may be that 'Rahab, saved as an act of reciprocated *hesed*, is ultimately a stumbling block to Israel's survival. The rescue of Rahab is Israel's first act of apostasy.'[31]

Lori Rowlett finds the significance of Rahab's story in its relation to Achan's story in Joshua 7. She claims:

> Rahab was transformed from the quintessential Other into an insider deemed worthy of protection (and life). She accepted the structures of control and was allowed a place within the hierarchy of insiders. Achan, on the other hand, forfeited his place within the hierarchical system, although he was a born insider, by his attempt to circumvent the structures of control.[32]

In contrast to those who emphasize Israelite and Canaanite distinctions, Rowlett argues that comparing Rahab's and Achan's stories 'reveals that the true organizing principle of the narrative is not primarily ethnic identity

26. Dora Mbuwayesango, 'Joshua', in Daniel Patte *et al.* (eds.), *Global Bible Commentary* (Nashville, TN: Abingdon Press, 2004), pp. 64-73 (68-69).

27. Fewell, 'Joshua', p. 72.

28. Tikva Frymer-Kensky, 'Reading Rahab', in Modechai Cogan, Barry Eichler, and Jeffrey Tigay (eds.), *Tehillah le-Moshe: Biblical and Judaic Studies in Honor of Moshe Greenberg* (Winona Lake, IN: Eisenbrauns, 1997), pp. 57-67 (65).

29. See Exod. 23.23-24; Deut. 7.1-2; 12.2-4, 29-31; 16.21-22; 18.9-14; 20.16-18; Josh. 6.17, 18, 21; 10.40; 11.11-12 and elsewhere.

30. Frymer-Kensky, 'Reading Rahab', p. 64.

31. Frymer-Kensky, 'Reading Rahab', p. 65.

32. Rowlett, *Joshua*, p. 178.

but voluntary submission to authority structures, including the patriarchal political arrangement as well as the central ruling establishment represented by Joshua'.[33] A simplistic identification with 'woman Rahab' is thus not advisable according to feminist interpreters.

Feminist scholars and postcolonial critics have also taken up Robert Allen Warrior's challenge to read the biblical narrative from a Canaanite perspective.[34] Native American scholar, Laura Donaldson, notes Rahab's connection with another Canaanite woman, Ruth: 'Like her daughter-in-law Ruth, Rahab embodies a foreign woman, a Canaanite Other who crosses over from paganism to monotheism and is rewarded for this act by absorption into the genealogy of her husband and son—in this case, into the house of Salmon and, ultimately, of David'.[35] Kwok Pui-lan summarizes Lori Rowlett's comparison of Rahab to Disney's popularized Pocahontas story:

> Rowlett discerns four disturbing parallels between Rahab and the Pocahontas of Disney/popular media: the Native woman falls in love or has sex with the conqueror(s); she saves the conquerors and offers them assistance against her own people; she embraces the colonizing culture wholeheartedly; and her body and reproductive powers are co-opted in the conquest.[36]

Describing herself as 'a critic from Asia, where sex tourism is a flourishing business and some countries can be considered "the brothel of the world"', Kwok Pui-lan reads Rahab's story 'from the perspective of women compelled to provide sexual labor as an integral part of global markets and military buildup...[where] prostitution [is] a new form of colonization... [and where] larger societal forces and global structures...join hands to keep her in her place'.[37] Perhaps Rahab is a survivor.

In modern times, when Israel's survival and her relationship to surrounding nations and occupied peoples is again an issue, such texts call feminists and others to careful interpretations. Perhaps we concur with Musa Dube's postcolonial reading of the text: Rahab asks the powerful 'to begin to measure their relationship on the basis of their meeting and knowing the

---

33. Rowlett, *Joshua*, pp. 178-79.

34. Robert Allen Warrior, 'Canaanites, Cowboys, and Indians: Deliverance, Conquest, and Liberation Theology Today', *Christianity and Crisis* 49 (September 1989), pp. 261-65.

35. Laura E. Donaldson, 'The Sign of Orpah: Reading Ruth through Native Eyes', in R.S. Sugirtharajah (ed.), *Vernacular Hermeneutics* (Bible and Postcolonialism, 2; Sheffield: Sheffield Academic Press, 1999), pp. 20-36 (30).

36. Kwok Pui-lan, 'Sexual Morality and National Politics: Reading Biblical "Loose Women"', in Choi Hee An and Katheryn Pfisterer Darr (eds.), *Engaging the Bible: Critical Readings from Contemporary Women* (Minneapolis: Fortress Press, 2006), pp. 21-46 (37), citing Rowlett, 'Disney's Pocahontas', p. 68.

37. Kwok Pui-lan, 'Sexual Morality and National Politics', pp. 38-39.

very humanness and vulnerability of each person'.[38] Rahab also 'challenges them to read her text, the red ribbon that she hangs out, a text that calls them against their mission of killing and destroying lives, to a mission of saving life'.[39]

Feminist Scholarship on the Book of Judges: Achsah, a Dutiful Daughter? (Judges 1.12-15; cf. Joshua 15.13-19)

As Rahab did, Achsah, named in both Joshua and Judges, works with the gender expectations of her situation. The narrator presents Achsah, Caleb's daughter, positively, in Judg. 1.12-15. Like Tamar in Genesis 38, Achsah is a survivor, 'doing what must be done to insure a good life for her and her family'.[40] While she confronts her father, insisting that she be given water along with fields so that her dry land may be fruitful, she does so respectfully, deferring to male authority.[41] Indeed, Lillian Klein claims that the book of Judges offers her as 'an image of a model woman in a model male–female relationship'.[42]

However, deconstructive reader, Danna Nolan Fewell, raises questions about Achsah. Should she be seen as a trinket (her name means 'bangle' or 'anklet') given away by her father? Is she tethered or hobbled, as an Arabic cognate suggests; is she a 'spoil of war', 'bait', her husband's 'due reward', or a 'bargaining chip'?[43] In this brief text, part of our view of Achsah comes from the way we translate and interpret Judg. 1.14. Fewell presents several translations and comments on their differences:[44]

NRSV:	When she came to him, she urged him to ask her father...
REB:	When she became his wife, Othniel induced her to ask...
Tanakh:	When she came [to him], she induced him to ask...

38. Musa W. Dube, 'Rahab Is Hanging Out a Red Ribbon: One African Woman's Perspective on the Future of Feminist New Testament Scholarship', in Kathleen O'Brien Wicker, Althea Spencer Miller, and Musa W. Dube (eds.), *Feminist New Testament Studies: Global and Future Perspectives* (New York: Palgrave Macmillan, 2005), pp. 177-202 (180).

39. Dube, 'Rahab', p. 180.

40. Fewell and Gunn, *Gender, Power and Promise*, p. 122.

41. Fewell, 'Joshua', p. 83; Lillian R. Klein, 'A Spectrum of Female Characters', in Athalya Brenner (ed.), *A Feminist Companion to Judges* (FCB, 4; Sheffield: JSOT Press, 1993), pp. 24-33 (27).

42. Lillian R. Klein, 'The Book of Judges: Paradigm and Deviation in Images of Women', in Brenner (ed.), *A Feminist Companion to Judges*, pp. 55-71 (55).

43. Danna Nolan Fewell, 'Deconstructive Criticism: Achsah and the (E)razed City of Writing', in Gale A. Yee (ed.), *Judges and Method: New Approaches in Biblical Studies* (Minneapolis: Fortress, 1995), pp. 119-45 (133).

44. Fewell, 'Deconstructive Criticism', pp. 130-31, 135.

Boling, *AB*:   When she arrived, he nagged her to ask...
Soggin, 1981:   When he came to her, he prompted her to ask...
                       [Here Soggin emends the MT, following LXX and
                       Vulgate.]

Who is the subject of the verb: Achsah or Othniel? Fewell muses:

> If Achsah is the subject of the verb, we get an Othniel who is easily manipu-
> lated by his wife (God forbid!)... If...Othniel is the subject, we get a greedy
> hero who nags his wife to do something he is not willing to do himself. Some
> hero! In the end we see how interpreters are preoccupied with how the
> biblical text models men.[45]

Another perspective comes from Mieke Bal, who sees Achsah as acting
autonomously in a world of men, boldly but properly challenging Caleb's
fatherly authority with her bodily speech-act, claiming water for her life-
producing body.[46] But Fewell wonders if Achsah is an assertive, self-moti-
vated woman, who communicates by her action 'that she is willing to travel
no further until she gets what she wants' or is she a 'deferential, unassuming
young woman...[a] modest and respectful daughter'?[47] As interpretations of
Achsah's story show, one regular challenge for feminist scholars is how to
understand the depiction of women in biblical texts in relation to their
presumed androcentric historical, sociological, and narrative contexts.

Leaders, Warriors, Mothers, and Poets:
Deborah and Jael (Judges 4–5)

Feminist scholars like to examine women in pairs, such as Sarah and Hagar
or Rachel and Leah, and to explore their relationships. Yet the redactor of
Judges is either disinterested in such a potential friendship or seems keen to
keep the women warriors of Judges 4–5 apart. As queer commentator, Deryn
Guest, observes: 'Deborah and Jael never meet each other in the text... Only
in the song of chapter 5[.24] does Jael's name cross Deborah's tongue as
she praises Jael's actions.'[48] Guest summarizes the imaginative, midrashic
reading of Sara Maitland in which Deborah and Jael smile at one another,
laugh and grin over 'the smashed head of Sisera'. They reach 'out hands,
unspeaking, almost shy with excitement, [they] touch each other very gently.
They know their husbands will never want to touch them again.'[49] Guest

---

45.   Fewell, 'Deconstructive Criticism', pp. 135-36.
46.   Bal, *Death*, pp. 153, 155-56.
47.   Fewell, 'Deconstructive Criticism', pp. 137-38.
48.   Deryn Guest, 'Judges', in Deryn Guest *et al.* (eds.), *The Queer Bible Commentary*
(London: SCM Press, 2006), pp. 167-89 (177).
49.   Guest, 'Judges', p. 179, citing Sara Maitland, 'Of Deborah and Jael', in Maitland,
Telling Tales (London: Journeyman Press, 1983), pp. 1-4 (4).

finds joy in Maitland's creative rereading 'of biblical women who, despite being married, might have resisted their heterosexual script and harboured other loyalties'.[50]

In contrast to Maitland's inventive midrash, Gale Yee places the characters in their historical context and examines the metaphor of the 'woman warrior' within its history of interpretation. She observes that the proximity of military and domestic roles in pre-monarchic Israel made it possible to depict women as warriors.[51] Yee's analysis suggests that the author of Judges 4 reinforces 'negative stereotypes of women in general. Instead of a warrior defending her people and her household, Jael becomes at the hands of the male author a temptress, deceiver, and ultimately a castrator.'[52] Yee also notices that subsequent interpreters find it difficult to view women as warriors. The discussions demonstrate the limited assumptions and manifold interpretative prejudices about proper ambitions and gender roles for women.[53] Hence, Yee views these stories about women warriors 'as cautionary tales to keep women in their place'.[54]

Feminist scholars have also discussed the origins of these passages. For instance, Jo Ann Hackett holds on to the traditional view that Judges 5 is 'generally considered one of the oldest pieces of literature in the Bible'. In contrast, Athalya Brenner maintains that it is unclear whether Judges 4 precedes Judges 5 or vice versa.[55] Feminist scholars also have different opinions about the female authorship of these chapters.[56] Hackett considers

---

50. Guest, 'Judges', p. 180.

51. Gale A. Yee, 'By the Hand of a Woman: The Metaphor of the Woman Warrior in Judges 4', in Claudia V. Camp and Carole R. Fontaine (eds.), *Women, War, and Metaphor: Language and Society in the Study of the Hebrew Bible* (Semeia, 61; Atlanta, GA: Scholars Press, 1993), pp. 99-132 (110-12).

52. Yee, 'By the Hand of a Woman', p. 117.

53. Yee, 'By the Hand of a Woman', pp. 117-24, provides glimpses of dozens of readings from Pseudo-Philo to more recent interpreters of the nineteenth and twentieth centuries.

54. Yee, 'By the Hand of a Woman', p. 108.

55. While Jo Ann Hackett presents a traditional view that Judg. 5 is 'generally considered one of the oldest pieces of literature in the Bible', Athalya Brenner maintains that opinions are divided over whether Judg. 4 or 5 is earlier. See Jo Ann Hackett, 'Violence and Women's Lives in the Book of Judges', *Int* 58 (2004), pp. 356-64 (357); Athalya Brenner, 'A Triangle and a Rhombus in Narrative Structure: A Proposed Integrative Reading of Judges 4 and 5', in Brenner (ed.), *A Feminist Companion to Judges*, pp. 98-109 (98).

56. Some male scholars have also argued for female authorship. Susan Niditch notes that Mordecai Levine argues for female authorship of Judg. 5; see her 'Eroticism and Death in the Tale of Jael', in Peggy L. Day (ed.), *Gender and Difference in Ancient Israel* (Minneapolis: Fortress Press, 1989), pp. 43-57 (52), citing Levine, 'The Polemic against Rape in the Song of Deborah', *Beth Mikra* 25 (1979), pp. 83-84.

the possibility 'that some of these stories in fact derive from women's literature, literature composed by and/or preserved in women's circles'.[57] Yet Athalya Brenner finds a distinction in narrative voice between the two chapters. She sees Judges 4 as 'predominantly male oriented' and Judges 5 as 'predominantly female oriented'.[58] Her colleague, Fokkelien van Dijk-Hemmes, attributes the Song of Deborah to a woman author.[59] In other words, feminist scholars are as divided about authorship issues as androcentric interpreters have been for a long time.

Adrien Bledstein's position is perhaps the most dramatic of them all. She argues for extending the female authorship of the Song of Deborah to the book of Judges as a whole.[60] In her view, the prophet Huldah, known for authenticating a scroll for King Josiah in 2 Kings 22, may in fact be the Deuteronomist and the author of the entire book of Judges. If the book is indeed a satire, designed 'to admonish the young monarch Josiah: "Beware of he-who-would-be-God"',[61] it would explain the humorous depictions of several male characters, such as Samson 'the dodo' or 'the greatest jackass in the Bible', '[t]hick-headed Manoah', and Gideon, a foolish hero prone to excess, who haggles and has a lousy son.[62] In short, Bledstein proposes

> that we imagine a woman recorded the period of Judges from a Divine, ironic perspective. Drawing upon stories told by women and men, she ridiculed Israelite men who experienced themselves, instead of YHWH, as the deliverers of Israel and consequently made a tragic mess of things. The anguish evoked by a review of the period of Judges was presented through the defensive shield of ironic laughter, so that all of Israel might remember that YHWH alone is Divine.[63]

The song's claim in Judg. 5.7 that Deborah arose as 'a mother in Israel', and Jael's epithet, 'most blessed of women', in Judg. 5.24 present another arena of feminist analysis. Feminist scholars wonder in what ways the rhetoric about Deborah and Jael as 'mothers' affects Israelite women or

---

57.   Jo Ann Hackett, 'In the Days of Jael: Reclaiming the History of Women in Ancient Israel', in Clarissa W. Atkinson, Constance H. Buchanan, and Margaret R. Miles (eds.), *Immaculate and Powerful: The Female in Sacred Image and Social Reality* (Boston: Beacon Press, 1985), pp. 15-38 (32).

58.   Brenner, 'A Triangle and a Rhombus', pp. 107-8.

59.   Fokkelien van Dijk-Hemmes, 'Mothers and a Mediator in the Song of Deborah', in Brenner (ed.), *A Feminist Companion to Judges*, pp. 110-14 (111). For more on gender and biblical texts, see Athalya Brenner and Fokkelien van Dijk-Hemmes, *On Gendering Texts: Female and Male Voices in the Hebrew Bible* (Leiden: E.J. Brill, 1993).

60.   Adrien Janis Bledstein, 'Is Judges a Woman's Satire on Men Who Play God?', in Brenner (ed.), *A Feminist Companion to Judges*, pp. 34-54.

61.   Bledstein, 'Is Judges a Woman's Satire on Men Who Play God?', p. 54.

62.   Bledstein, 'Is Judges a Woman's Satire on Men Who Play God?', pp. 49, 48, 45.

63.   Bledstein, 'Is Judges a Woman's Satire on Men Who Play God?', p. 53.

future readers who could be mothers. On the one hand, a 'mother' is praised. Alice Ogden Bellis reminds her readers that the 'phrase "most blessed of women" is used in the Bible only of Mary, Jesus' mother, and Judith'.[64] On the other hand, Fewell and Gunn point out that these biblical mothers justify violence. Sisera's mother 'reduces her enemy to a "womb"' while Deborah is a 'bellicose mother who pushes her "children" to victory'.[65] Hence, they conclude: 'There are some surprising images of motherhood in this story... Mothers who are leaders, protectors, counselors, and portraits of courage, are also mothers who condone violence, deceit, and the possession of other women.'[66] Exum also notes that Barak and Sisera are like little boys who need their mother.[67] Initially, then, it seems that Deborah is a good mother, the one who keeps her children safe, whereas Jael is a dangerous, head-smashing mother. Yet Exum also insists that the 'dangerous mother and the nurturing mother are one and the same'.[68] Indeed, 'it is not possible to experience only one side of the mother and not the other. Jael is both nurturing and deadly. Deborah not only gives life to Israel but also sends her "sons" off to war, where many of them will die.'[69]

The dangerous and nurturing mothers are presented with an array of sexual imagery in the book of Judges and its midrashim. Exum notes, for example, that Jael comes to Sisera, 'an expression often used of sexual intercourse'.[70] But this language must be rendered well so that its erotic force is felt. Accordingly, Niditch, who follows Alter's suggestion, translates Sisera as falling between Jael's *legs* in Judg. 5.27. She notes that 'between her feet' obscures 'the visceral sexual quality of the imagery' which is a euphemism for genitals.[71] Similarly, Fewell and Gunn imagine Jael as pounding the tent peg not through the sleeping Sisera's temple or head in 5.26, but through his *mouth*.[72] Their reading 'produces the even more graphic image of the woman approaching the man and thrusting a phallic tent peg into his mouth'.[73] Niditch captures the rhetorical force of Jael's effort: 'Having a woman do the womanizing, the man despoiled just as he is

---

64. Bellis, *Helpmates, Harlots, and Heroes*, p. 122.

65. Fewell and Gunn, *Gender, Power and Promise*, p. 125.

66. Fewell and Gunn, *Gender, Power and Promise*, p. 126.

67. J. Cheryl Exum, 'Feminist Criticism: Whose Interests Are Being Served?', in Yee (ed.), *Judges and Method*, pp. 65-90 (72).

68. Exum, 'Feminist Criticism', p. 72.

69. Exum, 'Feminist Criticism', p. 73.

70. Exum, 'Feminist Criticism', p. 73.

71. Niditch, 'Eroticism', p. 47.

72. Danna Nolan Fewell and David M. Gunn, 'Controlling Perspectives: Women, Men, and the Authority of Violence in Judges 4 and 5', *JAAR* 58 (1990), pp. 389-411 (393).

73. Exum, 'Feminist Criticism', p. 73.

in a position of sexual seducer himself, makes for an especially powerful portrait of the victor'.[74] Rabbinic readings engorge the sexuality. They suggest that the milk Jael gave Sisera was breast milk, and, perhaps counting Sisera's actions in 5.27 (he 'sank' three times; he 'fell' three times; and he 'lay' between Jael's legs), the rabbis conclude that Jael 'had sex with Sisera seven times'![75]

What should readers make of all of this? Mieke Bal invites readers to remember the violence and to think rhetorically about how the text affects and persuades those who read or hear it by involving them in feeling, experiencing, and participating. Bal states:

> *Writing* history is not just noting the facts. It is selecting what the writer finds relevant for his own purpose... The Song of Deborah is a good example... [It] is a commemoration... Deborah's poetic work consists of making the assembled people experience the triumph again, *feel* the pleasure and pride of victory, *experience* the shame of cowardice for those who did not participate, *participate* in the speech-act of blessing Yael for her act... The gap between this form of history-making and the epic version that *explains* the event rather than sharing it, that chooses to enhance the rational interpretation over the emotional revival, cannot be overestimated.[76]

Such active commemoration of unnecessary violence and courageous response characterizes the interpretations of feminist scholars when they turn their attention to the story of Jephthah and his daughter.

From Victim to Voice: Jephthah's Daughter (Judges 11)

Phyllis Trible includes Judges 11 among her texts of terror.[77] She reads Jephthah as a victimizer and his daughter as a victim. Feminist exegetes, following Trible's lead, have examined the vocabulary and literary details of the text, explored its social context, and developed nuanced, imaginative, and resisting readings. For example, Esther Fuchs points out that Jephthah's 'use of the pronoun *'ănōkî* (I myself) [in Judg. 11.35] stresses his own culpability...[dramatizing his] bitterness, despair and anger'.[78] Such an interpretation yields a new vision of Jephthah. Fuchs explains: 'Rather than exposing Jephthah as a selfish coward, the text depicts him as a victim; a victim through his own wrong-headed actions, but a victim nonetheless'.[79]

---

74. Niditch, 'Eroticism', p. 52.

75. Leila Leah Bronner, 'Valorized or Vilified? The Women of Judges in Midrashic Sources', in Brenner (ed.), *A Feminist Companion to Judges*, pp. 72-95 (89).

76. Bal, *Death*, p. 241 (original italics).

77. Trible, *Texts of Terror*, pp. 92-116.

78. Esther Fuchs, 'Marginalization, Ambiguity, Silencing: The Story of Jephthah's Daughter', in Brenner (ed.), *A Feminist Companion to Judges*, pp. 116-30 (122).

79. Fuchs, 'Marginalization', p. 124.

Feminist readers discuss the noun, *bĕtûlay*, which in Judg. 11.37-38 is often translated as 'virginity'. Mieke Bal maintains that this term refers to a transitional period in the life of a young woman,[80] and it should not be equated with sexual purity, as the narrator's phrase 'she had never known a man' (Judg. 11.39, RSV, NJPS) suggests.[81] Peggy Day notes a growing consensus about the translation of this term. It views the key issue as 'the social recognition of [the daughter's] transition to physical maturity'.[82] Drawing on Ugaritic cognates, Exum concurs.[83] The issue is a rite of passage through a dangerous, liminal state, not a reference 'to a woman who has not had sexual intercourse'.

Feminist scholars debate how Jephthah and his daughter regarded the vow. Did the vow signal Jephthah's unfaithfulness, as suggested by Trible,[84] or was this form of human sacrifice religiously acceptable with the vow emerging under the influence of the Spirit, as Exum contends?[85] Interpreters wonder if Jephthah considered that his daughter might be first to greet him and thus be doomed by his vow. They also discuss whether the daughter knows about her father's vow. Esther Fuchs contends that the daughter's joyful dance indicates dramatic irony since 'she does not know the gruesome meaning of her joyful actions'.[86] Yet Bal disagrees, arguing that such rituals

80. Bal, *Death*, p. 48.

81. Bal, *Death*, p. 46. There Bal also examines the word *bĕtûlâ* and the phrase 'that had not known man' in their context in Judg. 21.12.

82. Peggy L. Day, 'From the Child Is Born the Woman: The Story of Jephthah's Daughter', in Day (ed.), *Gender and Difference in Ancient Israel*, pp. 58-74 (58).

83. J. Cheryl Exum, 'On Judges 11', in Brenner (ed.), *A Feminist Companion to Judges*, pp. 131-44 (141).

84. Trible, *Texts of Terror*, p. 97.

85. On the Spirit's influence, see J. Cheryl Exum, 'The Tragic Vision and Biblical Narrative: The Case of Jephthah', in J. Cheryl Exum (ed.), *Signs and Wonders: Biblical Texts in Literary Focus* (SBLSS; Atlanta, GA: Society of Biblical Literature, 1989), pp. 59-83 (66). On human sacrifice, J. Cheryl Exum, 'Murder They Wrote: Ideology and the Manipulation of Female Presence in Biblical Narrative', in Alice Bach (ed.), *The Pleasure of her Text: Feminist Readings of Biblical and Historical Texts* (Philadelphia: Trinity Press International, 1990), pp. 45-67 (66), cites Alberto Green, *The Role of Human Sacrifice in the Ancient Near East* (Missoula, MT: Scholars Press, 1975), p. 199, who observes: 'During the formative period of the Federation of Israel, there is the strong implication that human sacrifice was practiced by the people as an acceptable aspect of their Yahwistic belief'. In contrast, Susan Niditch, *War in the Hebrew Bible*, p. 33, argues: 'It is important to note that the tale of Jephthah's daughter does not necessarily imply that ancient Israelite bandit chiefs regularly promised human sacrifices from their own households in order to obtain victory against enemies any more than the tale of Iphegenia indicates that ancient Greek generals generally sacrificed daughters to make the wind move their vessels'.

86. Fuchs, 'Marginalization', p. 120.

were common and would have been known both to Jephthah and his daughter. She writes: 'The "normal" procedure of celebration after victory included the participation of his daughter as the dancing and singing maiden to celebrate the victor'.[87] Danna Nolan Fewell and David M. Gunn concur when they note that Jephthah's vow was made in public to rouse a war effort, and his daughter certainly could have heard about it.[88] Thus, her actions may be viewed as protecting others from the fate of her father's cruel and thoughtless vow.[89] In short, Fewell and Gunn assert she greeted her father on purpose. They write:

> Her voluntary action passes judgment on her father's willingness to bargain for glory with the life of another. His priorities...stand condemned... If we can concede such initiative in this young woman, we can see her taking control of the vow, turning it from a weapon of victory accidentally causing unavoidable collateral damage to a chilling lesson about recklessness, thoughtlessness, and human worth... She chooses to take upon herself her father's vow, but she does not choose his company.[90]

Jephthah's daughter may thus have acquiesced to her own death because she knew her tragic fate: as a virgin, she was an acceptable sacrifice.[91] In other words, feminist interpreters debate whether to give the daughter agency over her fate.

In short, feminist readers struggle with Judges 11. Unsurprisingly, they hold a variety of positions. Fewell and Gunn find a tale of two abused children, Jephthah and his daughter.[92] At stake is whether a reader accepts the narrator's point of view. Following Renita Weems, Alice Ogden Bellis concludes: 'In Judges 11 the narrators...paint a stupid, self-serving vow as the action of a faithful man'.[93] If readers can carefully 'discern the difference between genuine piety and self-serving, ersatz versions [like Jephthah's] that destroy rather than build up...then perhaps Jephthah's daughter did not die in vain'.[94]

---

87.   Bal, *Death*, p. 45.

88.   Fewell and Gunn, *Gender, Power and Promise*, p. 127.

89.   David M. Gunn and Danna Nolan Fewell, *Narrative in the Hebrew Bible* (Oxford Bible Series; New York: Oxford University Press, 1993), p. 116.

90.   Fewell and Gunn, *Gender, Power and Promise*, p. 127.

91.   Exum, 'Murder They Wrote', p. 63.

92.   Fewell and Gunn, *Gender, Power and Promise*, p. 126.

93.   Bellis, *Helpmates, Harlots, and Heroes*, p. 130; informed by Renita J. Weems, 'A Crying Shame', in Weems, *Just a Sister Away: A Womanist Vision of Women's Relationships in the Bible* (San Diego: LuraMedia, 1988), pp. 52-69.

94.   Bellis, *Helpmates, Harlots, and Heroes*, p. 130.

Bellis is not alone in this assessment. Esther Fuchs also cautions feminist readers to be wary of the narrator's choices. For instance, why does the daughter not cry out when she learns her fate? Why does she not resist her father's vow? Fuchs explains:

> A protest or howl of despair on the part of Jephthah's daughter would have unduly highlighted the daughter's tragedy. The daughter's calm response and subsequent silence permit the reader to remain focused on the father's grief. Had Jephthah's daughter been shown to ask for pity, had she asked to be spared, had she turned to Yahweh with a plea for mercy, the narrative would have tipped the scales too much in her favor, so much so that Jephthah's refusal to grant her freedom would have cast both him and Yahweh in a questionable role.[95]

The daughter continues to be sacrificed by interpreters, Fuchs explains, when 'the center of attention continues to be Jephthah'.[96]

So what's a feminist reader to do? Deconstruct and resist, advises J. Cheryl Exum. In a series of several essays, Exum's interpretations depict Jephthah as a nearly tragic figure,[97] his daughter as an unwisely glorified victim[98] who accepts her fate with alarming composure,[99] the deity as implicated[100] or at least partially complicit,[101] and the text itself as a phallogocentric attempt to teach proper daughterly submissive behavior.[102] Yet some attempts by Jephthah's daughter to claim her voice,[103] nevertheless, can be retrieved by astute, resistant readers willing to deconstruct the text.[104] Exum

---

95. Fuchs, 'Marginalization', p. 126.

96. Fuchs, 'Marginalization', p. 116.

97. Exum, 'Tragic Vision', p. 76.

98. Exum, 'Murder They Wrote', p. 64. Indeed, Exum contends, to glorify Jephthah's daughter as a victim is to 'fall into a patriarchal pattern of thinking'; see 'Murder They Wrote', p. 60. How do we reject this concept without also sacrificing Jephthah's daughter through our reading? Exum explains in 'Feminist Criticism', p. 77: 'Recognizing that the narrator uses the women of Israel to elevate the willing victim to honored status allows us to expose the text's valorization of submission and glorification of the victim as serving androcentric interests'.

99. Exum, 'Murder They Wrote', p. 58.

100. Exum, 'Murder They Wrote', p. 49.

101. Exum notes the source of the tragic in Jephthah's story as divine silence ('Tragic Vision', p. 78, cf. p. 68 n. 5); the absence of divine censure for Jephthah's carrying out his vow raises doubts about the divine role and questions about divine benevolence ('Tragic Vision', pp. 78-79).

102. Exum, 'Feminist Criticism', p. 77.

103. Exum notes that 'within the confines of the patriarchal word...she makes some motions toward self-assertion...she attempts to define herself'; see 'Murder They Wrote', p. 62.

104. Exum, 'Murder They Wrote', p. 59, and Exum, 'On Judges 11', p. 143.

models how to do deconstructive, resistant readings. First, she advises to *recognize the narrator's position*: 'There is no..."Jephthah's daughter's story"'.[105] The story is not about her, and there is no negative judgment by the narrator for her father's actions. Second, she recommends *acknowledging the patriarchal bias*. While there is no blatant misogyny, the story reflects 'a culturally inherited and deep-rooted gender bias'.[106] Third, she proposes to *discern what specific interests are being served*. Jephthah's daughter is memorialized not as herself but *as a daughter*—that is why her name is not preserved.[107] The story functions to teach daughters to submit to paternal authority.[108] Fourth, Exum urges readers to *look for clues to how the text may subtly undermine itself*. In this case, a shift in pronouns in his daughter's speech notes Jephthah's responsibility. Like Moses responding to God after the golden calf incident by saying '*your* people whom *you* brought up', Jephthah's daughter places the blame and ownership of responsibility where it belongs. She reminds Jephthah and readers 'of his responsibility: *You* have opened *your* mouth to the LORD; do to me according to what has gone forth from *your* mouth'.[109]

Two womanist scholars, Renita Weems and Valerie Cooper, model the approach recommended by Exum. Weems encourages today's readers to take up our 'sacred responsibility' to speak out against domestic violence, to stop hiding tragedy, horror, and sin under silence, and instead to act in 'radical devotion to one another—and to the...truth'.[110] Similarly, Valerie Cooper moves beyond merely deconstructing the ancient text to bring it into conversation with Black women's realities today.[111] She wonders how many Black Jephthahs there are today, men who 'are as marginalized and historically have been as securely locked out of economic and political power as Jephthah was'.[112] Their plight, like his, often misguidedly leads 'Black Jephthahs [to] mistreat Black daughters as mute offerings to their own societal powerlessness, while the society that keeps Jephthah marginalized has some of his daughters' blood on its hands'.[113] She also notes that

---

105.　Exum, 'Murder They Wrote', p. 46.
106.　Exum, 'Murder They Wrote', p. 59.
107.　Exum, 'Murder They Wrote', p. 59; see Exum, 'Feminist Criticism', p. 77.
108.　Exum, 'Murder They Wrote', p. 59.
109.　Exum, 'Feminist Criticism', p. 78.
110.　Weems, 'A Crying Shame', pp. 52, 67.
111.　Valerie C. Cooper, 'Some Place to Cry: Jephthah's Daughter and the Double Dilemma of Black Women in America', in Cheryl Kirk-Duggan (ed.), *Pregnant Passion: Gender, Sex, and Violence in the Bible* (Atlanta, GA: Society of Biblical Literature, 2003), pp. 181-91.
112.　Cooper, 'Some Place to Cry', p. 187.
113.　Cooper, 'Some Place to Cry', p. 189.

frequently Black women, like Jephthah's daughter, 'accept choices that may ultimately mean death to them, if it will "save face" for the men they love'.[114] Cooper reminds womanist and feminist readers: 'What we see in Jephthah's daughter says much about who we are, what we believe about ourselves, what we believe about others, what we believe about society, and what we believe about God'.[115]

Mother or Temptress: Stereotypes and Women in Judges 13–16

Interpretations of Samson's women also tell us about ourselves and our society. Although Judges 13–16 mentions several women, male characters frame these chapters. They begin with 'a certain man', Manoah in 13.2, and end when Samson is buried 'in the tomb of Manoah his father' in 16.31. Feminist interpreters observe that men's interests shape the portrayal of the women in this text.

But the characterization of women is also similar to the depiction of women elsewhere in Judges. For instance, if Jephthah's daughter is a nameless model daughter, the first of Samson's women, his mother, is a nameless model mother.[116] A careful reading of Judges 13 shows that though she is nameless, Manoah's wife is more astute than her husband. The angel visits her and speaks only to her about her future child (Judg. 13.3-5, 9), even after Manoah requested his own hearing (Judg. 13.8) and later asks for instructions about the boy (Judg. 13.12). Exum concludes that the mother is perceptive, worthy, and shows theological insight while Manoah is obtuse and clueless.[117]

Yet the positive portrayal of Samson's mother merely reinforces the narrator's patriarchal interests. First, 'Mrs Manoah' is harmless because she does not challenge her husband's authority.[118] Second, she is an idealized woman. Though a mother, she is put on a pedestal, carefully guarded from any taint of sexuality. The text does *not* say what would normally precede a

---

114.   Cooper, 'Some Place to Cry', p. 187.

115.   Cooper, 'Some Place to Cry', p. 191.

116.   Exum, 'Feminist Criticism', p. 79.

117.   See Exum, 'Feminist Criticism', p. 79; J. Cheryl Exum, 'Samson's Women', in Exum, *Fragmented Women: Feminist (Sub)Versions of Biblical Narratives* (Valley Forge, PA: Trinity Press International, 1993), pp. 61-93 (65); and J. Cheryl Exum, '"Mother in Israel": A Familiar Story Reconsidered', in Russell (ed.), *Feminist Interpretation of the Bible*, pp. 73-85 (82). Compare Esther Fuchs, 'The Literary Characterization of Mothers and Sexual Politics in the Hebrew Bible', in Collins (ed.), *Feminist Perspectives on Biblical Scholarship*, pp. 117-36 (124).

118.   Exum, 'Feminist Criticism', p. 79.

birth announcement: Manoah 'went into his wife'.[119] Instead, there is a striking absence of sex in her story, especially when it is compared to the pervasive sexual liaisons, innuendo, and symbolism of her son's tales.[120]

Hence, the stories of Samson's women include a clear dichotomy of good woman/bad woman.[121] Women are either idealized as mothers or cast off as dangerous 'other'.[122] As J. Cheryl Exum observes, the division of women into respectable and disreputable 'also works to regulate female behavior by making gender solidarity impossible'.[123] Male supremacy can be maintained by threat, but it is more easily preserved by women's complicity.[124] In return for their subordination, cooperation, and controlled sexuality, women are rewarded by becoming mothers.[125] Motherhood is portrayed as a desirable way for women to attain status.[126]

The alternative to motherhood is the role into which Delilah and other women are cast—as alluring and dangerous 'other'. On his way to Delilah, Samson encounters two such 'other women'. First, he sees a woman from Timnah and, reminiscent of Hamor in Gen. 34.4, asks his parents to get her for him (Judg. 14.2). The road to Timnah is also where Judah sleeps with a 'prostitute' in Genesis 38. From both of these allusions, readers might expect some sexual/relational problems for Samson. What precisely happens is not clear. Mieke Bal suggests that Samson was insecure in his sexuality, perhaps bisexual,[127] and that he needed to grow up; hence, the Timnite woman's father tries to give his younger daughter to him.[128] Exum explains that the marriage was a *tsadiqah* marriage,[129] what Bal calls patrilocal, a custom by which a woman lives at her father's house after the wedding and the marriage is not yet consummated.[130] Danna Nolan Fewell believes that the prostitute whom Samson visits in 16.1-3 provides the key for explaining the relationship between the other women (the Timnite and Delilah) and Samson. They all do what they need to do in order to survive.[131]

119.   Exum, 'Feminist Criticism', p. 80.
120.   Exum, 'Samson's Women', p. 66.
121.   Exum, 'Feminist Criticism', p. 78.
122.   Exum, 'Samson's Women', p. 76.
123.   Exum, 'Feminist Criticism', p. 82.
124.   Exum, 'Feminist Criticism', pp. 79-80.
125.   Exum, 'Feminist Criticism', p. 82.
126.   Exum, 'Feminist Criticism', pp. 79-80.
127.   Bal, *Lethal Love*, p. 63.
128.   Bal, *Lethal Love*, p. 47.
129.   Exum, 'Samson's Women', p. 75.
130.   Exum, 'Samson's Women', p. 71 n. 19.
131.   Fewell, 'Judges', p. 80.

Delilah captures the attention of readers, poets, librettists, painters, and filmmakers in her role as *femme fatale*.[132] Yet interpreters often impose their views on the text, assuming, for example, that she is a Philistine prostitute. Yet Delilah has a name and owns her house,[133] and she seems interested in making money.[134] And with a Hebrew name, she might be Israelite,[135] and readers need not infer that she has had many lovers just because Samson seeks multiple sexual partners.[136] When reading the Samson–Delilah texts 'through a glass queerly', Lori Rowlett observes that a 'pattern of domination by the exotic Other in a tale of bondage and degradation emerges as a stock S/M scenario'.[137] In the context of rape, Susanne Scholz notes the root *'anah* in Judg. 16.5, 6, 19 and sees the potential 'for arguing that the Philistines and Delilah attempted to "rape" Samson'.[138] As we have seen before, feminist interpretations are diverse and rich in detailed discussions about gender, women, and issues of sexuality.

Trible's Literary Approach to Judges 19–21

Phyllis Trible's powerful 'literary-feminist' reading of the story of the Levite's concubine provides a helpful overview of the story in the final chapters of Judges.[139] Trible's interpretation calls readers, in homiletical fashion, to heed the concluding mandate of the Judges 19 text. Trible requests that we take the slain woman's story to heart, recognize that today's women suffer similar horrors, take counsel, and speak out. Trible's analysis

132. For a sampling of the history of interpretation of Samson and Delilah in epic, painting, opera, and film, see J. Cheryl Exum, *Plotted, Shot, and Painted: Cultural Representations of Biblical Women* (JSOTSup, 215; GCT, 3; Sheffield: Sheffield Academic Press, 1996), pp. 175-237.

133. Bal, *Lethal Love*, p. 51.

134. Hackett, 'Violence and Women's Lives', p. 359.

135. Exum, 'Feminist Criticism', p. 80.

136. Exum, *Plotted, Shot, and Painted*, p. 186.

137. Lori Rowlett, 'Violent Femmes and S/M: Queering Samson and Delilah', in Ken Stone (ed.), *Queer Commentary and the Hebrew Bible* (JSOTSup, 334; New York: Sheffield Academic Press, 2001), pp. 106-15 (106). Rowlett notes that Delilah functions in the role of dominatrix, and Samson as 'butch bottom' (p. 106), and that both forced shaving and submission to removal of hair are now 'classic element[s] of S/M play' (p. 111).

138. Susanne Scholz, *Sacred Witness: Rape in the Hebrew Bible* (Minneapolis: Fortress Press, 2010), p. 174. This helpful text includes feminist scholarship related to various aspects of rape (acquaintance rape, rape of enslaved women, marital rape, rape of men as male fear and reality) in relation to numerous texts in Judges, to texts elsewhere in the Hebrew Bible, and to ancient Near Eastern laws.

139. Trible, *Texts of Terror*, p. 66.

emphasizes several features in the Judges narrative: (1) women say nothing; (2) there are parallels in Dinah's rape story in Genesis 34 where Shechem attempts to 'speak to the heart' of the woman and in Abraham's near-slaying of Isaac in Genesis 22 where the father took '*the* knife';[140] (3) there is a double standard, also detailed in the Sodom story of Genesis 19, where rape is viewed as a vile breach of hospitality if done to a man, but becomes acceptable for women;[141] (4) the Masoretic Text (MT) is ambiguous but the Septuagint (LXX) is clear about whether the gang-raped concubine is dead when her master cuts her to pieces;[142] and (5) the feminine pronoun at the end of the story, 'consider *her*', may command readers not simply to consider the incident but to consider the destroyed *woman* herself.[143]

Trible reviews several responses to the story in the biblical text and beyond. In Judges 20–21, God joins tribal Israel in seeking vengeance, but the near annihilation of the guilty tribe of Benjamin leads to the capture of 400 additional women from Jabesh-Gilead and 200 women of Shiloh so that 'the rape of one has become the rape of six hundred'.[144] Trible wonders if the editor of Judges intends to commend kingship because of the book's conclusion, 'In those days, there was no king in Israel, every man did what was right in his own eyes' (Judg. 21.25). If so, then, ironically, neither the first king, Saul (also associated with Benjamin, Gibeah, and Jabesh-Gilead), nor the second, David (who commits adultery and whose sons rape Tamar and many concubines in 2 Sam. 11.2-27; 13.1-22; 16.20-23), provides a worthy contrast.[145]

For Trible, it is important to recognize that the biblical books following Judges emphasize hospitality and sympathetic attention to women: Hannah in 1 Samuel in the MT and Ruth and Naomi in the book of Ruth in the LXX. In other words, the canonical order offers a final 'healing word in the days of the judges' after the 'misogyny, violence, and vengeance' of Judges 19–21.[146] Still, Trible does not find the positive portrayals of women in subsequent biblical books or the prophetic condemnation of Gibeah in Hos. 9.9, 10.9, or the prophetic recommendation to be silent in evil times (as in Amos 5.13) to be sufficient.[147] The narratives of terror in Judges 19–21 are irredeemable.

---

140.   Trible, *Texts of Terror*, pp. 67, 80.
141.   Trible, *Texts of Terror*, pp. 74-75.
142.   Trible, *Texts of Terror*, p. 79.
143.   Trible, *Texts of Terror*, p. 81.
144.   Trible, *Texts of Terror*, p. 83.
145.   Trible, *Texts of Terror*, p. 84.
146.   Trible, *Texts of Terror*, p. 85.
147.   Trible, *Texts of Terror*, p. 86.

The only hope and challenge Trible finds in these biblical texts consists in readers who might interpret 'against the narrator, plot, other characters, and the biblical tradition because they have shown [the woman] neither compassion nor attention'.[148] Provocatively, then, Trible contrasts the concubine's unwilling sacrifice with a story more familiar to Christians, the Jesus story, though Trible is careful not to be overly explicit: 'Her body has been broken and given to many. Lesser power has no woman than this, that her life is laid down by a man' (cf. 1 Cor. 11.24; Jn 15.12).[149]

Some feminist scholars have criticized Trible's method because it ignores the historical setting and historiography of the book of Judges in its focus on the literary form of the biblical text.[150] Others are concerned that her reading reinforces patriarchal assumptions and find her effort to redeem an androcentric text, and the patriarchal culture and view of God it reinscribes, as misplaced.[151] Nevertheless, Trible's early evocative reading prompted many subsequent feminist exegetes to look anew at these troubling biblical texts.

Further Feminist Interpretations of Judges 19–21[152]

Feminist exegetes note matters of vocabulary, various textual difficulties, and ambiguities in the text. What does *pilegesh* mean? Should it be rendered 'concubine' (a traditional translation),[153] a wife living with her father,[154] a

---

148.   Trible, *Texts of Terror*, p. 86.

149.   Trible, *Texts of Terror*, p. 81.

150.   See Bal, *Death*, p. 34; and Susan Ackerman, 'Digging Up Deborah: Recent Hebrew Bible Scholarship on Gender and the Contribution of Archaeology', *NEA* 66 (2003), pp. 172-84 (172).

151.   See Fuchs, 'The Literary Characterization of Mothers', p. 117 n. 4; Exum, 'Murder They Wrote', p. 66.

152.   For a thoughtful review of several feminist and other interpretations of Judg. 19–21, see Scholz, *Sacred Witness*, pp. 139-50.

153.   Niditch, *Judges*, p. 185. After some discussion of the term in various biblical texts, Pamela Tamarkin Reis, 'The Levite's Concubine: New Light on a Dark Story', *SJOT* 20 (2006), pp. 125-46 (126), retains 'concubine', understanding it to mean 'like a wife, but not quite'. Karla G. Bohmbach, 'Conventions/Contraventions: The Meanings of Public and Private for the Judges 19 Concubine', *JSOT* 83 (1999), pp. 83-98 (88 n. 12), observes that in addition to *pîlegeš*, the woman is also referred to as 'maidservant' (*'āmâ*) in Judg. 19.19 and as 'the woman' (*'iššâ*) in Judg. 19.26, as well as implicitly being portrayed as daughter in Judg. 19.3-9, though she is never referred to explicitly with this term.

154.   Bal, *Death*, pp. 89, 84, claims that *pîlegeš* refers to a married woman who continues to live with her father—a sensible arrangement that allows her nomadic husband to visit her from time to time, while the woman's father continues to provide for her and her children.

'legal wife of secondary rank',[155] a 'secondary wife',[156] or simply 'wife'?[157] What did the woman do in 19.2 and shall we read *zanah* or *zanach*? Did the wife play the whore, prostituting herself in some way, or did she get angry with her husband?[158] And who is the subject in 19.3? Should the verse be translated 'When he reached her father's house' (e.g. NRSV, following LXX) or should readers prefer the MT, of 'she took him into her father's house' (NIV and others)?[159] There is also a *ketiv/qere* in v. 3, where the written (*ketiv*) text 'to return him' is conventionally read (*qere*) as 'to return her'. Here is how Reis translates the beginning of Judg. 19.2 to make sense of some of these difficulties: 'And his concubine whored for him'. She reads the preposition 'for' not 'as "against him" but as "for him", "on account of him", "on his behalf", "for his sake". The Levite was prostituting his wife.'[160]

In addition to textual and vocabulary matters, feminists note various literary features of Judges 19. For example, Karla G. Bohmbach observes that the text follows stereotypical gender conventions of women belonging (and being safe) *inside*, in the private realm, whereas men belong *outside*, and sometimes the text contravenes them.[161] Among the contraventions, Bohmbach notes, in particular, that the woman's most violent abuse, her dismemberment, occurs *inside* the house.[162] Given her safe arrival at her father's house, the woman is 'extremely self-reliant'.[163] She successfully

155.   J. Cheryl Exum, 'Raped by the Pen', in Exum, *Fragmented Women*, pp. 170-201 (177); cf. Gale A. Yee, 'Ideological Criticism: Judges 17–21 and the Dismembered Body', in Yee (ed.), *Judges and Method*, pp. 146-70 (161).

156.   Hackett, 'Violence and Women's Lives', p. 360 n. 7; and Koala Jones-Warsaw, 'Toward a Womanist Hermeneutic: A Reading of Judges 19–21', in Brenner (ed.), *A Feminist Companion to Judges*, pp. 172-85 (174).

157.   Fewell, 'Judges', p. 81.

158.   See Niditch, *Judges*, p. 189 n. b for a discussion of the manuscripts support-ing varied depictions of the woman's behavior. Fewell, 'Judges', p. 81, argues that the 'woman "resists" him (reading *zanach* instead of *zanah*)'. Yee, 'Ideological Criticism', p. 162, sees the woman's 'daring act of leaving a husband...as a metaphoric act of "fornication"'.

159.   Bohmbach, 'Conventions/Contraventions', p. 92, seems to favor the woman's subjectivity; see Bal, *Death*, p. 181.

160.   Reis, 'The Levite's Concubine', p. 129. She further argues: 'My translation enables the reader to understand why the concubine leaves her husband, why her father receives her, and why the Levite waits four months before trying to win her back. With this understanding, the *qere* need no longer supplant the *ketiv*, and the Bible can be read as it is written' (p. 129).

161.   Bohmbach, 'Conventions/Contraventions', p. 85.

162.   Bohmbach, 'Conventions/Contraventions', p. 96.

163.   Bohmbach, 'Conventions/Contraventions', p. 89.

made the long and treacherous journey that in reverse her master did not make safely with her. Indeed, in the first three verses (Judg. 19.1-3), she is depicted as 'a human being with thoughts and feelings of her own, who is able and willing to act independently in consequence of them'.[164] Later on, however, the woman reverts to the conventional representation of 'woman'. She is seen but not heard and 'all men speak, but no women do'.[165] Simultaneously, the story thus expands and complies with stereotypical gender conventions, as if it were only a play but with a deadly outcome.

J. Cheryl Exum presents a powerful reading of the concubine's story through the lens of ideological criticism. She observes that '[t]he anonymity of the woman who is gang-raped in Judges 19 encourages readers not to view her as a person in her own right'.[166] To counter that textual ploy, Exum gives her a name, 'Bat-shever (daughter of breaking)—a name that recalls her treatment by the men of Gibeah and her subsequent dismemberment by her husband'.[167] To Exum, this name indicates that feminist interpretations break open a text's androcentric ideology and expose its hidden messages about women.[168] Exum also explains that the concubine is dismembered due to the sexual nature of her offense against patriarchy: 'By leaving her husband, the woman makes a gesture of sexual autonomy so threatening to patriarchal ideology that it requires her to be punished sexually in the most extreme form'.[169] The woman's body is dismembered as a way to de-sexualize her. Exum views the woman's sexuality as 'a subtext motivated by male fear of female sexuality and by the resultant need of patriarchy to control women'.[170]

Given these and other observations about Judges 19, feminist interpreters articulate the overarching textual meaning variously. Some read the text's ideology in relation to violence in their own cultures. For instance, Katharina von Kellenbach presents a post-Holocaust reading that recognizes '[b]oth the Levite and his concubine...as foreigners and...victims of...racial and

---

164. Bohmbach, 'Conventions/Contraventions', p. 92.

165. Bohmbach, 'Conventions/Contraventions', p. 88 n. 13. Other scholars have also commented on the power of voice. Ken Stone notes that the Levite becomes an object of speech when the men of Gibeah address his host; 'Gender and Homosexuality in Judges 19: Subject-Honor, Object-Shame?', *JSOT* 67 (1995), pp. 87-107 (99). J.H. Coetzee observes that the Levite loses his voice when his life is threatened; see J.H. Coetzee, 'The "Outcry" of the Dissected Woman in Judges 19–21: Embodiment of a Society', *OTE* 15 (2002), pp. 52-63 (57).

166. Exum, 'Raped by the Pen', p. 176.

167. Exum, 'Feminist Criticism', p. 83.

168. Exum, 'Feminist Criticism', p. 83.

169. Exum, 'Raped by the Pen', p. 181.

170. Exum, 'Raped by the Pen', p. 181.

xenophobic violence'.[171] She interprets the Levite's plight as potentially similar to that of a Jewish ghetto policeman during the Nazi era who puts his wife and daughter onto a train that leads them to their death in Treblinka.[172] She explains why the Levite does not look at his concubine: 'The striking absence of empathy the morning after the deadly rape should perhaps not be attributed to the Levite's patriarchal attitudes or to feelings of male supremacy but rather to his victimization and powerlessness.[173] Thus, von Kellenbach concludes, 'Judges 19–21 portrays morally ambiguous decisions for survival and muddled pathways into the future'.[174]

Yet another perspective comes from Korean exegete, Yani Yoo, who reads Judges 19–21 in relation to the plight of Korean 'comfort women'. Under Japanese domination, Korean women, like the women in Judges, were 'nameless and thus demeaned', 'gifts and scapegoats', and 'victims of state-organized rape'.[175] Thus, unlike Exum who sees buried and encoded androcentric messages warning women against autonomy through threat of punishment, Yoo finds that the narratives in Judges invite 'the reader to witness and denounce the human evil against fellow human beings, especially women'[176] and to 'work together with women around the world to end violence against women'.[177]

Like Yoo, other feminist scholars see these texts as critiquing violence. Adrien Bledstein sees the portrayal of abuse in Judges 19 as 'censuring the low to which Israelite men have descended' and thus as condemning 'violent men'.[178] Alice Keefe finds in Judges 19–21 a critique of failed governance and a condemnation of violence.[179] Heidi Szpek suggests that the mosaic of biblical allusions in Judges 19 presents a hypothetical 'image of what Israel's destiny *might* become, what women's position *might* become, how brethren *might* become enemies and how this *might* all be (wrongly)

---

171.   Katharina von Kellenbach, 'Am I a Murderer? Judges 19–21 as a Parable of Meaningless Suffering', in Tod Linafelt (ed.), *Strange Fire: Reading the Bible after the Holocaust* (New York: New York University Press, 2000), pp. 176-91 (181).

172.   Von Kellenbach, 'Am I a Murderer?', p. 183.

173.   Von Kellenbach, 'Am I a Murderer?', p. 184.

174.   Von Kellenbach, 'Am I a Murderer?', p. 187.

175.   Yani Yoo, '*Han*-Laden Women: Korean "Comfort Women" and Women in Judges 19–21', in Phyllis A. Bird (ed.), *Reading the Bible as Women: Perspectives from Africa, Asia, and Latin America* (Semeia, 78; Atlanta, GA: Scholars Press, 1997), pp. 37-46 (41, 42).

176.   Yoo, '*Han*-Laden Women', p. 39.

177.   Yoo, '*Han*-Laden Women', p. 45.

178.   Bledstein, 'Is Judges a Woman's Satire…?', p. 35.

179.   Alice A. Keefe, 'Rapes of Women/Wars of Men', in Camp and Fontaine (eds.), *Women, War, and Metaphor*, pp. 79-98 (94).

accomplished in the name of the Lord'.[180] She invites readers to respond to the text and its violence because it is 'a horrific and effective metaphor of warning...for such a thing has *never* happened since the day that the Israelites came up from the land of Egypt until this day!...but it could!'[181]

While Susan Niditch finds in Judg. 21.1-11 'an implicit critique of the ban [*herem*] when that ideology becomes an excuse to kill and conquer',[182] she does not see it as critiquing violence against women. She responds neutrally to the androcentric narrator, explaining that Judges 21 describes a process of what feminist scholar Gayle Rubin describes as an 'exchange of females', and it does so 'for the purposes of reconciliation between warring groups of men'.[183] Acknowledging but not critiquing this male gaze, Niditch concludes: 'Judges does not end with chaos; it ends with wholeness, reconciliation, rehabilitation, and peace, made possible in men's eyes through the taking of women'.[184]

Susanne Scholz is not satisfied simply with an anthropologically informed analysis, but invites readers to bring our attention to contemporary realities and readers. She explains:

> In the metaphoric language of biblical prose, Judges 19–21 illustrates the misogyny during so-called peacetime and the prevalence of rape during war... [These stories] can help even contemporary readers to face the horrors of today's ongoing sexual violations of women, children, and some men during peacetime and war.[185]

The narratives of Judges 19–21 caution readers not to be complicit in biblical ideology but to be aware of it.

Perhaps Exum expresses it best when she asks feminist readers to start the interpretation process not with the biblical text but with 'the concerns of feminism as a worldview and as a political enterprise'.[186] Feminist interpreters ask questions like: How are women portrayed? Who has power, and whose interests are being served?[187] Hence, feminist readers 'expose the strategies by which men have justified their control over women' and they

---

180.   Heidi M. Szpek, 'The Levite's Concubine: The Story That Never Was', *Women in Judaism: A Multidisciplinary Journal* 5 (2007), http://wjudaism.library.utoronto.ca/index.php/wjudaism/article/view/3176/1337, p. 2 (original italics).

181.   Szpek, 'The Levite's Concubine', p. 8.

182.   Niditch, *War in the Hebrew Bible*, p. 137.

183.   Niditch, *Judges*, p. 208. See Gayle A. Rubin, 'The Traffic in Women: Notes on the "Political Economy" of Sex', in Rayna A. Reiter (ed.), *Toward an Anthropology of Women* (New York: Monthly Review Press, 1975), pp. 157-210.

184.   Niditch, *Judges*, p. 211.

185.   Scholz, *Sacred Witness*, p. 155.

186.   Exum, 'Feminist Criticism', p. 65.

187.   Exum, 'Feminist Criticism', pp. 69-70.

try 'to understand women's complicity in their own subordination'.[188] Interpretation involves not merely a descriptive process but also requires a stance outside the Bible's androcentric ideology.

Applying her hermeneutical insight to Judges 19, Exum focuses on the violated woman and names her Bath-sheber in order to 'restore her to the subject position the androcentric narrative destroys'.[189] She then identifies what the text is trying to communicate, stating that 'the message in Judges 19 is a cautionary one: if you do anything that even remotely suggests improper sexual behavior, you invite male aggression'.[190] Finally, she identifies additional strategies which, in the case of Judges 19, involve the blaming of the woman for her own victimization and using women's fear to control women. Exum explains:

> Biblical style typically suggests a causal connection by means of simple juxtaposition... Bath-sheber asks for it too, the text implies. Had she stayed in her place, under her husband's authority where she belonged, she would not have ended up at the wrong place—Gibeah of Benjamin—at the wrong time. By insinuating that women...are responsible for male sexual behavior, [this text relies] on a fundamental patriarchal strategy for exercising social control over women. Using women's fear of male violence as a means of regulating female behavior is one of patriarchy's most powerful weapons.[191]

Based on this analysis, Exum names Judges 19 for what it is: pornography and literary rape. She acknowledges that '[r]aped by the pen is not the same as raped by the penis', but she also contends that 'violence against women as it takes place in biblical narrative...like pornography—though not so blatantly...perpetuate[s] ways of looking at women that encourage objectification and violence'.[192]

Conclusion: 'Direct your Heart to Them, Take Counsel, and Speak'

In many ways, feminist interpretation of Joshua and Judges mirrors the state of feminist biblical scholarship more generally. Over the past thirty years, it has moved from primarily literary readings of biblical stories about women through various forms of biblical scholarship.[193] Phyllis Trible's early liter-

---

188.   Exum, 'Feminist Criticism', p. 65.
189.   Exum, 'Raped by the Pen', p. 177.
190.   Exum, 'Feminist Criticism', p. 85.
191.   Exum, 'Raped by the Pen', p. 189.
192.   Exum, 'Raped by the Pen', p. 170.
193.   See the second edition: Gale A. Yee (ed.), *Judges and Method: New Approaches in Biblical Studies* (Minneapolis: Fortress Press, 2nd edn, 2007) for an excellent survey, expanded to include essays on postcolonial (Uriah Y. Kim), gender (Ken Stone), and cultural (David M. Gunn) criticisms.

ary analysis and homiletical call to re-member the Levite's concubine, 'direct your heart to her, take counsel, and speak',[194] and Phyllis Bird's insistence that 'that adequate interpretation requires the employment of both literary criticism and social analysis'[195] lead to new questions and challenges. Which women (and men) are included among those to whom we should direct our hearts? About whom should feminist scholars 'take counsel' and 'speak' out? Will feminist biblical scholarship also include social analysis of contemporary women and involve itself in actively working for their liberation? Can serious scholars simultaneously be activists, and should we be?[196]

Two-Thirds World women and postcolonial scholars like Kwok Pui-lan and Musa W. Dube challenge feminist scholars and biblical scholars more generally to consider *all* of the women and marginalized peoples of the world in our scholarship. Simply exposing the underlying politics (e.g. of the Deuteronomistic Historian or a postexilic context) or deconstructing the biblical texts' ideologies (e.g. of insiders and outsiders) is not enough. Dube contends:

> [T]he main objective of a decolonizing reading is beyond just providing a deconstructive analysis that exposes the imperialist construction embedded in narratives. A decolonizing reading's main objective is liberation. It asks the question: 'How can we know and respect the Other?'[197]

Dube observes that white or Western feminist readers have the option of bracketing out postcolonial concerns, but doing so is an exercise of privilege.[198] Instead, Dube insists feminist readers must 'become decolonizing readers: they must demonstrate awareness of imperialism as a persistent and exploitative force at a global scale, they must demonstrate a conscious adoption of resistance to imperialism'[199] and 'become decolonizing readers who seek to build true conversations of equal subjects in our post-colonial and multicultural world'.[200]

---

194. Trible, *Texts of Terror*, p. 86; see Judg. 19.30; 20.7.

195. Bird, 'The Harlot as Heroine', p. 119.

196. Susanne Scholz, '"Tandoori Reindeer" and the Limitations of Historical Criticism', in Caroline Vander Stichele and Todd Penner (eds.), *Her Master's Tools? Feminist and Postcolonial Engagements of Historical-Critical Discourse* (Atlanta, GA: Society of Biblical Literature, 2005), pp. 47-69 (48), laments the fact that 'established scholars of the Bible are not even expected to relate to social, political, economic, and religious developments in our societies'.

197. Musa W. Dube, 'Toward a Post-colonial Feminist Interpretation of the Bible', in Kwok Pui-lan (ed.), *Hope Abundant: Third World and Indigenous Women's Theology* (Maryknoll, NY: Orbis Books, 2010), pp. 89-102 (99).

198. Dube, 'Toward a Post-colonial Feminist Interpretation', p. 97.

199. Dube, 'Toward a Post-colonial Feminist Interpretation', p. 99.

200. Dube, 'Toward a Post-colonial Feminist Interpretation', p. 100.

Kwok Pui-lan sees an even deeper level of accountability for scholars who benefit from US privilege. She argues that biblical interpretation is not just for Christians but 'is also a public and political discourse shaping the values and decision making of the nation'.[201] As was the case in Joshua and Judges, both in the narratives themselves and in the underlying political and social realities that they represent and to which they were addressed, the choices of the powerful affect the lives of real women. Kwok Pui-lan agrees with Dube that scholars have a responsibility to use our disciplines to serve liberation causes.

> Because sexual morality and national politics are currently so intertwined in the United States, with significant implications for the whole world, biblical scholars and theologians must assume the responsibility of searching for critical insights to illuminate the situation. Discourses about the Bible must always be seen in the wider contexts of cultural and religious ethos, as well as of changing economic and political configurations.[202]

As others have noted, one way to take feminist biblical scholarship into a productive and much-needed direction is to read the Bible with communities of 'ordinary readers',[203] such as the ones in Latin America that still find strength in the *ver, juzgar, actuar,* and *celebrar* method of liberation theology. Those Christian communities examine their own materialistic realities in conjunction with the biblical text (*ver*); they judge what God, through the Word, calls them to do (*juzgar*); they act on this call to make a liberatory difference for their communities (*actuar*); and they celebrate their actions (*celebrar*)—sometimes even in defiance of what may seem to be an unsuccessful attempt of creating change.[204]

Centuries ago, the ancient Israelite authors of Joshua and Judges wrote and edited their theological history of periods of transition—from wilderness, through conquest and settlement, transitioning to monarchy. They described times of violence and turmoil, with some sense of God's presence.

201. Kwok Pui-lan, 'Sexual Morality and National Politics', p. 24.
202. Kwok Pui-lan, 'Sexual Morality and National Politics', p. 24.
203. Gerald O. West, 'Difference and Dialogue: Reading the Joseph Story with Poor and Marginalized Communities in South Africa', *BibInt* 2 (1994), pp. 152-70, has done significant work in this area.
204. I thank Sister Nohemy Ortiz of the *pequeña comunidad* in Nueva Esperanza, El Salvador for teaching me this method. Scholars would also do well to note 'a process of reading practiced by many of the world's Native peoples [and others who faced unwanted proselytizing]—a process that actively selects and invents, rather than passively accepts, from the literate materials exported to them by the dominant Euro-Spanish culture'; see Laura E. Donaldson, 'The Sign of Orpah', p. 22, citing Rigoberta Menchú and Elisabeth Burgos-Debray (eds.), *I, Rigoberta Menchú: An Indian Woman in Guatemala* (trans. A. Wright; London: Verso, 1984), p. 135.

Whether one posits Assyrian, exilic, or postexilic context(s) for the books' composition and redaction, the ancient authors/editors brought their traditions into conversation with their own experiences. They wrote about insiders and outsiders, troubled relationships, imminent threats, identity, violence, and death, and in so doing they sought to speak words of hope, challenge, and/or caution to their communities.

As biblical interpreters of the twenty-first century, whether we view these ancient texts as scripture or read them as secular scholars, we have similar opportunities to bring the texts into conversation with our own time and challenges through our practices of interpreting. Feminist, queer, liberationist, and postcolonial scholars have brought a variety of questions, insights, and approaches to reading these texts. In our world of transition, where empire is destructive and current ways of living are unsustainable and wracked with violence, we may wonder whether using the 'master's tools' on texts viewed by many as scripture could aid us to 'dismantle the master's house' and lead to a transformed society.[205]

Certainly, feminist biblical scholarship on Joshua and Judges calls us to look at the women and men in *our* world who live amid war, under the legacy of past colonization or the cloud of newer empires, and whose lives are disrupted through patriarchal oppression and violence, to ensure that they are not 'raped by the pen' of the Bible's enduring cultural legacy. Following Trible's early call and the more recent challenges of her queer and postcolonial feminist sisters, we are advised to remember all people's lives, particularly those of unnamed marginalized women, and to 'direct our hearts to them, take counsel, and speak'.

205. The allusion is to Audre Lorde, 'The Master's Tools Will Never Dismantle the Master's House', in Lorde, *Sister Outsider: Essays and Speeches by Audre Lorde* (Berkeley: Crossing Press, 1984), pp. 110-13.

5

CLASS PRIVILEGE IN PATRIARCHAL SOCIETY: WOMEN IN FIRST AND SECOND SAMUEL

Lai Ling Elizabeth Ngan

The First and Second books of Samuel are often cast as narratives in which male characters such as Samuel, Saul, and David dominate and the transition from tribal structure to monarchy is central. Yet, as feminist scholarship of the past few decades has shown, women play significant roles in both biblical books. Jo Ann Hackett points out that '[w]omen play a larger role in the books of Samuel than in most of the rest of the Bible'.[1] As active characters in the narratives, these women can be found in the private and public domains of the story, as well as 'in the gray area that is the domestic sphere of a ruling family, where private decisions have public consequences'.[2] To be sure, none of the women rose to become heads of tribes or kingdoms. Their highest political status within the Israelite monarchy was to be a king's daughter or a king's wife, or, as in the case of Bathsheba, to become eventually a queen mother. Female characters are portrayed to fit stereotypical roles of women in a male-dominated society as envisioned by the narrator(s). Those who become mothers, such as Hannah and Bathsheba, are depicted as having fulfilled their womanly purpose in life; they live on through their sons. Those women who do not have sons, such as Michal and Tamar, are silenced and killed off by the narrator.[3] To put it succinctly, in the narrative of the Samuel books, women have two choices: 'Motherhood or death'.[4] The

---

1. Jo Ann Hackett, '1 and 2 Samuel', in Carol A. Newsom and Sharon H. Ringe (eds.), *Women's Bible Commentary* (Louisville, KY: Westminster/John Knox Press, exp. edn, 1998), pp. 91-101 (101).

2. Hackett, '1 and 2 Samuel', p. 101.

3. J. Cheryl Exum, 'Murder They Wrote: Ideology and the Marginalization of Female Presence in Biblical Narrative', in Alice Bach (ed.), *The Pleasure of her Text: Feminist Readings of Biblical and Historical Texts* (Philadelphia: Trinity Press International, 1990), pp. 45-68.

4. Karla G. Shargent, 'Living on the Edges: The Liminality of Daughters in Genesis to 2 Samuel', in Athalya Brenner (ed.), *A Feminist Companion to Samuel and Kings* (FCB, 5; Sheffield: Sheffield Academic Press, 1994), pp. 26-42 (35).

stories report that tragedy befalls women who fail to give birth to sons. As
Karla Shargent notes: 'The text is unable (or unwilling) to envision any
other livable alternative for them'.[5]

Women's stories in 1 and 2 Samuel, furthermore, as in the Hebrew Bible
as a whole, are not usually told in their entirety. Their characters remain
underdeveloped. The narrator mentions only parts of a woman's story to use
her as a foil for the development of male characters. A prime example is
Michal whose story is fragmented into four parts.[6] She first appears as Saul's
daughter and David's wife in 1 Samuel 18–19. After a long hiatus, she
reappears in 2 Samuel 6 when David is king in Jerusalem, married to
multiple wives and the father of many sons, but this time she appears only as
Saul's daughter. In these two incidences, Michal is the subject of verbs and
has a voice. In 1 Sam. 25.44 and 2 Sam. 3.14-16, however, she is an object
that is transferred from one male's house to another's; she has neither voice
nor agency. Another example of an underdeveloped female character is
Bathsheba. She hardly utters a word in 2 Samuel 11–12,[7] but when she
reappears in 1 Kings 1, she gives a long speech (1 Kgs 1.17-21), as an older
woman with a grown son who is about to be named king. None of the
narratives provide detailed information on the lives and accomplishments of
these and other women. We do not know who they are or what they want.
They conform to the androcentric status quo for the most part, appear in the
story in relation to the male characters, and their aim is to give birth to sons.
Feminist readers have to fill the gaps by imagining and hypothesizing about
their fates, often based on feminist critical insights, hermeneutical considerations, and theological understandings.

In the 1970s, feminist interpreters began to rely on feminist theory and
criticism, anthropological research, and women's experiences as lenses for
reading women's stories in the Hebrew Bible. They recognize that various
assumptions have shaped interpretations, usually from androcentric perspectives. They seek to unveil patriarchal assumptions in text and interpretation,
to critique androcentric bias, and to 'reconstruct' and 'reclaim' women's
stories as worthy to be heard and told.[8] They seek to rehabilitate tarnished
images of biblical women and explore possible alternative views of their

5. Shargent, 'Living on the Edges', p. 34.

6. J. Cheryl Exum, 'Michal: The Whole Story', in Exum, *Fragmented Women:
Feminist (Sub)versions of Biblical Narratives* (Valley Forge, PA: Trinity Press International, 1993), pp. 42-59 (42). 'The irony in the title of this Chapter is intentional. By
"the whole story" I refer to the whole fragmented story of Michal.'

7. The two words, 'I'm pregnant', is delivered by a messenger; they are at best an
indirect speech (2 Sam. 11.5).

8. Elisabeth Schüssler Fiorenza, *In Memory of Her: A Feminist Theological Reconstruction of Christian Origins* (New York: Crossroad, 1983), p. xiv.

stories. When they turn their attention to the books of Samuel, feminist interpreters highlight the stories of five women. They help to restore the portraits of Hannah, Michal, Abigail, Bathsheba, and Tamar; the following presents an overview of this work.

The Story of Hannah in Feminist Exegesis

First Samuel opens with the story of a woman. As feminist exegetes have pointed out, this account is not merely a prelude to the life of Samuel; this is Hannah's story. The frequent citation of her name in 1 Samuel 1–2 proves her prominence. Carol Meyers notes that the name 'Hannah' appears fourteen times in this pericope, as many times as the names of 'Elkanah', 'Peninnah', and 'Samuel' combined.[9] She prays, she vows, she names her son, and she brings the child Samuel and the sacrifices to Shiloh, all without the mention of Elkanah.[10] She exhibits agency and autonomy. Hannah also has a unique place in the stories of barren mothers in the Hebrew Bible. Joan Cook categorizes the stories of barren mothers into three models.[11] The first is the competition model as exemplified by Sarah, Rachel, and Hannah: 'the childless wife bears a son through divine intervention and he receives a significant name'.[12] The second is the promise model, as seen in the stories of Sarah, Samson's mother, Hannah, and the Shunammite woman. The barren woman encounters a messenger of God who 'promises a son and confirms the promise in spite of human doubt; the son is born and receives a significant name'.[13] The third is the request model whereby someone, either the barren woman or another person on her behalf, requests a son from God; God heeds the request and gives her a son. Examples of this model are stories of Rebekah, Rachel, Hannah, and the woman in Ezra's vision (2 Esd. 9.44-45).[14] Cook notes that 'Hannah is the only barren mother who fits all three models'.[15]

9.   Carol Meyers, 'Hannah and her Sacrifice: Reclaiming Female Agency', in Brenner (ed.), *A Feminist Companion to Samuel and Kings*, pp. 93-104 (96). 'Elkanah' is named eight times, 'Peninnah' is named three times, and 'Samuel' three times. 'Eli' is named ten times in 1 Sam. 1.1–2.21.

10.   Meyers, 'Hannah and her Sacrifice', p. 96. The MT only cites Hannah but the LXX adds Elkanah.

11.   Joan E. Cook, *Hannah's Desire, God's Design: Early Interpretations of the Story of Hannah* (JSOTSup, 282; Sheffield: Sheffield Academic Press, 1999), pp. 14-20.

12.   Cook, *Hannah's Desire*, p. 16.

13.   Cook, *Hannah's Desire*, p. 17.

14.   Cook, *Hannah's Desire*, pp. 18-20.

15.   Cook, *Hannah's Desire*, p. 24.

The first commentary to feature Hannah is Elizabeth Cady Stanton's *A Woman's Bible Commentary*. It portrays Elkanah as a Victorian romantic, an ideal husband who marries Hannah out of love, who is exceedingly kind and attentive to her needs, a man of feelings for Hannah's plight, who 'said to her one day in an exuberant burst of devotion, "Am I not more to thee than ten sons?"'[16] Yet this interpretation also reinscribes the stereotype that women are prone to jealousy and maliciousness; Hannah and Peninnah emerge as bickering wives who make life miserable for Elkanah, while he is an ever-loving, godly man. Another reading comes from Edith Deen in *All of the Women of the Bible*. She portrays Hannah from a different but still stereotypical perspective. To Deen, Hannah is an ideal wife and mother, a woman of prayer who has great faith in God. Deen writes: 'In her loving care of Samuel, Hannah becomes the prototype of the good mother everywhere, setting a stirring example of high morality and spirituality, which could bring a new order into the world'.[17] Thus, even with a focus on Hannah, the interpretation does not necessarily advance a liberationist stance. It still presents the character of Hannah as a woman typical of androcentric thought and imagination.

Only when feminist interpreters began using gender theory, family/relational dynamics, social scientific research, and feminist literary criticism did the reading of Hannah's story yield new insights into women in the Samuel books. For instance, Carol Meyers's observation that women in pre-monarchic Israel had authority in family and village life is widely accepted and supported by ethnographic research.[18] Feminist interpreters, nevertheless, wonder if Hannah, a woman in pre-monarchic Israel, had any agency. Historically minded feminist interpreters have tried to discern how much initiative and self-direction are available to her. They ask what her place was in a polygamous family. The text does not state clearly whether Hannah is the first or second wife, but the order of the wives usually affects the power arrangement in a family.[19] Furthermore, the Hebrew Bible includes other stories of co-wives who are in conflict such as Sarah and Hagar (mistress–maid) and Leah and Rachel (sister–sister). Yet it is unclear whether Hannah's and Peninnah's relationship is shaped by other factors besides

16. Elizabeth Cady Stanton, *A Woman's Bible (Part II)* (Boston: Northeastern University Press, 1993), p. 45.

17. Edith Deen, *All of the Women of the Bible* (New York: Harper & Row, 1955), p. 90.

18. Carol L. Meyers, *Discovering Eve: Ancient Israelite Women in Context* (New York: Oxford University Press, 1988).

19. As late as the mid-twentieth century, the first wives of polygamous Chinese families wielded tremendous power and control over the welfare of the other wives and their children.

being co-wives. Still barrenness is always a major cause for contention for all of the paired women. Does this problem reflect a historical reality or is it merely an androcentric narrator's attempt to play out one woman against the other?

Esther Fuchs argues that this is indeed the narrative strategy, pitting one woman against another. She states:

> By splitting the wife-figure into conjugal and maternal aspects, either by assigning each aspect a different literary context or by assigning each role to a different wife-figure, the conjugal narrative manages to keep the wife-figure in her proper place... [T]he strategy of role separation ensures that the wife-figure remains secondary and subordinate to her male counterpart.[20]

Not only was ancient Israel a patriarchal society, the text was written by redactors who shared the same patriarchal biases of their milieu. In other words, readers need to be aware of sexist leanings inherent in the text.

When interpreters assume an androcentric perspective, which may include women socialized and taught to read within the androcentric status quo, they often blame Hannah and Peninnah for causing family problems. Feminist interpreter Lillian Klein notes, however, that in the Hebrew Bible 'jealousy and seductiveness are the chief transgressions projected upon women'.[21] She applies René Girard's theory of 'mimetic desire' to analyze the jealousy and scapegoating between the two co-wives. 'Mimetic desire' is the desire to have what the other person has and can generate 'jealousy, rivalry and all the actions taken to gain the object of desire'.[22] In her analysis, Peninnah, not Hannah, is the one with expressed mimetic desire. She is jealous of Hannah because Elkanah loves the latter even though Yhwh has closed her womb (1 Sam. 1.5).[23] If young women in ancient Israel only had two acceptable roles, either as an unmarried virgin daughter in her father's household or as a son-bearing wife in her husband's household, obviously Hannah does not fit into either category, making her an 'Other'.[24] By taunting Hannah during the annual family sacrifice at Shiloh, Peninnah calls out Hannah's state of infertility, thereby socially and emotionally marginalizing her rival wife.[25]

---

20. Esther Fuchs, *Sexual Politics in the Biblical Narrative: Reading the Hebrew Bible as a Woman* (JSOTSup, 310; Sheffield: Sheffield Academic Press, 2000, repr. 2003), p. 171.

21. Lillian R. Klein, 'Hannah: Marginalized Victim and Social Redeemer', in Brenner (ed.), *A Feminist Companion to Samuel and Kings*, pp. 77-92 (78).

22. Klein, 'Hannah', p. 78.

23. Klein, 'Hannah', pp. 81-83.

24. Susan Niditch, 'The Wronged Woman Righted: An Analysis of Genesis 38', *HTR* 22 (1979), pp. 143-49 (145).

25. Klein, 'Hannah', p. 77.

In this triangulated relationship, Elkanah's role should not be ignored. Feminist interpreters have been quite vocal about Elkanah's contribution to the conflict between his wives. Surely he must have some inkling of the tensions in the family. Fuchs notes that the text is silent as to 'the husband's role in generating the bitter competition between the co-wives...(or) the advantage the husband derives, both from the polygamous setup and from the mutual hostility of his wives'.[26] Feminist exegetes have also unveiled Elkanah's privileged position. Hackett points out that Elkanah is not childless; he does not need a son from Hannah. He has 'both a wife to love and a wife to make children'.[27] The wives' grievances are not his concern and apparently he does nothing to alleviate the tension. David Jobling further suggests that 'he (Elkanah) cannot understand why the two women, enjoying their several marital satisfactions, are not just as happy with the situation as he is'.[28]

Though the text states explicitly that Elkanah loves Hannah, their interaction in 1 Sam. 1.8 has caused feminist interpreters to wonder about the veracity of that statement. Elkanah peppers Hannah with a quick series of 'why' questions, without giving her time to answer. His last question, 'Am I not more to you than ten sons?', uses a first-person subject pronoun with a second-person objective case.[29] The question is self-focused on the husband. While in Hackett's view, Elkanah's deficient understanding of Hannah's sadness shows that he is 'naïve or even insensitive',[30] Yairah Amit faults him as self-centered and self-serving. She emphasizes that Elkanah believes that he is better for Hannah than ten sons. He does not understand why Hannah is so distraught or why she needs a son. Accordingly, Elkanah's rhetorical question is not a comfort to Hannah and only reinforces her aloneness in this family. Amit states: 'Elkanah's words reveal him to possess the egocentricity of a child who perceives himself as the centre of his world and is disappointed when his behavior fails to receive the attention he expects'.[31] Feminists wonder what might change in the narrative if he were portrayed as making the quarrels of his wives his own. Indeed, Elkanah would have been a very rare husband and man if he had stood up against the patriarchal system and structures.

26. Fuchs, *Sexual Politics*, p. 158.

27. Hackett, '1 and 2 Samuel', p. 95.

28. David Jobling, *1 Samuel* (ed. David W. Cotter, Jerome T. Walsh, and Chris Franke; Berit Olam; Studies in Hebrew Narrative and Poetry; Collegeville, MN: Liturgical Press, 1998), p. 132.

29. Yairah Amit, ' "Am I Not More Devoted to You than Ten Sons?" (1 Samuel 1.8): Male and Female Interpretations', in Brenner (ed.), *A Feminist Companion to Samuel and Kings*, pp. 68-76 (75).

30. Hackett, '1 and 2 Samuel', p. 95.

31. Amit, 'Am I Not More?', pp. 74-75.

Feminist scholars observe that Peninnah is assigned a secondary role as the rival wife, the bad woman, and raise the issue of her marginalization. What would it be like to tell the story from Peninnah's perspective? Fuchs raises the possibility that 'Peninnah humiliates Hannah *because* of Elkanah's obvious preference for Hannah'.[32] Elkanah uses her body but there is no mention of love. The narrator portrays her as mean-spirited and vengeful. Her provocation, which is described as 'severe' and 'irritating', is juxtaposed to Elkanah's kindly action of portioning food to his family and the notice that he loves Hannah, the victimized wife. The narrative strategy highlights Elkanah's goodness at Peninnah's expense. Fuchs alerts readers that 'there is no explicit reference to Peninnah's feelings: her jealousy, her shame, her own anguish at being the less-favored'.[33] In fact, Peninnah does not have a voice in the story and does not defend herself against the narrator's accusations. Thus, readers sensitive to issues of oppression and marginalization read Peninnah's story with greater understanding and empathy.

Yet Hannah, emerging after Elkanah's questions in 1 Sam. 1.8, is a cause of delight for feminist readers. She is no longer the 'acted upon' but takes charge of her life and seizes control over her future. She does not wait for her husband's approval and goes directly to Yhwh (1 Sam. 1.9). Amit asserts that 'this distancing from her husband and from the family ceremony should be regarded as the resistance and protest of a woman isolated by her own family'.[34] Hannah pleads her case and vows to give back the son that God gives her as a nazarite for life. Meyers explains that, by naming her son, 'Hannah participates in the social authority implicit in giving of a name'.[35] Hannah acts independently of Elkanah's plan of yearly pilgrimages to Shiloh, taking the child and the sacrificial offerings to Shiloh as she plans (1 Sam. 1.21-24). Her prayer of thanksgiving (1 Sam. 2.1-10) serves as a model for the *Magnificat*, the song that Mary intones in Lk. 1.42-55. Hannah's story invites readings on many levels, among them one about the strength that women possess rising from the place of victimization to their rightful place in life.

The Story of Michal in Feminist Exegesis

Michal is Saul's younger daughter and David's first wife. Her story is fragmented into four brief segments in the Samuel books. Though she is the first person in ancient Israel to be both a king's daughter and a king's wife, scholars did not consider her an important character until the last few

---

32. Fuchs, *Sexual Politics*, p. 156. Emphasis in the original.
33. Fuchs, *Sexual Politics*, p. 156.
34. Amit, 'Am I Not More?', p. 75.
35. Meyers, 'Hannah and her Sacrifice', p. 99.

decades. In a 1991 anthology with a wide range of interpretations on Michal's story, the editors, David Clines and Tamara Eskenazi, intentionally entitled the book *Telling Queen Michal's Story*. I agree with the editors that addressing Michal as queen is an appropriate step 'to restore her to her rightful place in tradition and in memory',[36] as her reputation has been tarnished for far too long.

Michal's familial connection to both the villain and the hero complicates the interpretation of her story for conservative readers. Edith Deen, for example, praises Michal for her cleverness and courage to go against her father in order to save David, but she also faults Michal for worshiping idols, never mind that the teraphim are in David's house (1 Sam. 19.11).[37] Deen speculates that Michal's mother must have been a gentle woman, but Michal is not like her. Deen asks, 'How could there be any happiness for his daughter, Michal, who, like her father, had rejected God in her life?'[38] Whatever heroic achievement Michal may have accomplished is cut down with an accusation of idolatry, a grievous sin in Christian theology. Yet feminist scholars unmask the double standard with which readers judge Michal. Accordingly, Alice Laffey contends, 'Interpreters are accustomed to laud the character of men who act with such bravery', and then she urges that 'readers must begin to laud the character of such women also'.[39]

Deen's interpretation is a clear example of textual 'naturalization', which means that she fills the story's gaps. Cheryl Exum explains thus: 'We seek to bring textual events within our conceptual grasp, and we tend to apply particular notions of chronology, causality, coherence and contiguity, as well as particular cultural generalizations or stereotypes, in order to reduce their strangeness'.[40] She warns that in this process 'with its attendant urge to offer moral evaluation, the complexity of the biblical character is lost'.[41] A character such as Michal becomes flat, as readers inevitably blame the woman, and in Michal's case, they cast her as a shrew, a nagging wife, and all things negative.[42]

---

36. David J.A. Clines, 'Preface', in David J.A. Clines and Tamara C. Eskenazi (eds.), *Telling Queen Michal's Story: An Experiment in Comparative Interpretation* (JSOTSup, 119; Sheffield: Sheffield Academic Press, 1991), pp. 7-11 (8).

37. Deen, *All of the Women*, p. 98.

38. Deen, *All of the Women*, p. 100.

39. Alice Laffey, *An Introduction to the Old Testament: A Feminist Perspective* (Philadelphia: Fortress Press, 1988), p. 109.

40. J. Cheryl Exum, 'Michal at the Movies', in M. Daniel R., David J.A. Clines, and Philip R. Davies (eds.), *The Bible and Human Society: Essays in Honour of John Rogerson* (JSOTSup, 200; Sheffield: Sheffield Academic Press, 1995), pp. 273-92 (290-91).

41. Exum, 'Michal at the Movies', p. 273.

42. Exum, 'Michal at the Movies', p. 273.

Yet feminist scholars have begun the process of reclaiming Queen Michal's story. They notice that the 'window' frames the first and last episodes where she is active and the subject of verbs. In 1 Sam. 19.12, Michal, 'the wife of David', rescues her husband from Saul's scheme to kill him by letting him down through the window. She is the royal daughter and he is the married-in son-in-law. In 2 Sam. 6.16, Michal 'the daughter of Saul' looks out of the window and sees David dancing like a vulgar fellow (2 Sam. 6.20). Their social status is reversed in this scene: David is the king and Michal is merely one among many wives. Klein writes: 'The window which provided David freedom and saves his life becomes a window that confines Michal'.[43] She is behind the window and inside the house while David is outside in the world. Exum further comments that '[t]he text provides our window on Michal, offering us only a glimpse, the kind of view a window gives, limited in range and perspective. We are, as it were, outside, watching her, inside, watching David.'[44] The narrator limits access to Michal, but feminist readers must resist accepting the male perspective as the only one possible. Why not go inside the house and stand with Michal to see what she sees from behind the window? She has a clear view of the festivities on the street from her location. Clines suggests reading *with* Michal and not with the narrator.[45]

Feminist exegetes generally agree that Michal has female agency as evidenced by her active role in the first and last scenes in her story, but they diverge as to how her actions ought to be evaluated. Literary critic, Robert Alter, points out that Michal is the only woman in the Hebrew Bible who 'loves' a man.[46] This unique notation is interpreted by Klein as an indicator of her strength of character. In spite of her life circumstances as an object, used by men, and her childlessness that contributes to her emotional shame, Michal refuses to be a victim and she proclaims her love for a man of her choosing.[47] This capacity to love, however, is interpreted by Adele Berlin as an 'unfeminine trait'.[48] She cites three incidences that show Michal as failing to fulfill the female role as prescribed in the Bible. First, 'Michal is the aggressive and physical one' compared to Jonathan.[49] Second, she is

43.   Klein, 'Michal, the Barren Wife', in Athalya Brenner (ed.), *Samuel and Kings* (Sheffield: Sheffield Academic Press, 2000), pp. 37-46 (42).

44.   J. Cheryl Exum, *Tragedy and Biblical Narrative: Arrows of the Almighty* (Cambridge: Cambridge University Press, 1992), p. 89.

45.   David J.A. Clines, 'The Story of Michal, Wife of David, in its Sequential Unfolding', in Clines and Eskenazi (eds.), *Telling Queen Michal's Story*, pp. 129-40 (137).

46.   Alter, *The Art of Biblical Narrative*, p. 118.

47.   Klein, 'Michal, the Barren Wife', p. 39.

48.   Adele Berlin, 'Characterization in Biblical Narrative: David's Wives', *JSOT* 23 (1982), pp. 69-85 (70).

49.   Berlin, 'Characterization', p. 71.

childless in a social world where motherhood is of paramount importance. Third, Berlin points out that '[s]ignificant, too, may be the fact that Michal, unlike many women in biblical narrative, is never described as beautiful'.[50]

Exum, however, disagrees with Berlin's approach to the story. She warns that assigning 'unfeminine' and 'feminine' traits to Michal and Jonathan respectively is 'to risk reinforcing gender stereotypes'.[51] She agrees that Michal does have female agency and, to some degree, autonomy, but maintains that Michal's story is more about male rivalry than gender dynamics.[52] In 1 Samuel 19, Michal goes against her father and helps David escape, and in 2 Samuel 6, she goes against David and criticizes his vulgar dancing. Yet '[t]he alternating descriptions of Michal as "David's wife" or "Saul's daughter" draw attention to Michal's difficult position between the two men'.[53] She is caught in the men's struggle for power between Saul and David and then between David and Ishbaal. Exum further observes that Michal is 'hemmed in' both politically and narratively. She explains: 'The scenes where she is a subject are surrounded by scenes in which she is "acted upon". This narrative imprisonment underscores the impossibility of autonomy for Michal.'[54]

A significant change has taken place in Michal between the first and last episodes. How does the woman who once loved David become one who despises him? The only dialogue between the royal couple turns out to be a public display of mutual contempt (2 Sam. 6). Exum points out that '[s]exual jealousy, lack of proper religious enthusiasm, royal arrogance—these are all ways of naturalizing Michal's outburst'.[55] Notice that all of these explanations place the blame on Michal, including calling this quarrel her 'outburst', while David is absolved of any responsibility for his behavior or for causing Michal's revulsion.

Clines makes a strong case that to see the issue of the quarrel as a conflict over kingship is to take David's perspective. He states, 'that is how *he* would like this altercation to be regarded, as a conflict between the king that *is* and the representative of the king that *was*'.[56] He also concurs with Exum that Michal is disgusted with David's sexual vulgarity, but adds that the issue is David's neglect of her.[57]

50. Berlin, 'Characterization', p. 72.
51. Exum, *Fragmented Women*, p. 52.
52. Exum, *Fragmented Women*, p. 54.
53. Exum, *Fragmented Women*, p. 55.
54. Exum, *Tragedy and Biblical Narrative*, p. 84.
55. Exum, 'Michal at the Movies', p. 279.
56. Clines, 'The Story of Michal', p. 137. Emphasis in the original.
57. Clines, 'Story of Michal in its Sequential Unfolding', p. 138. He cited J. Cheryl Exum, 'Murder They Wrote: Ideology and the Manipulation of Female Presence in Biblical Narrative', in Bach (ed.), *The Pleasure of her Text*, pp. 45-67 (51).

The narrator purports that Michal castigates David for 'uncovering himself today before the eyes of his servants' maids as any vulgar fellow might shamelessly uncover himself' (2 Sam. 6.20b). His dancing shows that he is no better than any commoner and the maids to whom Michal refers are two social strata beneath her; they are David's (male) servants' maid-servants. Exum points out that 'class distinction' is one of the strategies of patriarchal ideology.[58] She asserts that '[i]t is used not to separate Michal from David as much as to isolate her from other women, making gender solidarity impossible and effectively humiliating the woman and eliminating her from the picture'.[59]

David gets the last word in this confrontation and the narrator ends Michal's story by noting that 'Michal the daughter of Saul had no child to the day of her death' (2 Sam. 6.23). Readers are tempted to attribute this comment as a punishment from God since the Hebrew Bible often portrays Yhwh as the one who closes and opens a woman's womb, effectively making Michal guilty of sin or of displeasing God. Another common explanation attributes it to David's refusal to have sexual relations with Michal in order to cut off any possibility of Saul's lineage in David's house. These suggestions perpetuate the patriarchal tendency to see woman as object and in a negative light, or perhaps not to consider the woman at all. Exum laments, 'The fact...that commentators do not even raise the possibility of Michal's refusal once again robs Michal of autonomy and is an example of what Esther Fuchs calls reinscribing patriarchal ideology'.[60] What if Michal is the one who rejects David? Exum notes that Clines is the first feminist interpreter to posit this causality for Michal's childlessness.[61] Exum considers it a distinct possibility because 'refusal would not be out of character for her'.[62] The portrayal of Michal as an agent of her life beyond the narrator's confinement is a readerly act of resistance to the androcentric erasure of this woman's story.

The Story of Abigail in Feminist Exegesis

Three factors have contributed to the indifference and neglect of Abigail's story (1 Sam. 25). First, her story is seen as an interlude in David's journey to kingship that provides readers with a glimpse of his life in the wilderness

58. Exum, 'Murder They Wrote', p. 195.

59. Exum, 'Michal at the Window, Michal in the Movies', p. 61.

60. Exum, *Tragedy and Biblical Narrative*, p. 88. She notes that Fuchs uses this term in her scholarly papers presented at the annual meetings of the Society of Biblical Literature.

61. Exum, *Tragedy and Biblical Narrative*, p. 88 n. 50; Clines, 'Story of Michal in its Sequential Unfolding', p. 139.

62. Exum, *Tragedy and Biblical Narrative*, p. 88.

as the leader of a band of outlaws, and explains how he acquired his second wife. Second, her story is the most benign among the stories of David's other wives, Michal and Bathsheba. There is neither bloodshed nor violence, neither war nor murder. In fact, Abigail prevents David from committing a massacre. Bach notes that David's acquisition of Michal and Bathsheba involves sexual violence but not so in the case of Abigail.[63] Third, Bach further notes that 'there is no allusion to sexual union or nonunion in the case of Michal'.[64] Abigail's role as the mother–provider and a good-sense wife without sexual scandals does not arouse in readers the kind of intrigue and curiosity that stories of a defiant princess/shrewd or a seductress/adulteress would elicit. She thus maintains: 'Perhaps that is why Abigail has no passionate admirers. Few have taken pleasure in her text.'[65] In other words, feminist interpreters, trying to uplift female characters in the Samuel books, bring Abigail out of the shadows of androcentric exegesis.

Feminist scholars emphasize that 1 Samuel 25 is first and foremost Abigail's story in which David and Nabal play their parts but she is clearly the prominent character. It is evidenced by the length and content of her speech to David (1 Sam. 25.24-31). Alice Bellis comments that Abigail speaks more than Nabal or David.[66] Bach observes that Abigail is the only character who interacts with all the other characters in the narrative.[67] Clearly, it is her story, but who is Abigail?

Feminist interpreters have tried to answer this question. To them, Abigail is the only woman whom the Hebrew Bible describes as having 'a good mind and lovely looks'.[68] Unlike Bathsheba and Tamar whose beauty draws unwelcomed attention from rapists, Abigail's beauty 'is apparently not the sort to inspire sexual desire'.[69] The citation of her winsome qualities is followed immediately with a description of her husband as 'hard and evil in deeds'.[70] Feminist exegetes notice that the narrator's praise serves another agenda. Fuchs, for example, states that 'Abigail's positive characterization emphasizes Nabal's villainy and presents her as a desirable and prized object. Her transference from Nabal to David signals God's support for

---

63. Bach, 'Pleasure of her Text', p. 36.

64. Bach, 'Pleasure of her Text', p. 36.

65. Bach, 'Pleasure of her Text', p. 28.

66. Alice Ogden Bellis, *Helpmates, Harlots, and Heroes: Women's Stories in the Hebrew Bible* (Louisville, KY: Westminster/John Knox Press, 1994), p. 148.

67. Bach, 'Pleasure of her Text', p. 26.

68. Robert Alter, *The David Story: A Translation with Commentary of 1 and 2 Samuel* (New York: W.W. Norton, 1999), p. 152. NRSV translates as 'clever and beautiful'.

69. Bach, 'Pleasure of her Text', p. 32. Bach's comment is a rather androcentric view of the cause of rape, as it seems to relate sexual violence with sexual desire that is inspired by the victim's beauty.

70. Alter, *David Story*, pp. 152-53. NRSV translates as 'surly and mean'.

David, as He enables his chosen king to win his enemy's beautiful and intelligent wife (1 Sam. 25:3).'[71] Nabal's name and characterization, on the other hand, predict his disastrous end.

Some feminist exegetes also consider Abigail's class status. They regard her as a wealthy upper-class woman because her husband Nabal is rich (1 Sam. 25.2b). Bach suggests that the description of the 'capable wife' in Prov. 31.12-31 'offers a clue to Abigail's many accomplishments. She considers a field and buys it; she perceives that her merchandise is profitable; she takes care of the poor, she makes all manners of garments and sells them. Clearly she does not eat the bread of idleness (when would she have time!), while her husband sits in the gates of the city.'[72] Abigail is a busy woman, a woman of action, and she hurries everywhere (1 Sam. 25.18, 23, 42). She is quick to make sound decisions and take bold steps. She knows when and what to say to the male characters in the narrative.

Hence, feminist interpreters describe Abigail as having verbal power. She speaks the words that defuse the crisis brought on by Nabal's arrogant refusal to give food to David's men. She dissuades David from slaughtering Nabal's household. Bach contends that Abigail is a redeemer to the men surrounding her and she acts as God's helper when she speaks prophetic words of assurance about David's future.[73] She suggests that the reader's focus should shift from David to Abigail, from 'the man who entered the arena to do violence' to 'the woman who led him out alive'. Instead of admiring David, the admiration belongs to Abigail.[74]

Unsurprisingly, then, feminist exegetes stress the agency of Abigail. Bach, for example, observes that in addition to her speeches, Abigail acts independently of Nabal and even goes against his wishes. She commands servants to prepare a large quantity of food and rides down the mountain without her husband's consent to meet David and his men.[75] Here is a character who is not only a one-dimensional 'model wife' but a complex character. The same set of actions that win Abigail the place as a mother-provider could also be viewed as the actions of a disloyal wife. As Bach notes: 'She refers to her husband as a fool (v. 25), sides with his enemy, and does not mourn his death'.[76] Katherine Sakenfeld thus wonders whether it would be appropriate to label Abigail as an opportunist who seeks to attach herself to a handsome young warrior.[77] This female character does not allow

71. Fuchs, *Sexual Politics*, p. 144.
72. Bach, 'Pleasure of her Text', pp. 30-31.
73. Bach, 'Pleasure of her Text', pp. 28-29, 40.
74. Bach, 'Pleasure of her Text', p. 29.
75. Bach, 'Pleasure of her Text', p. 29.
76. Bach, 'Pleasure of her Text', p. 34.
77. Katherine Doob Sakenfeld, *Just Wives? Stories of Power and Survival in the Old Testament and Today* (Louisville, KY: Westminster/John Knox Press, 2003), p. 86.

for a clear-cut positive or negative assessment. Abigail is a complex woman in the narrative, involved in issues of life and death.

Feminist readers are thus troubled by the way Abigail ingratiates herself to David and later to his servants when they take her to be David's wife. Bellis notices the incongruence between her speech and her power. She states: 'She constantly speaks of herself in very lowly terms, calling herself maidservant (*'amhâ*) [*sic*] and handmaid (*šiphâ*). These terms stand in contrast to the power she wields through her words.'[78] Fewell and Gunn suggest that she recognizes male power and knows how to work within the patriarchal structure to build a future for herself. These exegetes see Abigail as savvy and subversive, and so they write: 'Abigail's eloquence is voluble, meandering, and brilliantly persuasive. She knows the man's vanity and ambition and targets it to perfection (1 Sam. 25.28-29).'[79]

It seems that Abigail has a sinister side and readers are disinclined to consider it. Robert Alter, citing the work of Israeli novelist, Meir Shalev, believes that 'Abigail has matrimony in view, once her cantankerous old husband is out of the way'.[80] He is convinced by Shalev's strong argument that Abigail's plan to destroy his enemies (1 Sam. 25.29) is 'really suggesting herself as the agency for "Yhwh" when she repeatedly refers to God in David's life and God's intent to destroy God's enemies (1 Sam. 25.29).[81] To Alter, she is, in other words, proposing to David that she carry out a kind of contract killing of her husband, with the payoff that she will become the wife of the handsome young warrior and future king.'[82] How Nabal died is unclear; the text does not implicate Abigail as the assassin but credits Yhwh with the death of Nabal (1 Sam. 25.38). Thus, in his reading, Abigail is daring and ruthless although the textual gaps allow multiple readings of her narrative.

Readers who take seriously Bach's reminder that the Samuel books are male-authored and pro-Davidic must resist a negative evaluation of Abigail's cleverness. Should she be faulted for wanting to leave a bad husband and aim for a better future? Anna Shrikisson-Sharma's response is a resounding 'No!' She sees Abigail as a subversive woman who goes against the cultural expectations. Abigail is married to a mean man and cannot remove herself from this situation. Shrikisson-Sharma compares such a marriage to Caribbean women's experiences. They have to marry wealthy

---

78. Bellis, *Helpmates*, p. 148.

79. Danna Nolan Fewell and David M. Gunn, *Gender, Power, and Promise: The Subject of the Bible's First Story* (Nashville, TN: Abingdon Press, 1993), p. 156.

80. Meir Shalev, *The Bible Now* (Jerusalem: Schocken Books, 1985 [Hebrew]); cited in Alter, *The David Story*, p. 159.

81. Alter, *The David Story*, p. 158.

82. Alter, *The David Story*, p. 159.

men or '[i]n some cases, marriages are arranged as a business transaction for migration to the United States',[83] and many of them endure physical and emotional abuse from their husbands. Abigail's chance meeting with David proves to be a life-changing opportunity that allows her to leave her ill-tempered husband, and she recognizes that David, the 'guerrilla' rebel, is the future king with a sure house even though Saul, the present king, is still alive.[84]

Judette Gallares, a Filipino Roman Catholic nun, also reads Abigail's story positively. She explores the ethical implications of reading biblical women's stories from her perspective as an Asian and Third-World woman in the Philippines, a country that is beset with political and economic struggles and much violence between government troops and rebel groups. She pictures Abigail as 'a faithful pacifist, an advocate of active nonviolence and peace. She offers us an alternative value system, another set of ideals, another approach to leadership that relies more on the power of peace and reconciliation than on the power of hate and vengeance.'[85] Gallares's work with poor and uneducated women in crowded cities helps her see the image of Abigail in their faces and lives. She states: '[w]henever and wherever the spirit of nonviolence and efforts for peace and development abound, we are reminded of Abigail and all those who have followed the path of pacifism'.[86]

In short, feminists regard 2 Samuel 25 as Abigail's story. She is wise and beautiful, and not merely someone's wife, whether that be Nabal or David. Rather, she has impressive power to order and persuade men and redirect the course of their lives. Feminist interpreters should admire this strong woman with passion, taking pleasure in her text.[87]

The Story of Bathsheba in Feminist Exegesis

Bathsheba is one of the better-known female characters in the Hebrew Bible; yet, in fact, very little is known about her. The many gaps in her story have engendered multiple explanations, speculations, and interpretations from readers with the result that Bathsheba is often blamed for David's downfall and Uriah's death. Feminist exegetes such as Alice Bach remind us, however, that the women in the Hebrew Bible are male constructs. She notes that

---

83.   Anna Joycelyn Shrikisson-Sharma, 'Women Critiquing Culture: The Story of Abigail and a Guerrilla', in Patricia Sheerattan-Bisnauth (ed.), *Righting her-Story: Caribbean Women Encounter the Bible Story* (Geneva: World Communion of Reformed Churches, 2011), pp. 209-16 (210).

84.   Shrikisson-Sharma, 'Abigail and a Guerrilla', pp. 210-14.

85.   Judette A. Gallares, *Images of Faith: Spirituality of Women in the Old Testament* (Maryknoll, NY: Orbis Books, 1992), p. 124.

86.   Gallares, *Images of Faith*, p. 126.

87.   Bach, 'Pleasure of her Text', p. 28.

the 'women' are not real but 'idealized models' of types of women in the social world of the male authors. She writes: 'These stereotypes of the feminine, from virgin to whore, are defined in terms of the woman's sexuality'.[88]

The first issue feminist scholars call attention to is Bathsheba as the object of David's sexual desire and his voyeuristic gaze. Bach explains that 'the narratives are structured in frames: on the level of story the gaze of the male characters directs the narrative, making women objects of their gaze'.[89] Furthermore, '[o]n a narratologic level, the female figure's focalizing moment functions as a moment in which power is seized (as well as seen)'.[90] Bathsheba is particularly vulnerable because the narrator describes her as a very beautiful woman, bathing, presumably washing herself in the nude. Exum points out that '[t]he viewing is one-sided, giving him (David) the advantage and the position of power: he sees her but she does not see him'.[91] By following David's gaze, readers are complicit in sharing his voyeurism and seeing the bathing beauty through his eyes. She alerts us that '[r]eaders of this text are watching a man watching a woman touch herself'.[92]

Elna K. Solvang cites rabbinic tradition that describes Bathsheba as a clever seductress who plans the enticement by bathing naked on the roof where David would see her.[93] Solvang's research reveals that though many male commentators reached similar conclusions, their pronouncement of guilt on Bathsheba varies in degree. George Nicol, for example, is adamant that Bathsheba is the crafty seductress who wants to be seen by David so that he would desire and 'seduce' her. Solvang determines that Meir Sternberg is more restrained in his judgment; he admits that it is impossible to know Bathsheba's attitude, but nevertheless, she did bathe naked on the roof.[94]

Solvang, like many feminist exegetes, contends that Bathsheba is not the one on the roof. The preposition מֵעַל in 2 Sam. 11.2b should be translated as 'from'. Thus the NRSV renders the phrase as 'that he saw *from* the roof a

88. Alice Bach, *Women, Seduction, and Betrayal in Biblical Narrative* (Cambridge: Cambridge University Press, 1997), p. 130.

89. Bach, *Women, Seduction, Betrayal*, pp. 128-29.

90. Bach, *Women, Seduction, Betrayal*, p. 130.

91. J. Cheryl Exum, *Plotted, Shot, and Painted: Cultural Representations of Biblical Women* (JSOTSup, 215; Sheffield: Sheffield Academic Press, 1996), p. 26.

92. Exum, *Plotted, Shot, and Painted*, p. 26.

93. Elna K. Solvang, *A Woman's Place Is in the House: Royal Women of Judah and their Involvement in the House of David* (JSOTSup, 349; London: Sheffield Academic Press, 2003), p. 128.

94. George Nicol, 'Bathsheba, a Clever Woman', *Expository Times* 99 (1988), pp. 360-63; Meir Sternberg, *The Poetics of Biblical Narrative: Ideological Literature and the Drama of Reading* (Bloomington: Indiana University Press, 1985), p. 526 n. 10. Cited in Solvang, *A Woman's Place*, p. 128.

woman bathing'.[95] The topography of Jerusalem dictates that, in ancient Israel, houses constructed on the steep eastern slope of the mount be built on terraces. It is reasonable to assume that the king's house is on the highest level, giving David an unobstructed view of the houses on the terraces below. The text does not specify the exact hour when Bathsheba is bathing. However, according to the Hebrew Bible and Jewish practice a new day begins after sunset, so it seems reasonable to assume that the ritual bath for menses performed after the required waiting period of seven days takes place after sunset.[96] If so, Bathsheba would be taking her ritual bath in the light of an oil lamp and David would be strolling on the roof of his house hidden in the darkness.

Exum observes that '[i]n the biblical account, David's erotic involvement with Bathsheba occupies only one verse of narrative time'.[97] The sexual encounter is stated tersely in 2 Sam. 11.4 with five actions: 'So David sent messengers to get her, and she came to him, and he lay with her. (Now she was purifying herself after her period.) Then she returned to her house' (NRSV). Exum notes that '[h]e sent, he took, and he lay: the verbs signify control and acquisition. In contrast, only her movement is described: she came and she returned.'[98] Are Bathsheba's two actions indicative of her willing participation? Tikva Frymer-Kensky suggests that '[h]owever much she might have been intimidated by kingship, she was not forcibly raped'.[99] But can coercion through intimidation be considered any less than rape? Exum states that '[t]he king sends for a subject and she obeys... An actual demand for her sexual services is not necessary to make her feel she must agree to sex. David is, after all, the king, so is she free to refuse?'[100]

Other feminist exegetes beg to differ. Klein proposes that Bathsheba has no intention to refuse. To Klein, the verbal clause 'she came' is redundant since David's 'sent', 'took', and 'lay' subsume adequately Bathsheba's involvement in the sexual liaison. Klein states, 'The superfluous words do serve to mitigate Bathsheba's passivity, to be sure; and the use of "come", with its connotations of sexuality, insinuates Bathsheba's complicity in the

95.   Francis Brown, S.R. Driver, and Charles A. Briggs, *A Hebrew and English Lexicon of the Old Testament* (Oxford: Clarendon Press, 1907), p. 758. Emphasis added.
96.   Tirẓah Meacham (leBeit Yoreh), 'An Abbreviated History of the Development of the Jewish Menstrual Laws', in Rahel R. Wasserfall (ed.), *Women and Water: Menstruation in Jewish Life and Law* (Hanover, NH: Brandeis University Press, 1999), pp. 23-39.
97.   Exum, *Plotted, Shot, and Painted*, p. 20.
98.   Exum, *Plotted, Shot, and Painted*, p. 21.
99.   Tikva Frymer-Kensky, *Reading the Women of the Bible: A New Interpretation of their Stories* (New York: Schocken Books, 2002), p. 149.
100. Exum, *Plotted, Shot, and Painted*, p. 21.

sexual adventure'.[101] Klein regards Bathsheba's complicity with David as stemming from her desire to be a mother, to bear a child. She suggests that 'Bathsheba may well have been purifying herself on her roof with the hope of seducing King David into "seducing" her'.[102] Thus, she postulates: 'If she (Bathsheba) has been married to an infertile man, warrior though he is, she may find it necessary to mate with another male to fulfill her biological and social function as a woman—to become a mother'.[103] But how would Bathsheba know that Uriah is infertile when infertility is seen as a woman's fault in the ancient world? Klein's proposal makes David the victim who is manipulated by a clever seductress, which only results in blaming Bathsheba and allowing David to be excused from his sexual aggression.

Feminist exegetes almost unanimously assert that David raped Bathsheba. David would have heard Nathan's story of the rich man and the poor man with his ewe lamb as a court case; the king pronounces the death sentence on the rich man, and the prophet pronounces judgment on the king. Solvang notes that Nathan's parable portrays a tender, loving relationship between Bathsheba and Uriah which 'sharpens the tragedy of the narrative event'.[104] Exum considers stories of rape in the Bible as literary rapes: 'one is recounted in the story and one takes place by means of the story'.[105] Exum does not diminish the trauma and violence that raped women suffer in the real world, but she also discloses another site of rape in which women in biblical stories suffer; they are 'Raped by the Pen'.[106] Exum uses 'the rape of Bathsheba' 'as a metaphor to describe Bathsheba's treatment at the hands of the andocentric biblical narrator, whose violation of her character consists both in depriving her of voice and in portraying her in an ambiguous light that leaves her vulnerable, not simply to assault by characters in the story but also by later commentators on the story'.[107]

In addition to reading Bathsheba's story as a rape narrative, feminist biblical scholars explore the literary strategy of the narrator that denies Bathsheba's voice. Her silence suggests to them that she is not an important character and that the story is about the three male antagonists. Considering the primacy of dialogues in biblical narrative, Bathsheba's silence serves to reinforce the patriarchal ideology that it is a man's world.[108] Only David and

---

101. Lillian Klein, 'Bathsheba Revealed', in Brenner (ed.), *Samuel and Kings*, pp. 47-64 (49).
102. Klein, 'Bathsheba Revealed', p. 53.
103. Klein, 'Bathsheba Revealed', p. 52.
104. Solvang, *A Woman's Place*, p. 135.
105. Exum, *Fragmented Women*, pp. 12-13.
106. Exum, *Fragmented Women*, pp. 170-76.
107. Exum, *Fragmented Women*, p. 171.
108. Alter, *The Art of Biblical Narrative*, pp. 79-110.

Uriah have direct dialogue; other speeches are monologues with messages sent back and forth through couriers.

Another technique diminishes the woman's position in this narrative. Fuchs notes that the Bible almost always presents the hero-husband as morally and religiously superior to the wife-figure. In cases where the behavior of the hero-husband is morally questionable, such as an adultery type-scene, the wife-figure is only allowed a secondary role where she is 'passive, object-like and mute'.[109] Any protest, hesitation, or expression of self-will could result in the wife-figure emerging 'not only as the real victim but also as the moral hero of the scene... Any objection on the part of Bathsheba would have jeopardized the moral status of David vis-à-vis his future wife.'[110] It is inconceivable in the texts that a woman could be morally superior to Israel's ideal king. Bach approaches this literary strategy from the angle of its effect on the reader. She states: 'By withholding from the reader Bathsheba's reaction to the sexual demands of the king or to her own act of adultery, the narrator has eliminated a direct route of sympathy between the reader and the female character'.[111]

Feminist readers have attributed a wide range of motives, desires, and characterizations to the silence. Their interpretations, however, reveal more about themselves, their ideologies, their biases, and their social world than about Bathsheba and/or the narrator. Bach proposes: 'A strategic move for a resistant reader is to acknowledge the persistent connection in David's house between sexual power and political triumphs'.[112] Instead of keeping our focus solely on David's exploits, Bach proposes that '[w]ith one eye on David, a reader can keep the other eye on the female objects of David's desire'.[113] Then readers reclaim control of what they see: 'As feminist readers we can employ insight, avert our gaze, and go somewhere else. When faced with an authoritative over-viewing narrator, we can cast a cold eye.'[114]

The narrator and the prophet Nathan concur that 'the thing' David does is evil in Yhwh's eyes, and according to Deuteronomistic theology, the one who sins is punished. Yet David is punished through his wives. It is outrageous that his punishment due him is inflicted upon the bodies of his wives and children. David rapes Bathsheba, and then his daughter Tamar is raped by her brother Amnon, and David's concubines are raped by his son

---

109. Fuchs, *Sexual Politics*, p. 145.
110. Fuchs, *Sexual Politics*, p. 145.
111. Bach, *Women, Seduction, and Betrayal*, p. 135.
112. Bach, *Women, Seduction, and Betrayal*, p. 141.
113. Bach, *Women, Seduction, and Betrayal*, p. 141.
114. Bach, *Women, Seduction, and Betrayal*, p. 165.

Absalom. David murders Uriah, and then four of David's sons die for it, beginning with Bathsheba's firstborn son. Alice Laffey asks: 'But who notices that David sinned and *Bathsheba* was punished? Few commentators mention that the loss of her son was an injustice rendered to Bathsheba.'[115] She is dealt a series of severe blows because David did as he pleased and he had the power to do so. She is raped and her husband is murdered; she becomes a widow carrying the child conceived from the rape; and she enters the harem and becomes her rapist's possession while her newborn child dies. How much trauma and pain must a woman endure in such a short span of narrative time? Bathsheba's survival is a testament to her tenacity. Feminist readers enter the suffering with Bathsheba but also celebrate her reemergence.

The Story of Tamar in Feminist Exegesis

Phyllis Trible is the first feminist exegete to give serious attention to the 'texts of terror' in the Hebrew Bible.[116] These stories about women who are victims of physical and sexual violence are generally ignored in churches and synagogues because they are not texts that can be readily used in homilies or lessons. Furthermore, in a misogynist context, women's stories are pushed to the fringes while men's stories are highlighted. Trible tells them because they need to be told. She uses rhetorical-critical method to interpret the stories of four women, including Tamar, from a feminist perspective. She cautions that '[s]ad stories do not have happy endings' but '[s]ad stories may yield new beginnings'.[117] Instead of shying away from these uncomfortable stories, she invites readers to hear them anew and with compassion.

Trible's careful analysis shows the narrative as an artfully structured chiasm with Tamar's rape at its center. When the characters are introduced in 2 Sam. 13.1, both Absalom and Amnon are identified as sons of David while Tamar is described as their beautiful sister, but not as David's daughter. Bach observes that in 2 Samuel 13, the word 'son' is used nine times, 'brother' thirteen times, and 'sister' nine times. She thus writes: 'It becomes clear through the patterning of language that the family microscope is focused upon the actions of men while the punishment is to be lived out through the pain of women, particularly Tamar'.[118]

---

115. Laffey, *An Introduction to the Old Testament*, p. 121.
116. Phyllis Trible, *Texts of Terror: Literary-Feminist Readings of Biblical Narratives* (Philadelphia: Augsburg Fortress Press, 1984).
117. Trible, *Texts of Terror*, p. 2.
118. Bach, *Women, Seduction, and Betrayal*, p. 152.

David tells Tamar to go to her half-brother Amnon's house to make food for him. Feminist exegetes wonder if Tamar as a royal daughter is better situated to refuse the king's order than Bathsheba. Since her story follows immediately after Bathsheba's rape, Uriah's murder, and Nathan's prophetic pronouncement of judgment, the juxtaposition of these tales suggests a causal connection between them. Bach posits that '[a]ccording to divine reasoning the taking of another man's wife (Bathsheba) is equivalent to the incestuous contact that Amnon effects'.[119] Just as David has raped Bathsheba, now he sends Tamar into the grasp of her rapist.

Feminist interpreters sympathize with Tamar when they focus on the story. Tamar is silent when she arrives at Amnon's house and sets about the task assigned to her. Her activities of preparing the cakes (*lbbt*) are depicted with six verbs, all seen through Amnon's eyes. Trible notes: 'In obeying David, Tamar has become the object of sight. Amnon, the narrator, and the readers behold her. Voyeurism prevails.'[120] Frymer-Kensky proposes that what Tamar prepares is not simply food. She relates *birya* to 'the Babylonian medicinal prescription, the *bultu*, which comes from the verb *balātu* ('to live'), with the causative *bullutu* ('to heal'). The *birya* is not simply food, and making it is not simply an act of cooking; it is the preparation of a medical concoction.'[121] She speculates that '[i]f Tamar was instructed in medicinal herbs and rituals, then Amnon's request for her would seem legitimate, and David might be expected to comply without becoming suspicious or alarmed'.[122] Preparing *bultu* involves making heart cakes (*lbbt*). Frymer-Kensky suggests that the name of the cake may be an indication of its shape or function, that is, 'to "enhearten" the sick person and make his life force flow'.[123]

Feminist exegetes are in agreement that Tamar is the victim of incestuous rape. Three verbs in quick succession, 'he was stronger (*ḥzq*) than she', 'he raped (*'nh*) her', and 'he laid (*škb*) her', dispatches the rape scene. Trible explains that for the third verb 'the Hebrew omits the preposition to stress his brutality...the direct object *her* underscores cruelty beyond the expected'.[124] Frymer-Kensky writes: 'There is no question of seduction here: Amnon has raped her by force. The word *'innah*, "degrade", used before the verb for intercourse rather than after it, indicates rape. It is not strange that a mere change of verb order can denote such a colossally different experience for the woman.'[125]

119. Bach, *Women, Seduction, and Betrayal*, p. 152.
120. Trible, *Texts of Terror*, p. 31.
121. Frymer-Kensky, *Reading Women*, p. 158.
122. Frymer-Kensky, *Reading Women*, p. 158.
123. Frymer-Kensky, *Reading Women*, p. 159.
124. Trible, *Texts of Terror*, p. 34.
125. Frymer-Kensky, *Reading Women*, p. 162.

Susanne Scholz suggests that this is a case of acquaintance rape in which the perpetrator is known to the victim and perhaps even a close relative. He betrays the woman's trust and coerces her into sexual intercourse, or, as in the case of Amnon, Tamar's half-brother, he overpowers and rapes her by force.[126] Scholz states: 'It is Amnon *alone* who is responsible for raping a woman who trusts and likes him while he objectifies and violates her'.[127] Many interpreters find the atrocity that Tamar suffered so appalling that they quickly avert their gaze, console themselves that she will be avenged in the subsequent development of the story, or discount Tamar's suffering as inconsequential because the story is about the throne's contestation. Laffey recalls that this rationalization is frequently used to soften the horror of Tamar's rape and its consequences. After all, two years later, Absalom kills Amnon to avenge his sister and Absalom names his only daughter 'Tamar', her namesake (2 Sam. 14.27). Laffey explains that '[t]o the extent that the text is interpreted from either a historical and literary perspective, the horror of the victimization of women is trivialized... These vindications, however, do not make Tamar any less a victim.'[128] Thus feminist interpretations see it as their task to stay with Tamar and not to look away.

They also admire Tamar's eloquence. When confronted with Amnon's evil intention, Tamar speaks emphatically: 'No, my brother, do not force *('nh)* me'. Her speech seeks to thwart Amnon's aggression but her words fell on deaf ears. Thus, contrary to Bathsheba, Tamar has a voice, but like Bathsheba, she too is raped. Trible notes the irony in Amnon's use of 'my sister' when he demands Tamar to lie with him, for Prov. 7.4-5 calls wisdom 'my sister'. Trible asks: 'If sister wisdom can protect a young man from the loose woman, who will protect sister wisdom from the loose man, symbolized not by a foreigner but by her very own brother?'[129] Apparently the answer is 'no one!' Frymer-Kensky cites the use of 'my sister' in Song of Songs. There the sister is the beloved, familial terminology that is also found in love poems of other ancient Near Eastern literatures.[130] Yet in Tamar's case, the terminology aims to assuage the fear of the victim as she is drawn into the trap.

Feminist exegetes and literary critics have noticed connections between Joseph's and Tamar's stories. Alter, for example, observes that in the Hebrew Bible only Tamar and Joseph wear a particular garment (*ketonet passim*), variously translated as 'robe of many colors', a 'long robe with

126. Susanne Scholz, *Sacred Witness: Rape in the Hebrew Bible* (Minneapolis: Fortress Press, 2010), pp. 29-32.

127. Scholz, *Sacred Witness*, p. 42.

128. Laffey, *Introduction to the Old Testament*, p. 124.

129. Trible, *Texts of Terror*, p. 44.

130. Frymer-Kensky, *Reading Women*, p. 160.

sleeves'. Following E.A. Speiser's suggestion, Alter translates the term for garment as 'an ornamented tunic'.[131] The garment is meant for someone who does not do manual labor. Bach recounts that '[i]n their similar garments Joseph and Tamar represent a powerless figure, yet one who paradoxically is at the center of the rupture of the family. The blood on Joseph's *ketonet* "coat" is goat's blood and ultimately does not signal Joseph's death. The blood on Tamar's garment is her own blood, a sign of her stolen virginity, death for a woman in the ancient world.'[132] Both Tamar and Joseph are beckoned with 'lie with me', she from her half-brother Amnon and he from Potiphar's wife. Bach observes that since Joseph, however, is '[n]ot completely powerless because he is under the protection of Yhwh, Joseph is able to flee. Apparently under no one's protection, Tamar is raped.'[133] Trible borrows the phraseology of the Suffering Servant in Isaiah 53 and applies it to Tamar. She intones: 'Raped, despised, and rejected by a man, Tamar is a woman of sorrows and acquainted with grief. She is cut off from the land of the living, stricken for the sins of her brother; yet she herself has done no violence and there is no deceit in her mouth.'[134] But her suffering neither brings redemption nor is her suffering redeemed.

Feminist readers stay with Tamar's perspective to the bitter end of the story. After the rape, Tamar is thrown out of Amnon's house as if she is yesterday's garbage, and Tamar mourns the violence that Amnon has thrust upon her. Frymer-Kensky notes that she 'creates a public spectacle. She draws attention to her own devastation by openly revealing her plight. Not trying to hide her shame, she performs an act of grief and lament.'[135] Citing Middle Assyrian law, she explains that Tamar's actions in 2 Sam. 13.19 declare that she is an innocent victim, as otherwise, her silence may have led to accusations of seduction and adultery.[136]

Feminist exegetes, however, interpret Absalom's response with far less sympathy. Absalom sees Tamar and suspects what has happened. He asks if she has been with Amnon and immediately admonishes her: 'Be quiet for now, my sister; he is your brother; do not take this to heart' (2 Sam. 13.20). Are these words of comfort or words to silence the rape victim? Fuchs points out that 2 Samuel 13 is 'unambiguous' in its depiction of the three characters: Amnon the villain, Tamar the victim, and Absalom the hero.[137]

---

131. Alter, *The David Story*, p. 270; E.A. Speiser, *Genesis* (AB, 1; New York: Doubleday, 1964).
132. Bach, *Women, Seduction, and Betrayal*, p. 155.
133. Bach, *Women, Seduction, and Betrayal*, p. 156.
134. Trible, *Texts of Terror*, p. 40.
135. Frymer-Kensky, *Reading Women*, p. 165.
136. Frymer-Kensky, *Reading Women*, p. 165.
137. Fuchs, *Sexual Politics*, pp. 202-203.

The admonition of the hero to be quiet 'is construed as an expression of loving care, not as a brutal act of suppressing a raped woman's bitter plea for justice'.[138] Trible admits that '[o]n the surface, his words appear to countenance the rape, only delicately alluded to at that. In the name of family loyalty, Absalom would silence Tamar, minimize the crime, and excuse Amnon.'[139] Trible's rhetorical analysis of the story suggests, however, that Absalom is Tamar's only advocate, one who plots revenge, and counters brother and father for his sister.[140] Trible thus wonders whether Absalom's murder of Amnon is for Tamar or for himself. She regards Absalom as the 'good' brother when compared to Amnon, but is he his sister's advocate?

Not all feminist interpreters, thus, agree with Trible's positive assessment of Absalom's action. Fuchs, studying the family dynamics, narrative strategy, and patriarchal ideology in the stories of Dinah's (Gen. 34) and Tamar's rapes (2 Sam. 13), notes that brothers of rape victims often avenge their sisters but they never consult with the women in the planning and execution of the punishment. Instead, they replace the women.[141] Thus, Fuchs questions the positive value of the brothers' responses when she states: 'The brothers' willingness to take up cudgels on behalf of their sisters justifies the elimination of the victim from the story of the rape's revenge'.[142] In considering the rape laws of Exod. 22.15-16 and Deut. 22.28-29, Fuchs maintains that 'both the rape laws and the narratives are based on the assumption that the real victim is the raped woman's father or brother. What has not been questioned by critics is the imperceptible shift from rape victim to male relative and the implicit premise that the latter has a right to represent the former.'[143]

Also Frymer-Kensky questions the intention of Absalom's revenge. She calls attention to the use of familial language in Absalom's one-verse response, stating: 'Absalom's use of "Aminon", a form of Amnon that stresses the *'ammi* ("my people") and his "*your brother*", are both reminders of Amnon's place in the family... By accusing him, Absalom implies, she will bring public disgrace upon the family.'[144] Frymer-Kensky accuses Absalom precisely of all the things that Trible considers a surface reading, and so Frymer-Kensky asserts: 'With Absalom's words, he betrays her... She is the victim of both brothers: first by Amnon's rape, then by Absalom's

138. Fuchs, *Sexual Politics*, p. 203.
139. Trible, *Texts of Terror*, p. 39.
140. Trible, *Texts of Terror*, p. 39.
141. Fuchs, *Sexual Politics*, p. 202.
142. Fuchs, *Sexual Politics*, p. 204.
143. Fuchs, *Sexual Politics*, p. 204.
144. Frymer-Kensky, *Reading Women*, p. 166.

silencing. Nobody looks at her as a person. To Amnon, she was an object of lust and then hate; to Absalom, she is a crisis that has to be contained.'[145]

The narrative ends with a depiction of Tamar's social situation after the rape. The verse is short and to the point: 'So Tamar remained, a desolate woman, in her brother Absalom's house' (2 Sam. 13.20b). Scholz observes that the story ends with Tamar never recovering from her trauma.[146] However, Tamar's story has never ended; it echoes in every victim of incest, child sexual abuse, acquaintance rape, and domestic violence. Bellis states it well: 'Tamar is not an ancient anomaly. She is all around us. If awareness can lead to change, let us remember Tamar's story and resolve that sexual abuse can and will stop.'[147]

Conclusion

The stories of these five women in the Samuel books portray the complexity of women's experience in ancient Israel. Feminist scholars have sought to recover and reclaim their stories, to point out patriarchal assumptions inherent in both texts and interpreters, and to offer different ways of reading and seeing. One such strategy is for interpreters to engage in dialogue with each other and with the women of the Hebrew Bible, to create a welcoming space where these women can inhabit and tell their own stories. What would it be like to step into their shoes, to feel what they might have felt, and to tell the story from their perspective? The women presented in this study are major characters but there are innumerable women who inhabited their world, know their stories, but remain unnamed, invisible, and have no voice. What would it be like for Michal's maid to tell her mistress's story or for Abigail to tell Bathsheba's story? What of Amnon's servant who is asked to cast Tamar out of the house? What did he see and how does he feel? Admittedly, these are imaginative work, but nevertheless a legitimate endeavor, because they, too, add texture to women's stories where they have been denied. As Bach proposes: 'An interpreter can resist such a monologic interpretation by supplying the dialogic voice herself. The narrative strategy, to refuse interpretive closure by adding another voice to the author's attempt at monologic imperialism, is essential to a feminist reading, one that intends to disrupt the order determined unilaterally by author/narrator.'[148] The narrator need not have the last word.

---

145. Frymer-Kensky, *Reading Women*, p. 167.
146. Scholz, *Sacred Witness*, p. 42.
147. Bellis, *Helpmates, Harlots, Heroes*, p. 153.
148. Bach, *Women, Seduction, and Betrayal*, p. 151.

6

'QUEENS' AND OTHER FEMALE CHARACTERS: FEMINIST INTERPRETATIONS OF FIRST AND SECOND KINGS

Julie Faith Parker

At first glance, the books of First and Second Kings seem like sparse terrain for feminist exploration.[1] The very name pithily combines patriarchy and hierarchy in a mono-syllabic tribute to androcentric hegemony. Men fill its pages as rulers and subjects, warriors and commanders, priests and prophets. Some feminist readers have approached these narratives with seasoned ennui or blatant disinterest in what appears to be yet another biblical bastion of masculine texts. However, Kings has proven to be rich terrain for feminist scholars, due largely to the pervasive presence of women spanning a wide range of roles.[2]

The list of named female characters of Kings is impressive. These characters function as goddesses: Asherah (1 Kgs 14.15, 23; 15.13; 16.33; 18.19; 2 Kgs 13.6; 17.10, 16; 18.4; 21.3, 7; 23.4, 6-7, 14-15), Astarte (1 Kgs 11.5, 33; 2 Kgs 23.13), and Ashima (2 Kgs 17.30); queens and queen mothers: Abi (2 Kgs 18.2), Athaliah (2 Kgs 8.18, 26; 11), Azubah (1 Kgs 22.42), Bathsheba (1 Kgs 1–2), Haggith (1 Kgs 1.5, 11; 2.13), Hephizibah (2 Kgs 21.1), Jecoliah (2 Kgs 15.2), Jedidah (2 Kgs 22.1), Jehoaddin (2 Kgs 14.2), Jerusha (2 Kgs 15.33), Jezebel (1 Kgs 16.31; 18; 19; 21; 2 Kgs 9), Maacah (1 Kgs 15.2, 10, 13), Meshullemeth (2 Kgs 21.19), Naamah (1 Kgs 14.21, 31), Nehushta (2 Kgs 24.8, 12, 15), Tahpenes (1 Kgs 11.19-20), Zeruah (1 Kgs 11.26), and Zibiah (2 Kgs 12.1); mothers and daughters of kings and officials: Basemath (1 Kgs 4.15), Jehosheba (2 Kgs 11.2-3), Taphath (1 Kgs 4.11), Zeruiah (1 Kgs 1.7; 2.5, 22); the prophet Huldah (2 Kgs 22.14-20); and the young woman, Abishag (1 Kgs 1.1-4, 15; 2.13-25).

---

1. I frequently refer to the combined corpus of 1 and 2 Kings simply as 'Kings' since the two books were originally one.

2. The following list has been culled from Carol Meyers, Toni Craven, and Ross S. Kraemer (eds.), *Women in Scripture: A Dictionary of Named and Unnamed Women in the Hebrew Bible, the Apocryphal/Deuterocanonical Books, and the New Testament* (Boston: Houghton Mifflin, 2000).

Many unnamed women, however, also have significant roles and achieve fame within the canon despite anonymity, such as the Queen of Sheba (1 Kgs 10.1-13). Often these characters are known primarily through their associations with men by marriage or birth, such as Solomon's wives and concubines (1 Kgs 3.1; 7.8; 10.8; 11.1-8), Pharaoh's daughter (1 Kgs 3.1; 7.8; 9.16, 24: 11.1), the mother of Hiram (1 Kgs 7.13-14), the wife of Jeroboam (1 Kgs 14), the mother of Elisha (1 Kgs 19.20), the wives of Ahab (1 Kgs 20.3, 5, 7), and the wives of Jehoiachin (2 Kgs 24.15). Queen Tahphenes's sister, while also known as the wife of Hadad, is twice associated with her sister and only once with her husband (1 Kgs 11.19-20). Two widows—one from Zarephath (1 Kgs 17.8-24) and the wife of the sons of the prophets (2 Kgs 4.1-7)—showcase the miraculous powers of Elijah and Elisha, respectively, while testifying to their own faith and determination. Another woman, the Shunammite, is married but overshadows her husband (2 Kgs 4.8-37; 8.1-6). Some women become known through their roles as a nurse (2 Kgs 11.2-3), prostitutes (1 Kgs 3.16-28; 1 Kgs 22.38), slaves (2 Kgs 5.26), weavers (2 Kgs 23.7), or even cannibals (2 Kgs 6.26-33). Others remain victims mentioned only briefly, such as the pregnant women killed in war (2 Kgs 8.12; 15.16) and the daughters passed through the fire (2 Kgs 17.17; 23.10). Feminist scholarship on Kings carefully reviews these stories to explore the varied roles of women and dynamics of power and gender.

Given the wealth of material on women and girls in Kings, this chapter focuses on a few female characters to review and critique feminist scholarship from different perspectives. Since the nature of Kings is hierarchical, I simultaneously work through and subvert the books' social hierarchy by focusing on goddesses, queens, unnamed women, and finally, girls. Asherah, Jezebel, Bathsheba, the Shunammite, two Prostitutes [with King Solomon], and the Israelite slave girl serve as guides as their stories offer vehicles for reviewing feminist approaches to Kings. I further note the work of brave feminists who challenge biblical scholarship to venture into realms of praxis, and then add a personal story that reflects on 1 Kgs 3.16-18. Through this discussion, I hope to demonstrate the varied ways in which feminists use the texts in Kings as a means of liberation and transformation in the hearts and minds of living, breathing people.[3]

    3.   On the role of feminist biblical studies as a vehicle for emancipatory scholarship, see Elisabeth Schüssler Fiorenza, 'Reaffirming Feminist/Womanist Biblical Scholarship', *Encounter* 67.4 (2006), pp. 361-73.

Goddesses, Especially Asherah

Goddesses appear in Kings more than any other book of the Hebrew Bible. Three of the nine references (singular or plural) to the goddess Astarte occur in Kings (1 Kgs 11.5, 33; 2 Kgs 23.13), as do sixteen of the forty mentions of Asherah (1 Kgs 14.15, 23; 15.13; 16.33; 18.19; 2 Kgs 13.6; 17.10, 16; 18.4, 21.3, 7; 23.4, 6, 7, 14, 15). Susan Ackerman also suggests the possibility of a third goddess, Ashima, mentioned in 2 Kgs 17.30.[4] Thealogian Mary Daly suggests that if God is male, then male is God; the presence of goddesses questions this assumption of deification as exclusively male in the Bible.[5]

One significant contribution of feminist scholarship on Kings has been to alert biblical readers to the presence of goddesses and their worship in the text, even though the word 'goddess' does not appear in the Hebrew Bible. Ancient writers, intent on vaulting Yhwh above other gods, minimized or vilified suggestions of goddess worship. Feminist scholars note that modern translators frequently abet this effort by obfuscating references to the goddess's name. For example, the NRSV renders *'ašerah* as 'sacred pole' in 1 Kgs 14.15, 23; 16.33; 2 Kgs 13.6; 17.10, 16; 18.4; 21.3; 23.14, 15 and 'Asherah' in 1 Kgs 15.13; 18.19; 2 Kgs 21.7; 23.4, 6, 7. While these translations are logical in context, depending on whether *'ašerah* refers to a cult symbol associated with the goddess or the goddess herself, any association with goddess worship disappears with the rendering of 'sacred pole'.[6]

Over the past few decades, the goddess Asherah has been brought into the scholarly spotlight through stunning archaeological discoveries. Most striking are inscriptions pairing Asherah with Yhwh, found at Khirbet el-Qom, near Lachish in southern Palestine and Kuntillet Ajrud in northern Sinai. Many scholars also interpret a cult stand from Taanach as depicting Asherah in an object of sacrificial devotion. Female pillar figurines may also testify to the presence and power of this goddess. Voluminous studies, too numerous to be recounted here, categorize and analyze these findings.[7]

4. Susan Ackerman, 'Ashima/Ashimah', in Meyers *et al.* (eds.), *Women in Scripture*, pp. 511-12.

5. Mary Daly, *Beyond God the Father: Toward a Philosophy of Women's Liberation* (Boston: Beacon Press, 1973), p. 19.

6. For the evolution of the proper name 'Asherah' to its designation of a pole, see Judith M. Hadley, 'Yahweh and "his Asherah": Archaeological and Textual Evidence for the Cult of the Goddess', in W. Dietrich and M.A. Klopfenstein (eds.), *Ein Gott allein? JHWH-Verehrung und biblischer Monotheismus im Kontext der israelitischen und altorientalischen Religionsgeschichte* (OBO, 139; Fribourg/Göttingen: Universitäts-verlag, 1994), pp. 235-68.

7. The study of Asherah is practically a sub-field in biblical studies. For comprehensive treatments and extensive bibliographies, see Steve A. Wiggins, *A Reassessment of Asherah with Further Considerations of the Goddess* (Piscataway, NJ: Gorgias Press,

Feminist scholarship points out that the text's own polemic against goddess worship inadvertently testifies to the power of Asherah and the threat she poses to Yhwh in the minds of the Deuteronomistic writers. Feminist scholarship also highlights varied worship practices that were not part of the official cult but were still integral to the ancient world and included worship of goddesses.[8] The composite evidence points to a goddess who was worshipped along with Yhwh in popular devotion and within the temple cult, as suggested in the writings of Carol Meyers, Susan Ackerman, Hennie Marsman, and Jennie Ebeling, among others.[9]

2007) (for a specific discussion of Kings, see pp. 123-37); William G. Dever, *Did God Have a Wife? Archaeology and Folk Religion in Ancient Israel* (Grand Rapids, MI: Eerdmans, 2005); Mark S. Smith, *Early History of God: Yahweh and the Other Deities in Ancient Israel* (Grand Rapids, MI: Eerdmans, 2002); Bob Becking *et al.*, *Only One God? Monotheism in Ancient Israel and the Veneration of the Goddess Asherah* (London: Sheffield Academic Press, 2001); Judith M. Hadley, *The Cult of Asherah in Ancient Israel and Judah: Evidence for a Hebrew Goddess* (New York: Cambridge University Press, 2000); John Day, *Yahweh and the Gods and Goddesses of Canaan* (Sheffield: Sheffield Academic Press, 2000); Tilda Binger, *Asherah: Goddesses in Ugarit, Israel, and the Old Testament* (JSOTSup, 232; Sheffield: Sheffield Academic Press, 1997); Raz Kletter, *Judean Pillar-Figurines and the Archaeology of Asherah* (Oxford: Tempus Reparatum, 1996); Saul M. Olyan, *Asherah and the Cult of Yahweh in Israel* (Atlanta, GA: Scholars Press, 1988).

    8.   The text repeatedly depicts the inhabitants of ancient Israel as tenaciously clinging to goddess worship, despite Deuteronomistic prohibitions (e.g. 1 Kgs 15.13; 2 Kgs 23.4-7) or prophetic warnings (Jer. 7.18-20; 44.15-30). On the differences between the religious realities of ancient Palestine and the orthodox agendas promoted by the biblical writers, see Francesca Stavrakopoulou and John Barton (eds.), *Religious Diversity in Ancient Israel and Judah* (London: T. & T. Clark, 2010); John Bodel and Saul M. Olyan (eds.), *Household and Family Religion in Antiquity* (Oxford: Blackwell, 2008); Karel van der Toorn, 'Nine Months among the Peasants in the Palestinian Highlands: An Anthropological Perspective on Local Religion in the Early Iron Age', in William G. Dever and Seymour Gitin (eds.), *Symbiosis, Symbolism, and the Power of the Past: Canaan, Ancient Israel, and their Neighbors from the Late Bronze Age through Roman Palaestina* (Winona Lake, IN: Eisenbrauns, 2003), pp. 393-410.

    9.   See references in 1 Kgs 15.13; 2 Kgs 21.7; 23.4-7 where *'ašerah* is associated with the royal family and her image resides in the temple. 1 Kings 15.13 may indicate that Asherah had a relationship with the *gĕbîrâ*, often translated as 'queen mother', underscoring the position of both queen and goddess within the king's court. See Susan Ackerman, 'The Queen Mother and the Cult in Ancient Israel', *JBL* 112 (1993), pp. 385-401. See the work of Carol Meyers, most notably in *Discovering Eve: Ancient Israelite Women in Context* (Oxford: Oxford University Press, 1988). See also Susan Ackerman, *Under Every Green Tree: Popular Religion in Sixth-Century Judah* (Atlanta, GA: Scholars Press, 1992). More recent and important works include Hennie J. Marsman, *Women in Ugarit and Israel: Their Social and Religious Position in the Context of the Ancient Near East* (OTS, 49; Leiden: E.J. Brill, 2003) and Jennie R. Ebeling, *Women's Lives in Biblical Times* (New York: T. & T. Clark, 2010).

Many of the scholars who study goddesses in the ancient Near East likely would not self-identify as feminists, yet nonetheless their work proves invaluable for feminist studies. However, feminists point out that academic assumptions accrue to the study of goddesses that rarely accompany the study of gods.[10] While gods are recognized as fulfilling a variety of functions, goddesses in the ancient Near East are often automatically viewed as consorts or associated with fertility, despite their varied attested roles as warriors, underworld rulers, or city patrons. Nor are goddesses in the ancient Near East *ipso facto* subservient to their male counterparts.[11]

Queens, Especially Jezebel and Bathsheba

Although many of the queens in Kings are mentioned only briefly, a key contribution of feminist scholarship has been to reexamine, reclaim, and reinterpret these texts.[12] Feminist scholarship notes the impressive power that the text bestows on some women as visiting rulers and installed monarchs, as seen with the Queen of Sheba and Athaliah, respectively.[13] Yet the most powerful woman of the book of Kings, and perhaps the entire Hebrew Bible, is also the most vilified.[14]

The name Jezebel has secured a place in biblical notoriety, as well attested not only in commentaries but in the wider popular culture.[15] Nearly

10. For further discussion, see Jo Ann Hackett, 'Can a Sexist Model Liberate Us? Ancient Near Eastern "Fertility" Goddesses', *JFSR* 5 (1989), pp. 65-79; also Joan Goodnick Westenholz, 'Goddesses of the Ancient Near East', in Lucy Goodison and Christine Morris (eds.), *Ancient Goddesses: The Myths and the Evidence* (London: British Museum Press, 1998), pp. 63-82.

11. For a discussion of goddesses in various roles, see Tikva Frymer-Kensky, 'Goddesses: Biblical Echoes', in Hershel Shanks (ed.), *Feminist Approaches to the Bible* (Washington, DC: Biblical Archaeology Society, 1995), pp. 27-44; also Tikva Frymer-Kensky, *In the Wake of Goddesses: Women, Culture, and the Biblical Transformation of Pagan Myth* (New York: Free Press, 1992).

12. For a discussion of mothers of kings in Kings, see Mignon R. Jacobs, 'Mothering a Leader: Bathsheba's Relational and Functional Identities', in Cheryl A. Kirk-Duggan and Tina Pippin (eds.), *Mother Goose, Mother Jones, Mommie Dearest: Biblical Mothers and their Children* (Atlanta, GA: Society of Biblical Literature, 2009), pp. 67-84 (68-71).

13. Athaliah reigns as an independent queen and retains her position for six years (2 Kgs 8.26; 11), testifying to her effectiveness as a politician. The Queen of Sheba is the only woman in Kings with the direct title of 'queen' (*malkah*) and she functions as a head of state on a diplomatic mission (1 Kgs 10.1-13), without regard to gender.

14. As Phyllis Trible observes: 'No woman (or man) in the Hebrew Scriptures endures a more hostile press than Jezebel'; see Phyllis Trible, 'Exegesis for Storytellers and Other Strangers', *JBL* 114 (1995), pp. 3-19 (4).

15. Even a standard dictionary (a seemingly benign reference) defines 'jezebel' as 'a wicked, shameless woman'; see http://dictionary.reference.com/browse/jezebel.

a storybook archetype, Jezebel appears as the wicked queen, ruthless in her quest for domination. She engages in the Deuteronomists' most dangerous game—competition among the gods—and pays dearly for her participation.[16] Throughout countless generations, many biblical interpreters joined in the writer's gloating defamation of this evil woman. Commentators recount how Jezebel viciously slaughters the prophets of Yhwh (1 Kgs 18.4, 13), selfishly promotes abhorrent apostasy (1 Kgs 18.19), and cruelly threatens Elijah's life (1 Kgs 19.2). Often viewed as an evil conniver, Jezebel calculates an innocent man's murder (1 Kgs 21.1-26). Justifiably, then, a prophet foretells her gory demise (2 Kgs 9.7-10) and ultimately Jezebel is hurled to her bloody death (2 Kgs 9.30-33). Both biblical text and androcentric interpretation leave Jezebel lying on the ground in pieces (2 Kgs 9.34-37), another woman dismembered only to be remembered as fragmented refuse (Judg. 19.1–20.7).

But feminist scholars do not let Jezebel lay waste in ignominious infamy. They instead portray Jezebel as the victim of a smear campaign by the Deuteronomistic writers who abhor powerful foreign women who dare to contradict their agenda.[17] As Tina Pippin observes: 'The complex and ambiguous character of Jezebel in the Bible serves as the archetypal bitchy-witch-queen in misogynist representations of women'.[18] Feminist scholars question interpretations that paradoxically seek to disenfranchize women through the biblical portrait of a strong woman. In a feminist popular treatment, *Bad Girls of the Bible*, Barbara Essex explains that the perceived threat of foreign women, such as Jezebel, testifies to their influence.

> It was believed that foreign women would lure their Israelite husbands away from God to Baal. This view is extremely unflattering to the heroes of Israel's history; they appear weak, pliable, easily influenced, and wishy-washy. By implication, patriarchy gives great power to these women—they appear strong, determined focused, persuasive, dangerous, compelling, and powerful.[19]

16.   As E.B. Johnston notes, the pointing of the MT obscures the original sense of the name 'Jezebel' which means: 'Where is the prince?' (i.e. Baal). The Masoretic vocalization draws a paranomastic connection to 2 Kgs 9.37, where Jezebel is described as 'dung'; see E.B. Johnston, 'Jezebel', in Geoffrey W. Bromiley (ed.), *The International Standard Bible Encyclopedia* (Grand Rapids, MI: Eerdmans, 1982), p. 1057.

17.   Foreign women receive Deuteronomistic approval when they promote strict adherence to Yhwh (see Josh. 2.1-21; 6.22-25; Judg. 4.17–5.27) or laud its adherents (1 Kgs 10.1-13). For fuller discussion, see Janet Howe Gaines, *Music in the Old Bones: Jezebel through the Ages* (Carbondale/Edwardsville, IL: Southern Illinois University Press, 1999), pp. 21-24.

18.   Tina Pippin, 'Jezebel Re-Vamped', *Semeia* 69–70 (1995), pp. 221-33 (222).

19.   Barbara J. Essex, *Bad Girls of the Bible: Exploring Women of Unquestionable Virtue* (Cleveland, OH: Pilgrim Press, 1989), p. 61.

Feminist scholars, then, seek to redress this injustice on Jezebel's behalf. They rescue her reputation by highlighting her royal pedigree, independent wealth, uxorial control, and regal demise. Jezebel is a Phoenician princess, brought to Israel for a political alliance (1 Kgs 16.31), yet quickly exercises her own power. She pursues her own political and theological agenda, unafraid to dispense with opponents (1 Kgs 18.3-13). She is rich and supports a large retinue of 850 prophets of Baal and Asherah who dine at her table (1 Kgs 18.19). So great is Jezebel's power that Elijah, the prophetic paragon, flees from this queen in fear (1 Kgs 19.1-3). When her spineless husband chooses to sulk over a vineyard he cannot acquire, Jezebel ably takes the issue into her own hands. Clearly well-educated, Jezebel writes the necessary documents and procures the property by dispatching its owner (i.e. Naboth in 1 Kgs 21). This queen meets death with dignity and even Jehu must recognize her status as a king's daughter (2 Kgs 9.30-34). Her bloody demise does not signal her end in the text, for even the New Testament recalls Jezebel's influence throughout the ages (Rev. 2.20-23).

As a formidable challenger to the male power in the text, Jezebel is a captivating figure for feminist scholars. For example, Phyllis Trible describes Jezebel as a 'a first-class theologian and missionary. She promotes her faith.'[20] Janet Gaines traces Jezebel through the ages to show her pervasive influence in the arts and popular culture.[21] This Israelite queen is exceptional, as Alice Ogden Bellis notes, 'because of the strength of her personality and her unwillingness to subordinate her religious traditions to those of her husband'.[22] While Jezebel arranges for Naboth's death in 1 Kings 21, Claudia Camp suggests that this action 'may be understood from her point of view as an appropriate royal response to insubordination'.[23] Judith McKinlay posits that Jezebel was set up as the villain by Deuteronomistic editors who hold her responsible for the downfall of Ahab's reign.[24]

Yet feminist interpretations laden with appreciation and even adoration for Jezebel come at a price. In their efforts to praise Jezebel for her decisive role in the story of Naboth's vineyard (1 Kgs 21), some feminists are quick to defend her actions. Athalya Brenner explains that Jezebel 'sees this matter

---

20. Trible, 'Exegesis for Storytellers', p. 7. Trible further contrasts Jezebel with Elijah to show how the paradigmatic prophet fears this Phoenician princess.

21. Gaines, *Music in the Old Bones*.

22. Alice Ogden Bellis, *Helpmates, Harlots, and Heroes: Women's Stories in the Hebrew Bible* (Louisville, KY: Westminster/John Knox Press, 2007), p. 143.

23. Claudia Camp, '1 and 2 Kings', in Carol A. Newsom and Sharon H. Ringe (eds.), *Women's Bible Commentary* (Louisville, KY: Westminster/John Knox Press, 2nd edn, 1998), pp. 102-16 (110).

24. Judith E. McKinlay, *Reframing Her: Biblical Women in Postcolonial Focus* (Sheffield: Sheffield Phoenix Press, 2004), p. 77.

as a test case of monarchic power (v. 7)' as she ultimately gets Ahab what he wants.[25] This Jezebel can easily be interpreted as the highly solicitous wife, focused on her husband's happiness above all else, including scruples. A feminist portrayal, then, can be used by traditional commentators to praise Jezebel for her unquestioned devotion to her man's desires. Mary Joan Winn Leith extols Ahab and Jezebel's relationship as a 'model partnership'.[26] Further, David Ussishkin admits: 'I have always viewed Jezebel with admiration. A woman who is willing to murder for the sake of improving her husband's bad mood is not easy to find in our world.'[27] Western feminist interpretation also tends to mitigate Jezebel's heinous crime of orchestrating an innocent man's murder.[28] As Makhosazana Nzimande observes, Jezebel can represent mean and corrupt monarchies. She appears as a heartless, greedy, killer who exploits and oppresses people of inferior status. Speaking from her African context, Nzimande asserts: '[T]o speak of Jezebel as wise and cunning is unsettling for black women at the receiving end of imperial oppression'.[29] This insightful critique calls much of feminist scholarship to accountability for its frequent Euro-centric approach. Feminist scholarship, then, needs to include the work of scholars in womanist, postcolonial, and cultural studies to guard against an ethnocentric bias.[30]

25.   See, e.g., Athalya Brenner, 'Jezebel 1', in Meyers *et al.* (eds.), *Women in Scripture*, pp. 100-2. See also Gale Yee, 'Jezebel', in *ABD, CD-ROM*, version 2.1 (1997).

26.   Mary Joan Winn Leith, 'First Lady Jezebel: Despite her Bad Reputation, her Marriage to King Ahab Was Actually a Model Partnership', *BR* 20.4 (2004), pp. 8, 46. For further discussion on the relationship between Jezebel and Ahab, see Helena Zlotnick, 'From Jezebel to Esther: Fashioning Images of Queenship in the Hebrew Bible', *Bib* 82 (2001), pp. 477-95. In her comparison between Elijah and Jezebel, Phyllis Trible suggests that Jezebel becomes the 'capable wife' of Prov. 31.11, 12, 16, 17. See Trible, 'Exegesis for Storytellers', p. 12.

27.   David Ussishkin, 'Jezreel: Where Jezebel Was Thrown to the Dogs', *BAR* 36.4 (2010), pp. 32-42, 75-76 (37).

28.   Gaines, for example, admires Jezebel's authority and astuteness, while categorizing Naboth as 'obstinate' and showing 'insolence' (*Music in these Bones*, p. 58). While Gaines's fuller discussion of 1 Kgs 21 retains more balance, she shows marked sympathy with the queen (pp. 56-69). Athalya Brenner praises Jezebel as 'a foreign royal princess by birth, [who] was highly educated and efficient' and wonders, 'It remains to be understood why she gets such bad press'; see Meyers *et al.* (eds.), *Women in Scripture*, p. 101.

29.   Makhosazana K. Nzimande, 'Reconfiguring Jezebel: A Postcolonial Imbokodo Reading of the Story of Naboth's Vineyard (1 Kings 21:1-16)', in Hans de Wit and Gerald O. West (eds.), *African and European Readers of the Bible in Dialogue: In Quest of a Shared Meaning* (Leiden: E.J. Brill, 2008), pp. 223-56 (245).

30.   See Choi Hee An and Katheryn Pfisterer Darr (eds.), *Engaging the Bible: Critical Readings from Contemporary Women* (Minneapolis: Fortress Press, 2006); Caroline Vander Stichele and Todd Penner (eds.), *Her Master's Tools? Feminist and Postcolonial Engagements of Historical-Critical Discourse* (Atlanta, GA: Society of Biblical

Feminist scholarship also focuses on sexual politics, as seen in discussions about Bathsheba. Feminist scholars speculate as to whether her encounter with David (2 Sam. 11) should be classified as rape.[31] Cheryl Exum notes that the narrator invites readers to join David in viewing the nude Bathsheba, while withholding her point of view. Readers and commentators then become accomplices in the king's crime.[32] However, other feminists read Bathsheba's story in Kings as a coming-of-age tale. Adele Berlin notes that the passive young woman who was desired, taken, and made into a wife (2 Sam. 11–12), later becomes the proactive mature mother who strategizes and works to orchestrate her son's ascension to the throne (1 Kgs 1–2).[33] Lillian Klein views David as Bathsheba's pawn, as this fertile, childless, sexually experienced woman positions herself to seduce the most popular man in the land. She uses *him* to acquire status not only as a mother, but also as a queen.[34] Yet at the center of feminist discussion is the question of choice. How much can Bathsheba actually decide?

Esther Fuchs points out that the text is soaked in a male-centered perspective, as Bathsheba's story demonstrates. Fuchs observes: 'More often than not biblical female characters reflect male fears and desires rather than historical women. The male narrator wields rhetorical control, he has the power of discourse.'[35] Male wants and needs, then, shape the hopes and

Literature, 2005); McKinlay, *Reframing Her*; Musa W. Dube (ed.), *Other Ways of Reading: African Women and the Bible* (Global Perspectives on Biblical Scholarship, 2; Atlanta, GA: Society of Biblical Literature, 2002); Musa W. Dube, *Postcolonial Feminist Interpretation of the Bible* (St Louis, MO: Chalice Press, 2000); Renita J. Weems, *Just a Sister Away: A Womanist Vision of Women's Relationships in the Bible* (San Diego: Lura Media, 1988).

31.   See Susanne Scholz, *Sacred Witness: Rape in the Hebrew Bible* (Minneapolis: Fortress Press, 2010), pp. 99-103; Alice Bach, *Women, Seduction, and Betrayal in Biblical Narrative* (Cambridge: Cambridge University Press, 1997), pp. 128-50; Mieke Bal, *Lethal Love: Feminist Literary Readings of Biblical Love Stories* (Bloomington: Indiana University Press, 1987), pp. 26-36. As Exum points out, in texts as in life, charges of rape are difficult to prove and in the sexual encounter of 2 Sam. 11 the woman has no voice; see J. Cheryl Exum, *Fragmented Women: Feminist (Sub)versions of Biblical Narratives* (Valley Forge, PA: Trinity Press International, 1993), pp. 200-1.

32.   Exum, *Fragmented Women*, pp. 173-74.

33.   Adele Berlin, *Poetics and Interpretation of Biblical Narrative* (Sheffield: Almond Press, 1983), pp. 25-30.

34.   See Lillian R. Klein, *From Deborah to Esther: Sexual Politics in the Hebrew Bible* (Minneapolis: Fortress Press, 2003), pp. 55-71.

35.   Esther Fuchs, *Sexual Politics in the Biblical Narrative: Reading the Hebrew Bible as a Woman* (JSOTSup, 310; Sheffield: Sheffield Academic Press, 2000), p. 15. The stakes are high, Fuchs maintains, as the biblical world provides a template for relationships that continue into the present age, in which women are the inevitable losers.

goals of female characters.[36] According to Fuchs, Bathsheaba's rape is indicative of her enslavement in the Bible's patriarchal worldview.[37]

These discussions about Bathsheba show that feminist scholarship is far from monolithic. Tensions arise within feminist discourse as some scholars find powerful role models in women characters, whereas others maintain that such approaches ultimately hurt women by adopting a text that is inherently and inescapably oppressive. This range of interpretations cautions feminist scholars to avoid traps set by biblical writers and interpreters who pit women against each other. Interpretative strategies should seek the best interests of real women when assessing biblical women. The strategies need to recognize the women's struggles, rejoice in their successes, and resist their subjugation.

Unnamed Women, Especially the Shunammite and Two Prostitutes

One of the most important elements of feminist biblical scholarship is its search and recovery mission, as it discovers, revives, and strengthens previously overlooked female characters who then join their better-known textual sisters. Of all the named characters in the Hebrew Bible, fewer than eight percent are female.[38] Adele Reinhartz notes that the appearance of anonymous women alongside named men further focuses attention on the male characters as deserving more than nominal attention.[39] Athalya Brenner

---

36. For example, scholars routinely point to the birth of a son as the happy denoue-ment for biblical women. For a range of perspectives on biblical women and their desire to bear children, see Timothy D. Finlay, *The Birth Report Genre in the Hebrew Bible* (FAT, 12; Tübingen: Mohr Siebeck, 2005); Leila Leah Bronner, *Stories of Biblical Mothers: Maternal Power in the Hebrew Bible* (Dallas, TX: University Press of America, 2004); Mary Callaway, *Sing, O Barren One: A Study in Comparative Midrash* (SBLDS, 91; Atlanta, GA: Scholars Press, 1986); J. Cheryl Exum, 'The Mothers of Israel: The Patriarchal Narratives from a Feminist Perspective', *BRev* 2 (1986), pp. 60-67; Esther Fuchs, 'The Literary Characterization of Mothers and Sexual Politics in the Hebrew Bible', in Adela Yarbo Collins (ed.), *Feminist Perspectives on Biblical Scholarship* (Chico, CA: Scholars Press, 1985), pp. 117-36.

37. Fuchs, *Sexual Politics in the Biblical Narrative*, pp. 14-16.

38. Karla G. Bohmbach, 'Names and Naming in the Biblical World', in Meyers *et al.* (eds.), *Women in Scripture*, pp. 33-39 (34).

39. Adele Reinhartz, 'Anonymous Women and the Collapse of the Monarchy: A Study in Narrative Technique', in Athalya Brenner (ed.), *A Feminist Companion to Samuel and Kings* (FCB, 5; Sheffield: Sheffield Academic Press, 1994), pp. 43-65. See also Mieke Bal, 'Tricky Thematics', in J. Cheryl Exum and Johanna W.H. Bos (eds.), *Reasoning with the Foxes: Female Wit in a World of Male Power* (Semeia, 42; Atlanta, GA: Scholars Press, 1988), pp. 133-55.

highlights some of the Bible's lesser-known women and tells their stories from a first-person perspective.[40] Robin Branch applies tools of narrative criticism to the stories of some of the Bible's lesser-known women to concentrate on their overlooked contributions.[41] Bringing gynocentric questions to the text frees little-known female characters from textual obscurity.

The Shunammite (or 'Gedolah')

One such character is the Shunammite woman. Fokkelien van Dijk-Hemmes names her 'Gedolah', which means 'Great One', in an effort to contribute to her characterization, whereas other scholars simply call her 'the Shunammite'.[42] Her relatively unfamiliar story is tucked into the Elisha cycle (2 Kgs 4.8-37; 8.1-6). On one level, her story is a straightforward account of a woman who hosts the prophet Elisha and is rewarded with a son. When the child dies, she insists that the prophet revive him, which he does miraculously (2 Kgs 4.8-37). Feminist scholars first call attention to this woman by noting that she defies typical stereotypes. Tikva Frymer-Kensky observes that she is the only woman in the Hebrew Bible who cannot have a child but does not express any desire for one.[43] The Shunammite woman is perfectly content without a male child, the standard biblical prerequisite for muliebral happiness. Mary Shields shows how this woman reverses power and control as she overshadows her husband and controls the outcome of the story beyond the work of the prophet.[44] This mostly unknown biblical character then emerges as a forthright woman unafraid of commanding and contradicting powerful men, offering a textual model for real women who push the

---

40. Brenner gathers selected women biblical characters in a fantasy round table. The only portrayal from Kings is the prophet Huldah (2 Kgs 22.14-20). Athalya Brenner, *I Am: Biblical Women Tell their Own Stories* (Minneapolis: Fortress Press, 2005), pp. 155-62. See also Claudia V. Camp, 'Female Voice, Written Word: Women and Authority in Hebrew Scripture', in Paula M. Cooey, Sharon A. Farmer and Mary Ellen Ross (eds.), *Embodied Love: Sensuality and Relationship as Feminist Values* (San Francisco: Harper & Row, 1987), pp. 97-113; Norma Rosen, *Biblical Women Unbound: Counter-Tales* (Philadelphia: Jewish Publication Society, 1996).

41. Robin Gallaher Branch, *Jeroboam's Wife: The Enduring Contributions of the Old Testament's Least-Known Women* (Peabody, MA: Hendrickson, 2009).

42. Fokkelien van Dijk-Hemmes, 'The Great Woman of Shunem and the Man of God: A Dual Interpretation of 2 Kings 4:8-37', in Brenner (ed.), *A Feminist Companion to Samuel and Kings*, pp. 218-30 (230); The Shunammite is the only woman in the Hebrew Bible extolled as *gedolah*, normally translated as 'great'. See Wesley Bergen, *Elisha and the End of Prophetism* (JSOTSup, 286; Sheffield: Sheffield Academic Press, 1999), p. 90.

43. Tikva Frymer-Kensky, *Reading the Women of the Bible* (New York: Schocken Books, 2002), p. 66.

44. See Mary Shields, 'Subverting a Man of God, Elevating a Woman: Role and Power Reversals in 2 Kings 4', *JSOT* 58 (1993), pp. 59-69.

confines of patriarchal boundaries within their own lives and communities. While the patriarchal narrator has the last word in this story, feminist scholars note with amazement and appreciation how much this unnamed woman has accomplished in this prophetic tale.

Two Prostitutes

While some may counter, indeed justifiably, that scholarship—not activism—is the work of academics, Avaren E. Ipsen demonstrates the provocative results that can ensue when the two are combined. She talks with sex workers about 1 Kgs 3.16-28, asking for their opinions about the story of Solomon with two prostitutes.[45] The sex workers observe that the prostitute who is willing to have a child cut in half is clearly the evil mother, but the king who suggests the idea and appears ready to follow through with it is viewed as the hero. One woman, Kimberlee, feels that the women had to be prostitutes because they are perceived as inherently immoral. Another sex worker, Veronica Monet, discerns that the women are prostitutes because if they had a man in their lives, he would be the one to come before the king. She also observes that the courtroom portrayed in the Bible is kinder to prostitutes than the modern judicial system, which frequently does not let prostitutes keep their children.[46] Sex workers instantly recognize the economic aspects of the story, as prostitutes then as now are typically poor women, sometimes working to support children. As Ipsen summarizes: 'A sex worker standpoint exposes the corrupt and violent nature of Solomon's court. This is invisible even to many liberation oriented biblical scholars.'[47]

Feminist scholars recognize the need to unmask social location. Just as the stories of the Bible point to truths in our lives, the stories of our lives point to truths in the text. Brenner notes, 'The pretense to critical objectivity is losing ground, not least because of feminist insistence'.[48] Feminist interpreters thus switch to the first person to explore the intersections between the Bible, culture, and their own experience.[49] I would like to demonstrate

45. Avaren E. Ipesen, 'Solomon and the Two Prostitutes', *The Bible and Critical Theory* 3 (2007), pp. 2.1-2.12.

46. Ipsen, 'Two Prostitutes', p. 2.7. On prostitutes as characters, see Phyllis Bird, 'The Harlot as Heroine: Narrative Art and Social Presupposition in Three Old Testament Texts', *Semeia* 46 (1989), pp. 119-39.

47. Ipsen, 'Two Prostitutes', p. 2.9.

48. Athalya Brenner, '"My" Song of Songs', in Athalya Brenner and Carole Fontaine (eds.), *A Feminist Companion to Reading the Bible: Approaches, Methods, and Strategies* (FCB, 11; Sheffield: Sheffield Academic Press, 1997), pp 567-79 (567).

49. See Gale A. Yee, 'An Autobiographical Approach to Feminist Biblical Studies', *Encounter* 67.4 (2006), pp. 375-90; Philip R. Davies (ed.), *First Person: Essays in Biblical Autobiography* (Biblical Seminar, 81; New York: Sheffield Academic Press, 2002); Ingrid Rosa Kitzberger (ed.), *Personal Voice in Biblical Interpretation* (New York: Routledge, 1999).

this autobiographical approach with a personal and true story that relates to 1 Kgs 3.16-28. Years ago, when Times Square in New York City was still a gritty and sleazy place, I worked as a counselor at a shelter on West 46th Street for homeless women with children. There I met a young woman named Suzanne who came from Florida to New York City, fleeing from her husband who used to beat her at gunpoint. She had gotten off a bus in Port Authority knowing no one. She was seven months pregnant and had her two-year-old son, Justin, in tow. Suzanne found her way to the shelter where I worked, and there I helped her navigate the dizzying social services system. After a few weeks, my mother invited Suzanne and Justin to come live in my parents' home on Long Island. She slept in my former bedroom. Soon we discovered syringes in the bathroom; Suzanne was a heroin addict who would prostitute herself to earn money for drugs. At one point she took the train into New York to collect her welfare check, not returning for two weeks and leaving my mother to care for her son. Of course, Suzanne was pregnant this entire time. She gave birth on Christmas Eve, and my mother and I went to the hospital after the midnight service. Suzanne knew she could not care for her new son, and with help from my mother, she found a lawyer to arrange an adoption. Like the mother of the living son in 1 Kgs 3.16-28, Suzanne was a prostitute ready to give up her baby boy. Yet while the biblical story presents itself as a fairy tale with a 'happily-ever-after' ending, it points to painful and timeless socio-economic realities. Prostitutes are often poor women who lead harsh and dangerous lives. Suzanne is now dead from AIDS. Feminist scholarship on Kings explores ancient and modern political implications of women in the text whose lives span a wide range of social locations mirrored in our own world.

Girls, Especially the Israelite Slave Girl

To date, feminist scholarship has focused almost exclusively on women characters and overlooked the Bible's girls. As Esther Menn points out: 'Perhaps because they are small, child characters are easy to dismiss or to stereotype as simple, innocent, and insignificant'.[50] One such young heroine is the Israelite slave girl of 2 Kgs 5.1-14. While some compendia of women in the Bible omit mention of this girl, she is nonetheless a significant character in the Elisha cycle.[51] The Israelite slave girl instigates the healing

---

50. Esther Menn, 'Child Characters in Biblical Narratives: The Young David (1 Samuel 16–17) and the Little Israelite Servant Girl (2 Kings 5:1-19)', in Marcia Bunge (ed.), *The Child in the Bible* (Grand Rapids, MI: Eerdmans, 2008), pp. 324-52 (324).

51. For example, she is missing from the chapter on Kings in Alice Ogden Bellis, *Helpmates, Harlots, and Heroes: Women's Stories in the Hebrew Bible* (Louisville, KY: Westminster/John Knox Press, 2007), pp. 139-55. She is mentioned briefly in M.L. del

of her great master, Naaman, with whom she offers a perfect contrast in nationality, class, age, status, power, and gender. Menn compares this small girl to the young David with Goliath, noting their resourcefulness, originality, and flexibility in scenes that cross ethnic boundaries.[52] Jean Kyoung Kim admires the small girl's power of persuasion.[53] Robin Gallaher Branch extols this girl as a model of belief, healing, and hope: 'Unnamed, probably orphaned and alone, and occupying the lowest position in a hostile, alien society, this child nonetheless makes one of the simplest, purest statements of faith in the Bible'.[54] She is the only girl explicitly noted as 'little' who speaks in the entire Hebrew Bible.

A new frontier in feminist scholarship is to discover the Bible's girls. Within Kings, characters who are sought for marriage, for example, Abishag (1 Kgs 1.1-4, 15; 2.13-25), Pharaoh's daughter (1 Kgs 3.1; 7.8; 9.16, 24; 11.1), and possibly the wives of Solomon (1 Kgs 11.1-3), may be understood as teenagers and therefore relatively young. Studies of households and their economic realities should not neglect consideration of young family members, as seen with the mother of the two children to be sold into slavery (2 Kgs 4.1-7) or the Shunammite's loss of land (2 Kgs 8.1-6). The daughters passed through the fire (2 Kgs 17.17; 23.10) also raise questions of power and vulnerability that are familiar to feminist scholars.

Looking Back and Ahead

First and Second Kings offer one of the Bible's richest collections of narratives for feminist scholars. Significant progress over the past four decades has first called attention to the women in these texts and introduced many new female characters into our biblical lexicon. Feminist scholarship has also defended women characters against portraits that malign women, as seen with Jezebel, and highlighted female characters whose stories have been overlooked, as with the Israelite slave girl. Yet the insights here go beyond simply noticing or championing female characters. Incorporating knowledge gleaned from archaeological discoveries with Kings texts on goddesses, feminist scholarship pushes readers to examine theological assumptions

Mastro, *All the Women of the Bible* (Edison, NJ: Castle Press, 2004), p. 93; Miriam Therese Winter, *Woman Witness: A Feminist Lectionary and Psalter* (New York: Crossroad, 1992), p. 336. In Meyers *et al.* (eds.), *Women in Scripture*, Naaman's wife and the slave girl are grouped in a single entry, p. 275.

52. Menn, 'Child Characters', pp. 324-52.

53. Jean Kyoung Kim, 'Reading and Retelling Naaman's Story (2 Kings 5)', *JSOT* 30 (2005), pp. 49-61.

54. Robin Gallaher Branch, *Jeroboam's Wife: The Enduring Contributions of the Old Testament's Least-Known Women* (Peabody, MA: Hendrickson, 2009), p. 147.

upon which the entire Bible is based. Hints of women's cults and goddess worship raise questions of religious practices that extend beyond the Yahweh-alone agenda of the writers. These texts also provide a merism of female roles with characters from goddesses to slaves and consistently grapple with issues of politics and power. Feminist scholarship has mined even brief stories on queens to show that women wielded significant power in the ancient world, most of which did not concern the Deuteronomistic historians. Feminist scholarship on Kings has also engaged women from their own social and political location, as with women who are sex workers, and ventured to intertwine scholarship with lived experiences.

Avenues for future feminist studies on Kings are many. The female characters in Kings stretch female biblical stereotypes of mothers, wives, and daughters, as they inhabit roles of goddesses, queens, and slaves, inviting scholars to ask how power structures change with women in key positions. Female characters in Kings can also raise questions of gender construction, as with Jezebel who acts in ways more typical of the male characters found in Kings.[55] Women, girls, and goddesses in Kings can challenge constructs of femininity and masculinity; this discussion merits further consideration. Future feminist biblical scholars also should question the text's biases about ethnicity, instead of accepting the text's insider/outsider paradigm of the 'foreign woman', which surfaces frequently in Kings (e.g. 1 Kgs 3.1; 7.8; 10.1-13; 11.1-8, 19-20; 16.31; 18.19; 21; 2 Kgs 9). Feminist biblical scholarship keeps finding ways to take risks, to expand the interpretive status quo, and to open minds and hearts to the power of the biblical text. Androcentric hegemony is no longer the final word decreed by Kings.

55. On the gender construction of Jezebel, see Victoria S. Kolakowski, 'Throwing a Party: Patriarchy, Gender, and the Death of Jezebel', in Robert E. Goss and Mona West (eds.), *Take Back the Word: A Queer Reading of the Bible* (Cleveland, OH: Pilgrim Press, 2000), pp. 103-14.

7

BIBLICAL METAPHORS AS PART OF THE PAST AND PRESENT: FEMINIST APPROACHES TO THE BOOKS OF ISAIAH, JEREMIAH, AND EZEKIEL

Sandie Gravett

The major prophets were not among the first biblical books feminist scholars investigated. On the surface, this prophetic literature appeared to offer scant material for feminist inquiry because the books carry male names, report the words of male prophets, and direct messages primarily towards kings, court officials, and the people of Israel, all understood as male. Only a few female characters appear, receiving only fleeting attention and apparently providing little insight into the activities of women in ancient Israelite society. By contrast, the prophetic books include many metaphors of women as prostitutes and adulterers, but unlike the earlier and much shorter book of Hosea, they show up largely in the margins of the major prophets.

It took some time for feminist exegetes to approach the major prophets with feminist perspectives. Once they did, they mined Isaiah, Jeremiah, and Ezekiel for various purposes. First, they turned their attention to the prophetic metaphors that depict cities and nations as women, often characterized as wives or daughters and presented as 'whoring'. Within this context, feminist exegetes also explored more positive aspects of the daughter/wife/mother metaphors to describe the relationship between Israel and God. Second, feminists discovered references to the so-called 'queen of heaven' in the book of Jeremiah and examined the prevalence and power of goddess worship in Jerusalem and elsewhere in the ancient Near East. Third, they studied female images, such as God as mother, in the prophetic tradition and their relationship to ancient religious practices and possible links to women prophets and women's significance within religious worship settings. The following discussion explores these three topics to present the developments of feminist scholarship on the major prophets.

Cites and Nations as 'Whoring' Women:
Feminist Work on the Pornographic Metaphors

In 1973, feminist philosopher, Mary Daly, stated bluntly that 'the imagery of Old Testament Prophets was very sexist' and exhibited 'a tiresome propensity for comparing Israel to a whore'.[1] Yet feminist Hebrew Bible scholars did not rush to examine these metaphors. Indeed, one of the first studies that carefully examined female metaphors in Hosea 1–3 appeared only in 1985.[2] The author, Drorah Setel, calls the biblical texts pornographic because they equate the covenant between God and Israel with the relationship between the prophet and his wife in sexually explicit and sexually violent ways. It took several additional years until similar metaphoric references in the books of Isaiah, Jeremiah, and Ezekiel received full attention from feminist interpreters.[3]

Depicting violated women, the metaphors stand in a long tradition of imaging cites and nations in feminine terms. In Hebrew, for instance, the construction of the word for daughter (*bat*) and a place name might simply

1. Mary Daly, *Beyond God the Father: Toward a Philosophy of Women's Liberation* (Boston: Beacon Press, 1973), p. 162.

2. T. Drorah Setel, 'Prophets and Pornography: Female Sexual Imagery in Hosea', in Letty M. Russell (ed.), *Feminist Interpretation of the Bible* (Philadelphia: Westminster Press, 1985), pp. 86-95.

3. See, for example, Susan Ackerman, 'Isaiah', in Carole A. Newsom and Sharon H. Ringe (eds.), *The Women's Bible Commentary* (Louisville, KY: Westminster/John Knox Press, exp. edn, 1998), pp. 169-77. Also in that volume, Kathleen M. O'Connor, 'Jeremiah', pp. 178-86, and Katheryn Pfisterer Darr, 'Ezekiel', pp. 192-200; Phyllis Bird, '"To Play the Harlot": An Inquiry into an Old Testament Metaphor', in Peggy Day (ed.), *Gender and Difference in Ancient Israel* (Minneapolis: Fortress Press, 1989), pp. 75-94; Athalya Brenner, 'On "Jeremiah" and the Poetics of (Prophetic?) Pornography', in Athalya Brenner and Fokkelien van Dijk-Hemmes (eds.), *On Gendering Texts: Female and Male Voices in the Hebrew Bible* (BibInt Series 1; Leiden: E.J. Brill, 1993), pp. 177-93; Athalya Brenner, 'Pornoprophetics Revisited: Some Additional Reflections', *JSOT* 70 (1996), pp. 63-86; Katheryn Pfisterer Darr, 'Ezekiel's Justifications of God: Teaching Troubling Texts', *JSOT* 55 (1992), pp. 97-117; A.R. Pete Diamond and Kathleen M. O'Connor, 'Unfaithful Passions: Coding Women Coding Men in Jeremiah 2–3 (4:2)', *BibInt* 4 (1996), pp. 288-310; Fokkelien van Dijk-Hemmes, 'The Metaphorization of Women in Prophetic Speech: An Analysis of Ezekiel 23', in Brenner and van Dijk-Hemmes (eds.), *On Gendering Texts*, pp. 167-76; Julie Galambush, *Jerusalem in the Book of Ezekiel: The City as Yahweh's Wife* (SBLDS, 130; Atlanta, GA: Scholars Press, 1992); Pamela Gordon and Harold C. Washington, 'Rape as a Military Metaphor in the Hebrew Bible', in Athalya Brenner (ed.), *A Feminist Companion to the Latter Prophets* (FCB, 8; Sheffield: Sheffield Academic Press, 1995), pp. 308-25; Mary E. Shields, 'Circumcision of the Prostitute: Gender, Sexuality and the Call to Repentance in Jer 3:1–4:4', *BibInt* 3 (1995), pp. 61-74; Mary E. Shields, 'Multiple Exposures: Body Rhetoric and Gender Characterization in Ezekiel 16', *JFSR* 14 (1998), pp. 5-18.

derive from the grammatical practice of viewing nouns for cities and countries as feminine.[4] Further, as Julia M. O'Brien suggests, 'Israel was not unique in the ancient world in associating cities with female images. Mesopotamian texts describe cities as having patron goddesses who fight on their behalf and weep over their destruction.'[5] Among the major prophets, the authors of Isaiah in particular stress female imagery for various geo-political units,[6] although the most common referent—a poetically personified daughter—appears in both the books of Isaiah and Jeremiah.[7] Metaphorical mothers, daughters, and sisters also assume prominence in Ezekiel 16 and 23. Most frequently, the women depicted in these texts suffer. Pamela Gordon and Harold C. Washington, for example, examine how the imagining of a city as woman often ends in violent destruction. They observe that in these pictures of sexual violence 'the language gives a grim and realistic reminder of the fate of women in war'.[8]

Possible Origins of the Metaphor

How did such associations between women and cities or nations take root? Perhaps most readily these personified figures symbolize women's roles in the social structure of ancient Israel. The image of the ideal family presents daughters as living under the protection and care of their fathers until they join another household as a wife, concubine, or (in some cases) servant or slave.[9] The depiction stresses the importance of a woman's virginity as a daughter—and then her fidelity as a sexual partner—in order to assure the known paternity of any children and the proper maintenance and inheritance

---

4.   Karla G. Bohmbach, 'Daughter', in Carol Meyers (ed.), *Women in Scripture: A Dictionary of Named and Unnamed Women in the Hebrew Bible, the Apocryphal/ Deuterocanonical Books, and the New Testament* (Boston: Houghton Mifflin, 2000), pp. 517-19 (518).

5.   Julia M. O'Brien, *Challenging Prophetic Metaphor: Theology and Ideology in the Prophets* (Louisville, KY: Westminster/John Knox Press, 2008), p. 126.

6.   Susan Ackerman, 'Women Sidon and Tyre', in Meyers (ed.), *Women in Scripture*, p. 556.

7.   See Daughter Ammon (Jer. 49.4); Daughter Babylon/Chaldea or Virgin Daughter Babylon (Isa. 47.1, 5; Jer. 50.42; 51.33); Virgin Daughter (Jer. 14.17); Daughter Dibon (Jer. 48.18); Daughter Egypt or Virgin Daughter Egypt (Jer. 46.11, 19, 24); Daughter Gallim (Isa. 10.30); Daughter Israel (Jer. 31.22); Daughter Jerusalem (Isa. 37.22); Virgin Daughter Sidon (Isa. 23.12); Daughter Tarshish (Isa. 23.10); Daughter Zion, or Virgin Daughter Zion (Isa. 1.8; 10.32; 16.1; 37.22; 52.2; 62.11; Jer. 4.31; 6.2, 23). A discussion on the various uses appears in Bohmbach, 'Daughter', p. 517.

8.   Gordon and Washington, 'Rape as a Military Metaphor, p. 322.

9.   Joseph Blenkinsopp, 'The Family in First Temple Israel', in Leo G. Purdue *et al.* (eds.), *Families in Ancient Israel* (Louisville, KY: Westminster/John Knox Press, 1997), pp. 48-103 (76).

of a household's assets.[10] Further, women work in the household to produce the necessities of life such as food and textiles, while also giving birth and tending to the children who ensured the family's survival.[11] Cities, then, assume a feminine gender as locations demanding defense and nurture in addition to serving as sources of basic life needs. As Christl Maier states:

> Cites, like women, can be desired, conquered, protected, and governed by men. A city provides the main sources of life such as food, shelter, and a home to the people, just as a mother for her children. Thus, the feminine gendering of the space is primarily based on its ideas about its use and usefulness for human habitation.[12]

The use of the term daughters with regard to locations could also reference satellite villages near a larger city. Jeremiah 49.2-3 and Ezek. 26.6, 8; 30.18 utilize this type of language. Frank Frick turns to the social structure of ancient Israel to explain the terminology. He explains: 'Mothers had considerable authority over their daughter—hence the analogy of a walled mother-city exerting control over the unwalled, dependent daughter villages. Just as a mother had responsibilities in caring for her children, so the city provided protection for its people.'[13]

Additionally, feminists look at the Torah to understand the development of the metaphor of Israel as a woman in relationship to God. As Tikva Frymer-Kensky observes, the terms of the covenant between Yhwh and the people show distinct similarities to the marriage bond. She states:

> Deuteronomy, which fully develops covenantal language, demands 'love' from Israel for God, a 'love' which manifests itself by fidelity and obedience to commandments and laws. The Pentateuch also uses marital language to express the breaking of this loyalty-bond and its consequences. Failure to maintain exclusive loyalty to God is called 'wantoness' or promiscuity (*znh*) and God's reaction is…his 'jealousy' (*qn'*).[14]

To Frymer-Kensky, the relationship of the deity with the people reflects aspects of the institution of marriage as practiced in Israel. Yet the descriptions vary dramatically from human marriage as the metaphors depict extreme violence perpetrated by God, the husband, on his wife. She is

10.　Blenkinsopp, 'The Family in First Temple Israel', p. 63.

11.　Blenkinsopp, 'The Family in First Temple Israel', p. 78.

12.　Christl Maier, *Daughter Zion. Mother Zion: Gender, Space, and the Sacred in Ancient Israel* (Philadelphia: Fortress Press, 2008), p. 73.

13.　Frank S. Frick, 'Mother/Daughter (NRSV, Village) as Territory', in Meyers (ed.), *Women in Scripture*, pp. 532-33 (533).

14.　Tikva Frymer-Kensky, *In the Wake of the Goddesses: Women, Culture, and the Biblical Transformation of Pagan Myth* (New York: The Free Press, 1992), p. 146.

allowed, even invited, to remarry her divorced spouse, God. Frymer-Kensky claims that '[t]he Israelite listener knew that God was different',[15] but many other feminist scholars debated this sharp distinction.[16]

The vast majority of the metaphors imagine the characters in situations of war and the dire consequences it has for them. As Brad Kelle explains: 'A close analysis of prophetic texts that personify cities as females...leads to a first observation: when these texts describe the *destruction* of the city, they frequently employ the metaphorical language of physical and sexual violence against a woman'.[17] In the major prophets, multiple references to women as mothers, wives, and daughters serve as the basis for symbolizing the failed relationship between God and Israel and the consequences expressed in the woman's eventual downfall.[18] Additionally, other nations are also imagined as 'daughters' and suffer a similar fate, as mentioned in Isa. 47.1-5 and Jer. 46.11. Most often these texts picture the women as prostitutes and blame them for their own victimization. Thus Gordon and Washington observe that 'before her violation, the young woman fulfills the role of virginal object of male fantasy; after she is abused, she becomes the "harlotrous"—yet still beautiful—object of male scorn'.[19]

The lengthiest treatment of the metaphor in which women are presented as prostitutes appears in Ezekiel 16 and 23. In Ezekiel 16, the city of Jerusalem is presented as the adulterous wife of Yahweh whereas in Ezekiel 23 Jerusalem and Samaria are sisters and unfaithful lovers of their husband, God. Both passages warn the people of Israel against relying on other deities and foreign alliances for protection, and they depict the disloyalty of the Israelite cities as the women's sexual voraciousness. Such 'whoring' receives, at least from the point of view of the writers, just and fitting punishment. The cities fall into the hands of their enemies like women who are brutalized and raped during wartime. The texts describe the female figures as losing their homes, facing the deaths of their children, and experiencing brutal physical and sexual assaults. Moreover, the imagery blames the women's suffering on their sexual promiscuity for theological reasons. The

---

15.   Frymer-Kensky, *In the Wake of the Goddesses*, p. 149.

16.   See, e.g., J. Cheryl Exum, 'The Ethics of Biblical Violence against Women', in John W. Rogerson, Margaret Davies and M. Daniel Carroll R. (eds.), *The Bible in Ethics* (Sheffield: Sheffield Academic Press, 1995), pp. 248-71.

17.   Brad Kelle, 'Wartime Rhetoric: Prophetic Metaphorization of Cites as Female', in Brad E. Kelle and Frank Ritchel Ames (eds.), *Writing and Reading War: Rhetoric, Gender, and Ethics in Biblical and Modern Contexts* (Atlanta, GA: Society of Biblical Literature, 2008), p. 98 (original italics).

18.   See, for example, Isa. 1.27; 3.16-24; 57.3-13; Jer. 2.33–3.20; 4.30; 13.20-27; 22.2-23; Ezek. 16.1-63; 23.1-49.

19.   Gordon and Washington, 'Rape as a Military Metaphor', p. 319.

metaphoric depictions absolve God of any responsibility for not protecting Israel. They also use pornographic language to justify sexual assault on the women, as they are accused of 'whoring' against their husband, God.

Feminist-Literary Studies on the Prophetic Metaphors
In her assessment of the development of feminist exegesis on these texts, Gerlinde Baumann observes:

> [S]ince the 1980s there has been a clear shift in exegetical treatment of prophetic marriage metaphors. Whereas in older (non-feminist) works the subject was most commonly discussed under the topic of 'God's love', the foreground is now occupied by the aspect of violence against the 'wife' in the marital relationship (with reference to concrete women's experiences), as well as the pornographizing of the imagery.[20]

The feminist discussion thus highlights the significance of sexual violence in the prophetic literature. Two central preoccupations drive much of this feminist commentary. First, feminist exegetes examine the gender bias in the interpretation of these passages, which often fails to interrogate the violence against women in the texts. Second, in a related effort, they debate the appropriate reactions to these texts by readers. Feminist exegete J. Cheryl Exum considers the interpretive reception of these passages on violence against women as problematic. She explores the biases prevalent in the history of interpretation not only of Ezekiel 16 and 23 but also of Isaiah, Jeremiah, Hosea, and Lamentations. She thus explains:

> In dealing with the ethical problems raised by passages in which a male deity is pictured as sexually abusing a female victim, we cannot confine ourselves to the issue of gender bias in representation, which we can describe and account for as a product of an ancient patriarchal society where the subordinate position of women was taken for granted. We also need to consider gender bias in interpretation.[21]

In other words, Exum's goal is not simply to study how biblical authors referred to women in androcentric ways, but to challenge the complicity of exegetes throughout the ages. Interpreters rarely criticized the sexist assumptions with which the biblical text constructs women as prostitutes and justifies women's 'punishment' with sexual violence and even murder. Exum further holds that centuries of male dominance in biblical scholarship

---

20. Gerlinde Baumann, *Love and Violence: Marriage as Metaphor for the Relationship between YHWH and Israel in the Prophetic Books* (Collegeville, MN: Liturgical Press, 2003), p. 8.

21. J. Cheryl Exum, *Plotted, Shot, and Painted: Cultural Representations of Biblical Women* (Sheffield: Sheffield Academic Press, 1996), p. 102.

made it impossible to highlight alternative readings. Androcentric readers were content to privilege the perspective of God, the angry husband whom the prophetic texts present as punishing, beating, and raping his adulterous wives. Thus, androcentric commentators reinscribed sexist conventions from the text into their own worlds. They read 'with' the divine voice and accepted as normative sexist theological views and the social practices derived from them. Exum states:

> In describing God's treatment of his wayward wife, the prophets rely upon a rhetorical strategy that encourages the audience to identify and sympathize with a male-identified deity... When readers privilege the deity, which most readers of the Bible still do, they are forced into accepting this position, for to resist would be tantamount to challenging divine authority. This is the position taken almost without exception by biblical commentators, who, until recently, have been almost without exception male. Typically these commentators either ignore the difficulties posed by this divine sexual abuse or reinscribe the gender ideology of the biblical texts; usually they do both in their ceaseless efforts to justify God.[22]

In short, Exum highlights how the interpretive history of these passages jettisoned concern for women, even in more contemporary settings, in favor of privileging a troubling image of the divine.

Other feminist commentators, such as Gordon and Washington, examine readers' responses to these violent metaphors. Pondering the impact of the metaphor's sexual violence in today's culture, they advise that resistance to the prophetic message is the only viable option, writing: '(N)o one is safe in the environment created by such rhetoric. Women are allotted the role of victim, and men are expected to pursue with equal enthusiasm both sexual domination and "war, the ultimate adventure".'[23] Fokkelien van Dijk-Hemmes pushes further when she explores the features and functions of pornography in the context of the biblical metaphor and the responses of male and female readers to Ezekiel 23. She suggests that the biblical material promotes the 'denial or misnaming of the female experience',[24] and labels what appears as pornographic. She also shows that translations such as the NRSV hide the serious violence depicted, as for instance in Ezek. 23.3: 'They played the whore in Egypt; they played the whore in their youth; their breasts were caressed there, and their virgin bosoms were fondled'. To Dijk-Hemmes, this translation obscures the bluntness of the Hebrew imagery, and

22. Exum, *Plotted, Shot, and Painted*, pp. 114-15.
23. Gordon and Washington, 'Rape as a Military Metaphor', p. 323.
24. Van Dijk-Hemmes, 'The Metaphorization of Women in Prophetic Speech: An Analysis of Ezekiel 23', in Brenner (ed.), *A Feminist Companion to the Latter Prophets*, pp. 244-55 (248).

she wants to make the bluntness visible in the English translation. Accordingly, she translates the same verse as follows: 'There they [grammatically masc., see also v. 8] pressed the teats of their [the women's] maidenhood'.[25] The phrase in Hebrew is vulgar, and by setting this action in the context of prostitution, the authors imagined women as sexually insatiable. This attitude, so Dijk-Hemmes, makes the text highly problematic and it ought to be understood as a depiction of sexual abuse.

Dijk-Hemmes makes another significant observation. She notes that the metaphor has a different effect on male and female readers. Men avoid identifying themselves as a sexually violated woman and resonate with the husband's perspective, condemning the woman who prostitutes herself. Dijk-Hemmes explains:

> The androcentric-pornographic character of this metaphorical language must indeed be experienced as extremely humiliating by a M (Male/Masculine) audience forced to imagine itself as being exposed to violating enemies. Nevertheless, it is exactly androcentric-pornographic character which at the same time offers the M audience a possibility of escape: the escape of identification with the wronged and revengeful husband; or, more modestly, identification with the righteous men who, near the end of the text, are summoned to pass judgment upon the adulterous women (v. 45).[26]

Thus, in the effort to avoid association with the punished woman, male readers agree with the negative casting of the woman's experience and exonerate the actions of the male deity who is portrayed as being wronged by his wife. Male readers empathize with God as a cuckold husband, justify the violence unleashed on the woman, and eagerly claim a position of privilege from which to interpret the sexual violence.

In sharp contrast, the text offers female readers 'no such possibility of escape',[27] asking women readers to identify with the violated female characters and to force them to take on her humiliation and subjugation. Female readers must accept the punishment as deserved when they follow the premise of the metaphor, namely that the male divinity is justified to punish his wives for their grave adulterous acts. More significantly, the metaphor reinforces the idea of women as objectified and powerless, an idea embedded in Western culture.

The feminist focus on the interpretive history and the role of readers shifts a common presupposition in biblical scholarship, namely that meaning resides in an authoritative text. Feminist scholars demonstrate that text and

25. Van Dijk-Hemmes, 'The Metaphorization of Women', p. 250.
26. Van Dijk-Hemmes, 'The Metaphorization of Women', p. 254.
27. Van Dijk-Hemmes, 'The Metaphorization of Women', p. 255.

readers can and do interact not only to generate a singular reading experience, but also to produce an interpretive history. By altering the balance of power between text and reader, feminist interpreters interrogate the norms of both the culture that produced the text as well as the cultures that receive it.

Historical-Feminist Approaches to the Metaphors

The feminist concern for the mental, emotional, and theological health of contemporary readers and the emphasis on gendered hermeneutical approaches has created a lively debate among feminist and androcentric exegetes. Among the latter is Robert Carroll who assumes a highly visible role in this conversation. In his view, feminist readers overreact to the female images in the prophetic poetry. He stresses that the metaphor attributes positive and negative characteristics to both male and female characters. He also emphasizes that these passages do not describe actual events. They are metaphors that pertain equally to women and men. He states:

> If the biblical writers only used negative images of women and positive images of men, then I could see the force of the objections made by feminist readers of the Bible. But that is not the case. The metaphorization processes represent negative *and* positive images of both men and women (as metaphors!) and because such representations are inevitably metaphoric their referential force is symbolic.[28]

In Carroll's view, feminists misunderstand the metaphors when they connect them to the lived realities of women and men. Most importantly, he charges that feminist exegetes ignore the gendered composition of the original audience which consisted largely of men, and so male behavior dominates in the metaphors. Carroll thus urges feminist readers to attend less to the form of the message, the metaphor, and more to the context in which the metaphor addresses men. In his view, contemporary feminist interpretations are inadequate in shedding light on ancient Israelite women's lives. Still, he also acknowledges that 'feminist oppositions to the text are one more way of doing a proper *Ideologiekritik* reading of the Bible'.[29]

Unsurprisingly, some feminist scholars, disagreeing with Carroll, maintain that the pornographic metaphors relate directly to the social world of ancient Israel. They contend that the ancient authors communicated effectively with their audiences because of this connection. Interestingly, the argumentation of these feminist interpreters differs from critics such as Dijk-Hemmes and Exum. They are less interested in the reception history

---

28. Robert P. Carroll, 'Desire under the Terebinths: On Pornographic Representation in the Prophets—A Response', in Brenner (ed.), *A Feminist Companion to the Latter Prophets*, pp. 275-307 (279).

29. Carroll, 'Desire under the Terebinths', p. 306.

of the poems than in the depiction of the gender dynamics at work in the Israelite production of the biblical texts. For example, Renita Weems shows that the metaphor succeeds as a literary device precisely because it conjures up a central element in the social environment of the audience to which it was directed. The Israelite listeners who heard the depictions of women as sexually promiscuous relied on their cultural foundations to make sense of the text. She writes:

> [T]hose metaphors that wind up finally as memorable and enduring in audiences' minds are the ones that tap into widely held, deeply felt values or attitudes within an audience. In other words, the audience must *care* about the social picture the metaphor is capturing.[30]

Accordingly, the original listeners understood the descriptions because they know them from their lives. Weems also explains that, by using the metaphors, the Israelite authors avoided conflict with their male audience. All of them shared the same assumptions which included the idea that a husband loses his honor when his wife is sexually independent. He must retaliate to keep his honor. Weems drives this point home when she states:

> The metaphor of the promiscuous wife expected its audience to share the values and attitudes of Hebrew society—the belief in a wife's exclusive sexual devotion to her husband, her failure to do so constituting shame on her part that brought dishonor upon her husband and warranted retaliation. The prophets expected their audiences to share these fundamental understandings. Otherwise, the metaphor would have made no sense to them.[31]

Another feminist exegete pursues a similar historically conceptualized argument. Gale A. Yee explains that in an honor/shame based androcentric society female sexual purity symbolizes a family's ability to protect its material resources and a large measure of a man's honor rests on the sexual behavior of women, whether she is his wife, daughter, sister, or mother. If women were sexually shameless in any way, it would reveal publicly that the husband, father, brother, or son had failed in the responsibility to pre-serve the family's honor. He had been unable to protect or control the woman or women in his household and, consequently, the man and his family would have forfeited honor in the community.[32]

In such an honor/shame society, Yee observes, a man has to punish a straying woman to re-establish his honor. She must also submit to him again because she lacks the resources to survive without her family's support.

---

30. Renita J. Weems, *Battered Love: Marriage, Sex, and Violence in the Hebrew Prophets* (Minneapolis: Fortress Press, 1995), p. 24.

31. Weems, *Battered Love*, p. 29.

32. Gale A. Yee, *Poor Banished Children of Eve: Woman as Evil in the Hebrew Bible* (Minneapolis: Fortress Press, 2003), p. 46.

Yee stresses that in the metaphors God functions as such a betrayed husband and Israel is the adulterous wife who needs to be punished and resubmit to her husband. Thus, the metaphoric speech makes cultural sense to the original and mostly male readers.

When feminist exegetes focus on the social world behind the prophetic text, they also explore the ancient construction of gender. This methodological approach is the cornerstone for Phyllis Bird who examines the metaphor of 'whoring' as part of ancient Israelite cultic activity. Bird parses the verb, *znh*, to distinguish it from common or cultic prostitution. She argues that the metaphor calls to mind an unfaithful wife who threatens the 'house of the father', which was the foundational social structure in ancient Israel. Bird demonstrates that the issue is not related to the practice of prostitution but to the image of an adulterous wife. This image speaks directly to powerful men because it identifies them as women and so challenges their authority as Israelite men in covenant with God. Bird explains this rhetorical move in a discussion on Hosea 2:

> By appealing to the common stereotypes and interests of a primarily male audience, Hosea turns up their accusation against them. It is easy for patriarchal society to see the guilt of a 'fallen women' [*sic*]; Hosea says, 'You (male Israel) are that woman!'[33]

Much like Robert Carroll, then, Bird contends that the Israelite authors assumed the ancient Israelite social structure in their rhetoric to communicate effectively with the men in their audiences and to criticize their behaviors. The social structure, however, is more an imaginative impress of the familiar for a specific object lesson than indicative of the social reality of women.

Normalizing Violence? A Plea for Compromise and Positive Women Metaphors

The feminist conversation, whether focused on the history of interpretation for contemporary readers or stressing the historical context in ancient Israel, does not provide easy answers in the effort to understand the sexually violent metaphors in the prophetic literature. It demonstrates the delicate struggle to balance modern standards about sexual violence with the customs of ancient communities. For instance, the contemporary debates on the exegesis of the prophetic metaphors do not usually consider that the construction of women as prostitutes may have generated opposition in its own time and place or been offensive to the original audience. Perhaps most

---

33. Phyllis Bird, '"To Play the Harlot": An Inquiry into an Old Testament Metaphor', in Day (ed.), *Gender and Difference*, pp. 75-94 (89).

significantly, attention to the historical at the expense of the contemporary underplays the continued power that these metaphors still have in shaping attitudes and behaviors toward women even today.

We also need to remember that positive feminine familial images, depicting cities and nations, appear in the prophetic literature. For instance, the descriptions of the restored Jerusalem in Isa. 54.1-10 and 62.4 present a bride prepared to celebrate her marriage. The same city gives birth and nurtures her infant in Isa. 66.7-11. Zion's speedy and painless delivery (Isa. 66.7) indicates the renewed life of the nation after the pain of destruction and loss. Indeed, the text equates the newly minted mother with God who comforts and cares for her children (Isa. 66.13). Susan Ackerman notes that 'maternal imagery for Jerusalem/Zion is further evoked in Isa. 51:17–52:2 and 54:1-10, especially in 51:18 and 20 and 54:1'.[34] However, as Katheryn Pfisterer Darr notes: '[I]n Israel's ancient Near Eastern world, the principle purpose of marriage was to produce children, especially sons'.[35] Thus, to her, these references are androcentric as they locate the only acceptable place for ancient Israelite women in the traditional roles of the dutiful wife and mother.

At stake is, then, how feminist scholars ought to assess these images. Do the images offer positive portrayals of women or are they inherently androcentric? In a discussion of 'daughter' language, Julia M. O'Brien observes that two options often emerge for feminist interpreters, neither of which is satisfying. She asks pointedly: 'Does the metaphor of Jerusalem as a daughter give women, however indirectly, a voice in the Bible, allowing their suffering to be heard? *Or* is the metaphor demeaning to women, supporting mentalities that lock women into the roles of dependent daughters?'[36] O'Brien acknowledges that both readings are valid. They work to reclaim a positive aspect in women's lives and experiences, but they also are open to a critique of the social structures that inform them. Thus both readings assume 'a fairly direct correlation between the fate of a female character and the status of women in society'.[37] Hence, readers ought to ask '*whose* perspective the metaphor reflects and *to whom* it grants power'.[38] No easy answers are indeed in sight for feminist interpreters of the major prophets.

34. Susan Ackerman, 'Woman Jerusalem/Zion in Isaiah', in Meyers (ed.), *Women in Scripture*, pp. 544-45 (545).

35. Katheryn Pfisterer Darr, *Isaiah's Vision and the Family of God* (Louisville, KY: Westminster/John Knox Press, 1994), p. 205.

36. O'Brien, *Challenging Prophetic Metaphor*, p. 144.

37. O'Brien, *Challenging Prophetic Metaphor*, p. 150.

38. O'Brien, *Challenging Prophetic Metaphor*, p. 150 (original italics).

The Queen of Heaven and Women's Worship and Prophetic Practices:
Feminist Interpretations on Female Images for God in Prophetic and
Ancient Near Eastern Literatures

'Whoring' in the prophetic texts is frequently linked to the worship of other gods and goddesses. References to the people venerating the 'Queen of Heaven' in Jer. 7.18; 44.15-19, 25 certainly appear to support the prophetic charge. Judith M. Hadley states that the 'discussion of the topic can be divided into two categories: those who concentrate on the identity and cult of the Queen of Heaven, and those who focus on a literary analysis of the biblical text'.[39] Most feminist interpretations focus on the former. Some feminist exegetes also want to know what can be understood from them about women's devotional practices although the texts mention religious activities of both men and women.

O'Connor expresses the most common understanding of the Queen of Heaven when she notes that the figure as presented in the text 'probably combines features of two or more fertility goddesses in the ancient Near East'.[40] Bauman adds that this lack of clarity is seen elsewhere.

> The cult of goddesses with the title 'queen of heaven' is nothing specific to Israel or Judah; it is found from Mesopotamia through Egypt (Isis) and into the western Mediterranean world during a period of more than two and a half millennia as a syncretistic phenomenon displaying, despite differences, the same characteristics as those that can be discerned from the book of Jeremiah'.[41]

With regard to identity, Hadley offers a comprehensive list of the possibilities. For example, she looks at the arguments for Shapsu, as advanced by Dahood; Anat, as held by Albright, Cogan, and others; Asherah, as mentioned by Freedman, Vawter, Koch, and Dijkstra; and Astarte or Ishtar (sometimes both combined) by Bresciani and Kamil, Driver, Holladay, and Ackerman.[42] In considering these options, we should note that Astarte receives the title 'Lady of Heaven', while Ishtar was known by the same title and also by 'Queen of Heaven' in the Akkadian literature.[43] Or we might

---

39. Judith M. Hadley, 'The Queen of Heaven—Who Is She?', in Athalya Brenner (ed.), *A Feminist Companion to the Bible: Prophets and Daniel* (FCB, 2nd Series, 8; London: Sheffield Academic Press, 2001), pp. 30-51 (30).

40. O'Connor, 'Jeremiah', p. 182.

41. Baumann, *Love and Violence*, pp. 111-12. She quotes Renate Jost, *Frauen, Männer und die Himmelskönigin. Exegetische Studien* (Gütersloh: Chr. Kaiser Verlag, 1995), p. 236.

42. Hadley, 'The Queen of Heaven', pp. 43-50.

43. Ackerman, 'And the Women Knead Dough', pp. 110, 114.

consider that the worship of Astarte and Ishtar involves the offering of cakes.[44] Similarly, women take leading roles in the worship of Ishtar and in the worship of her consort, Tammuz.[45]

The varied identifications depend on references to behaviors similar to those evidenced in the biblical text or to like terminology in extra-biblical references. Hadley reminds us that

> it is even possible that precisely which deity was responsible for what in those heady pre-exilic times was as confusing for the late post-exilic writers as it is for us today. Thus, all that was necessary for the writer to drive home the point was that there had been a time, generations ago, when the people worshipped the Queen of Heaven, who would represent, for the late author, *any* deity that was worshipped apart from Yahweh.[46]

In other words, the idea of the 'Queen of Heaven' becomes a catch-all for false worship rather than a specific charge against a particular cult.

When exploring the behaviors associated with such worship, feminist scholars seek connections to the devotional practices of women. But in Jer. 7.18 the text associates the activities of the Queen of Heaven with the whole family: children gather wood, fathers light the fire, women make cakes, and drinks are poured out. Interestingly, however, the generic word 'women' appears instead of the specific nouns for 'mothers' or 'daughters'. Hadley observes that 'this designation appears to remove the women from the family unit, perhaps in anticipation of ch. 44, where they will take more responsibility for worship of the Queen of Heaven'.[47] Also Angela Bauer holds that 'by not naming mothers and daughters in particular, [this activity] is not limited to the private sphere, but allows for the possibility of cultic positions for these women'.[48] Bauer further explains that the extreme negativity of a prophet, such as Jeremiah, to these practices demonstrates 'that worshipping the Queen of Heaven and other gods was at the time perceived as a major threat to Yhwh-only religion'.[49] Certainly, a text such

---

44.　Ackerman, 'And the Women Knead Dough', pp. 113, 115.

45.　Darr, for instance, notes that 'Tammuz was manifest in nature's fecundity: rising tree sap, the fruits of the date-palm, grains for making bread and beer, the quickening of the fetus in its mother's womb, and breast milk'. Historical interpreters indicate that commemoration of Tammuz's death include an accompanying mourning of women on a yearly basis. This ritual reflected concern over the sufficiency of the harvest and the impact of drought. Feminist scholars also mention Ezek. 8.14 with its depiction of women as mourners as a likely reference to an actual custom of women weeping for Tammuz; see Pfisterer Darr, 'Women Weeping for Tammuz', p. 335.

46.　Hadley, 'The Queen of Heaven', p. 51.

47.　Hadley, 'The Queen of Heaven', p. 32.

48.　Angela Bauer, *Gender in the Book of Jeremiah: A Feminist-Literary Reading* (New York: Peter Lang, 1999), pp. 77-78.

49.　Bauer, *Gender in the Book of Jeremiah*, pp. 78-79.

as Jeremiah 44 recognizes the prominence of non-Yahwistic worship activities, as Susan Ackerman indicates in her research on the Queen of Heaven:

> This women's cult did not prosper only in those spheres such as the home and the family where we might expect to find women's religion. To be sure, there is a strong domestic component to the cult, seen especially in Jer 7:18, where 'the children gather wood, the fathers kindle fire, and the women knead dough to make cakes for the Queen of Heaven'. But if Jer 44:17 and 21 are to be taken at all seriously, then the 'kings and princes' of Judah are also among those who worshiped the Queen. And, if the worship of the Queen of Heaven was part of the religion of the monarchy, the Queen's cult may also have been at home in what was essentially the monarch's private chapel, the temple. This is certainly suggested by Ezek 8:14.[50]

Ackerman's historical recounting of women's worship emphasizes that women's cultic practices enjoyed the support of the state and were practiced publicly. Similarly, Kathleen O'Connor states that 'from the perspective of women today the queen's worshipers in ch. 44 appear in a positive light. They are resourceful, independent women with their own subculture.'[51] Feminist historical investigations into women's worship practices thus view women as religiously and politically empowered in ancient Israel of the sixth century BCE.

Additional support for women participating in public ritual acts appears in the biblical material. Feminists often refer to Jer. 9.17-19, which depicts women as skilled mourners and of professional status. Carol Meyers stresses Jer. 17.20b, which mentions daughters as being instructed in dirge and female neighbors in lament songs. Meyers explains that this passage 'probably refer[s] to members of groups of women that gathered to develop and transmit Israelite mourning culture'.[52] Although not explicitly identified with Yahweh, Jeremiah describes the women mourners in a positive tone to indicate the important social function of their work.

Another biblical text, Ezek. 32.16, supports this historical reconstruction of women's significant roles as professional mourners. This verse recognizes 'women of the nations' for carrying out mourning duties. Ackerman calls attention to several passages in this regard. She mentions Isa. 5.1-7 and 32.9-14 as indications that women made music as part of their cultic responsibilities.[53] Further, she refers to Isa. 32.11-12 as a depiction of a ritual in which women wore sackcloth and beat their breasts. Ackerman ties this text

50. Susan Ackerman, '"And the Women Knead Dough": The Worship of the Queen of Heaven in Sixth Century Judah', in Day (ed.), *Gender and Difference*, p. 117.

51. Ackerman, 'And the Women Knead Dough', p. 182.

52. Carol Meyers, 'Mourning Women', in Meyers (ed.), *Women in Scripture*, pp. 327-28 (328).

53. Ackerman, 'Isaiah', p. 171.

to Isa. 3.16–4.1 which might mean something else besides its apparent reference to the abuse of daughter Zion. Sackcloth, bald heads, and sitting on the ground might refer to a highly stylized ritual, and so Ackerman exclaims: '[W]hat underlies the highly denigrating polemic of 3:16–4:1, then, is positive imagery describing women as mourners'.[54]

Biblical exegetes extend the conversation about women's professional work in ancient Israel by exploring evidence that women held prophetic roles. Leonard Swindler makes a succinct observation: 'The Hebrew word for prophet is *nabi,* and its feminine form is *nebiah.* It is used to refer to four specific women in the Hebrew Bible.'[55] Matthijs J. de Jong maintains that explicit references to Miriam (Exod. 15.20), Deborah (Judg. 4.4), Huldah (2 Kgs 22.14; 2 Chron. 34.22), and Noadiah (Neh. 6.14) as prophets stand alongside general references in Isaiah 8, Ezekiel 13, and Joel 2 to indicate familiarity with women in such an office. Jong thus asserts: '[T]he biblical picture suggesting that prophetesses only played a marginal role may be misleading'.[56]

Although it is clear that these few references do not compare to 'the situation in Old Babylonian Mari and seventh century Assyria, where we find references to many prophetesses',[57] they nonetheless demonstrate that some Israelite women took on such authority. Claudia Camp even suggests that 'prophecy was one religious vocation open to women on an equal basis with men'.[58] For other commentators, the historical depictions hold far less clarity. Susan Ackerman, for example, maintains that the context of Isa. 8.3 undercuts the use of the term 'prophet' for women. She explains: '[T]his suggests that her title "prophetess" is merely an honorific bestowed upon her because of her husband's role as prophet, in much the same way that the wife of a king is assigned the title queen'.[59] Esther Fuchs's analysis on female biblical prophets makes the most comprehensive observation. She maintains that 'the names of the women we encounter in the text suggest that they have played meaningful roles, but the exposition is so sparse, there are so many informational gaps and lacunae, that it is hardly clear what the prophetess's role consisted of'.[60] For Fuchs, biblical texts inscribe and erase

54. Ackerman, 'Isaiah', p. 171.

55. Leonard Swindler, *Biblical Affirmations of Women* (Philadelphia: Westminster Press, 1979), p. 85.

56. Matthijs J. de Jong, *Isaiah among the Ancient Near Eastern Prophets: A Comparative Study of the Earliest Stages of the Isaiah Tradition and the Neo-Assyrian Prophecies* (Leiden: E.J. Brill, 2007), p. 334.

57. De Jong, *Isaiah among the Ancient Near Eastern Prophets*, p. 335.

58. Camp, '1 and 2 Kings', *Women's Biblical Commentary*, p. 109.

59. Camp, '1 and 2 Kings', p. 317.

60. Esther Fuchs, 'Prophecy and the Construction of Women: Inscription and Erasure', in Brenner (ed.), *Prophets and Daniel*, pp. 54-69 (56).

women as prophets because later editors removed and modified the histori-cal reality according to their theological presuppositions. Fuchs explains: 'By representing female prophetic discourse as minor, false, insignificant, abstruse, unreliable and peripheral the biblical redactor validates the elimi-nation of women from the latter prophets'.[61]

Determining the public or official roles of Israelite women in the worship of any deity thus rests on scant biblical evidence. Some feminist scholars, such as Ackerman, suggest that the combined weight of these texts demon-strates that 'the heavily male orientation of biblical religion forced many women to seek spiritual fulfillment elsewhere'.[62] Likewise, O'Connor finds that 'they are resourceful, independent women with their own subculture'.[63] Others, such as Carol Meyers, contend that much feminist study 'has not successfully broken away from western male models of what constitutes religion, it often views women's experiences and practices, whether visible in the Hebrew Bible, as marginal—as not "real religion"'.[64] Meyers also asserts that 'it is becoming increasingly clear that women everywhere have critical roles to play in religious life, even if those roles are ignored or marginalized in the public record.[65] Yet without additional archaeological or textual evidence, the number of women as prophets and their influence in ancient Israel remain historically uncertain.

Motherhood and Other Female Images for God: The Feminist Search for Empowering Prophetic Metaphors

Feminist theologian Sallie McFague observes that 'the problem with introducing a feminine dimension to God is that it invariably ends with identifying as female those qualities that society has called feminine. Thus, the feminine side of God is taken to comprise the tender, nurturing, passive healing of aspects of divine activity.'[66] The prophetic literature contains a catalog of female images for God, especially in Second and Third Isaiah,

61. Fuchs, 'Prophecy and the Construction of Women', p. 68.

62. Ackerman, 'Isaiah', p. 172.

63. O'Connor, 'Jeremiah', p. 182.

64. Carol Meyers, 'From Household to House of Yahweh: Women's Religious Cul-ture in Ancient Israel', in A. Lemaire (ed.), *Congress Volume: Basel 2001* (International Organization for the Study of the Old Testament: Leiden: E.J. Brill, 2002), pp. 277-303 (278).

65. Carol Meyers, 'The Hannah Narrative in Feminist Perspective', in Joseph E. Coleson and Victor H. Matthews (eds.), *Go to the Land I Will Show You: Studies in Honor of Dwight W. Young* (Winona Lake, IN: Eisenbrauns, 1996), pp. 117-26 (124).

66. Sallie McFague, 'God as Mother', in Judith Plaskow and Carol P. Christ (eds.), *Weaving the Visions: New Patterns of Feminist Spirituality* (New York: HarperCollins Publishers, 1989), pp. 139-50 (140).

proving McFague's point. The passages in Isa. 42.14; 45.9-10; 49.14; 66.12-13 present God as mothering. They also include two instances in which terminology for God is associated with the womb (Isa. 27.11b and 46.3-4). It should not surprise that feminist scholars are interested in understanding what historical-social circumstances contributed to these images. They have also debated why the androcentric Bible characterizes the divinity with female metaphors. Some feminist exegetes suggest that private family life served as a balm to the trauma of warfare and exile that gave rise to these texts. Sarah J. Dille maintains:

> [T]he unusual prevalence of explicitly feminine language may be especially evocative of the home, since home is stereotypically and archetypically the realm of the mother. The captives are homesick. The longing they experience is for home—for mother Zion, and for the God who cared for them from the womb. The language of family is also the language of survival and the language of life.[67]

Other feminists propose different options. For instance, Ackerman hypothesizes that '[t]he positive portrayals in the exilic Isaianic materials of that which had been previously denigrated (Zion) or ignored (motherhood, childbirth, and the like) may be responses to a temporary increase in female status. When social stability returned, misogyny unfortunately reemerged.'[68] These positions stand side by side.

Another image of God appears briefly in Jer. 31.20-22, emphasizing the compassionate nature of the parent. The depiction in Jer. 31.22 is particularly striking in its evocation of the eschatological age when, as a symbol of God's new creative activity, a woman 'encompasses a man'. Angela Bauer notes that 'the verse's meaning is considered problematic and has elicited many explanations'.[69] O'Connor, for example, maintains that 'seed imagery suggests that the woman sexually encompasses man to become pregnant, as God builds and plants the nation anew. Rather than disappearing, the destroyed people receive the promise of fertility, offspring, and new generations, as well as livestock to feed them.'[70] Again, the figure of woman receives praise for her role as a mother.

Other images of fertility possibly include Ezek. 47.1-12, and Kathryn Pfisterer Darr links the waters of life flowing from the Temple with female reproductive power. Even though she acknowledges that this connection is

67. Sarah J. Dille, *Mixing Metaphors: God as Mother and Father in Deutero-Isaiah* (London: T. & T. Clark, 2003), p. 177.

68. Ackerman, 'Isaiah', pp. 176-77.

69. Bauer, 'Woman Encompassing a Man', in Meyers (ed.), *Women in Scripture*, pp. 330-31 (330).

70. Kathleen M. O'Connor, *Jeremiah: Pain and Promise* (Minneapolis: Fortress Press, 2011), pp. 110-11.

not explicitly made, for Darr, groundwater elicits ideas about reproductive possibility. She also holds that 'it is not irrelevant...that Israel's ancestors frequently encounter their future brides at a well, since well water symbolizes the virgin's as yet untapped fecundity'.[71] The equation of the waters of God with fertility becomes clear in v. 12, but Darr is alone in tying this passage to female imagery.

The catalog of female images for God indicates that some feminist exegetes are eager to identify representations of the divine as both fertile and nurturing. Many also draw theological conclusions from these depictions. Phyllis Trible, for example, claims that 'by repeatedly using male language for God, Israel risked theological misunderstanding. God is not male, and the male is not God. That a patriarchal culture employed such images for God is hardly surprising. That it also countenanced female images *is* surprising.'[72] In her view, the biblical text offers both ancient and contemporary audiences a positive corrective regarding the divine and makes a valuable contribution to historical-literary understanding of ancient Israel's and our contemporary notions of God as mother and caregiver.

Other commentators find the female imagery in the prophetic literature problematic. Kathleen S. Nash points out the problem when she asserts: 'If the male Yahweh can provide a mother's love for Israel, there is no need for a divine mother. In the same way, women themselves are seldom described as acting as mothers, other than giving birth. Absent from the divine world, mothers are quickly dispatched to the fringes of their narratives.'[73] In other words, the male God takes on all gender roles, crowding out the need for the goddess. Further, the depictions demonstrate a limited example of women's possibilities in a male dominated social structure by relying on images that trap women in traditional roles.

About Feminist Priorities Regarding Prophetic Metaphoric Speech:
Concluding Comments

Feminist exegesis on the major prophets has made invaluable contributions to the historical and literary understanding of ancient Israelite gender roles and societal life. As Athalya Brenner observes: 'Analyses of female images have been a priority of feminist biblical criticism and, to a large extent, they

71. Pfisterer Darr, 'Ezekiel', p. 199.

72. Phyllis Trible, 'Overture for a Feminist Biblical Theology', in Ben C. Ollenburger (ed.), *Old Testament Theology: Flowering and Future* (Winona Lake, IN, Eisenbrauns, 2004), pp. 399-408 (404).

73. Kathleen S. Nash, 'Mother', in David Noel Freedman, Allan C. Meyers and Astrid Beck (eds.), *Eerdmans Dictionary of the Bible* (Grand Rapids, MI: Eerdmans, 2000), p. 973.

still are'.[74] Feminist exegetes have devoted much attention to the excavation and explanation of these metaphors. Often they locate them in Israelite history and only then relate the rhetorical effectiveness of these metaphors to contemporary practices. Feminist interpretations thus indicate that prophetic literature contributes to religious and social attitudes still shaping Western societies. They suggest that we cannot leave unexamined prophetic images about women because we would then ignore their ongoing potency in contemporary gender dynamics.

The ongoing significance of prophetic texts is widely recognized in biblical studies. Gale Yee notes that these texts continue 'to be a significant *fons et origo* of religious and social attitudes about gender, race/ethnicity, class, and colonialism'.[75] Thus, as Carol Meyers and other feminist interpreters suggest, these texts challenge readers to think critically about our reconstructions of the ancient world. When we limit the inquiry to literary approaches, we miss what historical analysis has brought to light. Similarly, when we limit the questions to Israelite historiography alone, we miss the vibrant crossing of cultures that exist then and now. In the same way, when we limit the historiographical methodologies only to the androcentric ones, we limit the expressions of gender in ancient Israel and the biblical text. And, as Yee reminds us, modern readers must approach prophetic texts not only with feminist concerns, but also with other sociopolitical categories, such as ethnicity, class, and geo-political location, foregrounded. In other words, feminist readers should not try to escape the burdens of how contemporary culture and society influences feminist readings of the prophetic literature. Feminist scholars, then, have brought renewed urgency to examining the prophetic metaphors as part of the past and the present.

---

74. Athalya Brenner, 'Introduction', in Brenner (ed.), *A Feminist Companion to the Latter Prophets*, pp. 21-37 (21).

75. Yee, *Poor Banished Children of Eve*, p. 1.

8

ENGAGING IMAGES IN THE PROPHETS: FEMINIST INTERPRETATIONS OF THE BOOK OF THE TWELVE

Susan E. Haddox

The Book of the Twelve comprises several prophets from the eighth to the fifth century BCE, whose audiences, concerns, and lengths vary significantly. Some of these texts mention women or use female images extensively, whereas others hardly at all. The representation of women in the Book of the Twelve is predominantly negative. Women are typically either portrayed with a bad character or as objects of suffering and weakness, symbolizing the opposite of masculinity. Unlike in the narrative texts, but similar to the major prophets, there are few examples of positive femininity. Much feminist criticism has therefore focused on analyzing the imagery and considered its implications for ancient and contemporary audiences. This essay, examining significant feminist criticism of the prophetic books, illustrates various types of interpretations with specific examples from the texts. I have organized the contributions of individual scholars around several major types of imagery in the prophets.

Understanding Metaphor

Many of the prophets portray women metaphorically, and so some consideration of the nature of metaphor is warranted. A metaphor consists of two components that create a new way of understanding a concept, thereby structuring the way people think about that concept. For example, Hosea portrays the intimate relationship between Yhwh and Israel as a marriage. This trope conveys things about the closeness and commitment in the relationship that cannot be relayed in other ways, but a metaphor by its very definition brings together two elements that are different. Thus the 'is not' of the metaphor must be kept in mind in order not to distort the image by equating it with historical reality.[1] Caution is particularly necessary with

---

1. Richtsje Abua, *Bonds of Love: Methodic Studies of Prophetic Texts with Marriage Imagery* (SSN; Assen: Van Gorcum, 1999), p. 12.

metaphors for the divine, because of potential harmful effects of understanding the metaphors as prescriptive for relationships between the divine
and human or between real men and women. Renita Weems argues that the
men need to identify with the husband in the metaphor. They have to agree
that an adulterous wife is shameful and deserves punishment because only
then do they accept that their own punishment is justified.[2] Thus the male
audience must accept and propagate the power structures presented in the
metaphor. A metaphor can therefore have harmful effects even if it does not
represent reality. Much feminist criticism has been focused on such uses of
metaphor.

City-as-Woman Metaphor

The personification of cities, especially capital cities, is the most common
female imagery in the Twelve, found in Hosea 1–3, Micah 1, Nahum 3, and
Zephaniah 2. A number of scholars treat the image of the city-as-woman.[3]
The origin of this association is debated, but it is common in ancient Near
Eastern texts. Some hypothesize that the city represents a goddess married to
a patron god, but others dispute the evidence.[4] Cities are grammatically
gendered as female, which may spur the personification as a woman. The
image of the city-as-woman occurs most often in the context of warfare,
involving destruction and physical violence.[5] In Micah 1, for example, the

2. Renita J. Weems, *Battered Love: Marriage, Sex, and Violence in the Hebrew
Prophets* (OBT; Minneapolis: Fortress Press, 1995), pp. 41-42, 80.

3. See, e.g., Peggy L. Day, 'The Personification of Cities as Female in the Hebrew
Bible: The Thesis of Aloysius Fitzgerald, F.S.C.', in Fernando F. Segovia and Mary Ann
Tolbert (eds.), *Reading from this Place*. II. *Social Location and Biblical Interpretation in
Global Perspective* (Minneapolis: Augsburg Fortress, 1995), pp. 283-302; Brad E. Kelle,
'Wartime Rhetoric: Prophetic Metaphorization of Cities as Female', in Brad E. Kelle and
Frank Ritchel Ames (eds.), *Writing and Reading War: Rhetoric, Gender, and Ethics in
Biblical and Modern Contexts* (SBLSymS, 42; Atlanta, GA: Society of Biblical
Literature, 2008), pp. 95-112; Julie Galambush, *Jerusalem in the Book of Ezekiel: The
City as Yahweh's Wife* (SBLDS, 130; Atlanta, GA: Scholars Press, 1992).

4. Sophia Bietenhard, 'Micah: Call for Justice—Hope for All', in Luise Schottrof and
Marie-Theres Wacker (eds.), *Feminist Biblical Interpretation* (Grand Rapids, MI:
Eerdmans, 2012), pp. 421-32. For a summary of the scholarship, see Brad E. Kelle,
Hosea 2: Metaphor and Rhetoric in Historical Perspective (Atlanta, GA: Society of
Biblical Literature, 2005).

5. Kelle, 'Wartime Rhetoric'. Others who concur that sexual violence and rape are
metaphors for the conquering of a city, as well as real results of warfare, are Pamela
Gordon and Harold C. Washington, 'Rape as a Military Metaphor in the Hebrew Bible',
pp. 308-25, and F. Rachel Magdalene, 'Ancient Near Eastern Treaty-Curses and the
Ultimate Texts of Terror: A Study of the Language of Divine Sexual Abuse in the
Prophetic Corpus', pp. 326-52, both in Athalya Brenner (ed.), *A Feminist Companion to
the Latter Prophets* (FCB, 8; Sheffield: Sheffield Academic Press, 1995).

cities of Samaria and Jerusalem are subject to violent destruction. They are urged to mourn their exiled inhabitants as they would mourn their children. In Zeph. 2.13-15, the desolate, destroyed city of Nineveh mourns, brought down in her pride, and the passersby scoff at her. Destruction is often sexually tinged, as evidenced in Nahum. The fall of the once proud city of Nineveh is described with language symbolic of rape. Rachel Magdalene observes that the river portals in Nah. 2.6-8 represent the female genitalia, portrayed as wet, which are thrown wide before the city is taken into exile.[6] Nineveh is explicitly stripped, exposed to her enemies, and humiliated in Nahum 3. Julie Galambush observes that the imagery draws on a cultural connection between femaleness and helplessness. She writes:

> Nahum exploits the attributes of infidelity, helplessness, and shame, common-places culturally associated with 'woman', to reorganize the reader's perception of Nineveh from that of threatening power to that of a deceitful but ultimately helpless female victim who has earned her punishment at the hands of the male god.[7]

Galambush further observes that this imagery plays into the biblical por-trayal of the 'stereotypically seductive but deceitful foreign woman (cf. Prov. 2.16-19; 7)'. Her punishment represents the humiliation of the 'other' in both political and symbolic terms.[8]

Occasionally, the feminine is used to portray a country, rather than a city. One instance is Nah. 1.15 where Judah, oppressed by Nineveh, is atypically referred to by a female pronoun. Similarly in Obadiah, Edom, which is mostly represented by the masculine Esau, takes a feminine object pronoun in the first verse when the nations are urged to rise up against her. Jione Havea suggests the gender-bending may be intended to emphasize the countries' vulnerability to defeat.[9]

City-as-Daughter

A particular category of the city-as-woman image is that of city-as-daughter, which is typically applied to Jerusalem or Zion, though Babylon is so refer-enced in Zech. 2.7. Elaine Follis has compared the image of Daughter Zion with Greek traditions. She observes that woman and the city were symbolic

---

6. Magdalene, 'Treaty Curses', p. 346. Some propose the cult statue of Ištar, representing the city, is taken into exile; see, e.g., Judith E. Sanderson, 'Nahum', in Carol A. Newsom and Sharon H. Ringe (eds.), *Women's Bible Commentary* (Louisville, KY: Westminster/John Knox Press, exp. edn, 1998), pp. 232-36 (232).

7. Galambush, *Jerusalem*, p. 42.

8. Galambush, *Jerusalem*, p. 40.

9. Jione Havea, 'Releasing the Story of Esau from the Words of Obadiah', in Alegandro P. Botta and Pable R. Andiñach (eds.), *The Bible and the Hermeneutics of Liberation* (SBLSS, 59; Atlanta, GA: Society of Biblical Literature, 2009), p. 93.

of settled, secure contexts. Thus the situation of crisis in which the image frequently occurs in the prophets emphasizes upheaval and loss of security.[10] Julia O'Brien observes that while city-as-daughter is a more neutral image than city-as-woman subject to rape, it still conveys vulnerability. Male imagery tends to be used when a city is in a stronger position. God, portrayed as a king or warrior, most often rescues the city-as-defenseless-daughter (Zeph. 2.10-13; 3.14-20; 9.9-10).[11] In a state of current vulnerability in Micah 4, Daughter Zion is promised the return of a king and restoration. In the meantime, she is threatened with the raping gaze of the nations and subject to exile. Later, she is given horns and hooves to thresh the nations, which transforms the daughter image into an animal. The image of daughter has both positive and negative implications. On the one hand, it reflects a relationship of care and protection. On the other hand, it portrays a relationship of dependence and vulnerability, and so it is often problematic for feminist interpreters.

City-as-Wife

The image of city-as-wife, especially as found in Hosea, has received by far the most attention from feminist critics. The book describes a 'sign-act' in the marriage between Hosea and Gomer. A sign-act is a technical term for a prophet's literal action that has symbolic significance. The marriage serves as a metaphor of the relationship between God and Samaria/Israel. This image is further developed in the books of Jeremiah and Ezekiel, where the identity of the woman/wife is clear: she is Jerusalem and Samaria. Although the sign-act of the prophet and Gomer's marriage slightly complicates identification issues in Hosea, an understanding of the wife as representative of Samaria fits best into the context of the book.[12] Feminists use a number of hermeneutical frameworks to study the metaphor. I have divided them here into theological, religious, political, and economic approaches and then present the work of feminist scholars who follow each approach.

Theological Interpretations. The theological approach considers the effect of the metaphor on modern readers. In pre-feminist interpretations, Hosea is often identified as the 'prophet of love'. God's love for Israel is reflected in the great love of the male prophet for his wife. Even though his wife is unfaithful to him, he does whatever he can to make her see the error of her

10. Elaine R. Follis, 'The Holy City and Daughter', in Elaine R. Follis (ed.), *Directions in Biblical Hebrew Poetry* (JSOTSup, 40; Sheffield: Sheffield Academic Press, 1987), pp. 173-84 (177).

11. Julia O'Brien, *Challenging Prophetic Metaphor: Theology and Ideology in the Prophets* (Louisville, KY: Westminster/John Knox Press, 2008).

12. For a thorough discussion, see Kelle, *Hosea 2*, pp. 82-94.

ways and return to him. Interpreters emphasize that his desire for reconciliation outweighs feelings of vengeance, just as God's love persists for a continuously rebellious Israel.

The emergence of feminist criticism revealed many troubling aspects with this rendering of the metaphor. Rather than seeing a loving husband, a number of feminist interpreters identify a pattern of violence and reconciliation more suggestive of an abusive relationship. They are particularly concerned with the influence of such a portrayal of the divine–human relationship on human relationships. Rut Törnqvist explains:

> What makes prophetical texts so dangerous for women is that they have been interpreted as 'proof texts' and used to define and describe females and wives as generally morally and sexually corrupt, so females/women are consequently to be punished by males, i.e. husbands and other male authorities, and in the outermost instance by the husband *par preference*, Yahweh himself.[13]

Concomitant with the dynamics of an abusive relationship, the woman is said to deserve the punishment. The text portrays Gomer as an unfaithful and immoral partner, which reinforces the cultural stereotype of the woman as Other. Thus female sexuality is depicted as dangerous, derivative, and 'other', and associated with pollution, sin, and death. Alice Keefe maintains: 'In contrast, male sexuality is linked with God by the covenant in circumcision and protected in sacral law as inviolate (Deut. 25:11-12)'.[14]

Other feminist readers emphasize the limiting capacity of this metaphor on women's lives. Yvonne Sherwood discusses how the 'dangerous' nature of Gomer as an independent agent challenges the patriarchal hierarchy, which places women in subservient positions. Gomer is an uncontrolled woman who must be boxed in, her ways 'hedged up'. Her very presence in the text is thus a threat, although the text works hard to contain and to punish her.

---

13.   Rut Törnkvist, *The Use and Abuse of Female Sexual Imagery in the Book of Hosea: A Feminist Critical Approach to Hosea 1–3* (Uppsala Women's Studies A: Women in Religion, 7; Stockholm: Gotab, 1998), pp. 15-16. Fokkelien van Dijk-Hemmes also notes how use of this metaphor acts as propaganda 'extolling the ideal patriarchal marriage'; see her 'The Metaphorization of Woman in Prophetic Speech: An Analysis of Ezekiel 23', in Brenner (ed.), *A Feminist Companion to the Latter Prophets*, pp. 244-55 (246).

14.   Alice A. Keefe, *Woman's Body and the Social Body in Hosea* (JSOTSup, 338; GCT, 10; Sheffield: Sheffield Academic Press, 2001), p. 143. Athalya Brenner expresses a similar view, stating that in the marriage metaphor the marriage contract is always broken by an adulterous wife, never the husband. This placement of blame on the wife reinforces a negative view of female sexuality vs. a neutral or positive view of male sexuality; see Athalya Brenner, 'Introduction', in Brenner (ed.), *A Feminist Companion to the Latter Prophets*, pp. 21-37 (26).

In contrast to the conventional tableau of grace, Hosea 1–3 can also be read as a tableau of patriarchy, the establishment of a system by the systematic exclusion, entrapment and repression of the female will. The threat of the 'woman of harlotry' is that of the countervoice, the opposite which, if listened to, threatens to relativize and subvert the absolute and univocal main/male perspective.[15]

Through a review of representative interpretations, Sherwood shows that androcentric portrayals of Gomer expand upon the text's suppression and erase, debase, or rehabilitate her in ways that deny her a resistant voice.

The application of methods from feminist analysis of modern pornography illuminates further the control the text places on Gomer. Athalya Brenner coins the term 'pornoprophetics' to describe the violent imagistic rhetoric in Hosea and other prophetic texts, and she considers how it depicts the women as being complicit in their own punishment.[16] Similarly, Drorah Setel categorizes these images as pornography, which she views as 'both a description of and a tool for maintaining male domination of female sexuality'.[17] Hosea 2 in particular accents the wife's helplessness in the face of the husband's anger. All of her resources, including fertility and reproduction, are shown to be under the control of Yhwh, the husband. As a result of her promiscuity, the land embodied by the wife becomes barren. As Setel observes, the passage moves the imagery of sexual unfaithfulness from the economic into the ethical realm.[18]

The mixture of violence and love in the marriage relationship makes the issue of reconciliation particularly problematic. Gerlinde Baumann asserts that the violence shows the desire on the part of the husband/Yhwh to preserve the relationship at all costs, through exercising power over the wife and making the connection to the destruction of the land.[19] Similarly, Weems

---

15. Yvonne Sherwood, 'Boxing Gomer: Controlling the Deviant Woman in Hosea 1–3', in Brenner (ed.), *A Feminist Companion to the Latter Prophets*, pp. 101-25 (120).

16. Athalya Brenner, 'On Prophetic Propaganda and the Politics of "Love": The Case of Jeremiah', in Brenner (ed.), *A Feminist Companion to the Latter Prophets*, pp. 256-74.

17. T. Drorah Setel, 'Prophets and Pornography: Female Sexual Imagery in Hosea', in Letty M. Russell (ed.), *Feminist Interpretation of the Bible* (Philadelphia: Westminster Press, 1985), pp. 86-95 (87).

18. Setel, 'Prophets', pp. 86-95.

19. Gerlinde Baumann, *Love and Violence: Marriage as Metaphor for the Relationship between YHWH and Israel in the Prophetic Books* (trans. Linda M. Maloney; Collegeville, MN: Liturgical Press, 2003), p. 97. See also Renita J. Weems, 'Gomer: Victim of Violence or Victim of Metaphor?', *Semeia* 47 (1989), pp. 87-104 (97). Weems observes (*Battered Love*, p. 29) that 'the image of the promiscuous wife played upon a range of ideas that tapped into some of the deepest, most subliminal social codes within a culture'.

notes that the sexual violence shows the extent to which Hosea goes to maintain the marriage, manifesting the assumption that reconciliation can only happen after punishment.[20] The punishment of stripping the wife fits the crime of wearing the 'vulgar apparel' of adultery and promiscuity upon the woman's face and breasts, as mentioned in Hos. 2.4.[21] This type of 'poetic justice' is also present in the punishment of the harlot Nineveh for crimes of adultery in Nahum 3, though as Mayer Gruber observes, it ultimately feeds a cycle of violence.[22]

These studies demonstrate that writers and interpreters of the prophetic text, consciously or unconsciously, have used a concept of the divine–human relationship based on the subordination of women. Because the violent depictions in these texts are preserved without much question as part of the biblical canon, the metaphors have sometimes been used to justify violence against women. Thus feminist interpretations are important for both theology and religious practice.[23] Susan Thistlethwaite observes that the seeming justification of the abusive relationship in the text has serious repercussions for addressing the problems of domestic violence. It is an issue that the church has often ignored or even enabled.[24] She observes: 'But the metaphor of patriarchal marriage for divine-human relationship is not one of mutuality; it is an image of dominance and subordination in that cultural context. Likewise, tying marriage to the divine–human relationship clearly divinizes male superiority in that relationship'.[25] Naomi Graetz discusses the problematic inclusion of these verses in the Haftora, which tends to propagate their patriarchalism into the modern day, even though the men, reciting these verses when they put on their tefillin, place themselves in the woman's role with respect to God.[26] While contemporary marriage practices differ from those portrayed in the text, the structures that the marriage metaphor inscribes still have powerful effect today.[27] Because of

---

20. Weems, 'Gomer', p. 97.

21. Weems, 'Gomer', p. 98.

22. Mayer I. Gruber, 'Nineveh the Adulteress', in Athalya Brenner (ed.), *Prophets and Daniel* (FCB, 2nd Series; Sheffield: Continuum/Sheffield Academic Press, 2001), pp. 220-25.

23. Athalya Brenner, 'Pornoprophetics Revisited', *JSOT* 70 (1996), pp. 63-86.

24. See also Susan Brooks Thistlethwaite, 'Every Two Minutes: Battered Women and Feminist Interpretation', in Russell (ed.), *Feminist Interpretation of the Bible*, pp. 96-107.

25. Thistlethwaite, 'Every Two Minutes', p. 107.

26. Naomi Graetz, 'God Is to Israel as Husband Is to Wife: The Metaphoric Battering of Hosea's Wife', in Brenner (ed.), *A Feminist Companion to the Latter Prophets*, pp. 126-45.

27. See, e.g., Graetz, 'Metaphoric Battering', p. 135.

the problematic theological elements of the marriage metaphor, Weems mentions the need to use various metaphors in the effort to describe the nature of the divine–human relationship. Hosea itself provides numerous other examples from different image fields, which, as Baumann notes, serve to relativize the importance of the marriage metaphor.[28]

Religious Interpretations. In addition to challenging an easy acceptance of the gender roles and violence depicted in the marriage metaphor, several feminist scholars question the common assumption in eighteenth- and nineteenth-century androcentric scholarship that the marriage metaphor reveals information about the actual religious situation during the eighth century BCE. Since the language of 'harlotry' (*znh*) is used in the polemic against idols, high places, and *baalim*, scholars have often assumed they referred to actual religious practices. Scholars developed complex scenarios about the supposed sexual fertility rites associated with the temples of Baal and Asherah. They imagined these rites as degenerate, drunken orgies, led by holy women (*qĕdēšôt*) who were assumed to be cult prostitutes, whose service was intended to ensure the continued fertility of the land and the people. Often they interpreted Gomer's harlotry in light of these invented Canaanite sex cults.

Most feminist historians challenge this scenario. For instance, Alice Keefe questions the idea that sex cults associated with Baal ever existed. She examines the various propositions about sacred marriage, sacred prostitution, fertility cults, and the role of female religious figures, as commonly asserted in twentieth-century androcentric scholarship on Hosea. In each case, she points out the paucity of evidence from ancient texts and iconography.[29] Thus, despite the references to *baalim* in Hosea, there is little evidence that Baal was worshipped to any significant extent in eighth-century Israel.[30] In addition, Baal was a god of vegetative fertility and not connected with sexual excess, unlike El.[31] His associations with fertility spring largely from his ability to defeat chaos.[32] Thus, for Keefe, the widespread and

---

28. Baumann, *Love and Violence*, pp. 103-4; see also Weems, 'Gomer', pp. 99-101.

29. Keefe, *Woman's Body*. Chapters 2–3 of her book give a detailed analysis of the popularity and problems of the fertility cult hypothesis.

30. See Keefe for a discussion of this issue in *Woman's Body*, p. 119. Note that Amos make no mention of widespread apostasy, as one might expect if Baalism was practiced extensively in Israel.

31. Susan J. Sanders, 'Baal au foundre: The Iconography of Baal at Ugarit', in Wilfred G.E. Watson (ed.), *He Unfurrowed his Brow and Laughed* (AOAT, 299; Münster: Ugarit-Verlag, 2007), pp. 249-66 (263).

32. Keefe, *Woman's Body*, p. 52.

unshakeable belief in the notion of fertility cults underlying the marriage metaphor in Hosea indicates the ideological bias of male interpreters. Particularly scholars writing within the Christian tradition regard female sexuality as the 'other'. Keefe explains:

> In this way, Hosea's female metaphor appears self-evidently as a sign for that which is 'other' and which must be excluded from Israelite religion—a sacral orientation to the powers of sexuality and fertility... So self-evident has this reading become that many feminist scholars, in their eagerness to recover a lost history of women's religions, have failed to discern the androcentric determinants behind the fertility cult thesis.[33]

Another feminist exegete, Christine Bucher, examines the use of *znh* in Hosea and investigates the possibilities of the existence of a sex cult. Although a Sumerian (not Canaanite) text describes a sacred marriage between the king and the goddess to enhance the fertility of the land, Bucher notes that only the king participated in such a ritual marriage. Thus, the general population did not practice such a ritual and large numbers of cult prostitutes or male worshippers were unnecessary.[34] It is not even clear whether the text refers to an actual ritual. Bucher finds only one mythological text describing intercourse between a god and goddess that contains a rubric for an accompanying ritual, and the ritual itself does not involve intercourse.[35] Nor is there evidence of ritual defloration occurring at the temples, in which young brides had sexual intercourse at a temple of Baal to promote fertility.[36] Much of the supposed evidence for these rites comes from later polemical Greek texts, which did not even refer to Canaanites.[37]

Perhaps the most comprehensive study on the use of *znh* in biblical texts comes from Phyllis Bird. She shows that Hosea links the images of promiscuity with illicit cult activity for rhetorical effect: improper cult worship by males is equivalent to illicit sex by females. The connection was meant to catch the listeners' attention but it does not prove that the worship indeed involved sexual activity.[38] Feminist scholarship has thus shown that despite

33. Keefe, *Woman's Body*, p. 65.

34. See Christina Bucher, 'The Origin and Meaning of *ZNH* Terminology in Hosea' (unpublished PhD dissertation; Claremont Graduate School, 1988), pp. 41-42.

35. See Bucher, 'Meaning of *ZNH*', pp. 64-66. She observes that these texts support the idea of ritual intercourse only if one assumes myth is derived from ritual.

36. Dirk Kinet, *Ba'al and Jahwe: Ein Beitrag zur Theologie des Hoseabuches* (Europäische Hochschulschriften, 23/87; Frankfurt: Peter Lang, 1977), pp. 79-80. See also Tikva Frymer-Kensky, *In the Wake of the Goddesses: Women, Culture, and the Biblical Transformation of Pagan Myth* (New York: The Free Press, 1992), pp. 199-202.

37. Keefe, *Woman's Body*, pp. 55-56.

38. Phyllis A. Bird, '"To Play the Harlot": An Inquiry into an Old Testament Metaphor', in Peggy L. Day (ed.), *Gender and Difference in Ancient Israel* (Minneapolis: Fortress Press, 1989), pp. 75-94 (86).

the immense scholarly efforts that went into finding a historical basis for the female sexual imagery in Hosea, the results were the projections of androcentric scholarship based on little supporting evidence.

While not necessarily accepting a historical basis for the marriage metaphor, several feminist scholars still attribute a primarily religious meaning to the text. Their basic premise is that the 'lovers' in Hosea 2 are other gods, or at least that they represent a syncretism between Baal and Yhwh.[39] Israel as the wife pursues other gods, and so violates the covenant marriage with Yhwh. The punishments that Yhwh inflicts on the wife in Hosea 2 reflect the curses associated with breaking this covenant (see Deut 28).

One example of such a religious interpretation comes from Mary Joan Winn Leith, who focuses on the primary category of curses that concern the sterility of the land and, in effect, reverse the process of creation, taking away the land animals, the birds of the air, and the fish of the sea (Hos. 4.3).[40] She suggests that Hosea 2 demythologizes the creation story of Yhwh as divine warrior, an image shared with Baal. Leith identifies three 'movements' in the biblical chapter: accusation, punishment, and restoration. Initially, Israel is stripped of her identity as a wife, isolated, but then emerges with a new identity and a new relationship to Yhwh; the earth is restored to a peaceful state. Thus the description of the marriage has ritual elements, analogous to a rite of passage, culminating in a new creation.

Another religious approach to Hosea 2 is Else Holt's proposal to envision the development of a new relationship between Israel and Yhwh through Hosea's use of the concept of election found in the Exodus and Jacob traditions to proclaim a 'Yhwh alone' message. The prophetic text teaches that since Israel has been chosen, Israel needs to commit itself exclusively to Yhwh in return. In Holt's view, Israel has not abandoned the covenant with God but emerges from polytheism into monolatry or monotheism.[41] Gale Yee agrees that Hosea preached a Yhwh-alone ideology in response to turbulent domestic and foreign relations.[42]

Similarly, Rut Törnkvist regards the sexual metaphors as a technique the prophet uses to engage in a debate about 'which God is allowed and which is not, and which woman is allowed and which is not'.[43] She suggests that during Hosea's time the identity of Israel as a distinct ethnic and religious

---

39. See, e.g., Baumann, *Love and Violence*, p. 90; Abma, *Bonds of Love*, p. 257; Weems, 'Gomer', p. 87.

40. Mary Joan Winn Leith, 'Verse and Reverse: The Transformation of the Woman, Israel, in Hosea 1–3', in Day (ed.), *Gender and Difference in Ancient Israel*, pp. 95-108.

41. Else Kragelund Holt, *Prophesying the Past: The Use of Israel's History in the Book of Hosea* (JSOTSup, 194; Sheffield: Sheffield Academic Press, 1995).

42. Gale Yee, *Poor Banished Children of Eve* (Minneapolis: Fortress Press, 2003).

43. Törnkvist, *Use and Abuse*, p. 17.

people was still fluid. Importantly, it did not include exclusive worship of Yhwh. Hosea tried to define Israel's identity more narrowly, specifically excluding goddess worship. Törnkvist explains:

> In this sense adultery, rape, or the people 'going astray' are not just violations of commandments, they are violations of various identity-constructs of 'Israel'... [Chapters 1–3] reflect the anxiety and holocaust of the Goddess and her worship in the Israelite society. The text also mirrors the repression of women from the cultic sphere. The battle is fought on the cultural and symbolic level.[44]

In this historical-religious reconstruction, monolatrous worship of Yhwh led to increased male domination in the religious sphere. Other feminist scholars concur. Margaret Odell views the male domination as further strengthened through a struggle between Levitical and Aaronide factions of the priesthood. She uses Hos. 4.5 as evidence: 'I will destroy your mother'. Based on the observation that in northern Israel, priests and prophets are sometimes called 'father' (e.g. Judg. 17.10; 2 Kgs 2.12), Odell argues that 'mother' refers to a cultic official, a female leader in communal festivals.[45] Few feminist scholars postulate that Hosea protested against the official role for women in the cult. Only Marie-Theres Wacker speculates that the prophet's condemnation includes goddesses, which, based on the prevalence of female figurines found in Israel, may have been part of popular religion.[46] She sees shadows of goddess language and symbols throughout Hosea.

Political Interpretations. A third approach places the marriage metaphor in the realm of politics and international relations, rather than religion. In this approach, the lovers represent political entities with which Israel has relations. Julie Galambush, studying the personified Jerusalem, focuses on political implications of the marriage metaphor, which appears in Hosea, Jeremiah, and Ezekiel.[47] When she examines Hosea, she details the ambiguous nature of the tenor of the metaphor and notes the difficulties of a consistent identification of the wife as the land. Opposing those who identify the wife more generally as Israel, she maintains that the association of the wife with the capital city Samaria best accommodates the range of meanings. Galambush explains that Hosea uses the term 'the baal' only as a title, referring to human lords or political 'lovers' with whom Samaria had relations,

44. Törnkvist, *Use and Abuse*, pp. 17-18.

45. Margaret S. Odell, 'I Will Destroy your Mother: The Obliteration of a Cultic Role in Hosea 4:4-6', in Brenner (ed.), *A Feminist Companion to the Latter Prophets*, pp. 180-93 (181-82, 192).

46. Marie-Theres Wacker, 'Traces of the Goddess in the Book of Hosea', in Brenner (ed.), *A Feminist Companion to the Latter Prophets*, pp. 217-41 (232).

47. Galambush, *Jerusalem*.

as apparent in Hos. 8.9-10.[48] She states: 'Thus the condemnation of Samaria's various "baalim" may play on the name of Baal, but only in the context of condemning the capital's devotion to foreign political powers'.[49] Her interpretation rejects the idea that idolatry is the central issue, as suggested in the religiously oriented approaches.

Galambush suggests instead that the oracles as a whole criticize the political actions of the rulers of Samaria, who broke their vassal treaties with Assyria by taking on other foreign nations as 'lovers' or treaty partners. Thus, any religious language relates to the nature of ancient Near Eastern treaties, which were witnessed and guaranteed by the gods of both sides. The breaking of the covenant was an offense against one's god, who would then enforce the treaty curses against his or her own people. Breaking the treaties meant that one questioned the power of one's god, a grave transgression similar to the loss of honor and status of the husband whose wife committed adultery. Thus, as Galambush observes, the marriage metaphor was an apt vehicle to convey the nature of the offense.

> Not only would Yahweh suffer dishonor as a king whose vassals had disobeyed, but also as a god whose name had been defiled. This aspect of Israelite apostasy—the defilement of the divine name—may have contributed more than any other to the use of the adultery metaphor to describe apostasy.[50]

In short, when feminist interpreters comment on the political and religious obligations in international treaties, they are not confined to viewing the marriage metaphor as religious apostasy. Instead, the metaphor connects with political concerns expressed in Hosea 4–14.[51]

Another feminist interpreter, Teresa Hornsby, rejects the idea that the metaphor refers to marriage at all. She observes that references to the so-called marriage is either ambiguous ('taking' and 'loving') or imagined, as all of the events in Hosea 2 are envisioned, not reported. Hornsby thus sees Gomer not as a wife, but as an independent prostitute, who is pursued by an obsessive client, Yhwh. The client fantasizes about controlling Gomer and hires her for an extended period in Hosea 3. In Hornsby's interpretation, a native of the Yehud wrote Hosea 3 after the Babylonian Exile as a critique of the returning priestly factions who wanted to restrict Israel's autonomy by placing her under the control of Yhwh. Accordingly, Hornsby interprets all of the references to promiscuity as related to prostitution and not adultery, and she proposes that the author of the text viewed the autonomy of the

---

48. Galambush, *Jerusalem*, p. 49.
49. Galambush, *Jerusalem*, p. 50.
50. Galambush, *Jerusalem*, p. 34.
51. See Susan E. Haddox, *Metaphor and Masculinity in Hosea* (Studies in Biblical Literature, 141; New York: Peter Lang, 2011).

prostitute favorably.[52] Hosea 1–3 emerges as a text witnessing Israel's loss of political independence due to the rise of the priestly factions in the post-exilic era. In conclusion, some feminist interpreters advance politically defined readings of the marriage metaphor. These readings emphasize the fact that the marriage metaphor was directed at a male audience and reflects male concerns, rather than addressing the position or misdeeds of real women.

Economic Interpretations. Gale Yee and Alice Keefe typify a fourth approach to the marriage metaphor. It defines its main issue as the economic centralization in eighth-century Israel, driven in part by political centralization and by the pressures of foreign tributary relations. Yee provides what she calls a Marxist-influenced materialist-ideological interpretation. It is based on the insight that biblical literature is both grounded in a specific historical situation and constructed to promote a particular viewpoint.[53] Her analysis thus pays close attention to both the socio-political context and the way the text manifests the symbols and the rhetoric of ideologies at work during the text's production.[54]

Yee maintains that Hosea was written in a socio-political system in which Assyria dominated and greatly altered the Israelite economy. What was formerly a familial mode of production, in which peasants kept most of the surplus, changed into a tributary mode that was dominated by large estates or latifundia. It was a system in which peasants lost their land through indebtedness. Thus agricultural production shifted from diversified plantings to cash crops, such as oil, wine, and grain, in order to pay the heavy Assyrian tributes. The trend toward monoculture made agricultural economy more vulnerable to bad weather, diseases, and insects.[55]

To Yee, the wife's infidelity in Hosea symbolizes the oppressive foreign and domestic policies that result from the pressures of agricultural intensification, political instability, religious conflict, and socioeconomic relations among kings, priests, and prophets.[56] Although politics and economics are the primary targets of Hosea's polemic, the religious references denote the fact that cultic sites were centers of political and economic power, as well as of religious activity.[57] Yee suggests that Hosea critiqued how the cult colluded in economic and political affairs, leading to the disintegration of

---

52. Teresa J. Hornsby, 'Israel Has Become a Worthless Thing: Rereading Gomer in Hosea 1–3', *JSOT* 82 (1999), pp. 115-28.

53. Yee, *Banished Children*, p. 10.

54. Yee, *Banished Children*, p. 23.

55. Yee, *Banished Children*, p. 83.

56. Yee, *Banished Children*, pp. 83, 85.

57. Yee, *Banished Children*, p. 91.

society. To Yee, Hosea promoted a 'polemical monolatry', as a means of social reform.[58] Yee asserts: 'Hosea was principally concerned with how the public male face of the cult, found in the sanctuary and priesthood, served the state'.[59] In other words, religious polemic addressed political, social, and economic changes that threatened social stability in eighth-century Israelite society.

Alice Keefe also interprets Hosea as a socio-economic critique of policies that disrupted a family-centered system and promoted centralization of economic resources and power in the hands of the elite.[60] The actions of the wife, who represents the social body of Israel, lead toward ever more stratified social organization. The lovers she pursues represent particular economic and power structures that exploited the peasant classes through a focus on trade products and cash crops.[61] Hosea's language about fornication and worship of other gods 'serve as alternating and intersecting tropes for inappropriate alliances or commercial "intercourse", and point towards the situation of Israel in the midst of a booming international market economy'.[62] Keefe thus views the rhetoric against the wife as the social body in terms of a socio-economic critique of the elite. In short, when feminist interpreters are attentive to the economic dynamics in Hosea, the poetry depicts class conflicts in Israel.

The Marriage Metaphor in Malachi

The issue of marriage reappears in Mal. 2.11-14, where the men of Judah are condemned for abandoning the wives of their youth and marrying the daughters of foreign gods. Some feminist interpreters, including Beth Glazier-MacDonald and Marie-Theres Wacker, take an historical perspective and compare the text with the critique of foreign marriage in the books of Ezra and Nehemiah, which does not only lead to apostasy but to an unjust treatment of the first wives. The charge of apostasy rests on the idea that foreign women lead Israelite men to their gods, rather than the other way

---

58. Yee, *Banished Children*, p. 86.

59. Yee, *Banished Children*, p. 96. A side effect of this policy, however, was the suppression of women's popular religion.

60. Alice A. Keefe, 'The Female Body, the Body Politic, and the Land: A Socio-political Reading of Hosea 1–2', in Brenner (ed.), *A Feminist Companion to the Latter Prophets*, pp. 70-100 (75).

61. Keefe notes that the items mentioned in 2.10a that Yhwh threatens to take back are the grain, the wine, and the oil, three chief cash crops; see Keefe, *Woman's Body*, p. 197.

62. Keefe, 'Female Body', p. 93.

around, a concept found throughout the Hebrew Bible.[63] Julia O'Brien, however, argues that within the context of idolatry, marriage is a metaphor, in which Yhwh is the wife of Judah's youth. She cautions against reading too much into the portrayal of Yhwh as wife, writing: 'It would be an overstatement to claim that Mal. 2.10-16 provides a biblical precedent for gender-inclusive language for the deity, but this unit does underscore the metaphorical nature of language used for God'.[64] Gerlinde Baumann similarly sees this passage as a continuation of the prophetic marriage metaphor in Hosea. She draws two implications from her reading of Malachi. First, it refocuses the metaphor from a relationship between God and the nation to one between God and individuals. Second, for Baumann, the transformation of the marriage image from God as husband to God as wife causes the metaphor to break down.[65] Baumann states:

> By the textually-created confusion of genders he [Malachi] also destroys any further 'normal' application of the marriage imagery. Through this opening to other gender-attributions for Yhwh and Judah the metaphor as *metaphor* emerges more clearly, through its alteration it is revealed as a human construction. There is a measure of travesty of the prophetic imagery in this text: At the end of the Book of the Twelve Prophets the thing that had its origin at the beginning, with Hosea, is taken up in such a way that the metaphor is broken apart.[66]

Family Metaphors

In addition to the city-as-woman metaphors in the Minor Prophets, family metaphors have garnered attention from feminist critics. Helen Schüngel-Straumann focuses on Hosea 11, which employs imagery of parent and child. She argues that this imagery is explicitly maternal:

> Hosea does not speak of his God andromorphically here, but *gynomorphically*. Although he avoids the word 'mother', he describes the everyday actions and behavior of a mother bringing up an infant, and in the second section, he depicts Yhwh as a mother who cannot find it in her heart to subject this child to the punishment it deserves.[67]

63. Beth Glazier-MacDonald, 'Malachi', in Newsom and Ringe (eds.), *Women's Bible Commentary*, pp. 248-50; Marie-Theres Wacker, 'Malachi: To the Glory of God the Father?', in Schottrof and Wacker (eds.), *Feminist Biblical Interpretation*, pp. 473-82.

64. Julia O'Brien, *Nahum, Habakkuk, Zephaniah, Haggai, Zechariah, Malachi* (AOTC; Nashville, TN: Abingdon Press, 2004), p. 303.

65. Baumann, *Love and Violence*, pp. 213-19.

66. Baumann, *Love and Violence*, p. 218.

67. Helen Schüngel-Straumann, 'God as Mother in Hosea 11', in Brenner (ed.), *A Feminist Companion to the Latter Prophets*, p. 214 (original italics).

Emphasizing the maternal nature of the care described in the first part of Hosea 11, Schüngel-Straumann emends several ambiguous terms:

> When Israel was young, I loved him; out of Egypt I called my son... But it was I who nursed [*tirgaltî*] Ephraim, taking him in my arms. Yet they did not understand that it was I who took care of them. I drew them with cords of humanity, with bands of love. I was for them like those who take a nursling [*'ûl*] to the breast [*leḥyēhem*], and I bowed down to him in order to give him suck (Hos. 11: 1, 3-4).[68]

She highlights the connection between the words for compassion and womb, even emending the word *niḥûmāy* in Hos. 11.8 to *raḥᵃmāy*, perhaps linking it to the daughter Lo-Ruhamah in ch. 1.[69] There she claims that God specifically rejects the masculine as a way to relate to Israel proclaiming, 'I am not a man [*wᵉlô' 'îš*]'.[70]

Another feminist interpretation focuses on the parental image in the opening chapter of Malachi, a case where God is shown as the father. Julia O'Brien maintains that the prophet constructs a particular model of parenting with an authoritarian father who demands submission of the sons. Obedient sons are loved like Jacob while disobedient sons are shunned like Esau. As a feminist interpreter, O'Brien finds this model problematic because it reinforces patriarchal norms and power structures. The role of the mother, important in the Ten Commandments, is excluded in this text which makes its androcentric tendencies even clearer.[71] O'Brien also questions the theological implications of the parental metaphor in its entirety when she explains:

> In demonstrating that the image of God the Father reinforces not only scripts about gender but also scripts about parenting, ideological critique challenges 'simple fixes' to the metaphor. Simply substituting 'she' or 'mother' for 'he' and 'father' or even speaking of the divine as gender-balanced Father/ Mother, might indeed challenge certain gender stereotypes, but it does not address the inherent dangers of the parental metaphor.[72]

---

68. Schüngel-Straumann, 'God as Mother', pp. 195-96. The Masoretic Text uses the word *'ôl*, 'yoke', but a simple repointing to *'ûl* yields 'infant', yielding the translation found in the NRSV. See also Gale A. Yee, 'Hosea', in Newsom and Ringe (eds.), *Women's Bible Commentary*, pp. 207-15 (213). The latter pointing fits the context of parent–child more easily than 'yoke', which changes the language to an agricultural metaphor. Schüngel-Straumann uses an Arabic cognate to justify translating *tirgaltî* as 'nurse' rather than the usual 'taught to walk', and renders *leḥyēhem* as 'breasts', rather than the usual 'cheeks' because this translation makes better sense of the plural form in the context of the passage.

69. Schüngel-Straumann, 'God as Mother', pp. 200-202, 208.

70. Schüngel-Straumann, 'God as Mother', p. 210.

71. O'Brien, *Challenging Prophetic Metaphor*, pp. 85-86.

72. O'Brien, *Challenging Prophetic Metaphor*, p. 99.

She encourages people to challenge these metaphors and not simply to accept them or reject them, but to interact with them in order better to understand themselves and to come into a more adult relationship with God.

Women versus Warriors

The images discussed so far focused on the relationship of the people with God. Another area of feminist concern relates to the appearance of female figures in the Minor Prophets to denote action and suffering on the human level. Claudia Bergmann examines how the prophets use women as symbols for vulnerable and defeated soldiers in military contexts. She observes that there are two major types of such images used in the Bible: women in childbirth and weak, victimized women. These two types of women are commonly mixed together in the scholarly literature, but Bergmann asserts that they are distinct and have different connotations. The first image refers to a situation of crisis. It involves pain and fear, but not necessarily weakness. The second image indicates that the men are no longer able to fulfill their roles as strong fighters; they are defeated.

The childbirth imagery appears in Mic. 4.9-10, in which Daughter Zion writhes in labor pains as exile nears, and Zech. 9.5, as Gaza awaits its fate. In Mic. 5.2, the end of labor and the birth of the child mark the coming of a new age. Although Bergmann does not discuss Hosea, an example of childbirth appears in Hos. 13.13. While Ephraim is portrayed there as the fetus rather than the mother, the process of childbirth still represents a situation of crisis.

The image of soldiers as weak women is seen most clearly in Nah. 3.13, where the soldiers, protecting the city of Nineveh, become women. Bergmann explains that the biblical use of this imagery corresponds with ancient Near Eastern treaty curses. The goddess Ištar takes away the symbols of manhood (bow and staff) and replaces them with symbols of womanhood (mirror and spindle). In other words, she turns the men into weak women.[73] Susan Haddox analyzes this trope in Hosea. In addition to the widely noted idea that the male audience is transformed into a female, promiscuous wife, she observes that in Hos. 2.23, the son Jezreel is transformed into a woman as she is sown into the earth. This transformation is supported by the fact that the bow (a prime metonym of masculinity) is broken.[74] The image of defeated warriors as weak women also plays into the fate real women face in

73. Claudia D. Bergmann, "'We Have Seen the Enemy and He Is Only a 'She'": The Portrayal of Warriors as Women', in Kelle and Ames (eds.), *Writing and Reading War*, pp. 129-42.
74. Haddox, *Metaphor and Masculinity*, pp. 147-48.

warfare, as apparent in many examples scattered throughout the Minor Prophets. They are sold into slavery (Joel 4.3, 8), raped (Zech. 14.2), or oppressed as widows (Mal. 3.5; Zech. 7.10).

Unrighteous Women

The prophet's vision of woman Wickedness in Zech. 5.5-11 has also drawn attention from feminist interpreters, because of its association of unrighteousness with a woman. Ulrike Sals notes that there is a lot of ambiguity in the passage.[75] The prophet sees an *ephah* basket with a lid. When the lid is removed, the angel names the woman in the basket 'Unrighteousness'. The *ephah* is then carried away to the land of Shinar by two other women with storks' wings, where it is set up and worshipped. Interpreters sometimes link the woman with Eve and thus with all women. Because the *ephah* is associated with a Mesopotamian cult room, the woman may also represent a goddess or a foreign woman in parallel to foreign wives in Ezra and Nehemiah, a connection made by Beth Glazier-MacDonald.[76] Sals explains that the different readings often blend in the history of interpretation:

> The text gives rise to the reading that the woman in the *ephah* is at one and the same time the strange woman *and* every woman, and that woman is intrinsically linked to unrighteousness.[77]

Containing Unrighteousness, the *ephah* is carried away by two women with stork-like wings, in a scene with ritual elements similar to the sending of the scapegoat to Azazel in the Yom Kippur ceremony (Lev. 16.10). Rather than an elimination ritual, however, where evil is expelled from the land, Sals calls it instead an 'infection' ritual, in which Shinar is contaminated with unrighteousness, in the form of a strange woman or goddess. The description of woman Wickedness in a sealed container is analogous to the story of Pandora, a parallel that Sals explores, although she rejects any claims that one story was literarily dependent on the other. Instead she places the connection in the minds of interpreters, who have come to associate women with wickedness.

> To think of Pandora when reading Zech. 5.5-11 is a result of our associations of 'women–evil–vessel'. The history of the reception of these texts has diminished differences between famous 'bad' women and focused upon (possible and non-existent) similarities.[78]

75. Ulrike Sals, 'Reading Zechariah 5:5-11: Prophecy, Gender, and (Ap)perception', in Brenner (ed.), *Prophets and Daniel*, pp. 186-205.

76. Beth Glazier-MacDonald, 'Zechariah', in Newsom and Ringe (eds.), *Women's Bible Commentary*, pp. 245-47.

77. Sals, 'Reading Zechariah 5:5-11', p. 196.

78. Sals, 'Reading Zechariah 5.5-11', p. 205.

While the vision itself has different facets, the naming of the woman as Unrighteousness reinforces negative portrayals of women throughout the prophets.

Another example of a negative portrayal appears in Amos 4.1-3, which includes a polemic against the 'cows of Bashan', derided for basking in luxury at the expense of the poor. While acknowledging that rich women may have been deserving of censure, feminist commentators such as Judith Sanderson take Amos to task for singling out women of high social status but not specifying women at the bottom of the social heap. Sanderson observes:

> Amos specifically condemned wealthy women for oppressing the poor (4.1) but failed specifically to champion the women among the poor... As Amos singled out wealthy women—a small group—for special condemnation, a balanced analysis would also have singled out poor women—a much larger group—for special defense and a show of that solidarity of which he was so clearly capable.[79]

Hence, some feminist interpreters claim that Amos falls prey to the patriarchal ideology of his time and places an undue burden of blame on women. The prophet does not acknowledge the extent to which women suffer disproportionately from the very behaviors and structures he condemns. Yet elsewhere, Amos uses women, along with men, to represent suffering, including women mourning (Amos 5.1-2), being murdered (Amos 1.13), turned into prostitutes (Amos 7.17), or suffering thirst along with the young men (Amos 8.13). Such images of suffering women serve to underscore the generally negative portrayal of women that feminist interpreters have found in the Minor Prophets.

Women Prophets

In contrast to associating women with apostasy, a few feminist scholars note cases in which women make positive contributions to Israelite religion. They comment on the description in Joel 3.1-2 of widespread prophecy with the spirit of God descending on many people in the eschaton. Both women and men will prophesy, young and old, slave and free.[80] In the day of God, at least, gender does not matter, although Wacker observes that the inclusion of women and slaves as prophets specifically serves as a symbol of confusion

---

79. Judith E. Sanderson, 'Amos', in Newsom and Ringe (eds.), *Women's Bible Commentary*, pp. 218-23 (221-22).

80. Beth Glazier-MacDonald, 'Joel', in Newsom and Ringe (eds.), *Women's Bible Commentary*, pp. 216-17.

and the overturning of the old orders.[81] For instance, Wilda Gafney examines Mic. 6.4, which mentions Miriam along with Moses and Aaron as the ones who led Israel out of slavery by God's hand. She speculates that the three may have been prophetic, rather than blood siblings. She also regards the reference as indicative of a tradition in which Miriam prophesies alongside Moses and Aaron.[82] Rainer Kessler identifies the figures of Moses as representing the Torah, Aaron as representing priestly functions, and Miriam as representing all prophecy. Prophecy during the Persian period, he argues, was suppressed because it tended to oppose alignment with the Persian state and favored independence for Judah. The choice of Miriam as a representative of prophecy not only echoes Numbers 12, but also resonates with the opposition of the prophetess Noadiah to Nehemiah (Neh. 6.14).[83] While these examples are few, feminist interpreters have noted their importance as positive images of women.

Issues in Feminist Interpretation of the Prophets

As a way to summarize some of the major concerns that have arisen in feminist analysis, Julia O'Brien discusses the ethical and theological use of the prophetic texts.[84] First, there is the problem of what she calls 'reading as male'. Only if one identifies with the male perspective in the text is God loving and just, such as in Hosea 1–3. However, such a hermeneutics ignores women's pain and value. Second, the prophets propagate a patriarchal ideology. While they may challenge other prevailing ideologies related to economics or monarchy, their oracles reinforce or even enhance hierarchical understandings involving women and children. Third, O'Brien asserts the feminist claim that 'all theological language is political language'. Talk about God cannot be separated from real human relationships. For a prophet to be considered ethical, the prophet must also be ethical toward women. Fourth, feminist criticism challenges the status of the text as a normative authority. O'Brien explains:

> Based on the 'What about women?' criterion, feminists insist that not all of what the prophets say faithfully describes the 'real' nature of the divine. Feminist analysis introduces a disjunction between what the Prophets say

81. Marie-Theres Wacker, 'Joel: God's Self-Justification', in Schottorf and Wacker (eds.), *Feminist Biblical Interpretation*, pp. 386-96 (390-91).

82. Wilda C. Gafney, *Daughters of Miriam: Women Prophets in Ancient Israel* (Minneapolis: Fortress Press, 2008), p. 116.

83. Rainer Kessler, 'Miriam and the Prophecy of the Persian Period', in Brenner (ed.), *Prophets and Daniel*, pp. 81-85.

84. O'Brien, *Challenging Prophetic Metaphor*, pp. 36-39.

about God and who God 'really' is. In contrast to earlier interpreters for whom description of what the Prophets say *itself* constitutes theology, feminists approach the Prophetic Books as (flawed) human testimonies that must be tested for their value.[85]

Feminist interpretations of the prophets foreground women's value and experiences in making theological and ethical judgments about the texts.

Beyond Female Images

Feminist interpreters of the Minor Prophets do not focus exclusively on female images although the emphasis on and analysis of those images has been a significant concern of their work. They have also dealt with non-gender specific texts and developed several approaches for them. One approach considers feminism's affiliation with other marginalized groups found in the text, such as minority ethnicities or oppressed social classes. For example, feminist scholars, such as Marie-Theres Wacker, think that Amos may serve as a resource for a vision of universal justice in the contemporary world, despite the critique that Amos unfairly singles out rich women for censure. Wacker maintains that feminist critics, who have come primarily from the first world, need to take into account global interpretations. She explains:

> Women have more occasion and reason than ever to bring into focus such global contexts that threaten to constrict their possibilities for action in new and different ways. In such a frame of reference, it makes sense, and is in fact essential for a feminist reading, to accentuate precisely the 'global' perspectives of the book, which are directed toward the world of peoples, cultures, and nations, on the one hand, and on the other, toward the cosmos, 'nature,' and creation.[86]

A second approach makes explicit patriarchal perspectives and social locations of the prophetic authors. For example, work in masculinity studies uncovers the particular masculine gender constructions underlying the rhetoric and assumptions of ancient and modern authors and audiences. Susan Haddox's study of Hosea elucidates the ways in which both gendered and non-gendered imagery critiques male elite leaders of Israel by playing off particular constructions of hegemonic masculinity. She shows that Hosea reinforces patriarchal gender norms but also repositions the male leaders within the social space. The text even contains a number of subversive elements.[87] Haddox observes:

85. O'Brien, *Challenging Prophetic Metaphor*, p. 39.
86. Marie-Theres Wacker, 'Amos: The Truth is Concrete', in Schottorf and Wacker (eds.), *Feminist Biblical Interpretation*, p. 398.
87. See, e.g., Haddox, *Metaphor and Masculinity*.

The general patriarchal nature of the text with its hegemonic definition of masculinity remains largely intact, but the variety of metaphors Hosea uses to create identity and relationships among people and with Yhwh create some play in the system.[88]

A third approach considers the effect of the prophetic rhetoric as a whole, not only specifically gendered imagery. For example, Judith Sanderson argues that Zephaniah's tirade against pride is a useful critique of those in power. However, the text may also be harmful to women who already have problems with self-esteem or dependence. She suggests distinguishing arrogance from pride and specifying the former as the sin.[89] Wacker offers hope that feminist readings open patriarchal texts to broader meanings. While noting Malachi's thoroughgoing use of male images, she finds its presentation of an authoritarian relationship between fathers and sons, and its focus on an elect people as hints in the text to the interpreter to open it up to a more inclusive reading.

To employ a feminist critical outlook, the reader must find a framework in which women can occupy new symbolic places and highlight the moments that are critical of patriarchy within this patriarchal book.[90]

Conclusion

In conclusion, feminist interpreters have continually engaged the vivid portrayals in the Book of the Twelve. The violence of the city-as-woman images, particularly in format of the marriage metaphor, has been a catalyst for the development of feminist biblical criticism. The prophetic passages made feminists question the assumptions of androcentric readings of the historical and cultural contexts of the texts, as well as the implications for the continued use of these texts in communities of faith. As feminist criticism moves forward, it will surely develop additional ideological and theological perspectives, shed new light on these texts, and reveal the prophetic voice.

88. Haddox, *Metaphor and Masculinity*, p. 156.

89. Judith E. Sanderson, 'Zephaniah', in Newsom and Ringe (eds.), *Women's Bible Commentary*, pp. 240-42.

90. Wacker, 'Malachi', p. 481.

9

DISCOURSE OF RESISTANCE:
FEMINIST STUDIES ON THE PSALTER
AND THE BOOK OF LAMENTATIONS*

Carleen Mandolfo

The book of Psalms and the book of Lamentations have received disparate degrees of attention from feminist scholars. The book of Psalms has received only marginal attention in sharp contrast to its elevated stature in Judaism and Christianity. The book of Lamentations, on the other hand, occupies a fairly minor position in those traditions, but has especially lately been the recipient of intense study by feminist biblical scholars. Both are more or less poetic in form, which probably accounts for the relative lack of feminist interest until recently. Narrative, featuring gendered 'characters', has always been more amenable to feminist interests. A recent concern with the literary phenomena of metaphor and voicing accounts at least in part for the atten-tion Lamentations is enjoying, insofar as the city of Jerusalem is figured as a woman in dialogue with the narrator/poet of chs. 1 and 2. The book of Psalms includes few gendered references, and virtually none that are feminine, except for occasional feminine imagery referring to the deity. In general, the shift away from characterization and toward formal features that marks feminist Lamentations scholarship has potential for feminist Psalms study.

The Book of Psalms

There have been strikingly few feminist studies on the book of Psalms. One might think that after a couple of decades of furious feminist work on the Bible we might see more work devoted to this important book. Yet if one considers the kinds of questions with which most feminist biblical scholars have concerned themselves we probably should not be too surprised.

*   I am grateful to Wilson 'Beau' Harris for his conscientious reading of the penultimate draft of this manuscript.

Melody D. Knowles and Esther Mann explain the lack of feminist scholarship in the following way: '[T]he relative absence of women in the Psalter in both content and authorial voice is mirrored by the absence of explicit, focused, and sustained feminist scholarship on the text'.[1] Pioneering feminist readers, focusing on narratives and poetry in the Pentateuch and the former prophets,[2] mostly concerned themselves with obviously gendered texts featuring female *characters*. They asked such questions as: *Where* do we find women in the text? *How* are women characterized in the texts?[3] Understandably, then, narrative texts were primarily mined for answers to these questions. The poetic form of the psalms precludes the inclusion of female 'characters', and its decontextualized nature reduces the opportunity for even metaphoric portrayals of women. Socio-historical questions were also part of the initial scholarship: *What* do we learn about the lives of ancient Israelite women from these texts?[4] Not only do the Psalms lack references to female characters, personae, or interests, but they are also conspicuously biased toward 'masculine' images and themes, such as war (Ps. 144) or other kinds of implied violent struggle (Ps. 137). Often they have to do with the king's activity against enemies (Ps. 20) or God's activity against Israel's enemies (Ps. 21) or against Israel (Ps. 79).

As part of his ongoing work on masculinity in the Bible, David Clines identifies six 'masculine' categories that exercise thematic primacy in the Psalter: 'the ideology of honour and shame; the construction of "enemies";

1. Melody D. Knowles and Esther Mann, 'Feminist Criticism and the Psalms', in Esther Menn (ed.), *Cambridge Methods in Biblical Interpretation: The Psalms* (New York: Cambridge University Press, forthcoming). This observation is echoed in Athalya Brenner, 'Introduction', in Athalya Brenner and Carole R. Fontaine (eds.), *Wisdom and the Psalms* (FCB, 2nd Series; Sheffield: Sheffield Academic Press, 1998), pp. 23-30 (29).

2. See, e.g., Phyllis Trible, *Texts of Terror: Literary Feminist Readings of Biblical Narratives* (OBT; Philadelphia: Fortress Press, 1984); and *God and the Rhetoric of Sexuality* (Philadelphia: Fortress Press, 1986). Readings in this vein have continued, though many with a more cultural-critical emphasis; see, e.g., Renita Weems, *Battered Love: Marriage, Sex, and Violence in the Hebrew Prophets* (OBT; Minneapolis: Fortress Press, 1995). Some literary readings have been more theory-driven: Mieke Bal, *Lethal Love: Feminist Literary Readings of Biblical Love Stories* (Bloomington: Indiana University Press, 1987).

3. Subsequently, the questions posed by feminist readers have become less literal. For example, there has been a flurry of studies on metaphor, particularly the ways in which figurative women have been deployed by biblical authors for the purpose of understanding the divine/human relationship. Not surprisingly, the prophetic marriage metaphor featured in several prophetic texts, primarily Hosea, Isaiah, Jeremiah, and Ezekiel, has become a favorite subject for feminist inquiry.

4. See, e.g., Carol Meyers, *Discovering Eve: Ancient Israelite Women in Context* (Oxford: Oxford University Press, 1991); and *Households and Holiness: The Religious Culture of Israelite Women* (Minneapolis: Fortress Press, 2005).

the role of women; the concept of solitariness; the importance of strength and height in its metaphorical system; and the practice of binary thinking'.[5] Melody Knowles also finds male concerns emphasized in the Psalms. She points out that the attribution of authorship to David in many psalms' headings slants readings toward male concerns. Analyzing psalmic images for the deity, she notes that they are overwhelmingly masculine although the Psalter includes a smattering of references that could be construed as feminine, especially metaphors for the deity. In Ps. 22.9-10 (Eng.), for example, the deity is portrayed as delivering David from his mother's womb.[6] There is no need to rehearse how the Psalter projects a masculine bias. Suffice it to say that it is particularly gendered and that gender is male, even though the language lacks contextual particularity. Clines even suggests, albeit tongue in cheek, that inscriptions for the book of Psalms include 'God helps you kill people' and 'God will make a man out of you'.[7] Despite so little obvious fodder, some feminists have attempted to read several psalms with feminist concerns in mind.[8]

The following review sorts previous feminist readings into three categories that are loosely drawn from Paul Ricoeur's hermeneutical work. First, some studies concern themselves with issues understood as originating 'behind the text'. Second, other studies advance readings that capitalize on possibilities for interpreting 'in front of the text'. Third, several works remain fundamentally focused 'in the text'.[9] The interests of historical-critical approaches to recover textual 'origins' have little to do with what a text *means* in the Ricoeurian sense, as he explained: '[T]he essential question is not to recover, behind the text, the lost intention but to unfold, in front of the text, the "world" it opens up and discloses'.[10] Genuine understanding results, then, only when a text has been appropriated and the world of possibilities it

5.   David Clines, 'The Book of Psalms, Where Men Are Men: On the Gender of Hebrew Piety', unpublished article at www.academia.edu/2469780, used with permission. Even in Ps. 10.18 where we would expect to have a reference to 'orphans and widows' female interests have been purged in favor of 'judge for the widow and orphan'.

6.   I am indebted to my research assistant, Carolyn Patterson, who ferreted out this and other instances of 'feminine' language in the psalms. She uncovered other interesting references on the deity's role in David's birth, deserving a study in their own right.

7.   Clines, 'Where Men Are Men'.

8.   Melody Knowles ('Feminist Criticism') surveyed the history of feminist interpretation of the Psalms. I am indebted to her bibliography for my own survey, which, however, takes a different tack.

9.   These categories should be understood as strategic and heuristic. Paul Ricoeur was interested in how these different hermeneutical elements *together* constituted meaning.

10.   Paul Ricoeur, 'Phenomenology and Hermeneutics', in Ricoeur, *From Text to Action: Essays in Hermeneutics*, II (Evanston, IL: Northwestern University Press, 1991), pp. 25-52 (35).

projects apprehended by a reader. This should not, however, be understood as a capitulation to extreme relativity and non-negotiated subjectivity.[11] That is, the integrity of the text itself must be maintained in the process of interpretation, and readers must by-pass neither the historical context nor the form of the literature itself to get 'in front of the text'.

Feminist works on the psalms, addressing what lies 'behind the text', are primarily interested in recovering origins. They might look for references to ancient Israelite women, either as *subjects* behind the psalms or as *composers/performers* of the psalms. Because getting behind the psalms is so challenging, a significant percentage of the (scant) feminist work done on the psalms has concerned itself with exploring the world 'in front of the text', that is, it appropriates the language of the psalms for contemporary women's concerns. The most underrepresented approach in feminist Psalms scholarship focuses 'in the text'. So far, few feminists have explained the structure and genre of psalmic literature to evaluate if the language, *per se*, might reflect women's realities and/or feminist concerns.

Behind the Text: Addressing Historical Questions[12]
Early feminist biblical scholars were trained in historical-critical methodologies, typical of much biblical scholarship. Thus some of the early feminist work on the Psalter follows this pattern and looks for the lives of real women in the texts under consideration. Knowles and Mann explain: 'The recovery of the details and stories of women within the psalms has two major facets vis-à-vis the ancient world: examining the texts for details about women in their daily life and cultic participation, and reading the texts as the prayers of ancient women'.[13] Similarly, Erhard Gerstenberger suggests that certain psalms have their *Sitz* in family cult (Pss. 127; 128; 131, which he calls 'family hymns') rather than the 'official', centralized cult, which may reflect situations of women in leading roles.

One straightforward feminist-historical reading of the psalms is Kathleen Farmer's work, published in *The Women's Bible Commentary*.[14] Assessing the plausibility that women's voices are recorded in the Psalter, she notes that

11. Paul Ricoeur, 'Phenomenology and Hermeneutics', in Ricoeur, *Hermeneutics and the Human Sciences: Essays on Language, Action, and Interpretation* (ed. and trans. John B. Thompson; Cambridge: Cambridge University Press, 1981), pp. 93-120 (113).

12. The observations made in the following categories are representative rather than exhaustive.

13. Knowles and Mann, 'Feminist Interpretation of the Psalms'.

14. Kathleen Farmer, 'Psalms', in Sharon H. Ringe and Carol Newsom (eds.), *The Women's Bible Commentary* (Louisville, KY: Westminster/John Knox Press, 1992), pp. 145-52.

in other biblical traditions (outside the book of Psalms) prominent women are portrayed as singers of hymns in Israel's worship (Miriam in Exod. 15.20-21 and Deborah in Judg. 5). In Ps. 148.12-13 women are commanded to praise Yahweh along with the rest of creation, and in Ps. 68.25, girls are pictured as playing musical instruments in a liturgical procession of praise.[15]

Farmer also mentions that five biblical women (Miriam, Deborah, Hannah, Judith, and Mary) responded to their respective life experiences by singing 'psalm like songs and prayers'. In each case their song recounts a changed circumstance not unlike the apparent situation reflected in the songs of thanksgiving recorded in the Psalter.[16]

Similarly, Lisa Davison evaluates the historical possibilities of women in the psalms. She states that some psalms are explicitly masculine, like the royal psalms. Yet she also observes that the subject matter of many psalms suggests that they *could* have been sung by women.[17] To bolster this possibility, she points out that many biblical texts mention women singing dirges (e.g. Jer. 9.19). Yet the flimsiness of the historical record gets the best of her when she recommends using one's *imagination* to hear the echo of women's voices in the psalms. She asks her readers to *imagine* the words of Psalm 123 being spoken by the women that Jeremiah urged to raise a dirge over the people. Even this example of imaginative retrieval falls short when one considers that Psalm 123 is not a dirge, but rather a lament, two genres that are not interchangeable. In any case, it is certainly true that any number of psalms *might* be applicable to the lives of women and *could* have been sung by women. But this kind of reading illustrates that historical analyses aiming to recover the place of women in the Psalter often fall well short of an acceptable critical hermeneutic.[18]

In contrast, Melody Knowles offers a substantial historical study that recovers the lives of women in the psalms. Also employing a text-critical approach, she mediates the debate over how to translate Ps. 131.2b. Many scholars translate the verse according to the pointing in the Leningrad Codex: 'As a weaned child on its mother; as the weaned child on me am I'. She argues for a re-pointing of the first preposition to include a first person singular pronominal suffix and translates: 'As a weaned child on me, its

---

15. Farmer, 'Psalms', p. 146.

16. Farmer, 'Psalms', p. 147.

17. Lisa W. Davison, 'My Soul Is Like the Weaned Child That Is with Me: The Psalms and the Feminine Voice', *HBT* 23 (2001), pp. 155-67 (159, 161).

18. Maria Häusl also argues for reading a specific psalm as a reflection of the concerns of an ancient (childless) woman; see Maria Häusl, 'Ps 17—Bittgebet einer kinderlosen Frau?', in Hurbert Irsigler (ed.), *'Wer darf hinaufsteigen zum Berg JHWHs?', Beiträge zu Prophetie und Poesie des Alten Testaments* (Arbeiten zum Text und Sprache im Alten Testament, 72; St Ottilien: EOS Verlag, 2002), pp. 205-22.

mother; as the weaned…'[19] With this slight adjustment Knowles removes the ambiguity, making explicit the author's gendered identity.

Another example of a critically rigorous historical approach comes from Silvia Schroer, who suggests that the reference to 'wings' in the psalms (Pss 17; 36; 91) may refer to Egyptian goddesses, in particular the vulture mother goddess. Schroer states:

> A strong connection was made in the Ancient Near East between the Mother-Goddess and the vulture, to which rich notions of protection and regeneration were attributed. Whenever there is mention of the protective wings of YHWH, the motherliness of YHWH is not particularly emphasized. Nevertheless, it is definitely present. In this respect, YHWH is the successor of the Goddess.[20]

In opposition to the few historical 'success stories' are those that searched in vain for traces of women in the psalms.[21] While not identifying himself as a feminist interpreter, Marc Zvi Brettler undertook an exhaustive and persuasive analysis of the place of women's prayer in the cult of ancient Israel. He concludes that 'there is no positive evidence, from pre-exilic or postexilic sources, for the participation of women in the cult in some role connected to the singing of the psalms'.[22] In fact, much of Brettler's evidence suggests a deliberate marginalization of women and women's concerns in the Psalter. His extensive exegesis of Psalm 128, for example, demonstrates that the language of this psalm places the wife/mother figure on the periphery of her own home.[23] Quite significantly, he notes that 'there is not a single psalm that specifically concerns life-cycle events or other issues that would have been unique to the Israelite woman rather than the man'.[24] This lack is extraordinary for a collection of texts we often describe as running the gamut of life experiences mediated through religious practice and worship. Brettler's conclusion reinforces the intuition of many scholars that the psalms were composed by and for elite males in the context of an official, rather than familial, religion.

19. Melody D. Knowles, 'A Woman at Prayer: A Critical Note on Psalm 131:2b', *JBL* 125 (2006), pp. 385-91.

20. Silvia Schroer, 'Under the Shadow of your Wings: The Metaphor of God's Wings in the Psalms, Exodus 19.4, Deuteronomy 31.11 and Malachi 3.20, as Seen through the Perspectives of Feminism and the History of Religion', in Brenner and Fontaine (eds.), *Wisdom and the Psalms*, pp. 264-82 (280).

21. Of course, David Clines's work falls into this category.

22. Marc Zvi Brettler, 'Women and Psalms: Toward an Understanding of the Role of Women's Prayer in the Israelite Cult', in Tikva Frymer-Kensky and Victor H. Matthews (eds.), *Gender and Law in the Hebrew Bible and the Ancient Near East* (JSOTSup, 262; Sheffield: Sheffield Academic Press, 2009), pp. 25-56 (40).

23. Brettler, 'Women and Psalms', pp. 29-30.

24. Brettler, 'Women and Psalms', p. 39.

Yet another study finds few women-related concerns in the book of Psalms. Nancy Bowen's intertextual reading of Psalm 45 could legitimately be placed in the 'in the text' category, but ultimately her concerns are historical. Her study aims to discover whether the concerns of ancient women are reflected in the psalms. She reads Psalm 45 alongside other biblical 'romantic fairytales', such as Abigail, Esther, Ezekiel 16, and the Song of Songs. She concludes that Psalm 45 supports a feminist agenda even though this psalm does not mention a woman. She explains:

> Like most fairytales, Psalm 45 presupposes asymmetry in its gender relationships... This is, after all, a song *for the king*. It is *his* concerns and purposes that are the central focus. The bride is present not for what *she* might seek from or bring to (beyond children) the marriage but is present only to enable the king to fulfill his mandate regarding the kingdom.[25]

Bowen also argues that Psalm 45 commits the same violence against women as Ezekiel 16. Still, due to the decontextualized and metaphoric nature of the psalms, historical-critical approaches have proven less than satisfactory in the study of the book of Psalms and consequently, feminist historical interpretations have run into equal or even greater challenges than their androcentric counterparts.

In Front of the Text: Contemporary Appropriations
Many feminist 'readings'[26] appropriate the language of the psalms for the lives of contemporary women. Knowles suggests that the lack of sustained feminine concerns *in* the psalms and the lack of sustained feminist criticism *on* the psalms 'contrasts starkly with women's use of the psalms in earlier historical periods, and on a popular level, in the contemporary context as well'.[27]

Ulrike Bail provides a representative example of a feminist scholar who reads psalms as resources for contemporary women. Her intention is 'not to offer a reconstruction of a historically identifiable distress or of a so-called real problem as the background to a specifically female experience of violence'. Instead, she asks whether 'the structure of the language used in the Psalms can give space to the specific experience of violence suffered

25. Nancy Bowen, 'A Fairy Tale Wedding? A Feminist Intertextual Reading of Psalm 45', in Brent Strawn and Nancy Bowen (eds.), *A God So Near: Essays on Old Testament Theology in Honor of Patrick D. Miller* (Winona Lake, IN: Eisenbrauns, 2003), pp. 53-71 (56, original emphasis).

26. In my view, it is difficult to call some of these 'studies' as many lack what most biblical scholars would consider a critical sensibility.

27. See Knowles, 'A Woman at Prayer', pp. 7-8 and 20 for brief references to and bibliography of ancient and contemporary readers, and an example of an eighteenth-century New England woman who reads the psalms to deal with her situation of domestic abuse.

by women'.[28] Bail reads Psalm 55, especially vv. 13-14, as a potentially sustaining poem for women who have suffered domestic abuse or so-called 'date rape'. However, the links she makes do not go beyond basic thematic connections.

A more critically sophisticated example of the *use* of psalms, albeit not a primarily feminist one, is the work of Kristin Swenson. She reads the lament psalms alongside theories on illness and chronic pain[29] and suggests that a reading of biblical psalms provides 'a lens through which we see how pain both presses people to ask questions of meaning and finally may defy answers to those questions'.[30] Her focus on the non-linear, experiential, and embodied aspect of the psalms could fruitfully be harnessed for more sustained feminist reflection.

In the Text: Attending to Formal Features
Situating the hermeneutic enterprise 'in the text' means paying attention to genre, structure, and the semiotic codes that organize the text in meaningful ways. Relatively few feminist studies of the psalms have considered how the structure of the poems might contribute to a feminist agenda. I do not, however, advocate formalism as the *telos* of interpretation. Taking my cue from Ricoeur, I propose that feminist readings find ways for a given text to reach beyond itself and, in dialogue with its readers, to create new worlds. The point is 'to seek in the text itself, on the one hand, the internal dynamic that governs the structuring of the work and, on the other hand, the power that the work possesses to project itself outside itself and to give birth to a world that would truly be the "thing" referred to by the text'.[31] What is needed for this hermeneutical process to work is an equally firm commitment to the text and to the world being created by the interpretative process leveled at the text.

Although Beth Tanner's commitments lie largely 'in front of the text', her intertextual work demonstrates respect for the integrity of the text itself. It thus is a promising example of the direction to be taken by feminist psalm scholarship.[32] Tanner uses the readerly impulses of Patrick Miller as a springboard for her own different work:

28. Ulrike Bail, 'O God, Hear my Prayer: Psalm 55 and Violence against Women', in Brenner and Fontaine (eds.), *Wisdom and the Psalms*, pp. 242-63 (243).

29. Kristin M. Swenson, *Living through Pain: Psalms and the Search for Wholeness* (Waco, TX: Baylor University Press, 2005).

30. Swenson, *Living through Pain*, p. 49.

31. Paul Ricoeur, 'On Interpretation', in Ricoeur, *From Text to Action*, pp. 1-20 (17).

32. Beth LaNeel Tanner, 'Hearing the Cries Unspoken: An Intertextual-Feminist Reading of Psalm 109', in Brenner and Fontaine (eds.), *Wisdom and the Psalms*, pp. 283-301. See also Beth LaNeel Tanner, *The Book of Psalms through the Lens of Intertextuality* (Studies in Biblical Literature, 26; New York: Peter Lang, 2001).

> Miller stresses that the language of the Psalms is 'open and metaphorical' and
> it 'invites, allows and calls for interpretation that looks and moves forward
> into the present and future as well as for interpretation that looks backward'.
> The Psalms, then, engage both the ancient 'texts' of the Hebrew Bible and the
> 'texts' of the interpreter. This flexibility in the metaphorical language of the
> psalms should make them prime texts for a feminist interpretation.[33]

Tanner acknowledges that most readers understand the *Sitz im Leben* of
Psalm 109 as a court of law. But she asks what happens when we read it
through the lens of the Rachel and Leah narrative, in which case it becomes
the voice of the silent ones. She writes: '[B]y juxtaposing [Psalm 109 with]
the story of Leah and Rachel, the enemy is found in one's own house and is
a member of one's own inner circle...the metaphorical language of the
household take[s] on a different sense when read with the Genesis narrative'.[34] Space considerations do not permit a thorough review, but Tanner's
study makes some compelling intertextual connections.

Although one would not always know it in the context of biblical studies,[35] feminist scholarship in general has moved beyond a focus on 'women'
to a focus on 'gender'. The only work on psalms currently available in this
category is the queer-critical analysis of the psalms by Tamar Kamionkowski.[36] In fact, Kamionkowski avers the impossibility of recovering
women's lives in the Psalter. Among the central claims she makes are that

> there are some psalms that are indeed gender-free and universal. However,
> these psalms are rare and constitute the exception rather than the norm. The
> majority of psalms exhibit predominantly binary thinking and do not allow for
> grays and fluidity... I will further argue that the psalmists and the God of the
> psalms reflect the view points and perspectives of stereotypical masculinity.[37]

Her research comes to the conclusion that, read in an historical context, the
psalms were written by and for men to a male God.

This overdetermined masculinity also leads Kamionkowski to discuss
how the psalms offer a variety of male-to-male relationships that are ripe
for queer appropriation.[38] Most useful is her attention to the way psalmic
poets structured their discourse in terms of binaries. The binarism is 'useful' because, as she notes, the strict binary structure of psalmic language
('I' vs. 'the enemy', the paths of righteousness vs. wickedness) reinforces

---

33. Tanner, 'Hearing the Cries Unspoken', p. 283.

34. Tanner, 'Hearing the Cries Unspoken', p. 298.

35. There are exceptions, of course, such as the work done in the area of postcolonial
feminist, queer, and masculinist biblical studies.

36. Tamar Kamionkowski, 'Psalms', in Deryn Guest (ed.), *The Queer Bible
Commentary* (London: SCM Press, 2006), pp. 304-24.

37. Kamionkowski, 'Psalms', p. 305.

38. Kamionkowski, 'Psalms', p. 312.

typically masculine concerns such as military prowess and domination over others. In short, the psalmic presentation of 'homosociality...reinforces the hegemony of men over women'.[39] Yet she also asserts that there is potential for a recontextualization based on those very binaries although the binary oppositions represented in the psalms are problematic for feminist concerns and liberationist concerns, in general. She explains: 'A great number of psalms represent the voices of the oppressed and the marginalized. Both through individual suffering and through ancient Israel's national experience of exile and displacement, the psalms present a rich record of the perspectives of the "Other".'[40] In my view, this final observation has much to contribute to feminist thinking on the interpretation of the Psalter.

Looking Ahead in Feminist Psalter Study

Since feminist work on the psalms is at such an early developmental stage, I would like to suggest some ideas for future work. In a section of her book that discusses strategies for dealing with divine violence and theological logocentrism, especially in those texts described as 'prophetic pornography', Cheryl Exum advises that two effective strategies consist in 'looking for competing discourses' and conducting a 'systematic deconstructive reading of the texts in question'.[41] The two strategies are related, of course. The first regards competing discourses as traces of women's discourse that have not been completely erased and help to resist the claims of the dominant patriarchal–divine discourse. Exum writes that the traces of competing discourses help 'to uncover evidence of the woman's suppressed point of view in these texts'.[42]

The second focuses more generally on the disruption of binaries that structure the text. Exum explains: 'Deconstruction questions the fundamental logic of binary opposition (male/female, culture/nature, rational/emotional, objective/subjective) and staunchly refuses to privilege *either* side of an opposition, or violent hierarchy, over its opposite'.[43] This observation needs to be applied to the feminist study of the psalms because the disruption of the binaries upon which patriarchal discourse depends to legitimate its hegemony is a feminist move in its own right. Keeping in mind Kamionkowski's caveat about the staunchly binary nature of psalms discourse, I recommend the notion of linguistic subversion for future feminist psalm studies.

39. Kamionkowski, 'Psalms', p. 314.
40. Kamionkowski, 'Psalms', p. 320.
41. Cheryl Exum, *Plotted, Shot, and Painted: Cultural Representations of Biblical Women* (JSOTSup, 215; Sheffield: Sheffield Academic Press, 1996), pp. 125-27.
42. Exum, *Plotted, Shot, and Painted*, p. 127.
43. Exum, *Plotted, Shot, and Painted*, p. 128 (original emphasis).

There are three related primary observations about the psalms that qualify them as potentially subversive literature. It should be noted that most of these observations pertain especially to the genre of lament psalms. While many of the remarks offered here have applicability across genres, the issues are most immediately comprehensible if one considers them with lament psalms in mind.

First, as poetry, psalms are inherently non-linear discourses, a feature that is augmented by the fact that we are unable to provide an adequate description of their contexts. Psalms are not sustained discursive reflections on human existence or the cosmos or the human/divine relationship. They are an outpouring of metaphor, flashes of allusive images, and syntactic hodge-podges. The very structure of parallelism suggests an ongoing deferral of closure. On a formal level, it is nearly impossible to put this kind of open-endedness into the service of hegemonic demands. Of course, the psalms are not form without content, and much of the content is admittedly masculine, as critics like Clines, Brettler, and Kamionkowski emphasize. Still, it takes some work to make those connections because the formal structure of this literature does not surrender itself easily to such claims.

Second, the psalms are embodied discourses that find their *telos* in the 'truth' of *experience* rather than logocentric claims. From the beginning feminist thought has concerned itself with the notion of the body as a way of combating patriarchal insistence on objective truth, a truth that denied women's claims to alternate realities. Feminist theorists noted that men, white men in particular, rely on disembodied power and eschew truth claims that emerge from embodied knowing.[44] There are two studies on the psalms that address the issue of the body. Neither of them is specifically feminist, but both offer observations that could be mined fruitfully for feminist inquiry. Swenson's work has already been reviewed above. Speaking of lament psalms, she observes: '[T]hey are voices out of pain, not thoughts on pain or hypothetical ideas about pain management; they represent a sense of self that is not neatly divided body from mind from spirit from community…'[45] Her attention to the very visceral language of the psalms meshes well with feminism's epistemological commitment to embodiment.

Amy Cottrill's study of the construction of human subjectivity in the individual psalms of lament also has great feminist potential. Insofar as the female body (whether actual or symbolic) is the site where patriarchal prerogatives have been pressed, the potential of Cottrill's work should be obvious from the following statement:

44. Although there are differences in the ways each feminist theorist conceptualizes embodiment, all of them struggle to conceptualize the body in a way that resists essentialism and respects the integrity of the experienced body, as well as the body's political context and its relationship to power.

45. Swenson, *Living through Pain*, p. 11.

The [supplicant] employs a specific repertoire of imagery that characterizes the body as weakened, vulnerable, dependent, and without an effective mode of moral agency. The body rhetorically marks that site of the lamenter's public and private powerlessness, suffering, and incapacitation. This body discourse not only expresses profound suffering, however, but also negotiates social and relational power'.[46]

Furthermore, and of crucial importance for feminists, Cottrill demonstrates that the very embodiment of the psalms is a potent source of authenticity and personal power insofar as it effectively constructs a reality that demands response by the powerful.

Third, many of the lament psalms are polyphonic and, as such, resist the normative and hegemonic theological dogma of much of the rest of biblical discourse and its interrogators. My work on these psalms, while not explicitly feminist in orientation, has always struck me as trending in that direction. I used M.M. Bakhtin's notion of dialogism to challenge the monologic interpretations that historically had been a hallmark of psalms interpretation. Monologic formulations are particularly susceptible to logocentric abuse because they situate epistemological control in one voice. Bakhtinian linguistics requires some massaging to make it amenable to feminist concerns, but all the pieces are there. His notion of polyphony 'decenters patriarchal control...avoids the sovereign and authoritative, the dichotomous and binary... Bakhtin's insistence that...all construction is situational deprives the dominant angle from its claim to being natural and inevitable.'[47] Of course, Bakhtin demonstrated that *all* utterances are linguistic alloys, but I wanted to show how several lament psalms are explicitly dialogic, that is, composed of several voices, literally.[48] My linguistic analysis of dialogic psalms ultimately led to a consideration of the way the supplicant's voice challenges the hegemonic theological discourse of her interlocutor within the psalms, and serves as a countervoice to the broader canonical claims that overwhelm and silence the weaker voices in their midst.

I began this survey with the observation that little feminist work had been done on the Psalter. I also expressed little surprise at that fact given the dearth of feminine figures and issues in the psalms. I conclude on a much

46. Amy Cottrill, *Language, Power, and Identity in the Lament Psalms of the Individual* (New York: T. & T. Clark, 2008), p. 29.

47. Barbara Green, *Mikhail Bakhtin and Biblical Scholarship: An Introduction* (SBLSS, 38; Atlanta, GA: Society of Biblical Literature, 2000), p. 58.

48. Carleen Mandolfo, *God in the Dock: Dialogic Tension in the Psalms of Lament* (JSOTSup, 357; Sheffield: Sheffield Academic Press, 2002). Space constraints do not permit a demonstration of the dialogic structure of lament psalms, but see *God in the Dock*, pp. 35-36, for a chart that breaks down the voicing. On double-voiced discourse as women's discourse, see Athalya Brenner and Fokkelien van Dijk-Hemmes, *On Gendering Texts: Female and Male Voices in the Hebrew Bible* (Leiden: E.J. Brill, 1993), p. 27.

more hopeful note for the future of feminist criticism on the psalms. Some significant work has already been done, especially 'behind' and 'in front of' the text. I have outlined some directions for future feminist work on the Psalter that focuses on the internal dynamics of the texts, but also has potential for constructing realities outside itself with beneficial effects for real women.

The Book of Lamentations

Over the past ten years, scholarly activity on the book of Lamentations has noticeably increased. Interestingly, women have written the majority of the monographs[49] although few are explicitly feminist in orientation. Recently, Heath Thomas has chronicled feminist interest in the book of Lamentations and offered his own perspective. Thomas counts seven studies with explicitly feminist approaches or with significant interest in discussing feminist issues. Thomas notes that 'the issue of justice lay at the heart of the theology of Lamentations, and it is here that feminist approaches engage the book'.[50]

While I agree with Thomas that the issue of justice is at the heart of the poetic discourse of Lamentations, an additional element draws feminist attention. After all, as we saw above, relatively little feminist work has been done on the entirety of the psalms although many of those poems are centrally concerned with justice. Thus what has drawn feminist readers to the book of Lamentations has to do with the prominent place of 'Daughter Zion', the city of Jerusalem figured as woman, as well as daughter, wife, and mother (Lam. 1–2 and once in Lam. 4.22). Of course, the book of Lamentations is neither the first text in which Daughter Zion is featured in the Hebrew Bible, nor is it the first place that feminists have turned their attention to her. Daughter Zion, sometimes known as Lady Jerusalem, is a favorite trope among many of the especially pre-exilic prophetic writers, and has become a popular feminist topic.[51]

49. See T. Linafelt, *Surviving Lamentations* (Chicago: University of Chicago Press, 2000); F.W. Dobbs-Allsopp, *Lamentations* (Louisville, KY: Westminster/John Knox Press, 2002); A. Berlin, *Lamentations: A Commentary* (Louisville, KY: Westminster/ John Knox Press, 2002); N. Lee, *Lyrics of Lament* (Minneapolis: Fortress Press, 2010); K. O'Connor, *Lamentations and the Tears of the World* (Maryknoll, NY: Orbis Books, 2002); and C. Mandolfo, *Daughter Zion Talks Back to the Prophets* (Atlanta, GA: Society of Biblical Literature, 2007).

50. H.A. Thomas, 'Justice at the Crossroads: The Book of Lamentations and Feminist Discourse', in Andrew Sloane (ed.), *Tamar's Tears: Evangelical Engagements with Feminist Old Testament Hermeneutics* (Eugene, OR: Pickwick Press, 2012), pp. 246-73.

51. In Hosea, Isaiah, Jeremiah, and Ezekiel, Daughter Zion is commonly referred to in conjunction with the prophets' use of the marriage metaphor, in which Yhwh is the husband and the city of Jerusalem is personified as the (adulterous) wife. Because so

Since gendered Jerusalem is also centrally featured in the book of Lamentations, it is not surprising that feminists eventually turned their attention to her portrayal there. The book begins, 'How lonely sits the city that once was full of people! How like a *widow* she has become, *she* that was great among the nations!' (Lam. 1.1). The city is primarily referred to as 'Daughter Zion' (see Lam. 1.6; 2.1), but the appellations 'Daughter Jerusalem' (Lam. 2.13) and 'virgin Daughter Judah' (Lam. 1.15) also appear, in addition to feminine pronouns applied to the city. Several times she is also figured as a mother. In Lamentations 1, the narrator refers to 'her children' as going into exile (vv. 16, 18), and in Lamentations 2 she states, in her own voice, 'Those whom I bore and reared my enemy has destroyed' (v. 22).

In short, the explicitly feminist work on Lamentations has concentrated on the figuration of Daughter Zion. Most of these studies tease out the implications of this metaphor for women, ancient and contemporary. While many commentators agree that there is little redeemable in the figuration of Zion within the prophetic marriage metaphor, the conclusions are more mixed regarding the feminized representation of the city in Lamentations. Allowing for varying degrees of nuance, most feminist commentators read Daughter Zion in Lamentations 1–2 as an empowering figure or, conversely, as detrimental to the feminist ideal of female subjectivity.

B.B. Kaiser was one of the first to attend specifically to the image of Daughter Zion in the book of Lamentations.[52] She assumes that most biblical literature is authored by men, but she also suggests that sometimes these male authors adopt a female 'persona'. She explains: 'Although the female *person* undoubtedly had a secondary place within the cult, the female *persona* played a vital role in religious expressions of sorrow'.[53] Her goal is akin to the pioneering generation of feminist Bible scholars in that she is interested in *rehabilitating* the role of women in the Bible, and hence ancient Israel. While she does not feel justified in saying that women were directly responsible for text production, she finds solace in the notion that the experience of women was valued enough to be co-opted by male authors for specific and important purposes. Kaiser states: 'In Lamentations 1 the

much of this literature burns with graphic (albeit metaphoric) violence directed at Daughter Zion, the term 'porno-prophetics' has been coined in reference to it. In these texts, YHWH accuses the 'wife' of 'whoring' with other nations/gods and calls on the nations to be the instruments of spousal–divine wrath against the wife. As a result, Daughter Zion is metaphorically ravaged and brutalized with her 'husband's' consent (see especially Jer. 2–3 and Ezek. 16 and 23).

52. Barbara Bakke Kaiser, 'Poet as "Female Impersonator": The Image of Daughter Zion as Speaker in Biblical Poems of Suffering', *JR* 67 (1987), pp. 164-82. For her notion of 'persona' she draws on the work of William F. Lanahan, 'The Speaking Voice in the Book of Lamentations', *JBL* 93 (1974), pp. 41-49.

53. Kaiser, 'Poet as "Female Impersonator"', p. 182 (original emphasis).

Hebrew poet assumes the persona of menstruant Jerusalem, and in Lamentations 2 the poet becomes Mother Zion bitterly confronting the Murderer of her children… [T]he poet chooses the female persona to express the intensity of his grief… In a sense he becomes a "female impersonator".'[54] One of the hallmarks of Kaiser's work is that she is the first feminist scholar to attend to the voice of Daughter Zion as a *female* voice.

Deryn Guest objects to Kaiser's conclusions and is the only commentator that negatively appraises the female figuration of Zion in the book of Lamentations. She asserts that the metaphor itself is damaging, so long as it is the recipient of the violence inflicted by the deity. She wants to expose

> the strategy whereby women suffer physical affliction for the sake of typically male needs/fears/purposes, while men themselves evade the public glare of scrutiny. This tactic is evident in more than one Hebrew bible narrative, but pervades the image of Zion/Woman in Lamentations, facilitating an evasion of male responsibility and shunting the brunt of the blame onto a personified woman; and one cannot ignore the continuing effects this has upon contemporary readers.[55]

Her argument makes it clear that she sees little difference, qualitatively, between the treatment of Woman Jerusalem in the prophets and in Lamentations, 'for while the prophets threatened abuse in terrifyingly vivid detail, the book of Lamentations sees the fulfillment of those threats'.[56]

My monograph on Lamentations supports Guest's aversion to the negative treatment of the Woman in Lamentations. Yet I also argue that there is a crucial difference between the Woman's presentation in Lamentations and her presentations in the prophetic books.[57] This difference mainly has to do with the aspect of 'voicing'. In the prophets, Daughter Zion is given little or no subjective position. The fact that she is given an unfiltered voice in Lamentations 1–2, especially Lamentations 2, is of great consequence.[58] I draw on the work of philosopher Hilde Nelson to 'examine how the woman reconfigures the prophets' own words to construct a counterstory that better reflects her experiences from her point of view'.[59] A prime example of my intertextual reading occurs in the assessment of Zion's speech in Lam. 2.20-22.

---

54. Kaiser, 'Poet as "Female Impersonator"', p. 166.

55. Deryn Guest, 'Hiding behind the Naked Women in Lamentations: A Recriminative Response', *BibInt* 7 (1999), pp. 413-48 (428).

56. Guest, 'Hiding behind the Naked Women in Lamentations', p. 413.

57. Carleen Mandolfo, *Daughter Zion Talks Back to the Prophets: A Dialogic Theology of the Book of Lamentations* (SBLSS; Atlanta, GA: Society of Biblical Literature; Leiden: E.J. Brill, 2007).

58. See especially Mandolfo, *Daughter Zion Talks Back*, pp. 79-102.

59. Mandolfo, *Daughter Zion Talks Back*, p. 79. See also Hilde Nelson, *Damaged Identities, Narrative Repair* (Ithaca, NY: Cornell University Press, 2001).

At the end of this fiercely impassioned lament, Zion explicitly contradicts YHWH's construction of her and turns the prophetic rhetoric back against her accuser when she states: '*Those whom I cherished/formed and reared* my enemy has consumed' (v. 22). No ambiguity here about who 'my enemy' is... The prophets and God enact a false construction of Zion's body. It is a body of lust and treachery, not a body that births and nurtures children; but by accusing him with imagery evocative of the sacrificial crimes of which he accused her, she has commuted the moral liability as construed in the prophetic texts and has wrested back some of her moral agency by transforming YHWH's sexualized and violent portrait of her into one that powerfully evokes bereft maternity, as well as common humanity.[60]

Another feminist scholar who focuses on voicing is Zhe Li, who draws on the work of S. Goitein and A. Brenner and F. van Dijk-Hemmes. She is interested in finding traces of women's speech in biblical texts.[61] In the end, however, she does not claim to have proven a woman's voice in Lamentations 1 but finds a female persona that quite plausibly retains 'traces of the tradition of women's songs' in the Bible. In her view, these traces were, however, assimilated into an androcentric text in the canonization process.[62]

While not presenting a strictly feminist study, Nancy Lee also attends to voicing concerns in her fascinating and interdisciplinary study on the books of Jeremiah and Lamentations.[63] She examines mourning rituals across cultures and notes the unique role of women in these rites. This focus leads her to identify a female voice not only in Lamentations, but also in Jeremiah, a voice she calls 'Jerusalem's poet'.[64] She admits that the evidence for women's *actual* voices in Jeremiah or Lamentations is sparse, but she insists that this fact

---

60. Mandolfo, *Daughter Zion Talks Back*, pp. 99-100 (original emphasis).

61. Zhe Li, 'In a Different Voice: A Biblical Case of Women Singers in Lamentations 1', in Yeong Mee Lee and Yoo Yoon Jong (eds.), *Mapping and Engaging the Bible in Asian Cultures* (Korea: Christian Literature Society of Korea, 2008), pp. 251-63. See also Athalya Brenner and Fokkelien Van Dijk-Hemmes, *On Gendering Texts: Male and Female Voices in the Hebrew Bible* (Leiden: E.J. Brill, 1993); and Shelomo Goitein, 'Women as Creators of Biblical Genres', *Proof* 8 (1998), pp. 1-33.

62. Zhe Li, 'In a Different Voice', p. 262.

63. Nancy C. Lee, *The Singers of Lamentations: Cities Under Siege, from Ur to Jerusalem to Sarajevo* (BibInt Series; Leiden: E.J. Brill, 2002). For a brief summary of her monograph and other pertinent works, see also N. Lee, 'The Singers of Lamentations: (A)Scribing (De)Claiming Poets and Prophets', in Nancy Lee and Carleen Mandolfo (eds.), *Lamentations in Ancient and Contemporary Cultural Contexts* (Atlanta, GA: Society of Biblical Literature, 2008), pp. 33-46.

64. Lee, 'Singers of Lamentation', p. 34.

should not shut the door to more subtle and hidden possibilities. The woman's voice or perspective in Lamentations goes well beyond women's traditional mourning practice of the dirge, and beyond the lament genre's usual concerns. This voice helps spark a dialogical debate in *both books* about God's justice in the context and is very striking in terms of *challenging* both traditional theology and implicitly, traditional gender roles in Israel.[65]

In her commentary on Lamentations, Kathleen O'Connor shares with Lee and myself an interest in voicing as a means of ultimately challenging traditional theological and anthropological interpretations of the biblical book. O'Connor stresses that on the whole the book is far more concerned with Zion's suffering than with her 'sins', although she admits that in Lamentations 1, the narrator suggests that the Woman got what she deserved. Still, 'the immediacy of her speech as a victim gives her the moral authority of the survivor and undermines the narrator's perspective'.[66] In contrast stands the scathing language of Lamentations 2. O'Connor writes: 'Although the narrator [also] dominates the poem, his words concentrate on Zion's suffering. But now he no longer speaks as a distant observer; in this chapter he is an overwrought participant in Zion's unbearable reality. Again he addresses us instead of God, but it is God's involvement that obsesses him.'[67]

Most of the studies rehearsed so far have been, more or less, illustrative of the feminist tendency to read with a 'hermeneutic of suspicion'. That is, in theological terms they have been content, or even eager, to read *against* the deity and thus also against the Church's inclination to engage in theodic justifications of biblical violence. A couple of exceptions to this trend are still rightly considered feminist studies. The first is that of LeAnn Flesher in the *IVP Women's Commentary*, an evangelical commentary that examines the text from a 'hermeneutic of faith'.[68] Her position is that, as divine revelation, the book of Lamentations is authoritative as it stands. That does not mean, however, that Flesher ignores the language of complaint as a hallmark of the book and of Daughter Zion's speech, in particular. For Flesher, reading *with* Daughter Zion (presumably against God?) is not a subversive act, but rather an act of faithfulness because it is a discursive strategy that is modeled by the book itself.

---

65. Lee, 'Singers of Lamentation', p. 38 (original emphasis).

66. Kathleen M. O'Connor, *Lamentations and the Tears of the World* (Maryknoll, NY: Orbis Books, 2002), p. 18.

67. O'Connor, *Lamentations*, p. 31.

68. LeAnn Flesher, 'Lamentations', in Catherine Clark Kroeger and Mary J. Evans (eds.), *IVP Women's Bible Commentary* (Downers Grove, IL: Intervarsity Press, 2001), pp. 392-95.

A second example comes from Heath Thomas. He asserts that based on its own testimony Lamentations affirms God's just activity in relation to his people. More specifically, the suffering in Lamentations serves an eschatological purpose. He explains: '[A] variety of texts in the OT engage the theology of Lamentations and affirm that God is in control of his people, that he loves them, and that the punitive actions on display in Lamentations must be understood as only a moment in the full-sweep of Israel's history'. Thomas also suggests, however, that it is in the very nature of biblical complaint literature that God's justice is made plainest because it is there that humans are given the power to question God and demonstrate their firm belief in his ultimate justice.[69]

Difficult to fit into any of the broad categories referenced above is the work of Christl Maier. Her work is neither explicitly feminist, nor does it focus solely on Lamentations.[70] She wants to understand how throughout the canon the gendered figuration of Jerusalem creates a new image of the city, one that ultimately emerges 'as a religious symbol of salvation'.[71] In addition to tradition history and source and redaction critical methods she relies on French sociologist Henre Lefebvre's work on spatiality. She understands Lamentations 1–2 as key postexilic texts in the chronological development of Zion as a symbol. On her way to formulating her larger points, she makes a few feminist-friendly observations that resonate with the commentators already reviewed. For instance, she notes that

> the female body in Lamentations 1 works as a *site* and *sign* of imagination…
> On the one hand, the wounded body of Jerusalem…offers an explanation for
> the catastrophe: God overpowered like an enemy sacks a city… God's violent
> oppression contradicts the preexilic idea that the city has been chosen as
> divine dwelling place and, thus, is sacred… The wounded body of Jerusalem
> as a *sign*, however, signifies resistance against the hopeless situation in its
> unwillingness to surrender.[72]

Thus, according to Maier, the symbol of the stricken female body forces interpreters to grant agency to otherwise dehumanized victims of violence.

It should now be obvious why so much more explicitly feminist work has been done on Lamentations than the book of Psalms. Daughter Zion serves as a useful trope not only for ancient (probably male) authors who were

---

69. H. Thomas, 'Justice at the Crossroads'. Before offering his own reading of Lamentations, Thomas provides the most thorough review and analysis of feminist work on Lamentations to date.

70. Christl Maier, *Daughter Zion, Mother Zion: Gender, Space, and the Sacred in Ancient Israel* (Minneapolis: Fortress Press, 2008).

71. Maier, *Daughter Zion*, p. 4.

72. Maier, *Daughter Zion*, p. 152 (original emphasis).

struggling to understand the theological consequences of the devastations of the Assyrian (721 BCE) and Babylonian (587 BCE) invasions; but as it turns out this metaphor can be heuristically deployed with equally potent effect by feminist scholars who have sought to subvert traditional hermeneutical practices that side with the deity to the detriment of women.

Concluding Comments for Future Feminist Study

The books of Psalms and Lamentations evidence many formal similarities, but that has not resulted in a similar history of feminist readings. Feminist study of the psalms is marked by a lack of sustained and rigorous analysis. The absence of female characters has precluded traditional feminist literary analysis as well as any attempt to reconstruct the historical lives of women. The foregoing review makes clear that feminist psalms study would do well to take an entirely different tack. Future work should pay attention to the formal features of psalms as non-linear, embodied, and polyphonic discourses that undermine hegemonic, disembodied, and monolithic discourses with a tendency to overpower and to marginalize 'other' interpretations of the divine–human relationship. Such discourses do not reinforce patriarchy, monarchy, and domination which should be of great interest to feminist interpreters.

With regard to Lamentations, several feminist readers note that the book presents us with an embodied, gendered symbol in the figure of Daughter Zion. This figure poses a challenge to other scriptural (mostly prophetic) interpretations of the divine–Israel relationship that often serve as archetypes for male–female relationships in which sinful disobedience and violent punishment are justified and reinforced through the prophetic marriage metaphor.

In sum, feminist interpretation on the book of Psalms, in particular, would benefit from thinking 'outside the box' and exploiting more deftly the current trends in feminist theory. It is unlikely that female authorship, for example, will ever be settled conclusively, but methodologies focused on form over content (or context, for that matter) may offer promising insights into the feminist potential of this inspiring literature.

10

LOOKING IN THROUGH THE LATTICE:
FEMINIST AND OTHER GENDER-CRITICAL READINGS
OF THE SONG OF SONGS*

Fiona C. Black

It should not be surprising that a biblical book ostensibly about love and sex, with a woman as protagonist, has garnered considerable attention from feminist scholars. For the last thirty years, feminist work on the Song has been energetic, multi-vocal, and prolific. Until fairly recently, it has also largely been positive, with celebrations such as these ringing out about the protagonist:[1]

> [She] stands out in biblical literature as a woman who insists on her right to initiate love, to feel, to enjoy, and to explore the power of her sexuality. She feels good about herself and basks in her beloved's desire for her.[2]

> The amorous Shulamite is the first woman to be sovereign before her loved one. Through such a hymn to the love of the married couple, Judaism asserts itself as a first liberation of women.[3]

Her relationship receives equal praise as mutual, egalitarian, and a source of inspiration for contemporary readers:

> Remarkably, the Song seems to describe a non-sexist world, and thus it can act for us as an antidote to some of the themes of biblical patriarchy.[4]

---

* This essay is dedicated to Athalya Brenner and J. Cheryl Exum, whose works on the Song figure prominently here because they impacted feminist readings in many important and exciting ways. Their thought-provoking and dynamic studies of the Song inspired my own (and doubtless those of many others) and contributed greatly to my love of this text.

1. The woman in the Song is nameless and consequently does not receive a proper name in my analysis. The 'Shulammite' of 7.1 is not a proper name, nor is it an identifying appellation.

2. Renita J. Weems, 'Song of Songs', in Carol A. Newsom and Sharon H. Ringe (eds.), *The Woman's Bible Commentary* (Louisville, KY: Westminster/John Knox Press, 1992), pp. 164-66 (166).

3. Julia Kristeva, 'A Holy Madness, She and He', in Kristeva, *Tales of Love* (trans. L. Roudiez; New York: Columbia University Press, 1982), pp. 83-100 (99).

In this setting, there is no male dominance, no female subordination, and no stereotyping of either sex:[5]

> [It] advocates balance in female and male relationships, urging mutuality not dominance, interdependability not enmity...[6]

More recently, however, readers have questioned this positive evaluation of the woman in the Song and returned to matters of autonomy, body imagery, and sexuality, pondering the gender politics of the book anew. The matter of just how liberated a text and a protagonist we have in the Song of Songs is only a point of departure. As has been the case in biblical studies globally, feminist work on the Song has also begun to interact with more recent developments in gender criticism, eventually beginning to direct a critical eye at feminism itself.

This article explores the themes and strategies of feminist and gender-critical work on the Song, mapping the field as it has developed over the years.[7] I investigate four major and interrelated themes: authorship and canon, female autonomy, sexuality, and the body. Theoretical positions under consideration also occupy a wide range, including sociological, socio-historical, literary (poetics), feminist/gender and queer theories, psycho-analytical and cultural studies, broadly conceived. I conclude by floating directions for future research, both emerging from previous analyses and responding to the needs of a changing sub-discipline of gender and cultural criticism.

Approaches, Rule-Changers, and Allegorists

It is plausible to see Phyllis Trible's ground-breaking and extremely influential chapter in *God and the Rhetoric of Sexuality*, published in 1978, as the

---

4.   Marcia Falk, *Love Lyrics from the Bible: A Translation and Literary Study of the Song of Songs* (Sheffield: Almond Press, 1982).

5.   Phyllis Trible, *God and the Rhetoric of Sexuality* (Philadelphia: Fortress Press, 1978), p. 161.

6.   Weems, 'Song of Songs', p. 160.

7.   I use *gynocentric* as a general term to denote criticism from all time frames that is written with the female protagonist as its central concern and, often, with the perspective and experience of women readers in mind. *Feminist* is used in this essay to denote feminist biblical criticism—work that is self-consciously identifying itself as using a feminist hermeneutic to read the text. It is limited to the context of biblical scholarship (with one exception: Julia Kristeva, 'A Holy Madness'), which has been primarily influenced by second-wave feminism. Finally, I use *gender-critical* as an inclusive term to describe all work with an interest in gender that has been illuminated by gender-critical tools (feminist and beyond), e.g., post-feminist, masculinist, queer.

starting point for feminist work on the Song.[8] Indeed, Trible's work forms an important bridge[9] between interpretations of old, which wholly embraced the allegorical traditions—but which might not have been entirely comfortable with them—and later feminist writers, who would disavow allegory and eventually move away from any kind of theological reading.[10] Trible's

8.   One should consult J. Cheryl Exum, 'Developing Strategies of Feminist Criticism/Developing Strategies for Commentating the Song of Songs', in David J.A. Clines and Stephen D. Moore (eds.), *Auguries: The Jubilee Volume of the Sheffield Department of Biblical Studies* (JSOTSup, 269; Sheffield: Sheffield Academic Press, 1998), pp. 206-49, and Athalya Brenner's 'On Feminist Criticism of the Song of Songs', in Athalya Brenner (ed.), *A Feminist Companion to the Song of Songs* (FCB, 1; Sheffield: Sheffield Academic Press, 1993), pp. 28-37, for reviews of feminist work on the Song. Brenner's entire collection of essays, in fact, is set up as a history of research, and serious readers should consult it and the follow-up volume: Athalya Brenner and Carole Fontaine (eds.), *The Song of Songs* (FCB, 6; Sheffield: Sheffield Academic Press, 2000). For general histories of Song criticism (not explicitly pertaining to women's writing, but tracing the Song's movement from allegorical to modern readings), see Marvin Pope's lengthy introduction in his commentary, *Song of Songs* (AB, 7C; Garden City, NY: Doubleday, 1977).

9.   Thus, Trible's work is more than purely descriptive (*pace* Exum, 'Developing Strategies', p. 213). She does share theological impulses familiar to allegory, but she injects an innovative desire to contextualize the Bible for her time and place.

10.   Space does not permit us to begin at the beginning, which is with a tradition of pre-modern women writers on the Bible; see Gerda Lerner's 'One Thousand Years of Feminist Bible Criticism', in Lerner, *The Creation of Feminist Consciousness* (Oxford: Oxford University Press, 1993), pp. 138-66. This is unfortunate, since the scholarly record is shamefully lacking in its representation of female writers; see, for example, Richard A. Norris, *The Song of Songs: Interpreted by Early Christian and Medieval Commentators* (Grand Rapids, MI: Eerdmans, 2003). Though Genesis was the preferred choice of text for early women mystics and scholars, some, such as Clare of Assisi, wrote on the Song; indeed, some did so quite extensively; see, e.g., Teresa of Avila, *Meditations on the Song of Songs* and her *Life* in Kieran Kavanagh and Otilio Rodriguez (eds.), *The Collected Works of St Teresa of Avila*, I–III (trans. Kieran Kavanagh and Otilio Rodriguez; Washington, DC: ICS Publications, 1976–85). In all cases, these writers were guided by allegorical interpretations, in which the protagonist served as the soul or the Church, and Solomon as Christ. Allegorical parameters, however, were often stretched, as with the case of Teresa of Avila, who managed to subvert censors' expectations and concerns by veiling her brilliant theological insights as specialized women's discourse. Later women writers (in the eighteenth and nineteenth centuries) were also drawn to the Song, yet they seemed often to refrain from commenting on its erotic nature; see Elizabeth Cady Stanton, 'The Song of Solomon', in Brenner (ed.), *A Feminist Companion to the Song of Songs*, p. 55; and for a discussion on Mary Cornwallis and Sarah Trimmer, see Marion Ann Taylor and Christiana de Groot (eds.), *Recovering Nineteenth-Century Women Interpreters of the Bible* (Atlanta, GA: Society of Biblical Literature, 2007), especially the articles by Weir and Taylor. For all groups, it seems as though the Song's content served both as a source both of attraction (since it modeled the seeker's pursuit of God) and of anxiety.

thesis is that the Song should be held in readerly tension with the two creation accounts in Genesis, where, in the first, there is a harmonious view of the creation of humankind, but in the second (Gen. 2.4b–3.24), creation goes awry and the man, Adam, begins to dominate. In this process, the celebration of Eros that the initial creation account contains is badly perverted. Through the Song, however, Eros is redeemed, since the book shows an idealized relationship, restored by virtue of its mutuality and freedom from domination. In making a link between the two books, Trible's canonical interests follow other Christian readers[11] who identify the mismatch between the human relations in the creation accounts and those in the ideal world of the Song. Trible's work also hearkens back to allegorical interpretations, in which the tradition explores how earthly relationships could elucidate human–divine ones; they may be broken, but with God's grace, they are repairable.

The unique contribution for our purposes is Trible's gynocentric perspective. The reading draws metaphorical parallels between the Song and Genesis. For the Song, the woman's experience and her relation to her lover provide the key contrast to the primordial couple. Though thought-provoking, Trible's study requires, it has been suggested, a more 'sophisticated poetics', in that it glosses over some of the metaphorical nuances of the Song.[12] On the other hand, some have noted that her observations of the Song's synaesthetic qualities are meritorious, and, even more significantly, that her interpretation shows courage for its time.[13] Retrospectively and from a feminist perspective, it was significant that pioneering feminist scholars made the decision to reconsider a familiar connection between Genesis and the Song through a gynocentric lens. Where theological readings—especially Christian allegorical ones—interpreted relations between the two books in the typical creation–fall–redemption paradigm, Trible's introduction of the woman's voice as predominant was innovative, even iconoclastic. It did not exactly disrupt the typical theological paradigm, but it suggested radical gender- and literary-critical possibilities for Christian theology and biblical studies. It was a bold new way to focus literary readings of the biblical text.

Despite its boldness, Trible's reading of the Song still sought to smooth over or correct biblical problems of patriarchy. It is highly plausible that her innovative, but largely *theological* reading of the Song—in some ways

---

11. For a list, see Francis Landy, *Paradoxes of Paradise: Identity and Difference in the Song of Songs* (Bible and Literature, 7; Sheffield: Almond Press, 1983), pp. 183-84.

12. Landy, *Paradoxes of Paradise*, p. 185. Later Landy tempered his criticism of Trible in 'Mishneh Torah: A Response', in Brenner (ed.), *A Feminist Companion to the Song of Songs*, pp. 260-65.

13. So Landy, 'Mishneh Torah'.

echoing traditional readings of the book—prompted Carol Meyers and Athalya Brenner to address and ultimately to disavow theological readings of the Song, historical and contemporary. Meyers uses allegorical readings as a departure for her own work, asserting that the 'rise of critical biblical scholarship rescued the Song from the fanciful twists and turns of spiritualized biblical interpretation'.[14] Yet, she observes that some similarities with the past remain. Where she is willing to attend to the Song's erotic content and presentation of the body, for instance, Meyers finds that most modern readings are 'as unwilling to explore the use of physical imagery as...the traditional exegetes'.[15] In a similar vein, Brenner challenges modern allegorical interpretations because they obscure major interpretational issues in the Song, such as its plot (or lack thereof) and gynocentrism, and they impose an absent theocentrism.[16] Brenner states unequivocally that the book shows not gender mutuality, but female superiority.[17] Allegory 'perverts' and 'subverts' this situation since it 'requires a presentation of...[the woman] as submissive and inferior'.[18] She also observes the 'double change of focus' in allegory, from female to male and from human to divine, and thus asserts that 'the transmutation of gynocentrism into theocentrism in allegory passes through androcentrism'.[19]

It is doubtful that Meyers or Brenner would argue that modern secular scholarship is able to escape bias or be completely objective.[20] Rather, their complaints are with the *particular* effects of past scholarship's biases: they ignore imagery, impose a plot, and obscure the text's gynocentrism. What is not entirely clear, however, is whether Brenner's and Meyers's readings indicate a perception of a 'primary level' of meaning, and, by extension,

---

14.   Carol Meyers, 'Gender Imagery in the Song of Songs', in Brenner (ed.), *A Feminist Companion to the Song of Songs*, pp. 197-213 (197) (repr. from 1986).

15.   Meyers, 'Gender Imagery', p. 199.

16.   Athalya Brenner, 'To See Is to Assume: Whose Love Is Celebrated in the Song of Songs?', *BibInt* 1 (1993), pp. 265-84 (265).

17.   Brenner, 'To See', p. 273.

18.   Brenner, 'To See', p. 274.

19.   Brenner, 'To See', p. 274.

20.   Although many follow Meyers's and Brenner's lead, some feminist biblical scholars explicitly write on theological themes, or at least on the intersections between biblical studies and theology, e.g., Jonneke Bekkenkamp, 'Into another Scene of Choices: The Theological Value of the Song of Songs', in Brenner and Fontaine (eds.), *The Song of Songs*, pp. 55-89. Also, feminist writers have recently returned to allegory, not to employ it but to analyze it; see Jane Barr, 'Luis de Leon and the Song of Songs', in Brenner and Fontaine (eds.), *The Song of Songs*, pp. 130-41; Fiona C. Black, 'Unlikely Bedfellows: Allegorical and Feminist Readings of Song of Songs 7.1-8', in Brenner and Fontaine (eds.), *The Song of Songs*, pp. 104-29. Allegory also makes an appearance in queer readings; see below.

imply there is a (single?) correct way to interpret the Song's contents. This is an issue because feminist readings, for the most part, take a stance that is *corrective* to prior readings, and assume a 'critical' perspective that purports to replace 'spiritualized' (so Meyers) readings. This pioneering feminist work, however, does not generally allow for polyvalence in meaning, nor does it acknowledge that decisions about many features, such as recognition or denial of plot and determination of imagery, are readerly constructs. Such matters have become important as feminist study of the Song has developed and eventually has come to include other gender-critical interests as well.

Woman Authors and Female Culture

The gynocentrism of the text, as elaborated in early feminist work by Trible and Brenner, prompted an important thread in these initial years of feminist scholarship on the Song, namely, investigation into the probability of female authorship. As Brenner points out, the idea did not originate with feminist readers, but with S.D. Goitein, who suggested the possibility in an article penned in 1957.[21] It has primarily been Brenner, however, who has investigated the idea and contextualized it for feminist study of the Song. Brenner sums up the matter thus: 'There is virtual consent among scholars today that some, at the very least, of the poetry of the SoS should probably be attributed to female perspectives or even authorship. Hence, the text promotes opportunities for discussing female culture, its reclamation, and the affinities of the SoS with other female poems in the Bible...'[22]

Since, as all eventually admit, the question of female authorship is not provable, what is really at stake, for Brenner and others, is the idea of a feminine or gynocentric space. In other words, the question is whether the book reflects the cultural traditions of women. Important work in this area, by scholars such as Brenner, Meyers, Fokkelien van Dijk-Hemmes, and Jonneke Bekkenkamp, explores the social world of the Israelite woman and finds in certain song traditions an indication of women's culture.[23] The Song,

---

21. Reprinted in S.D. Goitein, 'The Song of Songs: A Female Composition', in Brenner (ed.), *A Feminist Companion to the Song of Songs*, pp. 58-66. Goitein observes that the sensibility of the book is feminine, that its worldview, themes and utterances clearly reflect feminine voice and interests.

22. Brenner, 'On Feminist Criticism', p. 28.

23. Eventually, Brenner and van Dijk-Hemmes joined forces in *On Gendering Texts: Female and Male Voices in the Hebrew Bible* (Leiden: E.J. Brill, 1993), labeling certain texts 'M' and 'F', the idea being that many texts reflect male or female interests. Their book also explores the possibility that the gender of readers can influence the determination of 'M' or 'F' for a given text, and that, in fact, a reader's gender can actually

by virtue of its inclusion of emotional perspectives, its (veiled) treatment of eroticism, the location of inspiration in daily life, and the fact that it is imagery-laden, lyrical, and addresses other women, is strongly suggestive as a repository for female cultural ideas and experience.[24] In addition, several texts clearly indicate a woman's perspective (e.g. 1.2-6; 3.1-4; 5.1-7, 10-16).

While Brenner and van Dijk-Hemmes work on genre and style, Meyers reaches similar evaluations of the Song as gynocentric space by focusing on its imagery. She posits that the images, as typically masculine figurations, when used of women can be read as locating power or privilege in the female realm. Thus, Meyers paints a picture of premonarchic Israel as a world with gender-balanced expressions of mutual intimacy.[25] In her analysis, the Song is not a 'chance aberration',[26] but, as a 'product of domestic life', it represents the miraculous survival of 'the cultural expression of female power in early Israel'.[27] It is also redemptive, as Meyers states: 'Luckily for feminists, who often despair of discovering meaningful material in the man's world of the official canon, a single biblical book has preserved this non-public world...'[28]

In sum, Brenner's claim that there is a 'virtual consent among scholars today' regarding female authorship is perhaps no longer as true in current scholarship as it may have been at the time of her writing it. Or rather, it may be true that some or most readers share this observation, but it is also true that they have ceased writing about it. Longer lasting has been the interest in female culture.[29] Yet in general, interest in the Song has shifted in

manipulate the perception of gender interests in biblical material. It is unfortunate that there has not been much serious engagement with this reading strategy in subsequent work on the Song, since the authors' efforts are a crucial step in tracing the lineage of both reconstructions of Hebrew Bible female culture and of gendered readings of the Song. Brenner continues this work in her important *The Intercourse of Knowledge: On Gendering Desire and 'Sexuality' in the Hebrew Bible* (Leiden: E.J. Brill, 1997).

24. Jonneke Bekkenkamp and Fokkelien van Dijk-Hemmes, 'The Canon of the Old Testament and Women's Cultural Traditions', in Brenner (ed.), *A Feminist Companion to the Song of Songs*, pp. 67-85 (79).

25. This proposal is based on her analysis of the images and on her observations about other gender peculiarities of the Song (such as the predominance of the female voice, the use of the phrase, *bet 'em*, and the presence of a 'folk culture' in the universality of the Song's love language).

26. Carol Meyers, *Discovering Eve: Ancient Israelite Women in Context* (Oxford: Oxford University Press, 1988), p. 196.

27. Meyers, *Discovering Eve*, p. 180.

28. Meyers, 'Gender Imagery', p. 212.

29. See, e.g., Robin C. McCall, '"Most Beautiful among Women": Feminist/ Womanist Contributions to Reading the Song of Songs', *Review and Expositor* 105 (2008), pp. 417-33; Melissa Raphael, '"Refresh Me with Apples, for I Am Faint with Love" (Song of Songs 2.5): Jewish Feminism, Mystical Theology and the Sexual

feminist work to other types of gender-related critiques of sexuality, sexual autonomy, and the body. In short, current feminist work tends to explore more reader-related matters rather than historical questions about authorship and original setting.

Body Imagery in the Song of Songs

One such reader-related matter is the imagery that describes the body in the Song. The descriptions bring the body together with a collection of natural, military, and architectural features in ways that, for first-time and habitual readers alike, are surprising, perhaps shocking. In commentaries, scholars usually debate the sense of a particular image, arguing for an interpretation that makes sense in their greater understanding of the Song as love poetry. Generally, interpreters maintain that those who are not able to appreciate the imagery as beautiful and pleasing have missed the point, or worse, are literal-minded. For instance, Michael Fox comments on Song 4.4: 'The incongruity is so great that there is, to be sure, the risk of losing many readers, who may find the image so abrasive, they never get around to sensing how the tower fits harmoniously into the atmosphere the image creates'.[30]

This difficulty in interpreting the images has implications for the matter of gender: figured in an erotic context and employed as part of the language of love, both lovers describe each other's bodies as part of the expression of their mutual desire. The descriptions usually appear in a series of poetic forms named by scholars as *wasfs* after their counterparts in Arabic poetry.[31] There are, however, some important differences between each lover's figurations. First, the woman's body is described many more times than the man's, which appears rarely. His descriptions of her draw heavily on dynamic images of nature. They are sometimes extremely intimate, and appear, on at least one occasion, to present the woman's body for the scrutiny of an assembled group of men. By contrast, the woman's description seems to be uttered as a means of describing her lover (whom she admires and seeks) to a group of women. Her images are more static or statuesque, and her perspective seems removed. Unsurprisingly, therefore, these texts

Imaginary', in Lisa Isherwood (ed.), *Good News of the Body: Sexual Theology and Feminism* (Washington Square, NY: New York University Press, 2000), pp. 54-72; Yael Almog, '"Flowing Myrrh upon the Handles of the Bolt": Bodily Border, Social Norms and their Transgression in the Song of Songs', *BibInt* 18 (2010), pp. 251-63.

30.   Michael Fox, *The Song of Songs and the Ancient Egyptian Love Songs* (Madison, WI: University of Wisconsin Press, 1985), pp. 226-27.

31.   Marcia Falk, 'The *wasf*', in Brenner (ed.), *A Feminist Companion to the Song of Songs*, pp. 225-33.

did not escape the notice of feminist scholars. As Brenner notes: '[T]he subject [the *waṣf*]…affords the opportunity for discussing matters of form, author's intent, reader's involvement, points of view, imagery, gender differentials, authorship, and so forth'.[32] Despite such an enticing challenge, though, for many years only two sustained studies of the images (Brenner's and Meyers's) were in evidence.

Implicitly, Brenner's and Meyers's work might be seen as a response to a general debate that had been brewing in scholarship on how to interpret the Song's imagery. Though not initially gender-critical, part of this debate involved a reading strategy advanced by Richard Soulen, which has been considered sexist by some feminist exegetes. Soulen's work explains the different characterizations of the man and woman in the metaphors, finding that the woman's 'poetic imagination' evidenced in Song 5.10-16 yields descriptions that are 'less sensuous and imaginative' than the man's descriptions of her body. In his view, '[t]his is due in part to the limited subject matter [i.e. the male body] and may even be due to the difference in erotic imagination between poet and poetess'.[33] Understandably, such evaluations raised feminist concerns. Marcia Falk responds that 'Soulen's evaluation… perhaps derives from a preconception that the description of a man's body…is necessarily "limited subject matter". Indeed, such a preconception is not surprising in a culture where men are taught to believe that exaltation of male beauty is frivolous or, worse, embarrassing.'[34] She further calls his evaluations naïve, since, once he has attributed the text to a female author, he dismisses it as inferior.[35]

Clearly, difference in poetic expression does not have to imply inferiority, but should signal to readers an opportunity ripe for exploration. Why do the Song's lovers express themselves so differently where the body is concerned? And why do readers respond differently to these disparate images? In their separate studies, Brenner and Meyers begin the important work of investigating the imagery for its gender implications. Instead of suggesting totalizing evaluations of female or male poetry as Soulen has done, they offer complex and subtle interpretations of the imagery that overturn the gender norms of the socio-historical or literary context in which the Song was written. Meyers's study, discussed above, explores the metaphors on the body in terms of their significance for the relation of the sexes in the book. She asserts that the imposition of stereotypically 'masculine' imagery on the female body serves to illustrate female power in the domestic sphere. Her

32. Brenner, 'On Feminist Criticism', pp. 35-36.
33. Richard N. Soulen, 'The *Waṣfs* of the Song of Songs and Hermeneutic', in Brenner (ed.), *A Feminist Companion to the Song of Songs*, pp. 214–24 (216 n. 1).
34. Falk, *Love Lyrics*, p. 85.
35. Falk, *Love Lyrics*, p. 85.

proposition is appealing, although there is little evidence for the effectiveness of such transfers of power, just as it is difficult to evaluate whether the attributions of 'masculinity' or 'femininity' of a given image are based on contemporary stereotypes or ancient ideas.[36] Brenner follows up her evaluation of the potential for a feminist study of the Song's images with a provocative examination of Song 7.1-10, in which she argues that this text is a parody of the other *wasfs*.[37] It may be understood as comedy, although it must not be taken to relay a real or photographic image of a woman.[38] She maintains that the comedic perspective allows for a fuller understanding of this image and helps us to understand the other images. And yet, the possibility that a text might stand as a potential source of ridicule may not sit well with readers; indeed, it may not have sat well with Brenner. She seems to accommodate the potential discomfort of the ridiculing male gaze by advocating that we read the image as women: if we understand it as women's writing about the female body, the language is readable as an 'in' joke, rather than the words of a potentially ridiculing lover. In so doing, Brenner recognizes that the image undermines ancient and contemporary practice that idealizes and idolizes love and women as objects of that love.[39]

Meyers and Brenner provide much-needed dissenting approaches to other feminist interpretations of the Song. Nevertheless, their readings also raise questions about readers' expectations, the stereotyping of imagery, and the protagonist's autonomy. Responding in part to these challenges, I problematize the body imagery by taking a word that exists in Song criticism, *grotesque*, as a heuristic. I interpret the images (*wasfs*) as grotesque, according to the literary and artistic construct that holds its audience in a conflicted state of fascination/attraction and horror/repulsion. So, for example, the image of the neck as a tower of David is discussed not only in terms of the usual interpretive resonances (its length and stateliness), but also for its grim, military connotations, replete with shields and signs of war. This reading strategy is not offered as a definitive or singular solution for the images, but as a way to allow for dissonance and indeterminacy in an otherwise rosy interpretive tradition that privileges symmetry, beauty, and allure. Most importantly, through these circumventions of traditional interpretation, the re-reading offers a fresh look at the Song's gender politics and at love and desire. I explore gender as implicated in looking and speaking, and I

36.　See my critique of Meyers's work in *The Artifice of Love: Grotesque Bodies and the Song of Songs* (JSOTSup, 392; London: T. & T. Clark, 2009), pp. 52-53.

37.　Brenner, '"Come Back, Come Back, the Shulammite": (Song of Songs 7.1-10): A Parody of the *Wasf* Genre', in Brenner (ed.), *A Feminist Companion to the Song of Songs*, pp. 234-57.

38.　Brenner, 'Come Back', p. 235.

39.　See my critique of Brenner's position in *Artifice of Love*, pp. 56-57.

conclude that, like love and the body, gender is fluid and pliable in the Song, exhibiting pitfalls and liberations. The grotesque provides opportunities to ponder refigurations and amatory constellations that quite exceed Hebrew Bible norms, making the Song a problematic and subversive text indeed.

Marriage and (Sexual) Autonomy

Doubtless, the odd body imagery in the Song is complicated by its presence in connection with sex. For earlier modern readers, the confirmation that the couple were married helped to temper concerns about the sexual and erotic contents of the text.[40] Briefly, feminist readers were interested in the possibility of the couple's marriage, too. On the one hand, the idea that a woman, unmarried, could be free to articulate her desire and direct her actions was incredibly appealing. On the other hand, if she were married, the constraints of marriage in ancient near Eastern culture troubled feminists' enthusiastic celebrations of the protagonist's experience. Which was it to be? Significantly, the question of marriage cannot be definitely settled in the text. Thus, feminist readers eventually abandoned this issue in favour of others.[41]

The subject of the woman's autonomy was more promising, since it did not explicitly deal with the possibility of marriage, but went to the heart of the issue: the verbal and physical freedom that the woman ostensibly enjoys. Early feminist readers emphasized that she seemed free to express her love, to seek out her lover, presumably to engage in lovemaking, and to be at a certain liberty to move around, although sometimes her apparent autonomy exists merely in a dream. This evaluation had a far-reaching effect on research on biblical women. Similar to Trible's assertion that the Bible's patriarchal failures in the garden are redeemed in the Song, feminist readers thought that the Song might redeem an entire Hebrew Bible corpus of oppression, misogyny, and neglect of women.[42]

Yet could it? Although initially feminist readers embraced the woman's perceived autonomy, some feminist interpreters, such as Ilana Pardes, wondered how this woman—and this book—ever made it past biblical

40. I refer here especially to the 'modern' tradition of criticism, which came into being after the rise of historical criticism in biblical studies in the nineteenth century. This tradition moved away from earlier allegorical readings (which did not dwell on human players in the text, married or not), but was still naturally influenced by the social mores of the nineteenth and early twentieth centuries.

41. See the critique offered by Burrus and Moore, 'Unsafe Sex: Feminism, Pornography, and the Song of Songs', *BibInt* 11 (2003), pp. 24-52, that even Trible, who insists on the absence of marriage, implicitly argues for it in her construction of heterosexual, egalitarian relations in the Song.

42. See the readings quoted above, and also Exum, 'Developing Strategies', for a lengthier list and discussion.

censors.[43] Moreover, celebratory feminist statements about the autonomy of the protagonist conflicted with several verses in which the woman addresses her lack of freedom (e.g. 1.6; 2.15; 5.7; 8.10)[44] and with the depictions of several ostensibly oppressive events, such as her beating at the hands of the watchmen of the city (5.7).

In the late 1990s, feminist readers began to interrogate the book and its potentially autonomous protagonist in earnest. They asked why a sexually autonomous woman did not check her actions, or have them checked by others. The beating scene of 5.7 in which the woman goes in search of her lover, is beaten by watchmen, and stripped, was a sticking point in such deliberations. Oddly, a stained glass window in a church in Darley Dale, Derbyshire prompted a fuller exploration of the scene.[45] In our reading of it, Exum and I observed that the window, in its surprising selection of the beating scene and its display in the viewer's direct line of vision, brings the question of sexual freedom to the forefront. The window emphasizes a scene that critics of the Song, feminist or not, have tended to downplay and to marginalize. In response, Exum and I made this matter central in our reading.[46] We used the visual confrontation of the scene to expose the important ideological issue of how readers evaluate and interpret texts. Later, I took up the scene again to consider the woman as a transgressive subject, in line with Kristeva's work on the concept of the abject.[47]

43.   Ilana Pardes, *Countertraditions in the Bible: A Feminist Approach* (Cambridge, MA: Harvard University Press, 1992); see esp. pp. 118-43. Daphne Merkin cast a similar doubt a few years later, foregrounding the implications of these readings for women in her tradition; see her 'The Woman in the Balcony: On Rereading the Song of Songs', in C. Büchman and C. Spiegel (eds.), *Out of the Garden: Women Writers on the Bible* (New York: Fawcett Columbine, 1994), pp. 238-51, 342. Alicia Ostriker has more recently considered Pardes's questions ('A Holy of Holies: The Song of Songs as Countertext', in Brenner and Fontaine [eds.], *The Song of Songs*, pp. 36-54).

44.   Though not explicit, 2.15 and 8.10 imply that the woman has been experiencing some undetermined difficulty (2.15), or is negotiating with her family members over her freedom (8.10). In the latter case, she seems to assert it, despite the previous words form her brothers.

45.   Fiona C. Black and J. Cheryl Exum, 'Semiotics in Stained Glass: Edward Burne-Jones's Song of Songs', in J. Cheryl Exum and Stephen D. Moore (eds.), *Biblical Studies/Cultural Studies: The Third Sheffield Colloquium* (GCT, 7; JSOTSup, 266; Sheffield: Sheffield Academic Press, 1998), pp. 315-42. Other studies of visual art and the Song of Songs are available; these are not explicitly gender-critical.

46.   Black and Exum, 'Semiotics in Stained Glass'.

47.   Black, 'Nocturnal Egressions: Exploring Some Margins of the Song of Songs', in A.K.M. Adam (ed.), *Postmodern Interpretations of the Bible* (St Louis, MO: Chalice Press, 2001), pp. 93-104. The abject is a psychoanalytical concept that attempts to articulate the process of discarding or resisting items (food, filth, the maternal body) or ideas (e.g. death, criminality) that is necessary for the maintenance of an individual's subjectivity.

After our reading of the Burne-Jones windows, Exum developed a manifesto of sorts, organized around the matter of autonomy, that identifies key issues for a feminist reading of the Song.[48] She states, for instance, that reading the Song is sometimes misleading and sometimes risky to critical faculties and/or to readerly desires; that there is no egalitarian relationship apparent in this text, even as much as feminist readers yearn to find one; and that the body is on display for male consumption, yet also absent—the book/lover conjures it up when it is needed or desired. It is important to note that Exum's article forms the backdrop for her commentary, *Song of Songs*, which is the first to involve gender-critical hermeneutics as a significant reading framework.[49]

Exum's and my study on the Burne-Jones window brings up yet another issue: the gazing of the male lover at his lover's body.[50] Looking at the body, or being looked at, has implications for the matter of autonomy, although in this case the woman's political freedom, rather than her physical or verbal liberties, is indicated. For Exum, the gaze is a significant feature in her commentary. It is also a crucial part of several articles on the presence/absence of the lovers and the implications of the language of love, including double entendre, conjuring, and dreaming. Brenner also raises these matters in her article on Song 7.1-10, and following her lead, I explore them fully in my study on the grotesque body.[51] For both Brenner and myself, the possibility that gazing is multivalent in its intention and impact is key. The implications of such readings are that the Song is opened to the possibility that if the gaze can shift, so, too, might the matter of autonomy.

For some dissenting readers, however, the problem of the Song's autonomous protagonist—along with the book's mysterious presence in the Bible—persists, and for them, an answer is found in patriarchy's complex logic. Gender-critical readers, Donald Polaski and David Clines, argue that the woman's central position and apparent autonomy were actually functions of male fantasy (Clines) or a complex presentation of woman in an

---

48. J. Cheryl Exum, 'Ten Things Every Feminist Should Know about the Song of Songs', in Brenner and Fontaine (eds.), *The Song of Songs*, pp. 24-35.

49. Exum is particularly interested in writing about different ways of speaking about love and the body; see 'Developing Strategies' for comments about the formulation of the commentary.

50. See J. Cheryl Exum, *Song of Songs: A Commentary* (Louisville, KY: Westminster/John Knox Press, 2005); Exum, 'Developing Strategies'; and Exum, 'In the Eye of the Beholder: Wishing, Dreaming and *Double Entendre* in the Song of Songs', in Fiona C. Black, Roland Boer and Erin Runions (eds.), *The Labour of Reading: Desire, Alienation and Biblical Interpretation* (Atlanta, GA: Society of Biblical Literature, 1999), pp. 71-86.

51. Brenner, 'Come Back'; Black, *Artifice of Love*.

observed and controlled position, resembling Foucault's panopticon (Polaski).[52] While these important counter-voices make intriguing arguments, readers should be aware that they continue to privilege the male gaze and the androcentric perspective that has dominated other readings of the book in the past (e.g. Soulen's), notably in terms of the woman's fantasy of her lover's body. These are important additions to the debate, but they cannot be aligned politically with the feminist readings we have considered thus far.[53]

It should be noted, too, that a number of feminist and gender-critical readers acknowledge the problem that readers, affected by the Song's beauty and lyricism as well as its difficulties, feel an attraction to the Song.[54] Carole Fontaine frames the dynamics of this conflict expertly:

> [I]t is hard for many of us *not* to love the Song of Songs... [F]or the most part even the inclusion of a *hypothetical* female voice that rejects patriarchal restrictions on her body and her choices is hailed as a bit of unlooked-for intertextual critique in support of the full agency of women as persons... At the same time, there may be a concomitant desire by those who love the Song and see it as hopeful to *downplay* what I see to be clear indications of social restraint imposed on the Beloved for the very behavior on her part that we praise.[55]

It is not only a matter of aesthetic appreciation for the book that is problematized, but for some, the prolonged cultural and spiritual history with

52. David J.A. Clines, 'Why Is There a Song of Songs and What Does It Do to You if You Read It?', in Clines, *Interested Parties: The Ideology of Writers and Readers of the Hebrew Bible* (JSOTSup, 205; GCT, 1; Sheffield: Sheffield Academic Press, 1995), pp. 94-121; Donald C. Polaski, 'What Will Ye See in the Shulammite? Women, Power and Panopticism in the Song of Songs', *BibInt* 5 (1997), pp. 64-81.

53. I have argued this more fully elsewhere; see Black, *Artifice of Love*, pp. 197-200.

54. See Exum, 'Ten Things', 'Developing Strategies', and *Song of Songs*; and Merkin, 'The Woman in the Balcony'. For more general issues around the problems of reading the Song and gender criticism, see Black, 'Beauty or the Beast: The Grotesque Body in the Song of Songs', *BibInt* 8 (2000), pp. 302-23, and *Artifice of Love*, Chapters 1 and 4; Brenner, 'Whose Love', 'Come Back', and *I Am: Biblical Women Tell their Own Stories* (Philadelphia: Fortress Press, 2005), pp. 163-90. The question of readerly responses is a related one, but not explored fully here because it is not always undertaken with a gender-critical perspective. The matter of readerly response or interpretive context will eventually form the backdrop to all gender-critical readings as the practice develops in Song criticism to include musicological, queer, and other approaches.

55. 'Watching out for the Watchmen (Song 5.7): How I Hold Myself Accountable', in Charles Cosgrove (ed.), *The Meanings We Choose: Hermeneutical Ethics, Indeterminacy and the Conflict of Interpretations* (JSOTSup, 411; London: T. & T. Clark, 2004), pp. 102-21. See also Carol Fontaine, 'The Voice of the Turtle: Now it's *my* Song of Songs', in Brenner and Fontaine (eds.), *The Song of Songs*, pp. 169-85.

the text exacerbates the tension.[56] These matters are important to mention. To be sure, they are not uniquely feminist concerns, but they often accompany feminist investigations of the Song.

As these varied approaches indicate, the matter of the woman's autonomy remains unsettled. At stake here are not only the woman's physical movement and any perceived impediments to it, but other features in the Song as well, such as how the protagonist is depicted or named.[57] Clearly, the question of her autonomy is also impacted by the freedoms that gender-attuned readers exercise when they 'have [their] sexy text and eat [their] critical cake too'.[58] Most importantly, autonomy as a critical concept or category bears the mark of contemporary thinking about gender and sexuality. As such, it is a concept that 'travels well' into recent gender-critical work on the Song and benefits from further theoretical elaboration. It is to this contemporary development in the scholarship that I now turn, and with it to some much-needed critique of existing feminist approaches to the text.

Sexing Up the Song of Songs

The dissenting readers discussed above, or, if I may, the practice of reading *dissentedly*, prepares the way for a final group of gender-critical readings, which foreground counter- or 'alternative' perspectives, such as queer, S/M, and pornographic sexualities. These readings represent a crucial development in gender-critical scholarship, but one must be cautious about seeing them as a radical break with what has gone before. More accurately, they continue with the impulses of earlier criticism in that they, too, critique the dynamics of power in sexualities and explore the experience of the book's protagonist.

Several differing approaches should be mentioned here. In one direction, Stephen Moore explores the Song as a text revealing the affective or intimate relationship that male adherents in Judaism and Christianity have enjoyed with the deity, or had thrust upon them.[59] Accordingly, Moore calls

---

56. See, most particularly, Athalya Brenner, 'My Song of Songs', in Brenner and Fontaine (eds.), *The Song of Songs*, pp. 154-68; *I Am*, pp. 163-90. Fontaine also comments on an extended personal history ('The Voice of the Turtle').

57. See my discussion of the woman's political autonomy, through a discussion of the woman's name and her self-representation, in 'Writing Lies: Autobiography, Textuality and the Song of Songs', in Fiona C. Black (ed.), *The Recycled Bible: Autobiography, Culture, and the Space Between* (SBLSS; Atlanta, GA: Scholars Press, 2007), pp. 161-83.

58. Exum, 'Developing Strategies', p. 248.

59. Stephen D. Moore, *God's Beauty Parlor and Other Queer Spaces in and around the Bible* (Stanford: Stanford University Press, 2001).

his work an 'outing' of the male religious Jew or Christian.[60] His reading is provocative, for not only does it read allegory differently (and somewhat naughtily), but it explores numerous queer subject positions in the Song's history of interpretation and traces the 'whitening' and (hetero)-sexing of the Song over its long history, to a point where, in the current literal readings, there is a somewhat prurient interest in female sexuality (in a heterosexual framework of course) and the body. Eventually, we come to see the Song as offering possibilities quite beyond those of its former, apparently rather demure, self.[61]

In another direction, and in response to Moore's challenge to create a 'carnal allegory' of the Song,[62] Roland Boer pens a series of thematically linked articles and book chapters on the sexual language and imagery of the Song. In one article, Boer creates a 'linguistic register' for sexual activity (actions, items, places, etc.), and explores the repetitive nature of the Song as a key to its erotic success.[63] In the context of a study of popular culture and censorship,[64] he continues the work as an experimental reading of the Song as pornography, interspersed with porn-narrative featuring 'Beth Rabbim' and 'Sue Lammith', among others. Boer is not at all concerned with the problematic possibilities of pornography. To flaunt them is, in fact, part of the point in his discussion of censorship.

The problematics of pornography are, however, what Moore and Burrus trade on in a publication entitled, 'Unsafe Sex'.[65] Building on Moore's work on allegory and responding to Boer's work, as well as critiquing previous feminist work on the Song,[66] they explore the possibility of reading the Song

---

60. Moore, *God's Beauty Parlor*, p. 3.

61. See also Heidi Epstein's important work on queer theory and musicology with respect to musical settings of the Song of Songs: 'Penderecki's Iron Maiden: Intimacy and Other Anomalies in the *Canticum Canticorum Salomonis*', in Ken Stone and Teresa Hornsby (eds.), *Bible Trouble: Queer Reading at the Boundaries of Biblical Scholarship* (SBLSS; Atlanta, GA: Society of Biblical Literature, 2011), pp. 99-130; 'Sour Grapes, Fermented Selves: Musical Shulammites Modulate Subjectivity', *The Bible and Critical Theory* 5.1 (2009): http://bibleandcriticaltheory.org/index.php/bct/article/view/235/218.

62. See R. Boer, 'The Second Coming: Repetition and Insatiable Desire in the Song of Songs', *BibInt* 8 (2000), pp. 276-301 (276): [A] carnal allegory…would be concerned with a range of questions: the function of sexual language and poetry, narrative and sexual description, explicitness and realism, repetition, fetishism and the range of sexual practices suggested in the Song…'

63. Boer, 'Second Coming'.

64. R. Boer, *Knockin' on Heaven's Door: The Bible and Popular Culture* (London: Routledge, 1992), pp. 53-70.

65. Virginia Burrus and Stephen D. Moore, 'Unsafe Sex: Feminism, Pornography, and the Song of Songs', *BibInt* 11 (2003), pp. 24-52.

66. Notably, Trible, *God and the Rhetoric of Sexuality*; Ostriker, 'A Holy of Holies'; Exum and Black, 'Semiotics in Stained Glass'.

as counterpleasure, that is, against the grain of traditional readings, feminist and pre-feminist, typically read 'through the prism of an unproblematized heterosexuality'[67] and which display, therefore, their abiding attraction to heteronormativity. Moore and Burrus turn their attention to Song 5.7 and consider the possibility that the Song is readable from an alternative perspective in the form of S/M practice. In their view, the Shulammite's preferences might function as a corrective for feminist readers' neglect of problematic power dynamics in heterosexual relationships—even those evident in the Song.

It is exciting that the trajectory of Song scholarship has developed to allow for possibilities such as Moore and Burrus's essay. However, their work is not without its problems, as Julie Kelso argues. She shows that the plotting of the scene in Song 5.7 as S/M fantasy—an idea that should be corrected to masochistic, following Boer's observations—fails to acknowledge the liberal underpinnings of the assumption that a woman is able to 'contract' for masochistic sexual relationships in which she is a willing partner. Kelso also warns that Irigaray's contribution to the discussion (*contra* Burrus and Moore) is its elaboration of monosexuality, which problematizes heterosexual and queer readings alike.[68]

These are serious matters and they deserve further elaboration. In discussing them, however, one should not obscure the playfulness of the more recent approaches.[69] In order to ask the necessary questions, the work of Boer, Moore, and others needs to be open to textual play. Some readers might find this off-putting—to re-quote Fox in a way that he did not at all intend: 'The incongruity is so great that there is, to be sure, the risk of losing many readers, who may find [it]...abrasive', or worse, offensive. However, a willingness to play with our own assumptions about the text and its interpretive history and to play with the text's components themselves is necessary in order to trouble the usual subjects of love and desire.[70] But playfulness, of course, no matter its intentions, has political consequences. In these new theoretical constellations and subject configurations, critics invite much-needed opportunities to critique past gender-critical approaches,

67. Burrus and Moore, 'Unsafe Sex', p. 28.

68. Julie Kelso, 'A Woman Is Being Beaten and Maybe She Likes It: Approaching Song of Songs 5:2-7', in Roland Boer, Michael Carden, and Julie Kelso (eds.), *The One Who Reads May Run: Essays in Honour of Edgar W. Conrad* (LHBOTS, 553; London: T. & T. Clark, 2012), pp. 160-75.

69. Playfulness does not mean, though, that Boer's work should not be subject to criticism; in this case, one might observe that his reading appears to clobber the Song's subtlety; see discussion in Black, *Artifice of Love*, pp. 221-29.

70. Indeed, such play is already apparent in earlier work (Brenner, 'Come Back', and Black, *Artifice of Love*), and is a necessary part of these alternative readings.

to explore new directions, and perhaps—again to continue with Fox's observations in ways that he may not have intended—to allow the Song 'to convey a radically different vision of love'.[71]

Future and 'Irregular' Readings: Some Concluding Comments

We have come some distance from the medieval musings of mystics on the Song, through contemporary feminist celebrations and explorations, to pornographic, queer, and S/M readings. Indeed, we have come some distance from the rejection of allegory on feminist terms to its re-embracing (albeit in somewhat stickier terms) by queer readers. This evident dynamism is, I propose, a sign of vigour and enthusiasm in the critique of this small but impactful book. In part, the fluidity of the text and its polyvalent imagery are significant indicators of why the Song sustains so much variety in readings. It is also evident that the Song's subject matter meets readers on personal and provocative terms.

Where do we go from here? I would like to see sustained responses from feminist or gender-critical scholars to some of the recent work by Boer, Moore, Kelso, Epstein, and Burrus and Moore. What, for instance, are the implications of reading *dissidently*? In general terms, feminist biblical scholars have not engaged with recent approaches, appearing instead to step out of the way. Should they do so, or will they respond, as Kelso has begun to? The critique that the above-mentioned queer readings have brought to feminist readings is important. Feminist readers need to look seriously at the heteronormative nature of their work. For that matter, they must also look at the largely Western perspective from which they write. There is an urgent need for work that brings the Song into conversation with postcolonial theory, and/or with interpretive communities from the Two-Thirds World.

The general areas of my discussion on body, sexuality, and authorship are not exhausted in gender-critical readings. The body imagery could be que(e)ried further, and the matter of affect remains pervasive and thought provoking. Although Brenner contextualized the Song in other biblical discourses on sexuality, other intersections and connections remain to be explored more fully, such as those between the so-called pornoprophetic texts and the Song. Further, we might consider the broad divide between theological (allegorical) readings and the literal turn. Surely, as in all areas

---

71. See Fox, *Song of Songs*, p. 227, although I hasten to add that the spirit of his commentary, which is itself iconoclastic in its linking of the imagery with Egyptian poetry, might be very much in line with the spirit of such newer iconoclasms, if not their content or intent.

of biblical interpretation, there is an opportunity to rethink these relation-ships and to see how they might rub up against each other in pleasant and insightful ways. And the cultural afterlives of the Song in art, film, and music offer many opportunities for gender-critical analysis, as Exum and Heidi Epstein are indicating.[72] In any case, traditional criticism on the Song cannot avoid the loud, creative, feminist, and gender-critical voices that have brought insight into the book. It also cannot ignore the wide range of features these voices have brought to light: a vocal protagonist, perplexing imagery, the problem of the gaze, and the implication of the reader. The future of the Song of Songs in biblical criticism remains bright and alluring indeed.

72. Epstein, 'Sour Grapes' and 'Penderecki's Iron Maiden'; J. Cheryl Exum, 'See-ing the Song of Songs: Some Artistic Visions of the Bible's Love Lyrics', in John Barton, J. Cheryl Exum, and Manfred Oeming (eds.), *Das Alte Testament und die Kunst* (Münster: Lit Verlag, 2005), pp. 91-127.

11

SITTING AROUND THE FIREPLACE AT WISDOM'S HOUSE: A REVIEW OF FEMINIST STUDIES ON PROVERBS, JOB, AND QOHELETH

Madipoane Masenya (ngwan'a Mphahlele)

Perhaps it should not be surprising that feminist Hebrew Bible scholars have given less attention to the wisdom books than to other books of the biblical canon. The literature does not prominently feature female characters or topics of interest to feminist scrutiny, and the male elitist tone and agenda of the wisdom books have contributed to the initial reticence. However, it has given way to feminist interpretations that appreciate the emphasis on the experiences of individuals, such as Job and Qohelet. Feminist exegetes have also found value in poetry that questions tradition as authoritative, such as the 'acts-consequences' construct or the idea that you reap what you sow. The following examines feminist interpretations on the books of Proverbs, Job, and Qoheleth. I imagine us sitting around the fire place at Wisdom's house and learning how feminist scholars have used feminist ingredients for cooking delicious meals in their pots.

Managing to Give Voice to the Voiceless: Feminist Approaches to the Book of Proverbs

When feminists began examining the book of Proverbs, they produced chapter-long articles on it in anthologies and one-volume feminist commentaries on the Bible. The essays include Carole Fontaine's entry on Proverbs in the first two editions of the *Women's Bible Commentary* and the *Harper's Bible Commentary*, Athalya Brenner's piece in the *Global Bible Commentary*, and Naomi Franklin's entry in the *Africana Bible*.[1] Only slowly did

---

1. Carole Fontaine, 'Proverbs', in Carol A. Newsom and Sharon H. Ringe (eds.), *Women's Bible Commentary* (Louisville, KY: Westminster/John Knox Press, 1998), pp. 153-60; Fontaine, 'Proverbs', in J.L. Mays (ed.), *Harper's Bible Commentary* (San Francisco: Harper & Row, 1988), pp. 495-517; Athalya Brenner, 'Proverbs', in Daniel Patte (ed.), *The Global Bible Commentary* (Nashville, TN: Abingdon Press, 2004),

feminist scholars produce book-length investigations on the book of Proverbs,[2] beginning with dissertations. A case in point is Claudia V. Camp's first comprehensive treatment on Proverbs in 1985. Her study analyzed the function of the female figure of Woman Wisdom in the patriarchal canon. Camp examined the various meanings of personified Wisdom and the theological significance of the Wisdom poems in Proverbs. She sought to understand the female roles and images to highlight the profound symbolic impact of Woman Wisdom in the postexilic era.[3] Almost twenty years later, my own dissertation focused on the Woman of Worth in Prov. 31.10-31, examining the poem within the entire book of Proverbs.[4] In that work I hypothesized that despite patriarchal bias Prov. 31.10-31 offers liberating possibilities to people, including African women in South Africa. For instance, the Woman of Worth cares for the entire household which should not be understood as a separation from the public domain. The Woman of Worth's work confers identity and power to her in society. It gives her a position of strength, as it does to African South-African women working on behalf of their households. The Woman of Worth also engages with all kinds of people and is not restricted to 'an ivory tower'.[5] She is a wise teacher with a strong work ethic, a powerful and independent woman, trusted by her husband and caring for the needy. The biblical text thus emerges with both oppressive and liberative features; it is an androcentric text with some affirming messages for African women.

All of these studies point to the androcentric nature of the biblical material by hypothesizing on the historical context of the sayings. Feminist exegetes approach the wisdom literature with a hermeneutics of suspicion because they assume that these texts were produced by men in patriarchal cultures. Feminists thus read the texts to unmask androcentric ideologies, but they have also turned their attention to the female figures mentioned in several chapters in Proverbs. They explore the historical and literary meanings of the 'Woman Stranger' (*ishah zarah*), 'Woman Wisdom', the 'Woman of Worth' (*eshet hayil*), and the various combinations of these female characters.

pp. 163-74; Naomi Franklin, 'Proverbs', in Hugh Page (ed.), *The Africana Bible: Reading Israel's Scriptures from Africa and the African Diaspora* (Minneapolis: Fortress Press, 2010), pp. 244-48.

2. See, e.g., Kathleen M. O'Connor, *The Wisdom Literature* (Collegeville, MN: The Liturgical Press, 1998); Carole Fontaine, *Smooth Words: Women, Proverbs and Performance in Biblical Wisdom* (Sheffield: Sheffield Academic Press, 2002).

3. Claudia V. Camp, *Wisdom and the Feminine in the Book of Proverbs* (Sheffield: JSOT Press, 1985).

4. Madipoane Masenya (ngwana' Mphahlele), *How Worthy Is the Woman of Worth? Rereading Proverbs 31:10-31 in African South Africa* (New York: Peter Lang, 2004).

5. Masenya, *How Worthy Is the Woman of Worth?*, p. 104.

On the Male Elite Authorship of Proverbs

What irritates feminist exegetes about the book of Proverbs is its satisfaction with the socio-political status quo and the fact that many sayings justify the abuses in society. Feminists thus bemoan the 'act–consequence concept', assumed in many sayings. It blames victims for their misfortune and warns readers of their fate. Carole Fontaine clearly articulates this discomfort when she writes:

> Unlike the contents of the Prophets, which is often critical of abuses in society, most of the wisdom traditions of Proverbs are associated with the preservation of the status quo of the male elite. One of the ways this may be observed is through the sages' belief in the act consequence relationship that undergirds much of the thinking in the book... Though the sages know that the poor may be at the whims of the rich, the act–consequence concept makes it easy to blame victims for having caused their own misfortunes, as is the case in the book of Job. With this kind of worldview, the struggle for social justice lacks the energy and zeal observed elsewhere in the Hebrew Bible.[6]

Unsurprisingly, then, feminist interpreters do not endorse sayings in Proverbs that tolerate and even foster unjust human relationships, including contentment with unjust gender relations. Such attitudes are exactly what feminist scholars challenge in their exegetical work.

They explain that the reason for these unjust teachings of social and political complacency originates in the male elite authorship of this literature. Rejecting their views as inadequate for contemporary spirituality and theology, feminists suggest looking at other wisdom books instead, such as Qoheleth and Job. Accordingly, Athalya Brenner states that '[t]he problem is that when we need spiritual food, or food for the mind, we may not find it in Proverbs'[7] and she advises that feminists ought to read Qoheleth and Job for 'a deeper understanding of the divine'. Although these books were also written by elite men in ancient Israel, she believes they offer 'spiritual sustenance' from a universal perspective.[8]

Other feminist interpreters, however, do not want to let go of Proverbs. Carole Fontaine, for instance, highlights the feminist potential of Prov. 10.1–15.33 as countering the male elite perspective. She shows that in Proverbs 10 a woman is depicted positively as a mother who instructs her children and is disappointed by her offspring's foolishness (10.1, 15, 20);[9] she is a gracious woman (11.6) and a good wife (12.4) in contrast to her negative counterparts.[10] Her approach makes a broader view on the material's

6.   Fontaine, 'Proverbs', p. 154.
7.   Brenner, 'Proverbs', p. 165.
8.   Brenner, 'Proverbs', p. 165.
9.   See also Masenya, *How Worthy Is the Woman of Worth?*, p. 84.
10. Fontaine, 'Proverbs', p. 157.

potential for feminist interpretations possible although, in the end, Fontaine recognizes the androcentric nature of the book. She exposes the androcentric ideology of Proverbs when she comments on the politics of inclusion and exclusion in the depiction of this woman. The female character appears only as mother and wife, the stereotypical roles for women in patriarchy. Since this female character complies with societal expectation, she is praised in Proverbs, but women of other roles and with other responsibilities are absent or negatively portrayed. For instance, many sayings bemoan the misfortune of living with a quarrelsome wife, but what of the plight of a wife forced to endure a violent husband? Men hackle with men, as in sayings that condemn men as fools, scoffers, drunkards, and sluggards. Yet no saying addresses the devastation of a drunken man wreaking havoc upon his family or the damages done by a male liar or adulterer. Fontaine thus emphasizes that the book of Proverb presents a generally unfair and unbalanced portrayal of women. It illustrates how the 'sages view their society and its ills through the narrow focus of the privileged male, so the picture presented is a lopsided and partial one at best'.[11] It describes society 'from one perspective only'[12] offering unreliable information on women in ancient Israelite society.

Explorations on Woman Stranger and Woman Wisdom
The female figures of 'Woman Stranger' (*ishah zarah*) and 'Woman Wisdom' in Proverbs have attracted considerable attention from feminist exegetes. Among them is Meike Heijerman who examines the figure of the Woman Stranger. Heijerman explains that this figure is portrayed as a rival to mothers. She admonishes a son and thereby undermines what the presumed task of a father was.[13] The Woman Stranger is also designated as a scapegoat for men, as she is reprimanded for having seduced them. She appears as a needy woman who even sells herself into prostitution.[14] Many male commentators do not listen to her perspective but accept the depictions of the speaker-in-the-text. Heijerman states unambiguously that Proverbs 7 is 'at the very least, a partly misogynistic text'.[15] She suggests four coping mechanisms to women readers. First, she advises women to ignore this text as it was not meant for them. Second, she proposes that women may decide to teach 'women's wisdom' as an alternative to other women, their daughters, and also their sons. Third, she proposes to view Proverbs 7 as 'a

11. Fontaine, 'Proverbs', p. 159.
12. Fontaine, 'Proverbs', p. 159.
13. Meike Heijerman, 'Who Would Blame Her? The "Strange" Woman of Proverbs 7', in Athalya Brenner (ed.), *A Feminist Companion to Wisdom Literature* (FCB, 9; Sheffield: Sheffield Academic Press, 1995), pp. 100-109 (105).
14. Heijerman, 'Who Would Blame Her?', p. 106.
15. Heijerman, 'Who Would Blame Her?', p. 108.

beautiful example of transference and projection'[16] by the text's speaker. Fourth, the female figure teaches about the connection between chaos and creativity. The Woman Stranger lives outside the confined roles of society and is thus able to say and do what is socially unacceptable. Herein consists her unanticipated power.

Other feminist interpreters, such as Gale A. Yee, focus on the Woman Stranger, examining the function of the seduction in the texts.[17] Yee assumes that the various references to the Woman Stranger describe the same woman and do not refer to several different women, as biblical scholars sometimes maintain.[18] The Woman Stranger is also a figure contrasted with other women, such as Woman Wisdom, a loving and faithful wife. Yee points out that the father encourages his son to be seduced by the love of his wife and to avoid the seductive glances of the Woman Stranger (Prov. 5.19-20).[19] Yee exposes the text of its androcentric content, communicated by men to each other. She states: '[O]nly man pursues Wisdom like a lover, and it is a woman who seduces him away from her. How does one mitigate such imagery when it touches a person at the most elemental and symbolic level, for instance the sexual?'[20]

But it is probably Claudia Camp who takes the discussion on Woman Stranger the furthest when she examines the historical origins of this character, its significance in Judea, and the socio-political, religious, and economic factors that contributed to the development of this figure in the book of Proverbs.[21] Camp identifies the theme of strangeness in other biblical non-wisdom texts, such as in Ezra, Nehemiah, and even Genesis 34, and makes important intertextual connections among the divergent materials.[22] For instance, she observes:

16.   Heijerman, 'Who Would Blame Her?', p. 108.

17.   Gale A. Yee, 'I Have Perfumed my Bed with Myrrh: The Foreign Woman (*'iššâ zārâ*) in Proverbs 1–9', in Brenner (ed.), *A Feminist Companion to Wisdom Literature*, pp. 110-30.

18.   Some feminist exegetes also defend this view; see, e.g., Camp, *Wisdom and the Feminine in the Book of Proverbs*; Camp, *Wise, Strange and Holy: The Strange Woman and the Making of the Bible* (GCT, 9; JSOTSup, 320; Sheffield: Sheffield Academic Press, 2000).

19.   Some feminist scholars suggest that the mother played this role; see, e.g., Heijerman, 'The "Strange" Woman of Proverbs 7', p. 105; Athalya Brenner and Fokkelien van Dijk-Hemmes, *On Gendering Texts: Female and Male Voices in the Hebrew Bible* (Leiden: E.J. Brill, 1993), pp. 55, 120.

20.   Yee, 'I Have Perfumed My Bed with Myrrh', p. 126.

21.   Camp, *Wisdom and the Feminine in the Book of Proverbs*, p. 31.

22.   Camp, *Wise, Strange and Holy*, pp. 29-35.

[F]emale ethnic foreignness is intimately linked, via several different modes, to other significant conceptual fields; it is linked by ideological framing, to worship of foreign gods; by metaphor…to sexual strangeness (adultery, prostitution and, in general, women's control of their own sexuality); by extension of the sexual metaphor, to deceitful language; by metonymy to correct ritual practice; by moral logic to evil; by onto-logic to death; and by patri-logic, to loss of inheritance and lineage.[23]

In other words, Camp exposes the Woman Stranger as a negative figure in the rhetorical repertoire of Proverbs and elsewhere. There, Woman Stranger is depicted as 'other' whom Israelite males should avoid.

Studies on the socio-historical setting affirm Camp's analysis. For instance, Harold C. Washington demonstrates that the 'strange female foreigner' (*zarah nokkriya*) posed an immediate and particular threat in postexilic Judea and her condemnation was motivated by concern for economic and corporate survival. In postexilic Judean society foreign women were branded as those from the 'outside' in an effort to preserve the socio-economic integrity of the inside people.[24] Hence, the vehemence of the Woman Stranger's condemnation should be understood as a reminder of the considerable social cost with which postexilic Israel imagined its reestablishment after the Babylonian exile.

Yet sometimes feminist interpreters see in the Woman Stranger a negative character. In one of my own studies I interpreted the Woman Stranger within the African South-African context, explaining that the African South-African woman is strange in her own country because of her race and gender, and as such she resembles the Woman Stranger.[25] Both have little control over their sexuality and life and both are marginalized figures in their respective contexts and considered to be impure. Yet in my earlier study I maintained that these characterizations of Woman Stranger and African women must be understood as male projections made during changing religio-political-economic conditions. At the heart of these androcentric characterizations is the effort to control women's bodies. If a woman attempts to resist such control, she is portrayed as a stranger, a deviant, a pollutant, which is a strategy that aims to keep women submissive to the oppressive status quo.

23. Camp, *Wise, Strange and Holy*, pp. 28-29.

24. Harold C. Washington, 'Strange Woman (אשה זרה/נכריה) of Proverbs 1–9 and Post-Exilic Judaean Society', in Brenner (ed.), *A Feminist Companion to Wisdom Literature*, pp. 157-84.

25. Madipoane Masenya (ngwana' Mphahlele), 'Polluting your Ground? Woman as Pollutant in Yehud: A Reading from a Globalised Africa', in McGlory Speckman and Larry T. Kaufmann (eds.), *Towards an Agenda for Contextual Theology: Essays in Honor of Albert Nolan* (Pietermaritzburg: Cluster Publication, 2001), pp. 185-202.

In general, however, feminist interpreters agree that the writers of Proverbs constructed opposite female characters in the Woman Stranger and the Woman Wisdom. In Proverbs this construct functions similarly to the Christian dualism of the Madonna and the Whore in which woman is the object of a man's choice leading him either to life or to death. This view of the sexes is, of course, inherently problematic because it regards women as the cause for good and evil whereas men are either benefactors or victims. Kathleen M. O'Connor exposes this dualism when she observes that it does not occur in real life. Both women and men have qualities of good and evil, and both are responsible for their choices. Thus, neither women nor men are completely to be blamed or excused.[26] O'Connor advises that readers recognize the misogynist depictions of women of the wisdom literature and approach it with caution. This stance is particularly needed in the reading of Prov. 11.12 and 21.9, and so she states:

> This means that we must be conscious of its [i.e. wisdom literature's] preju-
> dices against women and of its exclusion of women's experience from its
> purview. Otherwise, its powerful word will only continue to harden gender
> prejudices which dwarf humanity and which negates the lives of women.[27]

In other words, feminist exegetes propose that readers interpret wisdom literature with a hermeneutic of suspicion even when the female figure is portrayed positively, as in the case of Wisdom Woman. They recognize the androcentric interests behind positive portrayals, and they emphasize the pitfalls of Wisdom Woman's depiction as a potential marriage partner. This advice is, however, not always carried out. Some feminist exegetes show that Wisdom Woman also appears as *hokmah*, Sophia herself, who invites everybody to full existence and thus represents God.[28] Linda Day fore-grounds this positive divine-like depiction of Wisdom Woman who is a participant in the Creation.[29] The portrayal of Wisdom Woman shows her as being everywhere (Wis. 7.24; Sir. 24.3-7), and she is good with her words (Prov. 8.6-9). In sum, feminist interpreters emphasize the positive sides of Woman Wisdom but they also recognize the dangers of being seduced by androcentric literature into the positive depiction of this female character.

---

26. Kathleen M. O'Connor, *The Wisdom Literature* (Collegeville, MN: Liturgical Press, 1988), p. 62.

27. O'Connor, *The Wisdom Literature*, p. 62.

28. O'Connor, *The Wisdom Literature*, p. 63.

29. Linda Day, 'Wisdom and the Feminine in the Hebrew Bible', in Linda Day and Carolyn Pressler (eds.), *Engaging the Bible in a Gendered World: An Introduction to Feminist Biblical Interpretation in Honor of Katharine Doob Sakenfeld* (Louisville, KY: Westminster/John Knox Press, 2006), pp. 114-27 (122).

Explorations on the Woman of Worth

Equipped with the hermeneutics of suspicion, feminist interpreters also examine Prov 31.10-31, the poem on the Woman of Worth (*eshet hayil*). This poem has received high praise throughout the history of androcentric interpretation. Athalya Brenner explains that the Woman of Worth personifies the metaphorical and metaphorized Wisdom Woman. The metaphor indicates that the essence of feminine or female achievement is a woman who has completely adapted to the role demanded of her in androcentric society. Brenner emphasizes that the collapse of the Woman of Worth with Wisdom Woman is the ultimate patriarchal victory. It teaches that a useful woman is a wise woman; she is the antithesis of the Woman Stranger.

Hence, generally, feminists have a negative view of the Woman of Worth and criticize her depiction in the poem. To them, she is not an independent woman but pursues classic patriarchal concerns. She is only focused on her husband and children. For instance, Anne Braude observes that the portrayal of the Woman of Worth may have been avant garde in ancient Israel but in our time her depiction is regressive.[30] Other feminist interpreters point to the ambivalent portrayal of the Woman of Worth. They maintain that she may appear to be powerful and independent, as for instance Maryse Waegeman and Ellen L. Lyons stress,[31] but her family, husband, and children define her as a woman well adapted to patriarchal expectations.[32] In one of my own studies, I argued that the poem offers both liberating and oppressive possibilities for African women in South Africa.[33] Still others explain that Prov. 31.10-31 is entirely paternalistic and does not offer any liberating perspectives.[34] All of them agree: depictions of the Woman of Worth in Prov. 31.10-31 reinforce patriarchal ideology.

Sometimes, however, feminist exegetes manage to infiltrate the patriarchal space designed to exclude women. Even the heavy androcentric bent of Proverbs did not keep them away forever. Linda Day articulates this important move made by contemporary feminist interpreters when she states:

30. Anne Braude shared this view with me in a personal conversation in 1995.

31. Marsye Waegeman, 'The Perfect Wife of Proverbia 31:10-31', in Klaus-Dietrich Schunck and Matthias Augustin (eds.), *Goldene Äpfel in silbernen Schalen* (Frankfurt am Main: Peter Lang, 1992), pp. 101-107; Ellen L. Lyons, 'A Note on Proverbs 31:10-31', in Kenneth G. Hogland *et al.* (eds.), *The Listening Heart: Essays in Wisdom and the Psalms in Honor of Roland E. Murphy* (Sheffield: JSOT Press, 1987), pp. 237-45.

32. Denise L. Carmody, *Biblical Woman: Contemporary Reflections on Scriptural Texts* (New York: Crossroad, 1988), p. 72.

33. Masenya, *How Worthy Is the Woman of Worth?*, pp. 143-57.

34. Rosemary Radford Ruether shared this view with me in a telephone conversation in 1995.

> To join those who seek wisdom, women are thereby forced to include our-
> selves, where we have been, by tradition, excluded. We must write ourselves
> into the text. Modern women's appropriation of this tradition represents an
> example of how women, when facing the androcentric biblical text—to say
> nothing of patriarchal religious and social institutions—must make new
> patterns, must read ourselves into places we were not previously envisioned
> as inhabiting.[35]

In short, women readers have inserted themselves into the text, insisting on
making meanings that expose the androcentric ideology behind, within, and
in front of the texts. They have begun to appreciate wisdom from the perspective of feminist experience und uttered wisdom in their own voices.

The Recognition of Experience and beyond a Patriarchal God:
Feminist Wrestling with the Book of Job

Only a few feminist exegetes grapple with the heavily androcentric book
of Job. They expose and critique the interlocking systems of sexism and
classism, and offer women-friendly interpretations. In particular they highlight the female character of Mrs Job, redeeming her from centuries-long
interpretative violence. Some feminist scholars also regard Job's suffering as
analog to the sufferers of the world; they portray him as an anti-patriarch,
one of the oppressed. Yet, overall and especially in the 1970s and 1980s, the
book of Job did not enjoy much attention from feminist scholars due to its
glaring androcentric slant and omission of female characters. Christl Maier
and Silvia Schroer point to this problem when they write:

> Can a book which is so clearly and explicitly written from an androcentric
> point of view claim to deal with questions that are relevant for both men *and*
> women? Are we women touched by Job's suffering, his protest and his
> righteousness? Surely some skepticism is in order here... Suffering has its own
> female face—this is true today as, probably, in ancient Israel. How do we, in
> the view of this knowledge, read this book about the righteous sufferer? Are
> the well-known speeches of Yhwh plausible answers to the questions of Job or
> to our questions?[36]

---

35.   Day, 'Wisdom and the Feminine', p. 126.

36.   Christl Maier and Silvia Schroer, 'What about Job? Questioning the Book of
"the Righteous Sufferer"', in Athalya Brenner and Carole Fontaine (eds.), *Wisdom
and Psalms: A Feminist Companion to the Bible* (FCB, 2nd Series, 2; Sheffield: Sheffield
Academic Press, 1998), pp. 175-76. See also Lillian R. Klein, 'Job and the Womb: Text
about Men, Subtext about Women', in Brenner and Fontaine (eds.), *Feminist Companion
to Wisdom Literature*, pp. 186-200.

Feminist interpreters thus approach the book of Job cautiously and, unsurprisingly, few of them have written commentaries on it.[37] When they work on Job, their exegesis is not comprehensive but mainly focuses on specific passages. Predictably, Mrs Job received some attention, as for instance from Choon L. Seow and Sarojini Nadar.[38] Many of these studies rely on literary and ideological approaches, sidelining historical-critical issues.

Re-reading Job: Female Characters within the Androcentric Text

Although the plot is dominated by the male protagonist, his male friends, the male characters of God, and *ha-satan*, feminist interpreters attempt to recover Mrs Job and her role in the story. Mrs Job appears in 2.9 and has usually been evaluated negatively in the androcentric history of interpretation. As C.L. Seow notes, androcentric readers condemned her for not supporting her husband and called her 'an unthinking fool, an irritating nag, a heretic, a temptor, an unwitting tool of the devil, or even a personification of the devil himself'.[39] This hostile reception of Mrs Job has been untenable to feminist interpreters. Carol A. Newsom, for instance, praises Mrs Job for foreseeing the future events, as developed in the book's plot. In fact, so Newsom, Mrs Job's assessment of the situation shapes the gist of the content of Job's speeches in subsequent chapters. Newsom explains:

> What gets overlooked in this approach is that Job's wife is the one who recognizes, long before Job himself does, what is at stake theologically in innocent suffering: the conflict between innocence and integrity on the one hand and an affirmation of the goodness of God, on the other. It is the issue with which Job will struggle in the following chapters.[40]

In feminist interpretations, therefore, Mrs Job emerges as a potential theologian and philosopher who understands the seriousness of her husband's

---

37. Carol A. Newsom, 'The Book of Job', in Robert Doran (ed.), *New Interpreter's Bible. IV. 1 & 2 Maccabees, Job, Psalms* (Nashville, TN: Abingdon Press, 1996), pp. 130-36; Carol A. Newsom, 'Job', in Newsom and Ringe (eds.), *The Women's Bible Commentary*, pp. 138-44; Masenya Madipoane (ngwan'a Mphahlele) and Rodney Saddler, 'Job', in Hugh R. Page (ed.), *The Africana Bible: Reading Israel's Scriptures from Africa and the African Diaspora* (Minneapolis: Fortress Press, 2010), pp. 237-43.

38. Choon L. Seow, 'Job's Wife', in Linda Day and Carolyn Pressler (eds.), *Engaging the Bible in a Gendered World: An Introduction to Feminist Biblical Interpretation in Honor of Katharine Doob Sakenfeld* (Louisville, KY: Westminster/John Knox Press, 2006), pp. 141-50; Sarojini Nadar, 'Barak God and Die!', in Musa W. Dube and Musimbi Kanyoro (eds.), *Grant Me Justice: HIV/AIDS and Gender Readings of the Bible* (Pietermaritzburg: Cluster Publications; Maryknoll, NY: Orbis Books, 2004), pp. 60-79.

39. Seow, 'Job's Wife', p. 141.

40. Newsom, 'Job', p. 140.

situation. Initially, he dismisses her but eventually he follows her suggestions, yet without acknowledging the debt he owes her. Ellen van Wolde
agrees with this reading of Mrs Job's role in the plot regarding Mrs Job as a
catalyst for her husband's intellectual, theological, and spiritual development. She states:

> On the one hand she is completely overshadowed by her husband, and seems
> irrelevant to the story. On the other hand, she sets Job thinking, although he
> dismisses her words as foolish... Thus the woman plays an important part in
> the development of the story. With her help, Job changes from a cocksure
> believer to an asker of questions.[41]

In these and similar feminist readings, then, the wife is a central but hidden
character in the story. She gives her husband intellectual courage but he does
not acknowledge her.

Perhaps unsurprisingly, non-feminist interpreters responded to this positive assessment of Mrs Job, and rejected it. Victor Sasson designates her as
foolish:

> She is, indeed, a foolish woman, speaking like one of those foolish female
> chatterers. She makes an outrageous, blasphemous suggestion: to curse God
> and incur the penalty of death... Typically, our politically-correct critic twists
> the evidence and accuses the victim, not the perpetrator—simply because the
> perpetrator happens to be female.[42]

What he calls politically correct ought to be regarded as yet another twist of
the centuries-old misogynist interpretation history. Sasson perhaps unleashes
his complaint because he writes from a comfortable social location, just as
Job; both have to be viewed as the elite rich men they are. It is no wonder
that this perspective leaves untouched the classist and sexist ideologies
inherent in the text. Is it surprising that Sasson claims that women have
always needed to be controlled by patriarchy? Sasson is so complacent that
he finds it unimaginable for anyone ever successfully to dislodge and eliminate patriarchy![43]

In contrast, feminist commentators have been the ones focusing on Job's
scathing response to his wife's exhortation. Carol Newsom explains that the
translation of the verb *barak* has led to negative views of Mrs Job. Translating the verb as 'curse', androcentric interpreters found their dismissal of the
female character as justified. In their opinion, she is a negative foil for the

---

41.   Ellen van Wolde, 'Development of Job: Mrs Job as Catalyst', in Brenner (ed.),
A Feminist Companion to Wisdom Literature, pp. 201-21 (203-204).

42.   Victor Sasson, 'The Literary and Theological Function of Job's Wife in the Book
of Job', *Bib* 79 (1998), pp. 86-90 (87).

43.   Sasson, 'The Literary and Theological Function of Job's Wife', p. 89.

morally superior Job. As David Clines states: 'Whatever Job's wife means by her speech, to curse and die (2.9), it is evident that she plays her role in the story only as a foil to Job, his patience being contrasted with her impatience, his piety with her blasphemy, his wisdom with her speech'.[44] Predictably, then, the story does not elaborate on her suffering, what the loss of a healthy spouse might mean to her, or mention her embarrassment of living with a man who is regarded as a heinous sinner. The story also disregards her many pregnancies although they certainly need to be imagined as involving great risks to her life. Instead, in typical patriarchal fashion, the epilogue celebrates the beauty of her daughters and places special emphasis on their inheritance.[45] Even when the book glances at women's lives, patriarchal bias characterizes the depictions.

Some feminist scholars counter the overpowering androcentrism of the book by highlighting the daughters and other marginalized women. Newsom uplifts Job's daughters and their unusual status within the patriarchal family household of Job. The daughters receive their share of the inheritance equal to their brothers. So surprised about this matter-of-fact report on the daughterly inheritance, Newsom also wonders if this mention does not indicate the author's effort of stressing the exceptional nature of everything related to Job. Yet other feminist interpreters are less generous and do not regard the inheritance and the naming of the daughters as a reference to Job's specialness. They associate it with male charm that is not threatened by the female inheritance. Lillian R. Klein makes this point when she explains that only the son's genealogy counts in patriarchy, irrespective of the daughters being named or becoming heirs. In fact, the narrative discriminates against elderly women,[46] and so, in her view, 'woman is either a womb that gives birth to man's grief or a failed womb. It is hard to know which is better. Either way, there is no potential for woman to be righteous in this text.'[47]

Identifying Feminist Principles in Job's Story
To some feminist interpreters, a positive or negative character evaluation does not go far enough in the quest for a feminist reading of the book of Job, and so they search for feminist principles in the androcentric plot. One such principle consists in the idea of experience, as it plays such a prominent role in Job's responses to his friends. For instance, Newsom finds Job's insistence on the validity of his own experience helpful because, in her view, it affirms

44.   David J.A. Clines, *Interested Parties: The Ideology of Writers and the Readers of the Hebrew Bible* (GCT, 1; JSOTSup, 205; Sheffield: Sheffield Academic Press, 1995), p. 123.
   45.   Clines, *Interested Parties*, pp. 129-30.
   46.   Klein, 'Job and the Womb', p. 192.
   47.   Klein, 'Job and the Womb', p. 200.

the feminist emphasis on valuing women's experiences in the articulation of feminist consciousness. Newsom observes that feminists insist on the validity of their experiences against patriarchal dismissal and denigration, similar to Job who refers to his experience to reject his friends' explanations.[48] Thus, Job's repeated references to his experience affirm the feminist insight although the debate of Job and his friends does not refer explicitly to women or women's issues. In both cases, the referral to experience critiques tradition and authority. To Newsom, then, Job emerges as a proto-feminist figure, cast in a highly androcentric plot line.

The androcentric narrative discloses yet another principle, feminist interpreters propose. The story depicts a system in which male hierarchies of age and class rule. As Job and his friends engage in discussions of prosperity and loss, definitions of good and bad, they perform their male authority as elderly men of the upper class. Yet these positions of power disable them to see injustice in the world, and to feminists their opinions sound all too familiar.[49] Male characters talk about the world as if misfortune were disconnected from unjust societal structures, a depiction of reality feminists work against. Male dominance appears in yet another dynamic in the narrative, well known to feminists. David J.A. Clines observes that patriarchy is not only expressed in relations between men and women, it also appears in the interaction between older, more powerful men and younger, less powerful men. Job's nostalgic speech in Job 29 reflects this dynamic, as Clines states:

> Job portrays himself here as the dominant male, and he behaves like any dominant male among primates: others must make gestures of submission to him. This dominance is what gives him identity and pleasure, and in the time of his loss of it he can only wish that it was restored.[50]

In accordance with this paradigm of male domination, Job's wife serves as a foil, and in Job's response to his wife's exhortation, he mocks the absence of any wise women.[51] Clines problematizes Job's classification of foolish women as a gross generalization. He suspects that these women would probably be lower class women with whom Job, the elite patriarch, would not ordinarily associate. Clines explains:

> Perhaps there is a class aspect here as well, and 'foolish women' means, in particular, 'lower class women'; perhaps also it is the pious snob, who has pitched his tent on the moral high ground, who speaks here, equating 'lower class' with 'godless'. But more likely, as I was suggesting, it is simply the

48. Newsom, 'Job', pp. 140-41.
49. Newsom, 'Job', p. 142.
50. Clines, *Interested Parties*, p. 131.
51. Clines, *Interested Parties*, p. 129.

male speaking, the patriarch, who lumps all women together as foolish chatters, expects better of a patriarch's wife, and is disappointed but not surprised when she shows herself typical of her sex.[52]

In this analysis, then, Job is a macho, elite male who speaks disparagingly about women.

Other feminist and liberationist interpreters, however, do not want to let go of Job as a role model. They maintain that Job's experience of unjust suffering enables him to appreciate the plight of those on the margins, such as widows, orphans, women, and children. Writing from a Latin American perspective, Elsa Tamez uses Job as a model for innocent sufferers.[53] To Tamez, Job's protests are reminders to the poor that life was not given to be lived in misery.[54] Similarly, Sarojini Nadar, presenting a HIV and AIDS gender-sensitive reading of Job, suggests that only when Job becomes poor does he associate with the plight of the poor.[55] Another Job-affirmative reading comes from Bible Study group members in Kwa-Zulu Natal, South Africa, coordinated by Gerald West and Bongi Zengele. It centers on Job's protest in Job 3 and affirms those who suffer from HIV and AIDS.[56] Masenya also focuses on Job 3 when she employs an African story-telling approach. She argues that Job's lament attacks female reproductive anatomy and is therefore not helpful in the context of mourning African South-African women.[57] In short, feminist interpreters go back and forth on reclaiming and rejecting the feminist potential of the book of Job. They struggle with its androcentric tendencies and search for ways to subvert them.

The Great Patriarch: Image(s) of God in the Book of Job
The hermeneutical decision to acknowledge the unabated androcentrism in the book of Job is much easier to carry out when feminist interpreters examine the various depictions of God as a patriarch and problematize this

52. Clines, *Interested Parties*, p. 129.

53. Elsa Tamez, 'From Father to the Needy to Brother of Jackals and Companion of Ostriches: A Meditation on Job', in Ellen van Wolde (ed.), *Job's God* (London: SCM Press, 2004), pp. 103-11. See also Gustavo Gutiérrez, *On Job: God-Talk and the Suffering of the Innocent* (trans. Matthew J. O'Connell; Maryknoll, NY: Orbis Books, 1995).

54. Tamez, 'From Father to the Needy to Brother of Jackals', p. 104; Gutiérrez, *On Job*, pp. 13, 24, 34, 39-49.

55. Nadar, 'Barak God', p. 71.

56. Gerald West and Bongi Zengele, 'Reading Job "Positively" in the Context of HIV/AIDS in South Africa', in van Wolde (ed.), *Job's God*, pp. 112-24.

57. Madipoane Masenya (ngwan'a Mphahlele), 'Her Appropriation of Job's Lament? Her-Lament of Job from an African Storytelling Perspective', *Theologia viatorum: Journal of Theology and Religion in Africa* 33 (2009), pp. 385-408.

image of the divinity. Lyn M. Bechtel, for instance, notes the difference between the book's depiction of God and Job's belief in a patriarchal God. In her view, readers witness 'God's functioning within the arbitrariness of life' whereas Job attempts to cling to 'his theology of God's absolute control of life'.[58] Other feminist interpreters distinguish between the anthropomorphic and androcentric views about God on the one hand and the portrayal of a cosmic God on the other hand. Carol C. Newsom observes that Job's speeches depict God as a God of justice; they remain within the human realm. Yet, God's speech in Job 38–40 aims to redirect Job toward a cosmic view about God. There, God appears as ordering the creation and as utterly disregarding the human realm. For instance, the text emphasizes that God lets rain fall in the desert where there is no human life.[59] Thus, this speech demonstrates that God is not merely focused on human welfare. Newsom explains that this depiction presents God 'as a power of life, balancing the needs of all creatures, not just humans, cherishing freedom, full of fierce love and delight for each thing without regard for its utility, acknowledging the deep interconnectedness of death and life, restraining and nurturing each element in the ecology of all creation'.[60] To Newsom, this kind of God talk is reminiscent of feminist theological thought because it expands Job's patriarchal God into the God of Creation.

In a recent study I contributed to this effort of appropriating the God of creation. I referred this image to my own African context and discussed Job 3 through an eco*bosadi* lens.[61] I explained that biblical exegetes have to recover their connections and harmonious links with nature, as traditionally practiced by African peoples. These links were especially close between African women and earth, and a eco*bosadi* African reading of Job 3 makes evident this proximity. It shows that nature takes center stage in God's response to Job, superseding androcentric and anthropocentric expectations. God is creator of earth and all that is in it; God is a nurturing mother and sustainer of nature. Accordingly, Job 3 is important because it illustrates Job's delusion of being in charge as a patriarch and for attacking women's reproductive abilities. An eco*bosadi* hermeneutic exposes his delusion because this approach is closely connected to nature, women, and a holistic worldview.

58. Lyn M. Bechtel, 'A Feminist Approach to the Book of Job', in Brenner (ed.), *A Feminist Companion to Wisdom Literature*, pp. 222-51 (235).

59. Newsom, 'Job', p. 143.

60. Newsom, 'Job', p. 144.

61. Madipoane Masenya (ngwan'a Mphahlele), 'All from the Same Source? Deconstructing a (Male) Anthropocentric Reading of Job (3) through an Eco-bosadi Lens', *Journal of Theology in Southern Africa* 137 (2010), pp. 46-60.

Lynn Bechtel mentions yet another aspect about the divinity to be used for feminist purposes. She observes that Job and his friends are portrayed as exhibiting the typical human need for attributing excessive control to God. They assume that God has absolute control over all aspects of existence, an idea also characteristic of Deuteronomistic theology. It is built upon the dualism that splits God as either being in total control or as being completely arbitrary. It also assumes that God eradicates chaos and arbitrariness, and punishes the evil doers and rewards the righteous ones. Bechtel states that this kind of belief in God, evidenced in the speeches of Job and his friends, requires the conviction that people get what they deserve.[62] Yet the divine speech illustrates that this belief is wrong, as prosperity and deprivation come from either the human economic system and the arbitrary interplay of oppositional forces. God's answer to Job problematizes the human need for believing to be in control by thinking about God in anthropomorphic ways.[63] Thus, the divine speech challenges the theological expectation that life ought not to depend on the interplay of oppositional forces or utter arbitrariness. Read accordingly, the book of Job views nature and creation as much more powerful than humanity, as out of control and arbitrary, and as impossible to be mastered by humans like Job and his friends.[64] Ultimately, this image of God explodes the notion of a divine patriarch. It turns the book of Job into a feminist theological treatise after all.

Closed to Women's Experiences?
Feminist Readings of the Book of Qoheleth

From the outset, feminist interpreters struggled with the book of Qoheleth that famously rejects the notion of retributive theology. The books of Proverbs and Job present a debate on the issue, but in Qohelet the discussion is decided. Taking the male experience as the starting point and directing the author's word toward a male-defined audience, the male speaker rejects unambiguously the position that expects reward for those doing good and punishment for the evil doers. As Kathleen M. O'Connor puts it, to Qoheleth 'life is wearisome and empty'.[65] Qoheleth is a proponent of a radical theology that rejects the belief of his day. He proclaims that a moral connection between cause and effect does not exist. Feminists emphasize that this position is articulated from a male elite position. Qoheleth explains that no

---

62. Bechtel, 'A Feminist Approach to the Book of Job', p. 231.
63. Bechtel, 'A Feminist Approach to the Book of Job', p. 229.
64. Bechtel, 'A Feminist Approach to the Book of Job', p. 248.
65. Kathleen M. O'Connor, *The Wisdom Literature* (Collegeville, MN: Liturgical Press, 1988), p. 121.

matter how many slaves, singers, mistresses, and pleasure gardens he had acquired, none of them gave his life meaning.[66] He also did not find meaningful relationships. Fontaine explains that Qoheleth suffers the boredom of male elites. In this world, nature, women, and social inferiors are objects to be used and the situation of the oppressed is dismissed as irrelevant. Thus, Qoheleth's plight exhibits 'the symptoms of the same self-centered, worldview of elite males (4:1-3; 5:8-9)'.[67] Obviously, then, this book does not address the needs of poor women who struggle to make ends meet. Interestingly, however, and as pointed out by Elaine A. Philips, the references to personal anguish mentioned in the book of Qoheleth resonate with women from the lower rungs of the socio-economic ladder.[68] Weariness and endless toil certainly play a prominent role in their lives, perhaps also reminding them of Gen. 3.17-19 that connects their toil with divine punishment.

Yet overall, feminists classify the book of Qoheleth as misogynist. Fontaine observes that Qoh. 7.26 is a particularly good example of the writer's misogyny. Similar to the warnings against Woman Stranger in Proverbs, the verse emphasizes the negative effects that women have on men. Fontaine questions why Qoheleth singles out women in this way. Worse, he even makes men's escape from women a theological merit. I suggest that a feminist position reads this verse as an indication of Qoheleth's difficulty to control his sexual urges. He projects his personal weakness upon all women, which is a deeply misogynist move. Fontaine argues differently. She sees the misogyny as unsurprising because Qoheleth does not like children or women. He depicts children as lazy usurpers who take what they have not earned and he disregards women's contributions to society.[69] To him, women are only useful when they bring entertainment and pleasure to men (3.5-6), so that in typical male elite fashion men may enjoy life to the fullest because soon it will be over anyway (3.9-22; 9.4-6). Feminist exegetes conclude that there is little use for the cynical views expressed in this book.

However, as in the case of Job, some feminists embrace Qoheleth's insistence on the significance of personal experience. As O'Connor observes:

66. Carole R. Fontaine, 'Ecclesiastes', in Newsom and Ringe (eds.), *Women's Bible Commentary*, pp. 161-63 (162).

67. Fontaine, 'Ecclesiastes', p. 162.

68. Elaine A. Phillips, 'Job', in Catherine Clark Kroeger and Mary J. Evan (eds.), *The IVP Women's Bible Commentary* (Downers Grove, IL: InterVarsity Press, 1988), pp. 343-46.

69. Fontaine, 'Ecclesiastes', pp. 162-63. For a discussion on the contribution of Qoheleth's androcentric text to misogyny within Christianity, see also Carol Fontaine, 'Many Devices (Qoheleth7:23–8:1): Qoheleth, Misogyny and the *Malleus maleficarum*', in Brenner and Fontaine (eds.), *Wisdom and Psalms*, pp. 137-68.

> In accord with the tradition of Solomon, his vision is based on the authority of human experience; it recognizes the unity of human existence with the life and events of the universe; it affirms the centrality of the fear of Yahweh in human relationship with God and finally, it validates ordinary human life as the arena of spirituality.[70]

The notion that humans are intimately connected with God even when we do not fully understand it appeals to feminist interpreters because such a theology does not view God as distant and uninvolved. Although Qoheleth's basic position is one of cynical disengagement, the idea about humanity's participation in the largely unknown divine purpose is of interest to feminist and liberation theologians. It affirms the divine–human encounter even when it is difficult to discern purpose and coherence. It also values positively the pleasures of nature and the body. In this respect Qoheleth's theology might even be regarded as a precursor of feminist theology, minus its pessimistic outlook on the purpose of life.[71] Thus, despite the book's deep pessimism towards life and its detached, elitist, and misogynist arguments, Qoheleth challenges the status quo and affirms individual experience. By focusing on these aspects of the book, feminist interpreters have been able to bring a feminist hermeneutics into conversation with this biblical book that seems so adamantly closed to women's experiences.

Continuing to Move into Woman Wisdom's House: A Conclusion

Feminist exegetes need to be commended for wading through the heavily androcentric wisdom literature. Although some feminists might criticize these efforts as relying on the master's tools while trying to challenge biblical patriarchy in text and interpretation history, they have made such interpretations accessible and relevant to women readers. However, it needs to be noted that the resulting feminist interpretations, focusing on the problems of patriarchy in the wisdom literature, neglect the ideologies of classism, ethnocentrism, ageism, and anthropocentrism. The insufficient attention to the interlocking systems of discrimination is typical for European and white American feminist readers. Only when a few Two-Thirds World feminist exegetes began engaging this literature in the contexts of poverty and HIV/AIDs did interpretations emerge that accounted for the interlocking systems of discrimination. For sure, more needs to be done, but the existing feminist scholarship on the wisdom books are the foundation for the next generation of feminist scholars to make these connections with full force. They are thus well positioned to seek Wisdom, to find her, and to inhabit her house, and to be continuously taught by her.

70. O'Connor 'The Wisdom Literature', p. 132.
71. Fontaine, 'Ecclesiastes', p. 162.

12

THE STORIES OF WOMEN IN A MAN'S WORLD:
THE BOOKS OF RUTH, ESTHER, AND JUDITH*

Yael Shemesh

The books of Ruth, Esther, and Judith have always enjoyed considerable feminist attention whether during the nineteenth or twentieth centuries. The female names of these books have guaranteed feminist attention in the search for biblical texts that go beyond the androcentric focus on men, the patriarchal marginalization of women, or male-dominated storylines. Looking for feminist empowerment, especially during the heyday of the Second Feminist Movement in the 1970s, feminist scholars have made much of the prevalence and prominence of the female characters, Ruth, Esther, and Judith. They hunted for feminist heroines in the biblical texts, for role models to defend against structures of domination in society and religious institutions in which the Bible had been used to put down women for the ages. The three biblical books, named after women and including a presumed abundance of female characters, thus presented themselves as unique opportunities for feminist exegesis.

Since then, feminist appropriations have, of course, become more complicated and less hopeful towards the goal of feminist empowerment, and more willing toward compromise positions. But so have the contexts in which these texts are read. Nowadays, feminist postcolonial critics rub exegetical shoulders with women-focused and religiously conservative interpreters. The feminist hermeneutical scene on the books of Ruth, Esther, and Judith has become considerably more complex and less feminist radical than in the 1970s. The hermeneutical movement of the past thirty to forty years has largely followed the same pattern: it went from emphasizing the women in the book of Ruth as heroines in a patriarchal world to stressing 'the man's world' in which the female characters function.

In other words, initial enthusiasm on finding empowered women in the androcentric literature morphed into adamant criticism of women's roles in the male-dominated texts. The search for middle ground is perhaps the

---
* I would like to thank Keren Beit Shalom of Japan for the generous support of this research.

phrase of the day, seeking a compromise between enthusiasm and rejection, with the hope of holding on to the stories regardless. The following discussion explores a plethora of feminist interpretations of each biblical book—Ruth, Esther, and Judith—as they emerged in the past few decades.

Empowerment of Women or Promoting Patriarchal Interest: The Feminist Hermeneutical Struggle over the Book of Ruth

In the early stage of feminist approaches to the book of Ruth, the female characters became heroines, sources of feminist empowerment, role models forging a women-empowered path in a man's world. Phyllis Trible published the first such interpretation. Her sensitive literary analysis recognizes briefly and directly that in the book of Ruth '[a] man's world tells a woman's story',[1] but a woman's story it is nevertheless. Ruth is the prominent and dominant character and she has a companion, Naomi, her mother-in-law. The two of them work out their own salvation, they cooperate with each other, and together with the women of Bethlehem they represent 'paradigms of radicality' because '[a]ll together they are women in culture, women against culture, and women transforming culture'.[2] To Trible, the book of Ruth is a feminist piece of literature, or at least it can be interpreted with a feminist perspective challenging patriarchal oppression and discrimination against women. This can be done at least by those 'who have ears to hear the stories of women in a man's world', as she advises.[3] At a moment when feminists proclaimed publicly and in writing the Bible's utter patriarchal bias, Trible's assertion opened up powerful, liberating, and inspiring ways of looking at the book of Ruth in particular and the Bible in general.

Many feminist interpretations followed Trible's trajectory. They emphasize the central role that women play in the book. The two women, Ruth and Naomi, occupy center stage, and Orpah (1.4-14) supports them, as does the chorus of women of Bethlehem (1.19; 4.14-17). In addition, they invoke the founding mothers of the nation, Rachel, Leah, and Tamar, when the people and the elders bless Boaz (4.11-12), as Adele Berlin highlights in her reading of the story. She explains that Ruth and Naomi, like Rachel, Leah, and Tamar before them, ensure the continuity of the family and the nation.[4] In the same vein, Irmtraud Fischer states that 'the book of Ruth is a book of

1. Phyllis Trible, *God and the Rhetoric of Sexuality* (Philadelphia: Fortress Press, 1978), p. 166.
2. Trible, *Rhetoric*, p. 196.
3. Trible, *Rhetoric*, p. 196.
4. Adele Berlin, 'Ruth and the Continuity of Israel', in Judith A. Kates and Gail Twersky Reimer (eds.), *Reading Ruth: Contemporary Women Reclaim a Sacred Story* (New York: Ballantine Books, 1994), pp. 255-60.

women'.[5] In other words, initial feminist readers enthusiastically support the various women characters. They become proto-feminists, not only surviving but flourishing in the androcentric story world. Feminists recover them and regard them as proto-feminist figures in support of today's feminist endeavors.

In particular, feminist interpreters emphasize the special bond of solidarity and love between the two women. To them, Ruth's declaration of loyalty to Naomi (1.16-17) reflects a unique attachment between women in the Bible. Where else do we find a declaration of love by one woman for another woman? The women's bond is further marked linguistically when the narrator uses the root *dbq* for Ruth's relationship towards Naomi (1.14), a clear allusion to Gen. 2.24. Furthermore, the root *'hb* that depicts Ruth's relationship with Naomi in the speech of the women of Bethlehem (4.15) is the only place in the Bible where this denotes a loving bond between two women. The unusual description of love between two women, employing verbs appropriate to the relations between a man and a woman (*'hb, dbq*), has led Jewish lesbians, seeking empowerment, to make midrashic use of the story. They see Ruth as a role model and in her declaration of fidelity to Naomi (1.16-17) they find legitimacy for love between women. Hence the story is often incorporated into lesbian wedding ceremonies.[6]

In contrast to the stereotypical model of competition and hostility in other tales about women, such as Sarah and Hagar, Rachel and Leah, and Hannah and Peninah, feminists stress that the book of Ruth supports the ideal of love and cooperation among women. Thus, for instance, Ilana Pardes regards the book as an idyllic revision of the relationship between Rachel and Leah.[7] She states: 'Hence, as the Book of Ruth revises the story of Rachel and Leah, the rivalry between the younger and the elder co-wives gives way to a harmonious sharing of the same man'.[8] Pardes also highlights the fact that Ruth and Naomi are daughter-in-law and mother-in-law, a family link that in her view makes their bond special and from a literary perspective invites conflict and oedipal drama.[9] As typical of early feminist approaches to the entire biblical book, even the story's end becomes an indication of the

5.   Irmtraud Fischer, *Women Who Wrestled with God: Biblical Stories of Israel's Beginnings* (trans. Linda M. Maloney; Collegeville, MN: Liturgical Press, 2005), p. 142.

6.   See Rebecca Alpert, 'Finding our Past: A Lesbian Interpretation of the Book of Ruth', in Kates and Reimer (eds.), *Reading Ruth*, pp. 91-96.

7.   Ilana Pardes, 'The Book of Ruth: Idyllic Revisionism', in Pardes, *Countertraditions in the Bible: A Feminist Approach* (Cambridge, MA: Harvard University Press, 1992), pp. 98-117.

8.   Pardes, 'The Book of Ruth', p. 105.

9.   Pardes, 'The Book of Ruth', p. 103.

ongoing cooperation between the two women. In 4.16, Naomi takes Ruth's son, Obed, to her bosom and serves as his nurse not in competition to the mother but as a manifestation of the women's 'joint parenthood'. Accordingly, the women of Bethlehem do not diminish Ruth when they declare that '[a] son has been born to Naomi' (Ruth 4.17 [RSV]).[10] To feminist readers of this hermeneutical stage, women of all ages and relationships support and nurture each other in the book of Ruth.

Several scholars thus noted the feminist tone of the book. One of them is Carol Meyers who considers the women of Bethlehem as an informal women's network. She also guards against contrasting the public versus the private domain in which the women of Bethlehem function.[11] Others, such as Zefira Gitay, observe that the women and not the men of Bethlehem offer Naomi support. They accept Ruth as a full member of Israelite society without any signs of hesitation or resistance.[12] Feminist exegetes also note the linguistic peculiarity of the book. It mentions the maternal rather than the paternal house of Ruth (Ruth 1.8).[13] Meyers examines this collocation here and in Gen. 24.28, Song 3.4, and 8.2. In her view, the phrase indicates that the book of Ruth is a 'female text'[14] because it refers to lineage and not merely to the woman's living quarters. Suffice it to say, then, that early feminist interpreters are indeed taken by the book of Ruth. To them, it is feminist literature indeed.

The next logical question is to ask if the book of Ruth was written by a female author. Some feminist exegetes emphasize that this book is populated by women who are in charge of their own destiny and breaks clearly with various patriarchal conventions. For them, the uninvestigated assumption of a male author does not hold. For instance, several articles in Athalya Brenner's edited volume, *A Feminist Companion to Ruth*, appear under the heading of 'Gendered Authorship'. In a field dominated by historical critical studies on authorship and historical setting, the quest for a female author has thus preoccupied feminist scholars for years. It should be noted that,

10. Pardes, 'The Book of Ruth', p. 106.

11. Carol Meyers, '"Women of the Neighborhood" (Ruth 4.17): Informal Female Networks in Ancient Israel', in Athalya Brenner (ed.), *Ruth and Esther: A Feminist Companion to the Bible* (FCB, 2nd Series, 3; Sheffield: Sheffield Academic Press, 1999), pp. 110-27.

12. Zefira Gitay, 'Ruth and the Women of Bethlehem', in Athalya Brenner (ed.), *A Feminist Companion to Ruth* (FCB, 3; Sheffield: Sheffield Academic Press, 1993), pp. 178-90.

13. For a first articulation of this view, see Trible, *God and the Rhetoric of Sexuality*, p. 169.

14. Carol Meyers, 'Returning Home: Ruth 1:8 and the Gendering of the Book of Ruth', in Brenner (ed.), *A Feminist Companion to Ruth*, pp. 85-113.

more than fifty years ago, Shlomo Dov Goitein—though not a feminist—
suggested for the first time that a woman wrote the book of Ruth.[15] More
recently, Adrien Bledstein, too, conjectures that the book was written by a
woman.[16] Fokkelien van Dijk-Hemmes and Athalya Brenner are more
cautious about making such a statement. Avoiding the hypothetical question
about the author's biological sex, they assert that a female voice speaks from
the text. They characterize it as an 'F voice', even if it was not written by a
biological woman.[17] To all of them, the book of Ruth centers on women,
whether they are characters or possible authors, and it endorses women's
solidarity and feminist goals of women's power.

In sharp opposition to these optimistic views about the feminist potential
of the book of Ruth, other feminist interpreters build on it pointing to the
inherent androcentrism in this literature. One of them is Esther Fuchs who,
in rebutting Trible, notes that the female character, Ruth, acts in accordance
with a patriarchal agenda. Characteristic of women in patriarchy, she gives
up her national, ethnic, and religious identity when she follows Naomi. She
leaves her home, her people, and her religion, perpetuating the line of her
late husband and father-in-law.[18] This is a serious objection about the first
part of the biblical story that early feminist readers found empowering.
Women's solidarity and support turns into Ruth devaluing her own tradition
over against male lineage.

Yet this problem is not limited to the beginning of the story and also
occurs at the end. For instance, Cheryl Exum argues that Ruth's marriage to
Boaz and the birth of her son are not part of 'a story about how two women
make a life together in a man's world (though it is that in part), but a story
about the continuity of a family, and this requires the presence of a man.

---

15. Shlomo Dov Goitein, *Studies in the Bible* (Tel Aviv: Yavneh, 1957 [Hebrew]),
p. 252.

16. Adrien J. Bledstein, 'Female Companionships: If the Book of Ruth Were Written
by a Woman', in Brenner (ed.), *A Feminist Companion to Ruth*, pp. 116-33. See also
Mishael Maswary Caspi and Rachel S. Haverlock, *Women on the Biblical Road: Ruth,
Naomi, and the Female Journey* (Lanham, MD: University Press of America, 1996),
pp. 185-86.

17. Fokkelien van Dijk-Hemmes, 'Ruth: A Product of Women's Culture?', in
Brenner (ed.), *A Feminist Companion to Ruth*, pp. 134-39 (136); Athalya Brenner,
'Naomi and Ruth: Further Reflections', in Brenner (ed.), *A Feminist Companion to Ruth*,
pp. 140-44. On the idea of the 'F voice', see also Athalya Brenner and Fokkelien van
Dijk-Hemmes, *On Gendering Texts: Female and Male Voices in the Hebrew Bible*
(Leiden: E.J. Brill, 1993); Irmtraud Fischer, 'The Book of Ruth: A "Feminist" Com-
mentary to the Torah?', in Brenner (ed.), *Ruth and Esther*, pp. 24-49 (33-34).

18. Esther Fuchs, 'The Literary Characterization of Mothers and Sexual Politics in
the Hebrew Bible', in Adela Yarbro Collins (ed.), *Feminist Perspectives on Biblical
Scholarship* (Chico, CA: Scholars Press, 1985), pp. 117-36 (117-18 n. 4).

Naomi and Ruth need a redeemer (*go 'el*).'[19] Exum also observes that Boaz's entry into the narrative shifts the focus away from the relationship between the two women to the relationship between a man and a woman.[20] Despite her objections of reading the book of Ruth as a feminist treatise, Exum recognizes the possibility that Ruth and Naomi had a lesbian relationship. Hence, Exum goes back and forth between a hermeneutic that reads this biblical book as women-empowering and as promoting patriarchal interests.

It also needs to be acknowledged that early and later feminist interpreters always observe that the genealogy in Ruth 4 indicates that the book's main interest is not in women but in one man, David. Mona DeKoven Fishbein makes this point when she writes:

> In one stroke of the biblical pen, all the tensions and anguish and connections of the women heroines in this text are done away with, or seem as though they never existed. What really matters is the reproduction of men and their power, resulting in King David. A final tension—perhaps the most painful—in the book of Ruth.[21]

In other words, early and later feminist exegetes recognize that the book of Ruth is not unequivocally a feminist narrative. Early interpreters highlight the possibilities for a subversive, unexpected reading of the narrative as a tale about women who trust each other and make a life together. Every feminist scholar knows that this biblical book allows for many different readings but the feminist debate has always been over the question whether there is hope for a women-liberatory meaning or whether the story promotes an androcentric ideology after all.

Female Solidarity in the Center or on the Margins?
More on the Book of Ruth

Another significant aspect of the book—the relationship between Ruth and Naomi—has also been the subject of qualified and sometimes guarded exegesis. It especially relates to Naomi's attitude towards Ruth and the concern that, as Vanessa Ochs states, Ruth 'annihilates herself'. Whereas the men of Bethlehem compare Ruth to Rachel and Leah (4.11), Ochs likens her

---

19. J. Cheryl Exum, 'Is This Naomi?', in *Plotted, Shot, and Painted: Cultural Representations of Biblical Women* (JSOTSup, 215; Sheffield: Sheffield Academic Press, 1996), pp. 129-74.

20. It should be noted that Exum (see her *Plotted*, pp. 169-74) also finds feminist empowerment in the book because of the flexible depiction of the gender roles.

21. Mona DeKoven Fishbane, 'Ruth: Dilemmas of Loyalty and Connection', in Kates and Reimer (eds.), *Reading Ruth*, pp. 298-308 (307-308). See also Vanessa L. Ochs, 'Reading Ruth: Where Are the Women?', in Kates and Reimer (eds.), *Reading Ruth*, pp. 289-97 (297).

to Bilhah and Zilpah, the maidservants of Rebekah and Leah. Ochs asserts that like Bilhah and Zilpah, Ruth provides surrogate services for Naomi.[22] Accordingly, the final scene of the narrative is not an ideal of joint parenthood and women's solidarity, but the moment in which Naomi's exploitation of Ruth is blatantly expressed. The deal benefits Naomi only.

Similarly, Danna Fewell and David Gunn consider Naomi far from being the loving and selfless mother-in-law that earlier feminist readers recovered. To them, Naomi prevents her daughters-in-law from coming with her to Bethlehem because she regards them as a burden and an embarrassing reminder of her family's assimilation into Moab. Furthermore, Fewell and Gunn stress that Naomi responds with silent withdrawal. Naomi's effort to marry Ruth to Boaz is mainly driven by protecting her own interests, as it is Naomi's way of guaranteeing her economic future. Ruth is a surrogate womb, which explains why Naomi does not respond when the women of Bethlehem praise Ruth.[23]

Yet the same criticism applies to Ruth, according to Fewell and Gunn's interpretation. Ruth's motives are equally self-interested. She follows her mother-in-law because she calculates that, as a widow of an Israelite man, she has no future in Moab. She figures that she should follow her mother-in-law as much out of a sense of commitment as out of personal gain.[24] Still, so Fewell and Gunn, the depiction of female characters as complex characters who act in their own personal interests has a certain degree of feminist flavor.[25] Moreover, the story repeatedly states that Ruth is an alien, an immigrant; she merely fulfills her duties to the nation of Israel and then becomes superfluous to the tale.[26] In general, then, these and other feminist exegetes are less sure than earlier feminist readers that the book of Ruth

22. Ochs, 'Where Are the Women?'

23. Danna Nolan Fewell and David M. Gunn, '"A Son Is Born to Naomi!"': Literary Allusions and Interpretations in the Book of Ruth', *JSOT* 40 (1988), pp. 99-108; Danna Nolan Fewell and David M. Gunn, *Compromising Redemption: Relating Characters in the Book of Ruth* (Louisville, KY: Westminster/John Knox Press, 1990). See the criticism of this view by Peter W. Coxon, 'Was Naomi a Scold? A Response to Fewell and Gunn', *JSOT* 45 (1989), pp. 25-37, and the original authors' fierce rejoinder: Danna Nolan Fewell and David M. Gunn, 'Is Coxon a Scold? On Responding to the Book of Ruth', *JSOT* 45 (1989), pp. 38-43.

24. This perception of Ruth is not mentioned in the article, but only in the book; see Fewell and Gunn, *Compromising Redemption*, pp. 30-31, 94-98.

25. Fewell and Gunn, 'Is Coxon a Scold?', pp. 39-40 (concerning Naomi); Fewell and Gunn, *Compromising Redemption*, pp. 94-95 (concerning Ruth).

26. See, for example: Ochs, 'Where Are the Women?', pp. 296-97; Bonnie Honig, 'Ruth, the Model Emigrée: Mourning and the Symbolic Politics of Immigration', in Brenner (ed.), *Ruth and Esther*, pp. 50-74 (60); Judith E. McKinlay, 'A Son Is Born to Naomi: A Harvest for Israel', in Brenner (ed.), *Ruth and Esther*, pp. 151-57 (152).

supports women's solidarity and power. They are ready to question the assumption that the story presents women as supportive of each other and as challenging androcentric conventions.

In recent years, the book of Ruth has been the subject of many feminist interpretations written from multicultural perspectives.[27] Many of them focus on Ruth and her decision to accompany Naomi. Judith McKinlay, for example, reads the book from the perspective of a New Zealander, a member of the dominant culture in her country (a non-Maori *pakeha*). Because of her sensitivity to the subordinate culture, she is troubled by Ruth's assimilation and transformation from Moabite to Israelite. McKinley raises the possibility that the people of Bethlehem did not fully accept Ruth. Her evidence is that, in ch. 4, Naomi holds the child Obed and is named as his mother. Her son is recognized as a full-fledged Israelite, all indications of the book's 'colonial ethos'.[28]

Another feminist interpretation makes references to colonizing tendencies in the book. Athalya Brenner reads Ruth in light of the experience of labor migrants in today's Israel who feel compelled to leave their home countries in search of a living. When they arrive in the closed Israeli society, which Brenner stigmatizes as xenophobic, they work in menial jobs and become almost invisible. The only way they find a place in the host society is through marriage—although full integration, as Brenner notes, remains impossible. Her reading paints Ruth as Naomi's foreign worker, who has joined her involuntarily but eventually improves her standing in Israelite society, achieving a measure of visibility because of her marriage to Boaz.[29]

Gale A. Yee approaches the book from the perspective of an Asian American biblical scholar of Chinese descent. She emphasizes two aspects of the story that are relevant both to Ruth and to the Asian American experience. First, they are perpetual foreigners, never accepted as members of the culture in which they are living, but they are no longer affiliated with their culture of origin. Thus, Ruth is repeatedly designated as 'the Moabite' (1.4, 22; 2.2, 6, 21; 4.5, 10), and she calls herself 'a foreigner' (2.10). Second, both Ruth and Asian foreigners are viewed as a model minority. They are expected to conform to certain stereotypes associated with their birth cultures. For example, in the Hebrew Bible, foreign women in general and

27. See the literature cited by Gale A. Yee, 'She Stood in Tears amid the Alien Corn: Ruth, the Perpetual Foreigner and Model Minority', in Randall C. Bailey, Tat-siong Benny Liew and Fernando F. Segovia (eds.), *They Were All Together in One Place? Toward Minority Biblical Criticism* (Semeia Studies, 57; Leiden: E.J. Brill, 2009), pp. 119-20.

28. McKinlay, 'A Son Is Born to Naomi', pp. 151-57.

29. Athalya Brenner, 'Ruth as a Foreign Worker and the Politics of Exogamy', in Brenner (ed.), *Ruth and Esther*, pp. 158-62.

Moabite women in particular are seen as flaunting their sexuality in unacceptable ways. Similarly, so Yee, Asian American women are victims of the same derogatory image. Thus Yee suggests that Ruth is exploited in Israel, just as Asian Americans are exploited and their contributions are downplayed in America.[30]

In contrast to the interpretations by McKinlay, Brenner, and Yee, all of whom emphasize the exploitation of foreigners in the story, Kuk Yom Han regards Ruth's foreignness as a source of inspiration for the appropriate treatment of foreigners and especially foreign women. Han refers to a phenomenon common in Korea. There foreign women, eager to improve their economic situation, marry Korean men. Yet many of the women are abused by their husbands, who view them as chattels. Sometimes, due to age disparity, the husbands accuse their foreign wives of infidelity and beat them. Han explains that, like in Israelite society, Korean society is hostile towards foreign women and takes a dim view of such mixed marriages. Yet to Han, the book of Ruth rejects prejudices against international marriage. Thus, Boaz treats Ruth with sympathy, makes sure that his hired hands do not harass her sexually, invites her to share his meal (symbolizing her acceptance in society), and encourages her with lavish praise. Furthermore, when he declares his intention to marry the Moabite woman, his fellow Israelites do not denounce her but praise and bless the union. In the blessing of ch. 4 Ruth appears next to Rachel and Leah, the founding mothers of the Israelite nation (4.11), and next to Tamar, Judah's daughter-in-law/wife, the long-ago ancestress of King David (4.11-12). The women of Bethlehem also praise Ruth for her affectionate devotion to Naomi (4.15).[31] In short, multicultural feminist readings have reached diametrically opposed conclusions about the attitude towards foreigners in the book of Ruth.

Importantly, Ruth is not the only character who has been the target of this hermeneutical multiplicity. Several multicultural readings bring to the center another woman in the book of Ruth whom earlier feminist interpreters largely ignored. Especially feminist postcolonial interpreters direct their attention to Orpah in Ruth 1.4-14. One of the interpreters is Laura Donaldson who reads from a Native American perspective.[32] She regards Orpah as a true heroine and a model for Native American women, especially Cherokee women. Donaldson explains that since colonial times Cherokee women were

30. Yee, 'She Stood in Tears', pp. 119-40.

31. Kuk Yom Han, 'Migrant Women and Intermarriage in Korea: Looking at Human Rights with Help from the Book of Ruth', in Kyung Sook Lee and Kyung Mi Park (eds.), *Korean Feminists in Conversation with the Bible, Church and Society* (Sheffield: Sheffield Phoenix Press, 2011), pp. 90-100.

32. Laura E. Donaldson, 'The Sign of Orpah: Reading Ruth through Native Eyes', in Brenner (ed.), *Ruth and Esther*, pp. 130-44, esp. 140-41.

forced to intermarry which eroded their native traditions and heritage. Donaldson thus praises Orpah for her decision to value her mother's house and return back to her family of origin. Orpah is a source of hope because she does not succumb to assimilation and abandonment of her culture. Hers is a counternarrative to the story of Ruth who assimilates to the 'alien Israel-ite Father'.[33] Orpah does not abandon her tradition and religion but returns to where she came from.[34] Hence, to Donaldson, feminist postcolonial readers have to resist the 'imperial exegesis'[35] and seek to empower native and aboriginal peoples everywhere by emphasizing Orpah's decision. They have to reject the earlier feminist reading that lifts up Ruth as the model woman because such an approach endorses the colonization of native peoples. Donaldson advises that feminist postcolonial readers have to break with the tradition to focus on Ruth and promote Orpah who respects herself and her people.

Another postcolonial feminist reader, Musa W. Dube, identifies with Orpah. Writing from the perspective of Botswana, she offers an alternative history of Moab by imagining Orpah's correspondence with Ruth in a series of letters. Each letter begins and ends with the words, 'I am Orpah, the one who returned to her mother's house and to her gods', with a slight variation at the end of the last letter. In these letters, Orpah tells her younger sister, Ruth, about the history of their Moabite nation and the annals of their own family. Dube draws on *Ruth R.* 2.9, which identifies the two as the daughters of King Eglon of Moab. Orpah also reminds Ruth of the hospitable reception that their father Eglon extended to Elimelech and his family, saving them from starvation during the drought; how Orpah and Ruth married Eli-melech's sons; and how, after their father's death, Mahlon and Chilion tried to supplant Eglon's son, their brother Balak, and usurp his throne. They assassinated him, but were themselves slain by his bodyguard. According to Dube's creative interpretation, Orpah approves of Ruth's staying with her mother-in-law, Naomi, because Ruth was like a mother to both of them and a special relationship had developed between them. However, she also makes it clear that her return to her own mother, people, and heritage would have been a good choice as one of them had to take care of their mother, a widow like Naomi.[36]

In conclusion, whether feminist interpreters highlight Ruth as the heroine, search for a female author, stress or contest the women's solidarity with each other, or bring attention to Orpah, all of them share two characteristics

33. Donaldson, 'The Sign of Orpah', p. 144.
34. Donaldson, 'The Sign of Orpah', p. 144.
35. Donaldson, 'The Sign of Orpah', p. 144.
36. Musa W. Dube, 'The Unpublished Letters of Orpah to Ruth', in Brenner (ed.), *Ruth and Esther*, pp. 145-50.

of feminist criticism. First, they attend to traditionally marginal characters by turning the margins into the center. Second, they use the biblical tale to raise contemporary social problems, such as colonial oppression. The book of Ruth has proven itself as particularly fertile ground for the articulation of a wide range of feminist readings.

The Periphery Becomes the Center: Vashti in the Book of Esther

Whereas only interpreters of a postcolonial feminist persuasion bring attention to Orpah, a secondary character in the book of Ruth, the exegetical situation is quite different in the book of Esther. From the beginning, feminist interpreters love Vashti, the secondary character, because they see her as 'the first "woman who dared"'[37] and 'the woman who said "no!"' Thus, feminist exegetes highlight Vashti and contrast her to Esther, the main character in the tale. Importantly, Vashti is the only woman in the Hebrew Bible who openly refuses to obey the orders of a powerful man who is, after all, her husband and the king of the land. In other words, feminist interpreters accomplish precisely what Memucan feared: 'For this deed of the queen will be made known to all women, causing them to look with contempt on their husbands, since they will say, "King Ahasuerus commanded Queen Vashti to be brought before him, and she did not come"' (Esth. 1.17). Vashti is a role model for feminists. Already in the late nineteenth century, Elizabeth Cady Stanton praised her for scorning the apostle's command, 'Wives, obey your husbands' (Eph. 5.22; Col. 3.18).[38] Thus, unlike Orpah, Vashti has received attention from feminist and androcentric interpreters alike.

Condemnation or Rejection of Exploitation?
Women in the Book of Esther

Although feminist critics are generally sympathetic of Vashti because she refuses to be turned into an object by her husband, the king, they do not agree on the feminist value of the story itself. Examining the narrative voice, some feminist exegetes regard the narrative's viewpoint as androcentric and as endorsing the patriarchal gender status quo. They are sure that the book of Esther serves as a warning to women to not even think of undermining the social order because otherwise they would be punished like Vashti. These

---

37.   Lucinda B. Chandler, 'The Book of Esther', in Elizabeth Cady Stanton (ed.), *The Woman's Bible*, II (New York: Prometheus Books, 1999 [1895, 1898]), pp. 84-93 (87).
38.   Elizabeth Cady Stanton, 'The Book of Esther', in Stanton (ed.), *The Woman's Bible*, II, p. 86.

interpreters place Vashti in opposition to Esther who instructs women to be obedient if they want to be rewarded.[39] Read as an androcentric tale, then, several feminist readers expose the depiction of Vashti as androcentric. She appears as an arrogant woman who acts foolishly in contrast to Esther who does the right thing. For instance, Susan Niditch finds the figure of the arrogant woman common in folk literature. She explains that this figure is used in the book of Esther to cement the male chauvinist perspective. Thus, to the writer of Esther, 'Vashti's foolishness is a foil for Esther's wisdom'.[40]

Other feminist interpreters, however, counter that the book does not endorse androcentrism. Rather, it criticizes the oppression of women with its clear presentation of the patriarchal order and men as its promoters. All of them are depicted mockingly. These feminist interpreters state that the author, though not wholeheartedly advancing the abolition of patriarchy, rejects its extreme manifestations in the Persian Empire and opposes the treatment of women as sexual objects.[41] Biblical interpreter Michael Fox even classifies the author as a proto-feminist[42] who depicts Vashti sympathetically.[43]

Feminist interpreters also identify parallels between Vashti and Mordechai, the only characters in the book of Esther who flouts the king's orders. Vashti refuses to display herself before the drunken revelers at Ahasuerus's party; and Mordechai refuses to prostrate himself before Haman (3.2), the king's favorite and number two in the government hierarchy. Both of them refuse to humiliate themselves and be treated as objects in order to glorify and to exalt the king and Haman. Both of them infuriate a person of authority (the king/Haman), who perceives the refusal as a slight to his dignity: 'The king was greatly incensed, and his fury burned within him' (Esth. 1.12); 'Haman was filled with fury' (3.5; cf. 5.9). In both cases, the individual fury triggers larger political developments, accompanied by sanctions that target not only the recalcitrant person, but also his/her entire reference

39. See, for example, Esther Fuchs, 'Status and Role of Female Heroines in the Biblical Narrative', *Mankind Quarterly* 23 (1982), pp. 149-60 (156, 158). According to Fuchs (p. 159), the story was told in a man's world and for men.

40. Susan Niditch, 'Esther: Folklore, Wisdom, Feminism and Authority', in Athalya Brenner (ed.), *A Feminist Companion to Esther, Judith and Susanna* (FCB, 7; Sheffield: Sheffield Academic Press, 1995), pp. 26-46 (33).

41. See, for example, Michael V. Fox, *Character and Ideology in the Book of Esther* (Columbia, SC: University of South Carolina Press, 1991), pp. 206-11; Yael Shemesh, 'The Metamorphoses of Vashti: Bible, Aggadah, Feminist Exegesis, and Modern Feminist Midrash', *Beit Mikra* 47 (2002), pp. 358-59 n. 10 (Hebrew).

42. Fox, *Character and Ideology*, p. 209.

43. See also Timothy K. Beal, 'Tracing Esther's Beginnings', in Brenner (ed.), *A Feminist Companion to Esther, Judith and Susanna*, pp. 87-110.

group: all women in the empire, in the case of Vashti (1.19-20, 22); all Jews, in the case of Mordechai (3.6-15). The penal decree is given legal and practical force by messengers who are dispatched throughout the empire to make it public. In addition to the parallel in the plot, the phrasing is almost identical: 'He sent letters to all the king's provinces' (Esth. 1.22); 'letters were sent by couriers to all the king's provinces' (3.13); 'to every province in its own script and to every people in its own language' (1.22); 'every province in its own script and every people in its own language' (3.12).[44]

Thus, feminist interpreters maintain that Vashti must be viewed in a favorable light because Mordechai is the hero of the story, and Vashti is parallel to him. Vashti is an outsider, 'other', from a gender perspective and Mordechai is an ethnic outsider. She is a woman in a man's world and he a Jew in a world of Persians. He is the savior, and so Vashti too is a positive role model.[45] Sometimes, however, this parallelism turns on itself, as in Mary Gendler's interpretation, which depicts Mordechai positively but Vashti negatively.[46] To Gendler, they are contrasting characters. Whether these interpretations should be classified as 'feminist' is yet another debate, but all of them center on Vashti and debate her position in the narrative.

Sometimes, however, feminist interpreters compare the women characters with each other. Praise for Vashti is accompanied with an investigation on Esther's role. They highlight the assertive Vashti, who preserves her dignity, and contrast her virtues to Esther's passivity, her meekness, and her obedient compliance. After all, she is roused to action only after Mordechai scolds her.[47] In these feminist readings, then, Vashti challenges expectations of patriarchy whereas Esther adapts to them.[48] Alice Laffey's evaluation of the two queens exemplifies the negative perception of Esther in contrast to Vashti when she states:

44. Mary Gendler, 'The Restoration of Vashti', in Elizabeth Koltun (ed.), *The Jewish Woman: New Perspectives* (New York: Schocken Books, 1976), pp. 241-47 (242-43); Shemesh, 'The Metamorphoses of Vashti', p. 360.

45. Timothy K. Beal, *The Book of Hiding* (London: Routledge, 1997), pp. 78-79. Beal follows Simone de Beauvoir in *The Second Sex* in his analysis; see, e.g., pp. 12-13, 16-17, 58, *et passim*.

46. Gendler, 'The Restoration of Vashti', pp. 242-43.

47. See, for example: David J.A. Clines, 'Reading Esther from Left to Right— Contemporary Strategies for Reading Biblical Text', in David J.A. Clines *et al.* (eds.), *The Bible in Three Dimensions* (JSOTSup, 87; Sheffield: JSOT Press, 1990), pp. 41-42; Jeffrey M. Cohen, 'Vashti: An Unsung Heroine', *JBQ* 24 (1996), pp. 103-106. Clines considers Vashti as the only radical feminist in the Bible; see Clines, 'Reading Esther', p. 32.

48. See, for example, Gendler, 'The Restoration of Vashti', pp. 241-47.

> In contrast to Vashti, who refused to be men's sexual object and her husband's toy, Esther is the stereotypical woman in a man's world. She wins favor by the physical beauty of her appearance, and then by her ability to satisfy sexually.[49]

Some feminist interpreters, however, see both Vashti and Esther as positive role models for contemporary women. Already nineteenth-century suffragette, Elisabeth Cady Stanton, mentions both of them among the four biblical women whom she considers worthy of admiration. However, in the introduction to the book, she mentions only Deborah, Hulda, and Vashti, omitting Esther. [50] Perhaps she sensed what contemporary feminist interpreters articulate openly. For instance, Katheryn Pfisterer Darr notes that Esther should not be reduced to her looks because she needs more than beauty to save her people. Thus in Darr's interpretation, Esther is a powerful woman, too.[51] Another feminist interpreter, Katharine Doob Sakenfeld, regards both Vashti and Esther as influential characters. Both women model how to oppose abusive authorities. Vashti chooses to oppose openly the system whereas Esther works within the system to change it.[52] Both strategies work for different women at different places.

blical interpreter Michael Fox even classifies the author as a proto-femini accomplishments as a woman character in the narrative. Sidnie Ann White stresses the ethnic-religious identity of Esther. In White's reading, Esther is a model for Jews living in the Diaspora because she adapts successfully to her surroundings and accomplishes what she sets out to do.[53] Other feminist interpreters point to Esther's gradual empowerment. She starts as an object but becomes a subject in the course of the narrative. She begins by obeying Mordechai's instructions (2.20) and ends by commanding him what to do (4.15-17). Esther, with her acumen, resolves the crisis created by Mordechai. What is more, there is even an unexpected parallel between Vashti and Esther: the former is summoned by the king but refuses to go to him, whereas the latter goes when she is not summoned. In the words of Athalya Brenner: 'Esther mirrors Vashti: she does voluntarily what Vashti has refused to do'. The joke is on the men in the story: look at what an

---

49.   Alice L. Laffey, *An Introduction to the Old Testament: A Feminist Perspective* (Philadelphia: Fortress Press, 1988), p. 216.

50.   See Stanton, *The Woman's Bible*, II, p. 13.

51.   Katheryn Pfisterer Darr, 'More than Just a Pretty Face: Critical, Rabbinical, and Feminist Perspectives on Esther', in Darr, *Far More Precious than Jewels: Perspectives on Biblical Women* (Louisville, KY: Westminster/John Knox Press, 1991), pp. 164-202.

52.   Katharine Doob Sakenfeld, *Just Wives? Stories of Power and Survival in the Old Testament and Today* (Louisville, KY: Westminster/John Knox Press, 2003), pp. 49-50.

53.   Sidnie Ann White, 'Esther: A Feminine Model for Jewish Diaspora', in Peggy L. Day (ed.), *Gender and Difference in Ancient Israel* (Minneapolis: Fortress Press, 1989), pp. 161-77 (esp. 166, 173).

ostensibly submissive woman can accomplish.[54] In my view, the assessment of White that Vashti is more congenial than Esther to the hearts of contemporary women, and especially of women with a feminist consciousness, is indeed true.[55]

One feminist interpreter makes yet another pertinent observation. Bea Wyler notes that after ch. 1 gender as an issue disappears entirely. What remains at stake in the remainder of the book is whether Esther succeeds in bringing emancipation to her people. She succeeds as a Jew and not as a woman, Wyler states disappointedly. What is needed is a midrash that recounts Esther's campaign to emancipate the women of Persia. Whyler presents such a feminist retelling in which Esther pays not only tribute to Vashti but also appoints her as a private counselor.[56] Whyler thus remedies what she finds lacking in the book of Esther. In her midrash, the women succeed on the basis of gender, support each other, have strong feminist consciousness. Most importantly, they are positive models for women today. Interpretations on the book of Esther thus mirror the same hermeneutical developments and feminist yearnings, as they have emerged in feminist approaches to the book of Ruth. Feminist appropriations on the book of Judith reflect more of the same dynamics.

Complex Attitudes vs. Absolute Rejection: The Feminist Debate on the Book of Judith

The book of Judith is not part of the Jewish or Protestant canon, but it is included in the Roman Catholic and Greek Orthodox Bible. Interestingly, all interpreters agree on one point; the heroine of the book, Judith, does not grow as a character. On the contrary, her striking personality is fully developed from the moment she first appears. Furthermore, unlike women figures in the books of Ruth and Esther, Judith never follows a man's instructions. She acts independently and always takes the initiative on her own.[57]

---

54. Athalya Brenner, 'Looking at Esther through the Looking Glass', in Brenner (ed.), *A Feminist Companion to Esther, Judith and Susanna*, pp. 71-80 (75-76). This idea recurs in the work of many scholars.

55. Sidnie White Crawford, 'Esther', in Carol A. Newsom and Sharon H. Ringe (eds.), *Women's Bible Commentary* (Louisville, KY: Westminster/John Knox Press, exp. edn, 1998), pp. 131-37 (134).

56. Bea Wyler, 'Esther: The Incomplete Emancipation of a Queen', in Brenner (ed.), *A Feminist Companion to Esther, Judith and Susana*, pp. 130-33.

57. On the similarities and differences between Judith and Esther, see Sidnie White Crawford, 'Esther and Judith: Contrasts in Character', in Sidnie White Crawford and Leonard J. Greenspoon (eds.), *The Book of Esther in Modern Research* (JSOTSup, 380; London: T. & T. Clark, 2003), pp. 61-76.

Accordingly, feminist interpreters never doubt that the narrative depicts her in extremely positive terms. Yet they debate whether the book is a feminist book or, as a minimum, whether it includes feminist elements with Judith serving as a role model for woman.

In light of this situation, it is not surprising that interpreters identify strong feminist elements in the book of Judith. For instance, they admire Judith's freedom of action and her cooperation with another woman to save her people.[58] They also suggest that the book undermines patriarchal culture by presenting a woman who is resourceful, wise, and bold and a role model for women everywhere.[59] Judith is also an example for both women and men who wish to make the world a better place.[60] In fact, some feminists conjecture that the rabbis excluded the book from the canon for this very reason. The rabbis found it difficult to accept this heroine's strong and independent character and saw it as undermining the very foundations of the patriarchal order. Some feminist readers even maintain that this reason for Judith's exclusion laid the foundation for the inclusion of Esther. For instance, according to Sidnie White Crawford, the rabbis included the book of Esther because this heroine is submissive and obedient, unlike Judith.[61] Feminist interpreters often agree with this assessment but view it as an asset of the tale. Thus, Sheila Shulman maintains that the book of Judith celebrates 'a woman of strong purpose'.[62] She opposes those who criticize the heroine for using her feminine wiles because Judith's beauty and sexuality are legitimate weapons in a guerrilla war. Judith had to use unconventional tactics if she wanted to succeed in her world.[63] Similarly, Alice Ogden Bellis asserts that '[t]he stories of Ruth, Esther, Susanna, and Judith convey the most liberating messages for women of any of the stories of women in the first

---

58. Thus, e.g., Toni Craven, *Artistry and Faith in the Book of Judith* (SBLDS, 70; Chico, CA: Scholars Press, 1983), esp. pp. 121, 122.

59. Elizabeth Schüssler Fiorenza, *In Memory of Her: A Feminist Theological Reconstruction of Christian Origins* (New York: Crossroad, 1984), pp. 115-18. And, following Fiorenza, Linda Bennet Elder, 'Judith', in Elizabeth Schüssler Fiorenza (ed.), *Searching the Scriptures. II. A Feminist Commentary* (New York: Crossroad, 1994), pp. 455-69.

60. Alice Ogden Bellis, *Helpmates, Harlots, and Heroes: Women's Stories in the Hebrew Bible* (Louisville, KY: Westminster/John Knox Press, 1994), p. 222.

61. Crawford, 'Esther and Judith', pp. 70-76. See also Craven, *Artistry and Faith*, pp. 117-18; Sheila Shulman, 'A Woman of Strong Purpose', in Sybil Sheridan (ed.), *Hear our Voice: Women Rabbis Tell their Stories* (London: SCM Press, 1994), pp. 71-80 (80).

62. Shulman, 'A Woman of Strong Purpose', p. 77.

63. Shulman, 'A Woman of Strong Purpose', p. 78. Compare the argument concerning the legitimacy of Judith's resort to lies because she is engaged in a guerrilla war, advanced by Denise Dombkowski Hopkins, 'Judith', in Newsom and Ringe (eds.), *Women's Bible Commentary*, pp. 279-85 (283).

testament'.[64] In her opinion, Judith 'is perhaps the strongest Hebrew hero in all of biblical literature'.[65] Even traditional scholars agree with this assessment. Jan Willem van Henten characterizes Judith as an alternative leader who is more positively described than male leaders, including Moses.[66] He does not deny the book's androcentric scaffolding, but also finds an F voice in it all the same.[67]

Despite the foregoing, Carey Moore's view that 'clearly, Judith is a feminist kind of person!'[68] is not really clear at all. Many feminist scholars have a guarded attitude about the gender message implicit in the book and often simultaneously reinforce and challenge the book's patriarchal ideology.[69] For instance, Claudia Rakel maintains that feminist exegesis ought to oscillate between the two poles of suspicion and trust because the tension between the poles can never be eliminated and there is always room for both.[70]

Yet some feminist readers have an exclusively negative attitude about the book and its heroine. Betsy Merideth[71] and especially Pamela Milne[72] take the most uncompromising stand against Judith as a feminist heroine and as a feminist's heroine. They recognize that Judith is portrayed in exceedingly positive ways. Yet in their views, the book uses this female character to promote an anti-female ideology and to endorse outright gynophobia. Thus, Merideth states: '[T]he message could not be more clear: woman's beauty

64. Bellis, *Helpmates*, p. 206.

65. Bellis, *Helpmates*, p. 219.

66. Jan Willem van Henten, 'Judith as Alternative Leader: A Rereading of Judith 7–13', in Brenner (ed.), *A Feminist Companion to Esther, Judith and Susanna*, pp. 224-52.

67. Van Henten, 'Judith as Alternative Leader', pp. 245-52.

68. Carey A. Moore, *Judith* (AB, 40; New York: Doubleday, 1985), p. 65.

69. See Amy-Jill Levine, 'Sacrifice and Salvation: Otherness and Domestication in the Book of Judith', in James C. VanderKam (ed.), *'No One Spoke Ill of Her': Essays on Judith* (Atlanta, GA: Scholars Press, 1992), pp. 17-30 (esp. 17, 28); Hopkins, 'Judith', p. 284. Hopkins cautions against a one-dimensional reading of the story. Compare the approach of Margarita Stocker, *Judith: Sexual Warrior: Women and Power in Western Culture* (New Haven: Yale University Press, 1998), who insists that this is not a feminist story (pp. 8-9) but that, nevertheless, Judith's action does have feminist implications (p. 10).

70. Claudia Rakel, 'Judith: About a Beauty Who Is Not What She Pretended to Be', in Luise Schottroff and Marie-Theres Wacker (eds.), *Feminist Biblical Interpretation: A Compendium of Critical Commentary on the Books of the Bible and Related Literature* (Grand Rapids, MI: Eerdmans, 2012), p. 516.

71. Betsy Merideth, 'Desire and Danger: The Dream of Betrayal in Judges and Judith', in Mieke Bal (ed.), *Anti-Covenant: Counter-Reading Women's Lives in the Hebrew Bible* (JSOTSup, 81; Sheffield: Almond Press, 1989), pp. 63-78.

72. Pamela J. Milne, 'What Shall We Do with Judith? A Feminist Reassessment of a Biblical "Heroine"', *Semeia* 62 (1993), pp. 37-58.

and sexuality are dangerous to men because women use their attractiveness to deceive, harm and kill men'.[73] In other words, to Merideth, the narrative's emphasis on Judith's physical attractiveness to men signifies the androcentric tendency of the story. Milne goes even further when she maintains that 'through the propaganda of the *femme fatale*/female warrior character, men are taught, above all, to fear women. The otherness of women is thereby emphasized and women become objects to be viewed suspiciously and trusted not at all.'[74] Instead of a feminist tale of liberation of women, then, the book of Judith further cements women's oppression and stereotypical behavior.

Another feminist interpreter concurs. Amy-Jill Levine notes that Judith influences her surroundings and implements change in the leadership when women join her in song and dance, while the men merely follow them. Yet this change, Levine asserts, is of limited duration. In the end, the book sends the women home,[75] including Judith, the heroine, whom it literally 'domesticates'.[76] Judith, too, ends up in her house. Feminist critics make additional observations against the book's liberating message and Judith as a feminist heroine. They maintain that the emphasis on Holofernes as being struck down by a female hand (Jdt 9.10; 13.15; 16.5 [RSV 6]) does not empower women. Instead, it mocks the enemy as being defeated by a weak woman and emphasizes that salvation comes from the male God alone.[77] Milne also asserts that God, and not Judith, is the true hero of the story, and so Judith's role is that of a helper and not of a hero.[78]

Yet Claudia Rakel expresses a more moderate view of Judith. She recognizes the problematic nature of the portrayal of Judith as a woman who exploits her beauty to deceive men,[79] but insists that Judith's success was achieved not only by her charms, but also by her brains.[80] Rakel adds that, according to the story, female beauty endangers not only men, but also beautiful women themselves, as exemplified by the fact that Judith was nearly raped by Holofernes.[81] Hence, in her view, Judith is the heroine of the

73. Merideth, 'Desire and Danger', p. 76.
74. Milne, 'What Shall We Do with Judith?', p. 47.
75. Levine, 'Sacrifice and Salvation', p. 24.
76. Levine, 'Sacrifice and Salvation', pp. 27, 28. See, also Rakel, 'Judith', p. 527, who follows Levine.
77. Milne, 'What Shall We Do with Judith?', pp. 54-55; Hopkins, 'Judith', p. 283; Stocker, *Judith: Sexual Warrior*, p. 10. By contrast, van Henten, 'Judith as Alternative Leader', p. 246, sees the repeated emphasis of Holofernes as being killed by a woman as evidence of the F voice.
78. Milne, 'What Shall We Do with Judith?', pp. 48-55.
79. Rakel, 'Judith', pp. 518-19.
80. Rakel, 'Judith', p. 522.
81. Rakel, 'Judith', pp. 524-25.

story, although this position does not make her into a positive role model for women.[82] Some feminist readers also argue that Judith does not free herself or her sisters from the patriarchal order.[83] Furthermore, Judith does not share her people's suffering and hunger during the siege. Her house does not lack food and Judith enjoys a bath (10.3) while her fellow citizens need water and faint of thirst (7.22).[84] Nor does Judith demonstrate any sign of female solidarity with the women of Shechem, some of whom were certainly raped by her Israelite ancestors. Her prayer mentions their enslavement as retribution for the rape of Dinah but it does not sympathize with their probable experience of sexual violence (9.4).[85]

In short, then, feminist interpreters range from enthusiastically supporting to adamantly rejecting the book of Judith. Importantly, several scholars occupy a middle ground. They recognize that it depends on how we read the apparently empowering elements in the narrative with those that seem to endorse the patriarchal order. To those interpreters, there is no either/or message in the book of Judith.

A Mainstay Document for Feminists: Concluding Comments

Feminist interpretations on the books of Ruth, Esther, and Judith abound. Their namesakes are women whose actions gain national significance and whose works deliver their people, at least according to the narratives. Ruth delivers her people in a broad sense. She supports her mother-in-law economically, and she saves the family lineage from extinction. Her actions have national significance as she is the great-grandmother of King David. Similarly, Esther and Judith deliver their people from annihilation. In my view, the topic of lifesaving women in the Hebrew Bible still awaits comprehensive study, including a consideration of similarities and differences among these female characters, the differences between female and male lifesavers, and a discussion on the significance of gender. One last point: in all of the three books, the heroines of the stories are portrayed in favorable terms although, as feminist scholars maintain, a favorable depiction does not in itself indicate a story's feminist ideology. It does seem, though, that the favorable characterization of women is important from a gender perspective,

---

82. Rakel, 'Judith', p. 517.

83. Milne, 'What Shall We Do with Judith?', p. 55; Rakel, 'Judith', p. 525.

84. Levine, 'Sacrifice and Salvation', pp. 18-19.

85. Levine, 'Sacrifice and Salvation', pp. 18-19. See also Hopkins, 'Judith', p. 283. However, Rakel, 'Judith', pp. 521, 527, ignores this aspect of Judith's prayer when she asserts that Judith's opposition to wartime rape is one of the few instances of the F voice in the story. In my view, Judith is opposed only to the rape of Israelite women and evinces no empathy for the women of Shechem.

because we can infer from it that the inferiority of women, as perceived by biblical narrative, is a matter of law and social norms while it is not essential and immanent. Biblical narratives do not present women as inferior to men whether on moral or intellectual levels and often women are depicted in just the opposite way.[86] The recognition of this fact provides some comfort to feminist critics, especially to religious ones, and perhaps convinces them to not abandon the Bible as a mainstay document in Western culture and society.

86.   See Uriel Simon, '"Manoah Followed his Wife": A Woman's Place in Biblical Society', in Simon, *Seek Peace and Pursue It* (Tel Aviv: Yedioth Ahronoth, 2nd edn, 2004 [Hebrew]), pp. 96-115.

13

READING SILENCE:
THE BOOKS OF CHRONICLES AND EZRA–NEHEMIAH,
AND THE RELATIVE ABSENCE OF A FEMINIST INTERPRETIVE
HISTORY

Julie Kelso

My brief was fairly simple: to provide a critical analysis, description, and discussion of the feminist scholarship that exists concerning the books of Chronicles and Ezra–Nehemiah. Well, this would be simple enough *were* there something we could call a history of feminist scholarship on these books. Really, there is not. These books, as whole literary units, have not been and are still not read critically by feminist biblical scholars. By this I mean that feminist scholars in our discipline do not provide sustained research on and debates about these books in their entirety. Indeed the few feminist engagements with these books can be characterized as 'micro-readings', to use Roland Boer's term for the small shards of texts that feminist biblical scholars, in general, seem to favor.[1] This dearth of scholarship around Chronicles and Ezra–Nehemiah is most clearly evidenced by the fact that in the two series of *The Feminist Companion to Biblical Studies* there is yet to appear a volume devoted to Chronicles and/or Ezra Nehemiah.

Of course, in conjunction with other more 'popular' biblical books and stories, various feminist studies mention these biblical texts, especially when they are broadly concerned with formulating a picture of what postexilic life was like in the Promised Land, with Chronicles usually understood as a postexilic recounting of Israel's history. We are all familiar with the problem of foreign women in Ezra–Nehemiah (Ezra 9–10; Neh. 13.23-24, 26-28), for example, and we have probably heard about women referred to as singers (Ezra 2.65; Neh. 7.67; 1 Chron. 25.5), possibly scribes (the

---

1. Roland Boer, 'No Road: On the Absence of Feminist Criticism of Ezra–Nehemiah', in Caroline Vander Stichele and T. Penner (eds.), *Her Master's Tools: Feminist and Postcolonial Engagements of Historical-Critical Discourse* (Leiden: Koninklijke Brill, 2005), pp. 233-52.

'Hassophereth/Sophereth' of Ezra 2.55/Neh. 7.57), even builders such as Sheerah (1 Chron. 7.24) and the daughters of Shallum (Neh. 3.12). In truth, however, it is fair to say that Chronicles and Ezra–Nehemiah are biblical texts that, compared with other books of the Hebrew Bible, paint a picture of a society functioning disconcertingly well enough *without* women. That a few women remain in the *literary* construction of this society is hardly cause for celebration, revisionist or otherwise. Indeed, certain women literally get expelled from the narrative frames (e.g. Ezra 10.44; 2 Chron. 8.11) and these diegetic excisions, read in the context of the relative absence of women from the text as a whole, seem to me crucial to the logic of these books as a whole.

And yet, the few feminist readers of Chronicles and Ezra–Nehemiah consistently downplay the relative absence and silence of women in the text, and this downplaying is enabled by a certain recuperative or revisionist interpretive strategy that I call 'at-first-glance-ism'. 'At-first-glance-ism' is the approach of first noting what *seems* like the absence of women from the text, followed by a roll-call of female figures or characters actually present there. Once these figures are foregrounded, the recuperative feminist makes one of two moves (sometimes both): she asserts that these scant references to women alert us to just how important and valued women really are in the text; or, she asserts that, despite the text, these references tell us of this importance, value, and power of women in the world beyond the text, that of postexilic, Persian Yehud. Tamara Eskenazi's 'Out from the Shadows: Biblical Women in the Postexilic Era', Christiane Karrer-Grube's 'Ezra and Nehemiah: The Return of the Others', Alice L. Laffey's 'I and II Chronicles' and Marie-Theres Wacker's 'Books of Chronicles: In the Vestibule of Women' are, apart from my own book on Chronicles, the only feminist works available on Chronicles and Ezra–Nehemiah.[2] All of these four essays undertake 'at-first-glance-ism'. Ultimately, a critical reading of three of these works[3] demonstrates that 'at-first-glance-ism' is a weak feminist interpretive

---

2. Tamara C. Eskenazi, 'Out from the Shadows: Biblical Women in the Postexilic Era', in Athalya Brenner (ed.), *A Feminist Companion to Samuel–Kings* (FCB, 5; Sheffield: Sheffield Academic Press, 1994), pp. 252-71; Christiane Karrer-Grube, 'Ezra and Nehemiah: The Return of the Others', in Luise Schottroff and Marie-Theres Wacker (eds.), *Feminist Biblical Interpretation: A Compendium of Critical Commentary on the Books of the Bible and Related Literature* (Grand Rapids/Cambridge, MA: Eerdmans, 2012), pp. 192-206; Alice L. Laffey, 'I and II Chronicles', in Carol A. Newsom and Sharon H. Ringe (eds.), *The Women's Bible Commentary* (London: SPCK, 1992), pp. 110-15; Marie-Theres Wacker, 'Book of Chronicles: In the Vestibule of Women', in Schottroff and Wacker (eds.), *Feminist Biblical Interpretation*, pp. 178-91; Julie Kelso, *O Mother Where Art Thou? An Irigarayan Reading of the Book of Chronicles* (London: Equinox, 2007).

3. Wacker essentially builds upon Laffey's work, so I shall focus on the former.

approach to reading Chronicles and Ezra–Nehemiah. Such an interpretive approach often does little more than side-step the androcentrism of the texts, even though their works supposedly challenge this androcentrism. Just as problematically, 'at-first-glance-ism' enables feminist biblical scholars to exaggerate *dramatically* the presence and perceived value of women in the biblical texts and in the ancient world itself, outcomes ultimately driven by a desire for this (sacred) history to be appreciative and inclusive of women.

As my title insists, my contribution pertains to the problem of reading silence. I insist on asking how to analyze the relative absence of women from the books of Chronicles and Ezra–Nehemiah and how to account for the dearth of feminist scholarship on these books. I maintain that methodological preferences and theological concerns account for the scarcity of feminist scholarship on Chronicles and Ezra–Nehemiah. We need different feminist modes of reading to enable us to approach these ignored texts. I then provide a critical analysis of Eskenazi's, Karrer-Grube's, and Wacker's interpretations, clarifying why their recuperative approach is inadequate for the interpretation of Chronicles and Ezra–Nehemiah. Finally, I will briefly draw from my own work on Chronicles to suggest how to read biblical texts that largely do not include women. In my opinion, a more sophisticated approach to understanding the absence of women characters and its relationship to silence is necessary to a proper analysis of the actual *presence* and speech of women in the Hebrew Bible, in general.

Why Have We (Had) Little to Say?

Scholarship on both Chronicles and Ezra–Nehemiah has long been monopolized by the critical questions and concerns of that broad umbrella of approaches known as historical criticism, with its various methodologies, including text criticism, form criticism, redaction criticism, rhetorical criticism, and so on. This has meant decades of debates about whether the 'Chronicler' authored both texts, or whether Ezra was the sole author (a position that dates back to the Babylonian Talmud), both positions suggesting that Chronicles and Ezra–Nehemiah should be read as a single entity; whether there are two distinct authors, despite the similarities between the two texts; whether Chronicles is the work of one author or many—the unity/compositional history of Chronicles; whether Chronicles originally ended at 2 Chron. 36.23, or whether it extended into Ezra to include the first 6 verses; whether the genealogical chapters of 1 Chronicles (1–9) were part of the original text or added later; whether Chronicles was written in the early Persian period or much later; the question of sources, earlier biblical and extra-biblical; the question of historical credibility; the genre and overall purpose of Chronicles (the Davidic line and the temple cult run by the priests); the theology of Chronicles, and so forth.[4] Obviously, the concerns of Ezra–Nehemiah scholarship overlap here, continuing the traditional biblical scholars' obsession with authorship, dating, compositional history, unity, or apparent ideology (exclusivist for Ezra–Nehemiah, inclusivist for Chronicles). Both texts, even Chronicles, long ignored and unliked by biblical scholars, have come to be viewed as important, especially with respect to our understanding of the construction of Jewish identity, indeed identit*ies*, in relation to nascent Judaism(s), but for some also with respect to the rest of the Hebrew Bible itself, understood to have been redacted, if not even entirely conceived, during this period. As Boer recently put it, with respect to Ezra–Nehemiah:

> After languishing for many years in the doldrums of the postexilic period, where it was felt that the historical record was especially opaque, Ezra–Nehemiah has emerged as a key text in the debates over Second Temple Judaism. In a return to the Teutonic skepticism of the nineteenth-century biblical criticism, a return that seeks to shrug off the more recent theoretical developments within biblical studies, some, such as Philip Davies and Thomas Thompson, have argued that the bulk of the biblical material must be dated to the Persian period, if not at times the Hellenistic. And even newer methods such as postcolonial criticism take such a late dating as the starting point for understanding the politics of textual interrelationships.[5]

In other words, Chronicles and Ezra–Nehemiah are currently enjoying their time in the spotlight because of the argument for late dating of most if not all the biblical texts.

In general, these approaches interpret texts in relation to the context of their production, their *Sitz im Leben*. Such biblical interpretation is driven by questions relating to the dating of the texts, whether as a whole or in parts, authorship, redactorship, intended audience, socio-political and cultic concerns, theological foci, and so on. As Tate explains:

---

4. See Rodney K. Duke, 'Recent Research in Chronicles', *Currents in Biblical Research* 8 (2009), pp. 10-50, for a detailed discussion of the dominant themes of Chronicles research. As a sidenote, as I was writing this list I recalled that when I went to study the Bible at the university level I most certainly did not do so because I wanted to be an ancient historian, nor did I do so for reasons of faith as I am an atheist. Mercifully, my teacher Edgar Conrad was prepared to engage with the newer approaches to literature that were taking place outside of biblical studies. Otherwise I do not think I could have continued. I find discussions about authorship and dating excruciatingly tedious. As I shall discuss, I think it is far more important to ask how we might engage with these texts in a manner that enables us to think about the questions of the future and how to make it better than to quibble over authorship and dating, debates that seem to go nowhere of great import beyond biblical studies.

5. Boer, 'No Road', p. 234.

The text is seen as a shell with many layers. If the layers were appropriately peeled away, the scholar could discover the core and its original setting. Perhaps underlying the approach is the assumption that the real meaning resides in the text's originating circumstances and that subsequent development and recontextualization have distorted this meaning.[6]

Second-wave feminist biblical studies of the 1970s and 1980s was largely a critical intervention into the androcentrism of such approaches, with the patriarchal nature of the Bible itself, separate from its interpretive history, proving a difficult problem. As is well known, since Phyllis Trible's ground-breaking work,[7] a lot of feminist biblical criticism has begun precisely from the premise that it is not the biblical text itself that is problematic but the subsequent interpretive traditions, which have been impaired by the blind spots of androcentric reading. Indeed, according to Trible, while the texts certainly emerged out of a patriarchal context, the scriptures themselves contain depatriarchalising principles that can be revealed by careful feminist analysis. This form of feminist interpretative strategy brings analytic techniques that reveal the true 'revelation', enabling a biblical faith the intentionality of which 'is neither to create nor to perpetuate patriarchy but rather to function as salvation for both women and men'.[8]

Suffice it to say, feminist biblical studies has developed in many directions since these early days.[9] However, it is still dominated by feminists who work within confessional frameworks. According to the authors of *The Postmodern Bible*, the three main forms of feminist and womanist interpretations of the Bible, loosely classifiable as the 'Hermeneutics of Recuperation', 'Hermeneutics of Suspicion', and 'Hermeneutics of Survival', all share 'an institutional location within religious traditions'.[10] In other words,

6. W. Randolph Tate, *Interpreting the Bible: A Handbook of Terms and Methods* (Peabody, MA: Hendrickson Publishers, 2006), p. 166.

7. Phyllis Trible, 'Depatriarchalizing in Biblical Interpretation', *JAAR* 41 (1973), pp. 30-48.

8. Trible, 'Depatriarchalizing', p. 31.

9. For useful surveys of feminist biblical studies, see Dora Mbuwayesango and Susanne Scholtz, 'Dialogical Beginnings: A Conversation on the Future of Feminist Biblical Studies', *Journal of Feminist Studies in Religion* 25.2 (2009), pp. 93-103; Julie Kelso, 'Why Should Feminists Read the Bible?', *Hecate* 33.2 (2007), pp. 4-16; Athalya Brenner, 'Introduction', in Athalya Brenner and Carole Fontaine (eds.), *A Feminist Companion to Reading the Bible: Approaches, Methods and Strategies* (FCB, 11; Sheffield: Sheffield Academic Press, 1997), pp. 17-28; P. Milne, 'Toward Feminist Companionship: The Future of Biblical Studies and Feminism', in Brenner and Fontaine (eds.), *Reading the Bible*, pp. 39-60; Heather A. McKay, 'On the Future of Feminist Biblical Criticism', in Brenner and Fontaine (eds.), *Reading the Bible*, pp. 61-83; Bible and Culture Collective. *The Postmodern Bible* (New Haven/London: Yale University Press, 1995).

10. Bible and Culture Collective, *The Postmodern Bible*, pp. 244-67 (254).

these differing hermeneutics are all possible for the critic who works within a theological institution, and presumably for those with theological issues guiding their criticisms.[11] Moreover, these dominant feminist hermeneutics share one other feature: they are methodologies more or less up to the task of analyzing texts that *include* references to women and/or the feminine but not so when it comes to reading texts that can, or rather *need* to be characterized by the *absence* of female characters or anything explicitly pertaining to the feminine. Related to my concerns here, to date feminist readers seem to demonstrate little interest in challenging the historical-critical approaches to reading Chronicles and Ezra–Nehemiah as they have done for so many other biblical books. Moreover, even feminist works that can be described as 'postmodernist', employing poststructuralist, deconstructionist, or psychoanalytic modes of reading, for example, have had little to say about Chronicles or Ezra–Nehemiah.[12] Again, the reasons for this are fairly obvious:

11. That feminist biblical studies is still predominantly taking place in institutions with links to theological colleges, and thus with the work of most feminist biblical scholars being underwritten by an allegiance to a faith system, validates the fears of many feminist scholars outside of biblical studies—that theological allegiances will always outweigh feminist allegiances; see Gerda Lerner, *The Creation of Patriarchy* (Oxford: Oxford University Press, 1986), pp. 176-77; Milne, 'Toward Feminist Companionship', pp. 44-48.

12. In general, while the so-called postmodern challenge to the presumed objective intentions behind historical approaches has had a paradigm-shifting effect on the disciplines of the Humanities, and has certainly impacted, opened up, and in my opinion enhanced biblical studies, the so-called newer, related approaches, such as ideological criticism, psychoanalytic criticism, and deconstruction, to name a few, have not had the same degree of success when it comes to Chronicles and Ezra–Nehemiah scholarship. However, things are changing (slowly). For more recent approaches to Chronicles, see Roland Boer, *Novel Histories: The Fiction of Biblical Criticism* (Sheffield: Sheffield Academic Press, 1997); Christine Mitchell, 'Transformations of Meaning: The Accession of Solomon in Chronicles', *JHS* 4 (2002), Article 3, http://www.jhsonline.org/; and Steven Schweitzer, *Reading Utopia in Chronicles* (LHBOTS, 442; London: T. & T. Clark, 2007). For more recent approaches to Ezra–Nehemiah, see Willa M. Johnson, 'Ethnicity in Persian Yehud: Between Anthropological Analysis and Ideological Criticism', *SBLSP* 34 (1995), pp. 177-86; Willa M. Johnson, *The Holy Seed Has Been Defiled: The Interethnic Marriage Dilemma in Ezra 9–10* (Sheffield: Sheffield Phoenix Press, 2011); and Christopher B. Hays, 'The Silence of the Wives: Bakhtin's Monologism and Ezra 7–10', *JSOT* 33 (2008), pp. 59-80. Johnson's work is an interdisciplinary analysis of ethnicity in Ezra–Nehemiah, one that includes narratology, sociology, anthropology, and something she calls 'critical theories', by which she seems to mean ideological analysis. Hays brings Bakhtin's theory of monologism to the analysis of Ezra 7–10. Despite the title of his paper, which certainly piqued my interest, the paper is not feminist so I cannot engage with it here. This is also the case with Johnson's work. Nevertheless, both are important works that will need to be engaged with by feminists in the future. I would also have loved to engage with Claudia Camp's fascinating arguments

feminist biblical scholars seem overwhelmingly interested in methods that seek to rectify or even complete the 'pictures' of the biblical literature and the ancient world that androcentric readings have constructed through the centuries, readings that either have ignored or biasedly presented the issues concerning female characters/women in the ancient world. And such methods only make sense if women are already, in some sense, 'in the picture'. I want to suggest that in order to be able to engage critically with inordinately masculinist biblical texts such as Chronicles and Ezra–Nehemiah we need feminist modes that can attend to the complexities of the absence and silence of women in these literary product(ion)s.

At-First-Glance-Ism

The essays by Eskenazi, Karrer-Grube, and Wacker can all be characterized as exercises in recuperative reading. They seek to demonstrate that women are present in the text in often interesting ways, or at least that their mere inclusion in these androcentric texts indicates the importance of women in the 'real' postexilic world beyond the text. Eskenazi, Karrer-Grube, and Wacker note the relative absence of women from their texts of interest, and observe that 'at first glance' the absence is merely a false appearance, rectifiable by a 'closer analysis'.

Eskenazi informs us of her three goals: to focus on the Ezra–Nehemiah material that deals with women 'for the purpose of shared communal inquiry';[13] to refute the claim of the diminished status of women in the postexilic period; and, to understand the context of the opposition to foreign women in Ezra 9–10 so as to shed light on the roles and rights of women in this period. The absence of women in Ezra–Nehemiah is recognized initially, but this absence is a feature of the narrative that is present only '(a)t first glance'.[14] Later on, she qualifies this by saying that 'at first glance women seem all but absent from Ezra–Nehemiah, except as a problem when they are foreign. As such, their very presence is a problem for which absence is a solution.'[15] (I would have thought 'expulsion' would have been a more

---

about Ezra–Nehemiah. However, her work brings Ezra–Nehemiah to bear on broader issues rather than focusing on it exclusively; see Claudia V. Camp, *Wise, Strange and Holy: The Strange Woman and the Making of the Bible* (JSOTSup, 320; Sheffield: Sheffield Academic Press, 2000), and Claudia V. Camp, 'Feminist- and Gender-Critical Perspectives on the Biblical Ideology of Intermarriage', in Christian Frevel (ed.), *Mixed Marriages: Intermarriage and Group Identity in the Second Temple Period* (New York/London: T. & T. Clark, 2012), pp. 301-15.

13.   Eskenazi, 'Out from the Shadows', p. 252.
14.   Eskenazi, 'Out from the Shadows', p. 252.
15.   Eskenazi, 'Out from the Shadows', p. 262.

appropriate word to describe the solution, but as we shall see, Eskenazi's apologetics will not allow for such a criticism of the text.) Eskenazi argues that when we look a little closer at the text 'we discover that, hidden in the shadows, stand several interesting Jewish women of the postexilic period, some even more visible at times than their pre-exilic sisters'.[16]

Similarly, in her contribution on Chronicles, Wacker writes:

> To date…no engagement with Chronicles focusing specifically on women has been written.[17] This need not surprise us, as at first glance these books seem to present a world devoid of women… On the other hand, of all the books of the Bible, these two contain by far the most names of women and notes about women. This paradoxical content spurs the feminist experiment of subjecting 1 and 2 Chronicles to an against-the-grain reading tracing the figures of women made visible here.[18]

Likewise, though concerning Ezra–Nehemiah, Karrer-Grube writes:

> An attempt at a feminist-theological exegesis of the book of Ezra–Nehemiah… is nearly always met with astonishment and bafflement: at first glance it seems that female figures and questions of gender difference play next to no role as regards the theme of this book. Hence there is almost no feminist literature on this subject. Only a closer analysis, and a questioning that gets below the surface of the text's intended statement, reveal a different picture. The attempt to make 'the women' simply disappear from the concept of the book has not been successful. When we uncover the traces of their significance, we, at the same time, obtain a new insight into the book and its problems.[19]

Of these writers, Eskenazi is the only one who explicitly designates her approach as recuperative.[20] As she points out, recuperation or recovery of the stories and traditions of women from the past is a form of feminist

---

16. Eskenazi, 'Out from the Shadows', p. 254.

17. I have to admit feeling annoyed when I read this statement, given my book, the first feminist reading of the book of Chronicles, was published in 2007.

18. Wacker, 'Book of Chronicles', p. 178.

19. Karrer-Grube, 'Ezra and Nehemiah', p. 192.

20. Eskenazi's essay is the first feminist study of Ezra–Nehemiah. However, it should be noted that while Eskenazi is an expert in the field of Ezra–Nehemiah studies, specifically, and Second Temple studies more broadly, her other work can hardly be thought of as pursuing feminist critical analysis. Furthermore, the essay (strangely) appears in A. Brenner (ed.), *A Feminist Companion to Samuel and Kings* (FCB, 5; Sheffield: Sheffield Academic Press, 1994). As I mentioned earlier, there has yet to be written a volume on Ezra–Nehemiah and/or Chronicles. Reading this essay again today one realizes that 'Out from the Shadows' is an exemplar of the feminist method known as the 'Hermeneutics of Recuperation', still the most popular method for feminist biblical scholars, especially for those working from within confessional frameworks, which applies to most feminist biblical scholars.

historiography, and as such is akin to revisionism. Feminist recuperation/ revisionism, whether historical or literary, has been an important tool in the feminist kitbag, largely because the method refuses to ignore questions concerning women and their relationship to historical or literary canons and their formations. Androcentric critical practices, as we all know, never really thought (or think!) such questions to be important. And yet, as I shall go on to demonstrate, this method is fraught with problems, particularly when the texts under consideration seem to have almost fully drained themselves of women and their voices.

Before I go into more detail about these problems, let me digress for a moment to discuss some other methodological issues in Karrer-Grube's and Wacker's essays. Both of them speak of reading against-the-grain. Of course, all feminist reading practices in biblical studies are in fact reading against the grain, or against the dominant voice of the text and of its interpretive history. Wacker, like Laffey before her, is interested in drawing our attention to the female names and characters in Chronicles, placing them into relief instead of ignoring them as non-feminist scholars have done for so long. The purpose of doing such a thing is to insist that these traces reveal something about the daily reality of women's lives in Persian Yehud, some-thing not clearly presented by Chronicles as such. This, by any definition, is a recuperative/revisionist strategy. Karrer-Grube, on the other hand, is a little trickier. She describes her approach as a 'feminist-theological exe-gesis',[21] 'deconstructive',[22] and 'reading against the grain',[23] which at times I think is a fair enough description of what she is doing. Of all these scholars Karrer-Grube is the one who most emphasizes the absence of women and rightly insists that there is an explicit strategy of making women invisible in Ezra–Nehemiah. However, her approach is mostly characterizable as recuperative 'at-first-glance-ism', as I shall show. Indeed, at one point her designation of 'deconstructive reading' is misleading. In relation to the problematic expulsion of foreign women she states: 'In the sense of "deconstructive reading", we can pose a whole series of further questions that open up a broader spectrum of meaning'.[24] All of the questions she goes on to list (for example, 'What would it mean to look at the divorce policy from the point of view of those affected')[25] are questions that a feminist using *any* method could and should ask. In other words, it is not the deconstructive reading that generates these questions at all but the feminist lens through which she reads.

21.   Karrer-Grube, 'Ezra and Nehemiah', p. 192.
22.   Karrer-Grube, 'Ezra and Nehemiah', p. 196.
23.   Karrer-Grube, 'Ezra and Nehemiah', p. 195.
24.   Karrer-Grube, 'Ezra and Nehemiah', p. 204.
25.   Karrer-Grube, 'Ezra and Nehemiah', p. 204.

Furthermore, when Karrer-Grube does engage in deconstructive reading proper, it is also problematic. Pointing out that the production of a dominant meaning in a text requires the suppression of other often contradictory meanings, with that act of suppression never fully complete and thus ensuring that traces of those alternative voices remain, she argues that her reading reveals the central weakness of this patriarchal ideology intent on constructing a pure notion of 'Israel' through the exclusion of 'others': the contradictory act of destroying families (Ezra 9–10; Neh. 13.23-34, 26-28) when the family is 'precisely the institution that must guarantee the continued existence of society'.[26] On the one hand, this is true; the problem of foreignness comes to the fore here concerning the make-up of the family. But it is not really the family *itself* (the very concept of it) that is being destroyed, only those versions of it that do not fit the agendas of Ezra and Nehemiah.

The Shadows of Ezra–Nehemiah

Returning now to 'at-first-glance-ism', all three critics declare that the absence of women is merely a false judgment of the texts based on a superficial encounter with them. They then go on to rectify this by bringing the women 'out from the shadows', as Eskenazi puts it. With respect to Ezra–Nehemiah, this process is virtually the same for both Eskenazi and Karrer-Grube, despite their supposedly different methodologies. They deal with both the general mentions of women in Ezra–Nehemiah, pointing out that women are included at certain points of communal gathering, before moving to the more 'interesting' women mentioned, all of which is leading to an argument about the expulsion of the foreign women. For Eskenazi, the 'problem' of the foreign women in Ezra–Nehemiah concerns the fear of losing property: if women can inherit and retain property after divorce, as the Elephantine documents suggest, then the concern is that the land might fall into the hands of 'foreigners'. For Karrer-Grube, this expulsion of foreign women pertains to the need for boundary definition; Nehemiah wants a separate '*ethnos of "Jews"*', while Ezra builds upon this by introducing '*concepts and imagery from the realm of sacred law*'.[27]

Now, given that we are left with only traces of women and their activities, the biblical text itself, they claim, is inadequate for really knowing what life was like for women at this time. For both, however, women *must* have had more influence on their society than the biblical text would have us believe. For this argument, both are dependent upon the Elephantine documents and their 'evidence' that women could inherit property even if they have brothers, initiate divorce without loss of property, buy and sell property, take

---

26. Karrer-Grube, 'Ezra and Nehemiah', p. 205.
27. Karrer-Grube, 'Ezra and Nehemiah', pp. 210, 203; her emphases.

on cultic roles, and lend money.[28] To be fair, Eskenazi is far more reliant on
these documents (along with the work of Carol Meyers)[29] than Karrer-
Grube, who states: 'We do not know the extent to which we can apply the
same conditions to Judah; however, this does relativize the depiction in
EN'.[30] This assertion that women must have had more influence in reality is
where the problems really begin, for it leads the feminist scholar to make
statements about the ancient world that, in relation to the really very scant,
and perhaps even irrelevant extra-biblical evidence,[31] along with the overwhelmingly androcentric picture presented to us by Ezra–Nehemiah, are
mostly unsupportable. I shall begin by focusing on Eskenazi's essay.
Putting aside the problematic foreign women of Ezra 9–10 for the moment,[32]
these 'interesting women' she wishes to bring 'out from the shadows' are
hassōperet, a name that appears in the list of returnees and literally means
'the female scribe' (Ezra 2.55; *sôperet* in Neh. 7.57); the daughter of
Barzillai the Gileadite, whose husband is known as Barzillai, having taken
their name (Ezra 2.61; Neh. 7.63); the female servants and singers mentioned as additional to the 42,360 returnees (meaning they were not counted
among the elite *golah*; Ezra 2.65; Neh. 7.67); Shelomith (Ezra 8.10; it is
unclear whether this is a male or female name, but Eskenazi argues for the
latter); Shallum's wall-building daughters (Neh. 3.12); the prophetess
Noadiah, named as one of Nehemiah's opponents (Neh. 6.14); and finally
the women twice mentioned as present at the pinnacle of the restoration,
when Ezra read from the Torah (Neh. 8.2-4). In total, in the context of the
whole of Ezra–Nehemiah, this amounts to two *possible* female names in the
lists; an un-named woman who seems to come from a clan who practice

28. Eskenazi, 'Out from the Shadows', pp. 254, 259.

29. Carol Meyers, *Discovering Eve: Ancient Israelite Women in Context* (Oxford:
Oxford University Press, 1988). Meyers argues that when we supplement the biblical
representations with insights garnered from the social sciences, especially archaeology,
we can develop a more comprehensive picture of what life was 'really' like for women in
the ancient Near East. Famously, Meyers insists that life for women in premonarchic
times was far better because of the egalitarianism between the sexes enabled by the
authority and independence of the family unit, the household being the basic socio-
economic and political unit of that era. Eskenazi wants to insist that postexilic life saw a
return of such a situation, and thus that women did not have diminished power during this
time (which is a pretty long period, actually) but in fact had greater power than they did
during the monarchic era. While Eskenazi recognizes that the weight of her own
argument is largely dependent on the veracity of Meyers's, she insists that her findings
are also dependent on 'hints in the biblical texts for this period combined with evidence
of Elephantine' (Eskenazi, 'Out from the Shadows', p. 261 n. 2).

30. Karrer-Grube, 'Ezra and Nehemiah', p. 199.

31. On the problem of assuming a consonance of marriage, divorce, and inheritance
practices of postexilic Yehud and Elephantine, see Boer, 'No Road', pp. 236-37.

32. Eskenazi does not deal with the equally problematic Neh. 13.23–24.28.

patrilocal exogamy; female servants and singers, who do not seem to count as official returnees or *golah*; a reference to some un-named women who helped build the Jerusalem wall; a prophetess who is problematic, but for reasons that do not seem important enough to warrant narrative detail (though it might indicate the ability of women to occupy the prophetic office); and the presence of women at a few important moments, especially the reading of the Torah. Are we really supposed to believe that these few references to women, and sometimes we cannot even be sure that a female *is* being referenced, rectify the Ezra–Nehemiah picture of postexilic Yehudite society as predominantly all-male, and certainly as a society for which all decisions are made by leading men? Surely not. Furthermore, we do well to consider that in a text filled with communication, in the form of decrees, letters, and speeches, not one woman speaks or communicates directly as subject in any way; no woman is given direct speech or is presented as the author of a letter. Even a response from the expelled foreign women and their children is unimportant in the context of Ezra–Nehemiah.

The names/words Shelomith and *hassōperet*, while feminine, could of course refer to male characters, just as the feminine *qōhelet* is masculine. As I pointed out in my work on the genealogies and lists in 1 Chronicles, 'we can only be sure [well, more or less] of the gender of Hebrew names when there is an associated verb or substantive such as "sister" because the gender of Hebrew names does not necessarily indicate the gender of the character'.[33] Nevertheless, it is intriguing to consider the possibility of female scribes that *hassōperet* suggests, which Eskenazi claims has been 'well documented'.[34] Furthermore, Eskenazi wants us to consider the possibility that not only is Shelomith a female, but that this may be a reference to the descendants of Shelomith, the daughter of Zerubbabel (1 Chron. 3.19), who might also be the same 'Shelomith, the maidservant of Elnathan' on the seal found in 1975. And, I agree with her that we should reject the foolish tendencies of male scholars to claim that the 'daughters' of Shallum who help build the Jerusalem walls (Neh. 3.12) are not in fact his daughters but members of his hamlets, or else that the meaning is unknown.[35]

Yet, it does seem as if Eskenazi has to draw some very long bows here. Shelomith *may* be the same 'famed princess' of Chronicles, who *may* be the same Shelomith married to the governor of Judah (Elnathan, c. 510–490 BCE). *Hassōperet may* indicate the presence of women in the scribal guild.

33. Kelso, *O Mother*, p. 224 n. 5. Even then there are no guarantees (e.g. 1 Chron. 2.48, 49).

34. See Samuel A. Meier, 'Women and Communication in the Ancient Near East', *Journal of the American Oriental Society* 111.3 (1991), pp. 540-47.

35. See Loring W. Batten, *A Critical and Exegetical Commentary on the Books of Ezra and Nehemiah* (New York: Charles Scribner's Sons, 1913), pp. 213-14.

We cannot know for sure because the authors of the biblical text have not seen fit to give us an adequate record of women's lives in the postexilic period or even because their intention may be to write women out of the picture. Maybe, even, by this stage women *had* a diminished role in 'public' Yehudite society. Who knows. However, it is not simply that the 'translators and commentators' of Ezra–Nehemiah have effaced the presence of women, but that the text itself can offer no certainties on these issues *because of the overwhelmingly masculine nature of this literary world.* A handful of specific, though sporadic mentions of women, while they *may* enable us to *imagine* a greater role for women in the ancient world, cannot change the fact that the biblical text has virtually drained them from its literary construction of that world.

Indeed, Eskenazi's (revisionist, apologetic) desire to convince us that it is not the biblical text itself that ignores or effaces the presence of women, but the 'translators and commentators'[36] leads her to make some extraordinary, even anti-feminist, remarks. It is quite strange to read that Eskenazi believes the naming of Barzillai and his clan after his wife's ('the matriarch's') family is somehow evidence that women had greater power than we previously were able to consider.[37] Actually, what this verse probably indicates is a different patriarchal marriage system whereby the husband leaves his family and comes under the rule of his wife's *father*, what Mieke Bal calls patrilocal marriage, as distinct from the more familiar virilocal model.[38] Moreover, Eskenazi claims that there is symmetry of prohibition in Ezra–Nehemiah: 'Ezra–Nehemiah considers foreign husbands as abhorrent as foreign wives… The intermarriage prohibitions of Ezra–Nehemiah are consistently symmetrical.'[39] This is just plain misleading. She cites Neh. 10.30, which reads: 'We will not give our daughters to the peoples of the land or take their daughters for our sons'.[40] How is this symmetrical, given that it is an exchange system wherein men exchange women? And is it really consoling to think that the presence of women at the reading of the Torah in Neh. 8.2-4 indicates 'religious egalitarianism, at least on this level of participation'?[41] Religious egalitarianism in a belief system that worships the male god of the fathers, with an all-male priesthood, in a social system that depends on the (conflict-ridden) exchange of daughters? How is that even remotely egalitarian?

---

36. Eskenazi, 'Out from the Shadows', p. 265.
37. Eskenazi, 'Out from the Shadows', p. 266.
38. Mieke Bal, *Death and Dissymmetry: The Politics of Coherence in the Book of Judges* (Chicago: University of Chicago Press, 1988).
39. Eskenazi, 'Out from the Shadows', p. 264.
40. All biblical quotations are from the RSV.
41. Eskenazi, 'Out from the Shadows', p. 270.

Which brings me to what must by far be the worst suggestion in Eskenazi's essay: that we need to understand that, given the precarious historical, socio-economic context, the expulsion of foreign women is *at the same time* validation of the legitimate women: 'Rather than being simply a misogynist act, this dismissal of foreign wives is an opposition to some women in favor of others'.[42] Eskenazi's insistence (leap of faith, we might say) that the women of postexilic Yehud were in all likelihood afforded the same 'rights' concerning inheritance as the Elephantine documents present leads her to the rational-enough conclusion that the expulsion of foreign women, while couched in religious and ethnic language, actually comes down to economic and political necessities. Drawing on the work of Hoglund especially, she claims that the fear of intermarriage with the 'people(s) of the land(s)' is a fear of the loss of property, should divorce occur.[43] As Boer points out, however, this does not really make much sense if we consider the fact that the children of the couple would probably inherit it one day, especially given that this is a patrilineal system, thus keeping the property inside Israel.[44] And that such an economic and political context enables Eskenazi to delete any sense of misogyny or xenophobia from the biblical text is quite remarkable indeed.

Returning to Karrer-Grube, even though all throughout her work she acknowledges the overt androcentrism of Ezra–Nehemiah, she too makes what are, I think, outlandish and largely unsupportable statements concerning the 'reality' of women's lives in Persian Yehud. After her discussion of *hassōporet*, Barzillai's wife, Shelomith, Noadiah, and Shallum's daughters, all more or less in keeping with Eskenazi, she states that these are 'the last traces of women of great significance which have everywhere else been eliminated'.[45] As I discussed above, we can be sure of no such thing based on these scant and sometimes vague references. She goes on to argue that '(e)ven these few references to women show that the overall impression EN gives at first glance must be nuanced'.[46] In other words, the overall impression of Ezra–Nehemiah—a society that functions without any clear and certain female contribution to the decision-making processes concerning governance, identity, economics, and so on—needs to be rectified because of these meager mentions. By 'nuanced' I take Karrer-Grube ultimately to mean that 'things are much better than we first thought', which is the classic position of 'at-first-glance-ism'. As further evidence, I offer the following:

42.   Eskenazi, 'Out from the Shadows', pp. 263-64.

43.   Kenneth G. Hoglund, 'Achaemenid Imperial Administration in Syria-Palestine and the Missions of Ezra and Nehemiah' (unpublished PhD dissertation, Duke University, 1989).

44.   Boer, 'No Road', p. 238.

45.   Karrer-Grube, 'Ezra and Nehemiah', p. 199.

46.   Karrer-Grube, 'Ezra and Nehemiah', p. 199.

> According to the ideas of EN, *women are to be considered part of the collec-*
> *tive 'Israel'*, which represents the whole of those who belong to the new
> community. The text mentions their responsibilities while also establishing
> the criteria for membership and the boundaries separating the community
> from the outside.[47]

Are we reading the same Bible? First of all, I struggle to figure out just who
this 'Israel' in Ezra–Nehemiah is.[48] How exactly does Karrer-Grube feel
confident enough to say that not only does 'Israel' represent the new
community (who are they?) but that women are certainly included, given
that far more often than not they are absent from the text? (Perhaps that is
why she feels the need for emphasis, to make it more authoritative a
position?) Karrer-Grube does go on to discuss the narrower definition of
'Israel' as the *golah*,[49] but this knowledge obviously does not compel her to
go back and revise her earlier, broadly confident statement about the
inclusion of women. And of the rejection of the foreign wives, she claims:

> [I]n the Ezra texts the collective of the assembled community has the ultimate
> authority to make decisions... Moreover, this is the sole concept in which
> *women* are expressly named as *members*. They join in ordering the divorce of
> the 'foreign women' (Ezra 10.1), and they are present when the Law is read
> aloud (Neh. 8.2). They are even accorded *religious and political competency*
> [I am beginning to think that Karrer-Grube italicizes the statements she
> knows are probably overstatements]... In other parts of the text the collective
> appears, with a variety of assignments, without anything being explicitly said
> about the degree to which women are included. It makes sense to think of
> women as participants unless the contrary is proved.[50]

First of all, does Ezra 10.1-4 really tell us that women 'join in ordering
the divorce of the "foreign women"'? Yes, women are present. But do they
speak as *members* of this community? The text reads:

---

47.   Karrer-Grube, 'Ezra and Nehemiah', p. 196; her emphasis.
48.   On the surface, it seems that there are three castes: the returnees ('nobles',
'mighty ones', 'officials' and 'leaders'); the 'rest of the people, the priests, the Levites,
the gatekeepers, the singers, the temple servants, and all who have separated themselves
from the people of the lands to the law of God, their wives, their sons, their daughters, all
who have knowledge and understanding, join with their brethren, their mighty ones'
(Neh. 10.29-30/28-29); and the people(s) of the land(s). The second group, as Roland
Boer states, is only recognized as political subjects because of their association with the
elites ('their mighty ones'). However, the second and third groups begin to slide together
when the menservants and maidservants, male and female singers are not included among
the 'whole assembly' (Ezra 2.64-67/Neh. 7.66-69). Boer suggests that such people are
necessarily excluded so that the elite *golah* maintains control; see Boer, 'No Road',
p. 250.
49.   Karrer-Grube, 'Ezra and Nehemiah', p. 197.
50.   Karrer-Grube, 'Ezra and Nehemiah', pp. 197-98.

> While Ezra prayed and made confession, weeping and casting himself down
> before the house of God, a very great assembly of men, women, and children,
> gathered to him out of Israel; for the people wept bitterly. And Shecaniah the
> son of Jehi'el, of the sons of Elam, addressed Ezra: 'We have broken faith
> with our God and have married foreign women from the peoples of the land,
> but even now there is hope for Israel in spite of this. Therefore let us make a
> covenant with our God to put away all these wives and their children, accord-
> ing to the counsel of my lord and of those who tremble at the commandment
> of our God; and let it be done according to the law. Arise, for it is your task,
> and we are with you; be strong and do it.'

It only can seem possible that they agree, but that is all. How can we be sure
when the text never tells us through the mouth of a female character (who
could just be a pawn in this literary propaganda anyway) what the women
might think about this? Only Shecaniah speaks, and when he does he does
not include the women, or the children, as subjects, the 'we' clearly referring
only to the men. Nevertheless, Karrer-Grube does insist that this (possible)
image of support from both men and women for the separation from
foreigners is consistent with the androcentric idea of the text. And yet, not
unlike Eskenazi, she suggests the following:

> But we must suppose that in fact women were also among the supporters of
> this idea. They could participate in the advantages of the separation and agree
> with its theological basis. The 'foreign' women could easily appear as a
> danger to them, too (and as competition? Cf. Mal 2:10-16).[51]

Such a sentiment—that some women benefit from patriarchy while others do
not, and that those 'other' women are even dangerous or threatening—
betrays, like Eskenazi before her, a frustratingly anti-feminist stance. And it
is quite simply outrageous to suggest that we are to read women *into* the
text's 'collective' simply because it makes sense to do so without evidence
to the contrary. If we are to presume egalitarianism unless presented with
evidence to the contrary, then I submit Ezra–Nehemiah as a whole.

Finally, Karrer-Grube engages in some apologetics of her own, despite
the frequent condemnation of the text's androcentrism. Again, concerning
the foreign women, and similar to Eskenazi and Meyers, she argues that
because of the importance of the family in postexilic Yehud women must
have had influence, despite the patriarchal structure of the family and society
more broadly, as demonstrated by the text at least: 'Despite the family structure, which, through the public dominance of leading men, had contributed
to making women invisible, the influence of women had to be considered'.[52]
Ultimately, her claim is that the expulsion of the foreign women is actually

---

51. Karrer-Grube, 'Ezra and Nehemiah', p. 203.
52. Karrer-Grube, 'Ezra and Nehemiah', p. 203.

evidence that women were important and influential: 'Their great influence within the family is the basis for the whole issue'.[53] The mind boggles.

In the Vestibule of Women?

Wacker's essay on Chronicles suffers from these same problems of exaggeration and fanciful ascription of value and influence to the women of the Persian era. Like Laffey before her, Wacker's essay is little more than a roll-call of the women present in Chronicles and some mention of those left out of this version of Israel's history, with side discussions of pertinent issues: text-critical issues around the presence and absence of women's names, along with extra-biblical academic research on related topics such as naming, city-founding by women, matrilineality in ancient Israel, the role of women in the temple cult, and the question of the extent of goddess worship during the Persian era. The effect of this approach of focusing mainly on the presence of women is, of course, to make the reader think that the text is not so devoid of women after all. When an entire essay is dedicated to focusing predominantly on the female figures and characters, those named and unnamed, the impression will always be that the biblical text is indeed replete with women. As cited earlier, Wacker points out early in the piece (after some 'at-first-glance-ism') that there are more women named and mentioned in Chronicles than in any other biblical book.[54] This is misleading because it does not take into account the fact that these names appear within a text that is overwhelmingly about men. The number of females in comparison to the number of males named is dramatically less. The genealogies take up nine chapters and, of the hundreds of names, there are only forty-two (give or take a few) females named. Even the masculine forms of the verb 'to bear' (*yalad*) seriously outnumber the feminine forms (91 masculine forms, 85 of which are active and six passive compared to 17 active feminine forms). And, while women are present in the narrative of Chronicles (1 Chron. 10–2 Chron. 36), notably the names of certain kings' mothers and notes about wives of the kings, there are only *seven* cases where a female figure appears as integral to the story in some way (Michal, Pharaoh's daughter, the Queen of Sheba, Maacah, Athaliah, Jehoshebeath, and Huldah).

Furthermore, Chronicles re-tells the story of Israel from Adam through to the Babylonian exile. It encompasses a long range of the biblical texts, from Genesis through to 2 Kings. As such, there are a number of female figures who are notably absent (Eve, Sarah, Leah, Rachel, Bathsheba, to name just a few). Laffey and Wacker argue that the absence of certain women can be explained away by virtue of the focus of the Chronicler: the Davidic line and the temple cult, according to Laffey, the holiness of the house of god,

---

53. Karrer-Grube, 'Ezra and Nehemiah', p. 203.
54. Wacker, 'Book of Chronicles', p. 178.

according to Wacker.[55] In other words, the absence of these female characters is, like the absence of any focus on Moses, the Exodus, and conquest
traditions, and the kings of the northern kingdom of Israel, understandable
because of the Chronicler's own specific interests, meaning it has nothing to
do with gender. No 'closer analysis' of the absence of women from the text
is undertaken at all. Indeed, like Eskenazi and Karrer-Grube, Wacker's own
intention is to demonstrate how Chronicles is not only replete with women,
but that we may glean from the text just how important and valued women
were in the Persian period. And, like Eskenazi and Karrer-Grube, this recuperative 'at-first-glance-ism' leads Wacker to draw some very long bows,
effectively letting the text off the hook and, at the same time, leading us to
believe that the text has many positive things to tell us about gender and the
Persian period. One example will suffice for what is her consistent approach
throughout her 'analysis' of Chronicles. This example demonstrates how the
recuperative feminist imports information from beyond the world of the text
before her so as to make the text seemingly acknowledge the importance of
women both in that text and in the 'real' world beyond it.

Wacker notes the problem of gender and names and the impossibility of
knowing with surety how many women are referred to in the genealogies,
especially if 'the sons of' is gender inclusive. She draws upon the work of
Kessler who, as Wacker states, 'has proved that the giving of names in
ancient Israel was de facto carried out by the mother, whereas stories of
name giving that read differently "talk past" the social-historical reality'.[56]
This leads Wacker to claim that this fact (which is surely debatable, despite
Kessler's 'proof') means that all biblical names are somehow traces of this
tradition: 'Under the assumption that children receive their names from their
mother, the Israelite personal names passed on biblically and textually
would in every case need also—even if not solely—to be evaluated as testimonies to women's traditions not least in the realm of personal and familial
piety'.[57] Wacker offers 1 Chron. 7.23 as an example of the text-critical
aspect of this issue, pointing out that while the majority of Hebrew manuscripts have the father naming the newborn child Beriah, other Hebrew
manuscripts and ancient translations (she does not say which) have the
mother do it. She makes no mention of the fact that, at least in the Masoretic
text, the name itself is given a puzzling etymology and that the verse is then
followed by yet another problematic verse that includes women.[58] Wacker
avoids any deeper analysis of the question of why there are so few women

55. Laffey, 'I and II Chronicles', p. 114; Wacker, 'Book of Chronicles', p. 184.
56. Rainer Kessler, 'Benennung des Kindes durch die israelitische Mutter', *Wort und
Dienst* 19 (1987), pp. 25-35; Wacker, 'Book of Chronicles', p. 181.
57. Wacker, 'Book of Chronicles', p. 181.
58. See Kelso, *O Mother*, p. 150.

relative to men named in the genealogies and why these curious, sometimes non-sensical moments erupt in the genealogies when mothers do come into the picture. Moreover, by drawing upon Kessler's research Wacker is even able to suggest that the mere presence of names in the biblical text, whether a naming narrative is included or not, gestures in some way to the influence of women in this period. Simultaneously, the text is let off the hook AND cast as a 'vestibule' that contains evidence of women's actual standing in the 'real' world beyond it.

Attending to the Complexities of Women's Absence and Silence: Beyond Recuperative 'At-First-Glance-Ism'

Recuperative 'at-first-glance-ism' exaggerates the presence, value, and influence of women in the text's depiction of postexilic Persian Yehud and erroneously leads to the largely unsupportable thesis that women were valuable and influential in the 'real' world beyond it, despite their relative absence and silence from texts such as Chronicles and Ezra–Nehemiah. This absence and silence is never robustly accounted for and essentially the text is let off the hook. In his critical analysis of Eskenazi's essay, Roland Boer[59] also provides what I believe are compelling reasons for us to move beyond the recuperative/revisionist strategies that still dominate feminist biblical studies, 'namely the inescapable tendency toward micro-readings and the isolation of women from the matrix of the text itself'.[60] As I have just outlined, the approach of recuperative 'at-first-glance-ism' is to sift the text such that only those shards of texts that mention women remain. We are then asked us to consider these brief narrative moments or (more frequently) genealogical notes either *in light of* or in themselves *as* 'evidence' of women's value and influence. From these fairly miniscule fragments, and the archaeological language is intentional here, these feminist scholars construct a largely woman-friendly, more egalitarian picture of postexilic Yehud that is quite dramatically at odds with what the texts of Chronicles and Ezra–Nehemiah actually present: a world virtually absent of women, indeed where certain women are removed from the narrative itself. Why, we might well ask?

As Boer points out, so much of feminist biblical scholarship focuses on the texts that mention women, which means the focus is usually on such things as marriage, divorce, sexuality, and the family. Again, as I mentioned earlier, this recuperative approach has historically been necessary in biblical studies, and most other disciplines, to put women into the scholarly pictures

---

59. Boer, 'No Road'.
60. Boer, 'No Road', p. 234.

of the past, as valid 'objects' of inquiry; obviously this relates to the broader feminist desire to put women back into the picture of the past, to acknowledge that women did in fact exist in meaningful and productive modes, all of this necessary because of the blind-spots of historically masculine-sexist methodologies. However, a major side-effect of this approach is that there are gaping textual holes left in feminist biblical studies, a lot of which pertain to texts that deal with economic, political, and cultic control. It is as if a feminist can have nothing to say about any text unless it includes female characters. And this explains the apparent need of feminist biblical scholars to over-state the presence of women in texts that should rather be characterized critically as actively silencing women and the feminine. Furthermore, where the text does include women, even if just names in passing, recuperative feminists feel the need to demonstrate just how resourceful, how important, indeed how *valued* women must have been in the ancient world. Perhaps it is because I am not a believer and do not work within a confessional framework, in other words, I do not have to maintain the 'goodness' of the text, that I feel no need for such phantasies in the face of usually appallingly androcentric literature. Moreover, I am not an ancient historian, so I do not read the biblical texts to improve my knowledge of ancient Israel. The criticism that so much of the historical obsession in our field is directly related to (concealed) theological concerns is of course well known. Biblical historiography is probably more often than not *Heilsgeschichte*. Boer's point is relevant here:

> This practice [micro-reading] is due to the limited amount of material available in the Bible for analysis, even if we add the various bits and pieces of extra-canonical literature and the other ancient Near Eastern texts. But it also has a lot to do with the appropriation by religious bodies of these disparate temporal and spatial texts, declaring them sacred and making small selections of the sacred texts the centerpiece of worship in both church and synagogue. Each word and each letter then becomes overloaded with meaning, and one may spend a lifetime or two chasing that elusive meaning.[61]

As I strongly suggested in my work on Chronicles, surely texts that, at the macro-level, go about constructing an image of society that is run by certain men and that function with barely even a handful of women mentioned *is precisely what should interest feminist scholarship*. In other words, what we need to analyze and understand are the various means, including the imaginary and unconscious means, by which 'man' is able to create and sustain this image of himself as self-made and self-sustaining. This entails a close and careful analysis of the text as a whole. However, if the goals of feminist biblical scholarship are in large part determined by religious desires (to put it

61. Boer, 'No Road', p. 240.

bluntly: to see how the god loves the ladies too) or a simplistic desire to pepper the past with pseudo-egalitarianism, then texts that do not include female characters will continue to be ignored; or, just as bad, 'at-first-glance-ism' will continue to dominate feminist readings of Chronicles and Ezra–Nehemiah.

In my own work on Chronicles, I maintained that the absence of women in Chronicles, relative to the alternative 'story' of Israel's past (Genesis–2 Kings), needs to be read as a symptom of the complex modes of silencing at work in the text. Scholars have never argued for the dearth of women as one of the defining features of Chronicles. Actually, the absence of women is not usually even considered noteworthy, and as I mentioned earlier, when it is, it is accounted for by the Chronicler's lack of interest in anything other than the Jerusalem cult and the monarchy of Judah. And yet, if we are to examine Chronicles paying attention to its uniqueness, surely we need to ask why the absence and relative silence of women seems necessary to this particular version of the past. Through a careful analysis of the genea-logical chapters (1 Chron. 1–9) and the narratives (1 Chron. 10–2 Chron. 26), I argued that along with the obvious silence of women that results from their absence and in some cases banishment from the textual action (e.g. 2 Chron. 8.11), there are two other discernible strategies of silencing women in Chronicles: disavowal and repression. Drawing on and developing the psychoanalytic reading mode of Luce Irigaray, and Michelle Boulous Walker's work on the complex nature of silence, I demonstrated that in Chronicles women are most effectively silenced through their association with maternity, because the maternal body itself, as an origin of the mascu-line subject, is disavowed and repressed. This disavowal and repression enables the phantasy of mono-sexual, masculine production (a world without women), and the logic of the production of meaning thus depends upon the logic of patrilineal succession for its consistency.

I contend that this thesis enables us to understand why a number of problems arise on those relatively rare occasions when women, especially mothers, do appear in Chronicles. In the genealogies, the mere mention of women causes great problems when it comes to the production of meaning-ful, genealogical sense and these problems generally erupt around the use of the *yalad* verb.[62] Furthermore, the narrative of Chronicles represses the debt of the masculine subject to nature, but more specifically to the maternal body. This repression enables and indeed naturalizes the temporal logic of the narrative: patrilineal succession from father to son. Time and story move forward through the production of sons. It is this association with, indeed reduction of women to symbolic maternity ('woman' equals 'mother', or

---

62. For a summary of these problems, see Kelso, *O Mother*, pp. 156-61.

more specifically the 'son's mother'), along with the disavowal/denial and repression/erasure of the 'fact' that women's bodies are the only bodies capable of reproduction, that effects and guarantees the silence of the feminine in Chronicles, thus enabling 'man' to imagine himself as self-made and self-sustaining. This is the dominant phantasy at work in Chronicles, and it is this disavowal and repression that gives coherence to Chronicles' literary reconstruction of the past: 'in being reduced to the symbolic maternal function and thus silenced because of the repressed and disavowed status of their maternal bodies, women have been silenced to enable the phantasy of monosexual, masculine production required to sustain this particular (masculine) literary (re)production of Israel's social, political, and cultic past'.[63]

Following Luce Irigaray, I insist that we need to analyze our dominant cultural texts, perhaps especially the biblical texts, with the primary purpose of ascertaining just how we have come to be silenced *as women* in our cultures. We need to search for the means by which we have been silenced, able only to be heard as long as we mimic the 'masculine'. Concomitantly, we need to develop modes of listening to and writing about those texts such that we might begin to hear new possibilities for our future. For this to happen, we need a different relationship between past, present, and future to emerge, especially to avoid a paralyzing nostalgia for the past. And just as importantly, our engagements with these texts need to acknowledge and rigorously analyze the means by which the silence and absence of women maintains patriarchal orders, rather than letting these texts off the hook. I think such an approach is not only possible, but needs to be taken up in future feminist analyses of biblical texts. This approach is necessary if we are to understand properly how we have been silenced in our Western cultures, but more importantly so that we might begin to undo this silence and speak for ourselves rather than continue to be spoken for. Recuperative 'at-first-glance-ism' cannot achieve this for us.

---

63. Kelso, *O Mother*, p. 212.

14

CROSSING BOUNDARIES: FEMINIST PERSPECTIVES ON THE STORIES OF DANIEL AND SUSANNA

David M. Valeta

The Daniel and Susanna narratives are replete with formal and social boundaries that create questions and cause confusion. Both Daniel and Susanna are situated on fault lines between differing worldviews, competing ideologies, and alternative versions of truth. Consider this partial list of oppositions one finds in this material: several languages, multiple literary genres, good vs. evil, exile vs. empire, events and revelations occurring in earthly vs. heavenly realms, legal testimony of the socially and religiously powerful vs. the word of a powerless young woman. The twelve chapters of the Masoretic Text of the book of Daniel contain multiple genres and languages within the two primary formal sections of Narrative and Apocalyptic, and recount a variety of scenes where social, spatial, ethical, spiritual, and personal boundaries are tested and sometimes transgressed. Susanna exists in various Greek versions and explores themes that include sexuality, lust, voyeurism, attempted rape, abuse of power, and punishment for the wicked, to name the most obvious themes. Boundaries are enacted and defended by royal edicts, megalomaniacal personalities, heavenly beings, and legal and social conventions.[1]

In spite of the fact that relatively few female characters other than Susanna have roles in the Daniel corpus, the boundary crossings outlined above should be fertile ground for the exploration of issues of feminist concern. For the most part, however, Daniel scholarship has not focused on feminist issues, and many analyses of the Susanna material ignore or cursorily mention obvious feminist concerns. This review examines existing feminist analyses of the Daniel and Susanna stories along with suggestions for future exploration in these areas.

---

1. The best recent commentary that covers most of these issues in a satisfactory manner is Daniel L. Smith-Christopher, 'Daniel', and 'The Additions to Daniel', in Leander E. Keck (ed.), *The New Interpreters Bible*, VII (Nashville, TN: Abingdon Press, 1996), pp. 17-194.

Daniel

Initial readings of the book of Daniel indicate a text that contains few direct subjects of feminist concern. Passages that reference specific female characters are of limited interest. Ross S. Kraemer notes the presence of the following unnamed women in the book: Dan. 5.2-3, 23—Wives and Concubines of Belshazzar; Dan. 5.10-12—Queen (Mother) of Belshazzar; Dan. 6.24—Wives of Daniel's Accusers; Dan. 11.6-7—Daughter of the King of the South; Dan. 11.17—Wife of the King of the South; Dan. 11.37—Women Worshippers of an Unnamed Deity.[2] The references in Daniel 11 are historical references to the family members of various Ptolemaic and Seleucid rulers of the second century BCE and the roles they play in Daniel's depiction of this time period.

The female characters of Daniel 5 and 6 have received more attention. The wives and concubines in Dan. 5.2-3, 23 lend an orgiastic and erotic overtone to the royal banquet scene where the undecipherable written apparition confronts the fearful monarch. Kraemer notes that their presence at the banquet heightens the culpability of Belshazzar in utilizing the temple vessels as party ware.[3] These scenes are overshadowed by the appearance of the female consort of Dan. 5.10-12, and this passage is examined in several articles with varying interpretations. Athalya Brenner explores this passage in an article examining the motif of the obtuse foreign ruler in the Hebrew Bible, including such examples as the midwives' encounter with Pharaonic authority in Exodus and the Ahasuerus/Esther relationship. These narratives portray supposedly capable and powerful foreign rulers who are parodied through satirical references to their ruling abilities, their sexual prowess, and other bodily functions. Their ineffectiveness is heightened by the contrast presented by competent female characters.[4] This is certainly true in Daniel 5 where King Belshazzar throws a royal party complete with Jerusalem Temple utensils, only to be upstaged by the writing on the wall that causes him great scatological discomfort! Brenner succinctly describes his humiliation.

2. Ross S. Kraemer, 'Wives and Concubines of Belshazzar; Queen (of Babylon); Wives of Daniel's Accusers; Daughter of the King of the South; Wife of the King of the South; Women Worshippers of an Unnamed Deity', in Carol Meyers (ed.), *Women in Scripture* (Boston: Houghton Mifflin, 2000), pp. 340-44.

3. Kraemer, 'Wives and Concubines', p. 341.

4. Athalya Brenner, 'Who's Afraid of Feminist Criticism? Who's Afraid of Biblical Humour? The Case of the Obtuse Foreign Ruler in the Hebrew Bible', in Athalya Brenner (ed.), *Prophets and Daniel: A Feminist Companion to the Bible* (FCB, 2nd Series, 8; London: Sheffield Academic Press, 2001), pp. 228-44 (231-38).

> He is demoted at once from sexual adult male to an asexual child who can't control his bowel and/or bladder movements. This is the plain meaning of the text. And who saves the situation? The queen does.[5]

She sees the queen as the mature stateswoman who is more ingenious and politically astute than her incompetent and incontinent husband Belshazzar. Thus there is a humorous satirical edge to the introduction of a powerful female character to mock and destabilize male kingship. In the same volume, H.J.M. van Deventer argues that on the basis of biblical and ancient Near Eastern wisdom traditions this female royal character is better understood as the queen mother, not the queen, muting issues of sexuality and presenting her as a wisdom symbol. While still negative and destabilizing of the role of the king, van Deventer argues that an identification as the queen mother is more congruent with the historical and social roles of the time period, and thus one should take care not to read gender and empowerment issues back into the text.[6] Brenner in a short rebuttal recognizes that, indeed, female images in the Hebrew Bible are not focused on female agency but serve as mirrors for male images and behavior.[7] Either interpretation highlights the weak cartoon-like image of the powerful king in contrast to the calm, wise presence of this female character. Daniel 6 contains another direct reference to female characters and recounts the grisly fate of the innocent wives and children of the 122 royal counselors who intended the same fate for Daniel at the jaws of the ferocious felines. This wholesale suffering by innocent family members may be an example of reversal of fortune biblical stories similar to the denouement of Esther and the wholesale slaughter of Egyptians at the Red Sea.[8] Or it may be one of the many examples of exaggerated menippean overstatement found in the book of Daniel.[9]

5. Brenner, 'Obtuse Foreign Ruler', p. 239.

6. H.J.M. van Deventer, 'Another Wise Queen (Mother)—Women's Wisdom in Daniel 5.10-12?', in Brenner (ed.), *Prophets and Daniel*, pp. 247-61 (248); van Deventer, 'Would the Actually "Powerful" Please Stand? The Role of the Queen (Mother) in Daniel 5', *Scriptura* 70 (1999), pp. 241-51 (246).

7. Athalya Brenner, 'Self-Response to "Who's Afraid of Feminist Criticism?"', in Brenner (ed.), *Prophets and Daniel*, pp. 245-46.

8. So Smith-Christopher, 'Daniel', pp. 95-96. He also notes the possibility of the 'righteous' retributive violence of the oppressed when the tables are turned as an explanation of this event.

9. Menippean satire contains multiple genres, languages, styles, reversals, and exaggerations in order to critique and judge existing social, political, and religious realities; see David M. Valeta, *Lions and Ovens and Visions: A Satirical Reading of Daniel 1–6* (Sheffield: Sheffield Phoenix Press, 2008), esp. pp. 55-66.

Carol Newsom identifies power and powerlessness as a motif of the book of Daniel that resonates with exiles, women, and ethnic minorities. She shows that the theme of not only confronting political authority but also comically resisting power through humor and satire pervades these narratives.[10] Women's movements and other movements for equality and justice can find stories of hope, strategies for change, and simply good laughter in an appreciation of these chapters. She reflects upon the sustained theological critique of the nature of state power in the book of Daniel:

> Whereas much of this critique is congenial to feminism's own understanding of the arrogance of power, a feminist analysis may also be able to show some of the limitations of the perspective from which the book of Daniel makes its critique.[11]

Newsom notes that the overarching theme of Daniel 1–6 is one of Redeeming and Judging Royal Power.[12] The Daniel stories and visions provide rich resources for those seemingly without power to reclaim their identity.

Daniel 1 confronts the reader with dietary and identity issues, strategies intended to destroy the sense of self and personal history of the four captives. The provision of food is a symbol of paternalistic power over those who receive it. Newsom notes that food is gendered in many cultures and the vegetables chosen by the captives represent the hidden power of weak/female foods that create superior courtiers.[13] Philip Chia forcefully illuminates the violence inherent in forced name change and identity manipulation in a postcolonial context:

> Identity and name are very personal belongings—being and existence are rooted in them. The change of one's name without one's consent or by force, not only is an insult to one's integrity and dignity, but also a denial of the right to ancestry.[14]

---

10.   Robert Gnuse, 'From Prison to Prestige: The Hero Who Helps a King in Jewish and Greek Literature', *CBQ* 72 (2010), pp. 31-45 (41), notes that these stories affirm the innate superiority of the people over ruling foreigners.

11.   Carol A. Newsom, 'Daniel', in Carol A. Newsom and Sharon H. Ringe (eds.), *Women's Bible Commentary* (Louisville, KY: Westminster/John Knox Press, exp. edn, 1998), pp. 201-6 (201). See also Linda Day, 'Power, Otherness and Gender in the Biblical Short Stories', *HBT* 20.2 (1998), pp. 109-27.

12.   Newsom, 'Daniel', pp. 203-204.

13.   Newsom, 'Daniel', p. 202.

14.   Philip P. Chia, 'On Naming the Subject: A Postcolonial Reading of Daniel 1', in R.S. Sugirtharajah (ed.), *The Postcolonial Biblical Reader* (Oxford: Wiley-Blackwell, 2006), pp. 171-85 (177).

Danna Nolan Fewell exposes the psychic damage inflicted on those who are forced to don the mask of another identity chosen and controlled by an oppressor.[15] Persons living in circumstances of subjugation, victimization, and powerlessness learn skills of survival and resistance, and Fewell utilizes the work of James C. Scott to explore covert and overt strategies persons use to maintain one's dignity, self-worth, and identity in such situations.[16] Daniel resolutely determines not to be defiled, to hold on to his identity no matter what happens. Mary E. Mills analyzes the ways that Diaspora border crossings are fraught with both positive and negative consequences as human bodies are the contested space of personal and cultural purity and identity. Daniel's refusal to eat the King's food is not only out of a desire to be pure, but symbolizes that the pain of the community and the loss of social identity can be resisted and mitigated by individual actions.[17] Pieter Venter utilizes the concepts of spatial theory to understand the importance of containment, of control of ones' physical spatiality in order to preserve personal identity.

> It is neither the physical substance of the food nor their physical bodies that are endangered here. It is their mental bodies and their idea world that is endangered and should be protected at any price.[18]

These analyses raise several important issues concerning the importance of the individual in times and periods where depersonalization threatens identity.[19] Daniel 1 is a chapter full of scenes that inform feminist reflection on issues of subjugation, resistance, ideology, and personal power.

Several other scenes in the tales of Daniel 1–6 provide episodes that resonate with feminist concerns. The three friends in the 'Fiery Furnace' episode in Daniel 3 and the 'Lion's Den' story in Daniel 6 illustrate the dangers of direct confrontation with powerful authorities. These stories illustrate the courage necessary to stand resolutely against unjust power structures despite the possibility of severe punishment.[20] Women's movements for justice and equality around the world often face fearful situations where persecution and the threat of bodily injury and death are very real. Smith-Christopher notes that Mahatma Gandhi found inspiration from the Daniel 6 story in his

15. Danna Nolan Fewell, *The Children of Israel: Reading the Bible for the Sake of our Children* (Nashville, TN: Abingdon Press, 2003), pp. 120-23.

16. James C. Scott, *Domination and the Arts of Resistance: Hidden Transcripts* (New Haven: Yale University Press, 1990).

17. Mary E. Mills, 'Household and Table: Diasporic Boundaries in Daniel and Esther', *CBQ* 68 (2006), pp. 408-20 (419-20).

18. Pieter M. Venter, 'A Study of Space in Daniel 1', *OTE* 19.3 (2006), pp. 993-1004 (1002).

19. Tokunboh Adeyemo, 'Daniel', in T. Adeyemo (ed.), *Africa Bible Commentary* (Nairobi: WordAlive Publishers, 2006), pp. 989-1012 (990-91).

20. Newsom, 'Daniel', p. 204.

engagement in nonviolent resistance to unjust laws.[21] André LaCocque notes that the limitless claims of regimes and ideologies ruthlessly attempt to quash dissent, but that the dissenting behavior of Daniel and his friends is both humble and heroic.[22] One may face difficult consequences when choosing to confront unjust power and authority. Daniel Berrigan reflects upon the personal price paid by those who stand against the terrors of the nuclear age in his expositions on the book of Daniel.[23] I am also reminded of events in Tunisia during the Arab Spring, and of Mohamed Bouazizi and his death by self-immolation as emblematic of such resistance.[24] The human desire for freedom, justice, and equality is powerful, sometimes dangerous, and always inspiring.

When entering the territory of the dreams and visions of Daniel 7–12, one encounters imagery that has inspired countless creative interpretations and accompanying movements. Portents of the imminent denouement of the current historical situation run the gamut from the enormous popularity of the Left Behind phenomenon to the insightful secular philosophical analysis of Slavoj Žižek in his recent tome *Living in the End Times*.[25] Apocalypticism is often related to the violent ending of time and this planet. Representative feminist approaches to this literary genre include liberating apocalyptic, an embracing of the potential for concrete social change and hope for the future;[26] anti-apocalyptic, a rejection of the often misogynistic and violent apocalyptic masculinity of both religious texts and popular culture;[27] and counter-apocalyptic, which 'avoid(s) the closure of the world signified by a straightforward apocalypse, and…avoid(s) the closure of the text signified by the anti-apocalypse'.[28] Perhaps this recognition of the problematic nature

21. Daniel L. Smith-Christopher, 'Gandhi on Daniel 6', *BibInt* 1 (1993), pp. 321-38.

22. André LaCocque, 'Daniel', in Daniel Patte (ed.), *Global Bible Commentary* (Nashville, TN: Abingdon Press, 2004), pp. 253-61 (257-60).

23. Daniel Berrigan, *Daniel: Under the Siege of the Divine* (Farmington, PA: Plough Publishing House, 1998).

24. Robin Wright, *Rock the Casbah: Rage and Rebellion across the Islamic World* (New York: Simon & Schuster, 2012), esp. pp. 15-20.

25. For an analysis of the Left Behind phenomenon, see Leann Snow Flesher, *Left Behind? The Facts behind the Fiction* (Valley Forge: Judson Press, 2006); Slavoj Žižek, *Living in the End Times* (Brooklyn, NY: Verso Books, 2011).

26. Emilie M. Townes, *In a Blaze of Glory: Womanist Spirituality as Social Witness* (Nashville, TN: Abingdon Press, 1995), esp. pp. 120-44.

27. Lee Quinby, *Millennial Seductions: A Skeptic Confronts Apocalyptic Culture* (Ithaca, NY: Cornell University Press, 1999); Tina Pippin, *Apocalyptic Bodies: The Biblical End of the World in Text and Image* (London: Routledge, 1999).

28. Catherine Keller, *Apocalypse Now and Then* (Minneapolis: Fortress Press, 1996); Catherine Keller, *God and Power: Counter Apocalyptic Journeys* (Minneapolis: Augsburg Fortress, 2005).

of violence in apocalyptic texts can be mitigated through an understanding of the purpose of such imagery. David Russell notes the thematic resonances of larger than life apocalyptic imagery with the art and techniques of political cartooning.[29] Such imagery is often of a grotesque and lampooning nature in order to highlight the inherent foolishness of the subject under consideration. E. Alan Perdomo demonstrates how the visions of Daniel 7 can be fruitfully compared to the Latin American traditions of satirical larger than life portrayals of powerful political leaders that are cut down to size by various alternative sources of resistance.[30] The Occupy movements illustrate well the use of various media; art, music, literature, street theater as ways of calling attention to issues and causes that share connections with the function of apocalyptic imagery.[31] These sources suggest avenues of understanding apocalyptic texts as rich resources of hope, change, and imagination.

Accordingly, several interpretations of Daniel 7–12 assert that dreams and visions are important in the narrative and apocalyptic sections of Daniel as they imagine social and political change that resonate with issues of feminist concern. Smith-Christopher and Sharon Pace give ample backing to the importance of dreams as a mode of resistance.[32] Smith-Christopher writes of the potential promise and perils of visionary experience:

> Dreams are the beginning of the release from oppression. Dreams are images of what could be, what may be, and most dramatically, what will be!… Visionary religion has always been dangerous and uncontrolled for any institutional status quo. Visionary religion draws deep from the hopes and passions of people, especially in dire and despairing circumstances. Visionary religion speaks to the failure of established attitudes and traditions, and it opens the way to new possibilities.[33]

29.   David S. Russell, 'Apocalyptic Imagery as Political Cartoon?', in John Barton and David J. Reimer (eds.), *After the Exile: Essays in Honour of Rex Mason* (Macon, GA: Mercer University Press, 1996), pp. 191-200.

30.   E. Alan Perdomo, 'La protesta satirica en Daniel 7: una lectura evangelica latinoamericana', *VS* 6 (1996), pp. 163-73.

31.   Noam Chomsky, *Occupy* (New York: Penguin Books, 2012); Carla Blumenkranz *et al.*, *Occupy! Scenes from Occupied America* (Brooklyn, NY: Verso Books, 2011).

32.   Sharon Pace, 'Diaspora Dangers, Diaspora Dreams', in Peter W. Flint, James C. VanderKam, and Emanuel Tov (eds.), *Studies in the Hebrew Bible, Qumran, and the Septuagint Presented to Eugene Ulrich* (Leiden/Boston: E.J. Brill, 2006) pp. 21-59; Daniel L. Smith-Christopher, 'Prayers and Dreams: Power and Diaspora Identities in the Social Setting of the Daniel Tales', in John Collins and Peter Flint (eds.), *The Book of Daniel: Composition and Reception* (VTSup, 1; Leiden: E.J. Brill, 2001), pp. 266-90.

33.   Smith-Christopher, 'Daniel', pp. 106, 108.

Dreams and visions can be powerful inspiration for those struggling in difficult personal, social and political situations.[34] Newsom describes the imagery of Daniel 7 as unambiguous as the four monstrous beasts rise out of the sea and threaten humankind. This threat can only be met by an over-powering manifestation of divine power represented by the Ancient of Days and one like a Son of Man. She notes the ancient Near Eastern background of the female gendered chaos monster that rises out of the sea and the possibility of a submerged sexual hostility in such imagery.[35] This struggle between good and evil represents the dualism at the heart of many apocalyptic analyses and Newsom rejects such a monologic reading of the struggle between good and evil:

> The criticism is rather that the vision of apocalyptic too radically schematizes the world and so leaves out much that matters...feminism, aware of the ways in which women's perspectives on the world have tended to be excluded from consideration, champions a diversity of voices from various social locations engaging in dialogue about important issues.[36]

Brenda E. Brasher and Lee Quinby have gathered a volume of essays that furthers the discussion of the importance of gender and apocalyptic:

> Yet the persistent absence of attention to gender that permeates studies of apocalypticism and millennialism leaves critical data consistently and system-atically invisible. This widespread gender blindness may, in large part, be why little progress has been made in accounting for the recurrent outbreaks of millennial enthusiasm and apocalyptic violence to the present day.[37]

Much work remains to be done, and a continuing reinterpretation and appreciation of apocalyptic texts is needed, as Keller opines:

> The bad dreams of a species locked outside its own world, cut off from its shadows by violence and ideation, will only be healed from within. Because the within contains the codes of its own self-overcoming. The bad dreams of a species locked outside of its own world, cut off from its shadows by violence and alienation, will only be healed from within its own narratives.[38]

---

34. See Rokeya Sakhawat Hossain, *Sultana's Dream: A Feminist Utopia* (New York: The Feminist Press at the City University of New York, 1988), for a delightful story of the power of dreams in Bengali feminist science fiction.

35. Newsom, 'Daniel', p. 205.

36. Newsom, p. 206.

37. Brenda Brasher and Lee Quinby (eds.), *Gender and Apocalyptic Desire* (Millennialism and Society, 1; London: Equinox, 2006), p. xi.

38. Catherine Keller, 'Territory, Terror and Torture: Dream-reading the Apocalypse', *FemTh* 14 (2005), pp. 47-67 (67).

Susanna

In feminist exegetical work, Susanna is often grouped together with stories such as Judith, Esther and Ruth as examples of adventure and romance stories.[39] It is surprising, however, how often many interpreters focus on topics other than feminist issues in their analysis of Susanna, and only mention, if at all, how these issues are raised by this text. Amy Jill-Levine notes that,

> [T]he woman and the book are incorporated into the canonical version of Daniel and so safely tucked away into a story revolving around men's concerns.[40]

Lawrence Wills highlights the Hellenistic novelistic features of Susanna, such as elements of erotic sexual overtones and the exploration of the theme of social shame for her family and the wider community. The ultimate purpose of the story is to introduce Daniel as a wise young man, foreshadowing his heroic career in the rest of the book of Daniel.[41] LaCocque sees this story as an indictment of unjust religious leadership in Israel and the need for proper implementation of the Law:

> A subversive piece of literature, Susanna satirizes the Jewish 'establishment'. It contrasts the virtuous Jewess Susanna with lecherous elders, and wise children with aged scoundrels.[42]

Interpreters such as George J. Brooke and Sarah J.K. Pearce emphasize the focus on theological themes such as the physical location of the Susanna story in a garden and the Edenic overtones of the narrative, identifying Susanna as a second Eve.[43] Susanna's ordeal in the garden and subsequent vindication serve a much larger purpose:

39.   André LaCocque, *The Feminine Unconventional: Four Subversive Figures in Israel's Tradition* (Minneapolis: Fortress Press, 1990); Alice Ogden Bellis, 'Subversive Women in Subversive Books: Ruth, Esther, Susanna and Judith', in Bellis, *Helpmates, Harlots, and Heroes: Women's Stories in the Hebrew Bible* (Louisville, KY: Westminster/John Knox Press, 1994), pp. 206-26.

40.   Amy-Jill Levine, ' "Hemmed in on Every Side": Jews and Women in the Book of Susanna', in Fernando F. Segovia and Mary Ann Tolbert (eds.), *Reading from This Place*, I (Minneapolis: Fortress Press, 1995), pp. 179-90 (190), explores many of the ways that feminist issues have been muted in the history of scholarship.

41.   Lawrence M. Wills, *The Jewish Novel in the Ancient World* (Ithaca, NY: Cornell University Press, 1995), pp. 53-60.

42.   LaCocque, *Feminine Unconventional*, pp. 27-28.

43.   George J. Brooke, 'Susanna and Paradise Regained', in G.J. Brooke (ed.), *Women in the Biblical Tradition* (Studies in Women and Religion, 31; Lewiston, NY: Edwin Mellen Press, 1992), pp. 92-111; Sarah J.K. Pearce, 'Echoes of Eden in the Old Greek of Susanna', *FemTh* 4 (1996), pp. 11-31.

Rather, Susanna, the Second Eve, displays exemplary obedience in the garden and is vindicated; the end of it all is nothing other than that God is praised. Through her decisive example Susanna shows straightforwardly that Paradise is regained every time evil men are bravely confounded by a faithful woman.[44]

For Adele Reinhartz the textual and architectural space of the garden plays a key role in understanding the purpose of this story:

The role of the garden both in plot and in characterization suggests that the garden stands in for or symbolizes Susanna herself... Read in this way, the story underscores the need for piety and steadfastness in the face of the elders' threat of assault in the garden.[45]

In a similar fashion, both Patrick Henry Reardon and Catherine Brown Tkacz focus on piety and faithful obedience to God as the surest way to achieve justice and blessings.[46] Their readings of the Susanna narrative highlight the themes of suffering and vindication that are common in the history of Christian interpretation of this text.

Surely these readings illuminate facets of this text and are valuable, but to consider any one of these readings as the primary storyline of this text is to miss the obvious from a feminist, even more so a justice point of view. Alice Bach notes the silencing of Susanna by examining the parallels with the Joseph stories of Genesis and the *Testament of Joseph*. These narratives make use of their characters to reify acceptable community standards of the value of chaste and acceptable behavior.[47] Levine concurs in her assessment of Susanna's function in the story:

Apparently, when the threat is external, women/community can act; when the threat is internal—that is, when it threatens the very core of community—a man, or, more precisely, the deity whom the man represents, must preserve the existence of the male-defined community and must reinstate its honor. Although she speaks, Susanna is not (first and foremost) subject, she is object. And she is abject.[48]

44. Brooke, 'Susanna and Paradise Regained', p. 111.

45. Adele Reinhartz, 'Better Homes and Gardens: Women and Domestic Space in the Books of Judith and Susanna', in Stephen G. Wilson and Michel Desjardins (eds.), *Text and Artifact in the Religions of Mediterranean Antiquity* (Waterloo, Ont.: Wilfrid Laurier University Press, 2000), pp. 325-39 (335-36).

46. Patrick Henry Reardon, 'Susannah's Virtues: The Prayer of Distress and the Cause of Justice', *Touchstone* (US) 13.5 (2000), pp. 17-24; Catherine Brown Tkacz, 'Susanna and the Pre-Christian Book of Daniel: Structure and Meaning', *HeyJ* 49 (2008), pp. 181-96.

47. Alice Bach, *Women, Seduction, and Betrayal in Biblical Narrative* (Cambridge: Cambridge University Press, 1997), pp. 65-72.

48. Levine, 'Hemmed in on Every Side', p. 181.

Thus the voice and experience of the character is often muted and lost in service of larger issues. There are several interpreters who help Susanna regain her voice, to bring to life her experience.

This exploration of interpretations sensitive to feminist concerns of the Susanna narrative utilizes and adapts the taxonomy of Tikva Frymer-Kensky in her acclaimed work *Reading the Women of the Bible*. She classifies Hebrew Bible stories about women under four categories, alliteratively labeled 'woman as victor', 'woman as victim, 'woman as virgin (bride-to-be)', and 'woman as voice (of God)'.[49] Frymer-Kensky does not consider apocryphal texts in her analyses, and generally classifies each Hebrew Bible text she considers within a single category, but all four types are helpful in appreciating the richness of the Susanna narrative. While the Susanna narrative may exemplify one or more of these categories better than others, all four have degrees of resonance and explanatory value.

Victim, Victor, Virgin, Voice

Frymer-Kensky identifies important reasons why interpretations of women's stories in biblical texts are constrained by the presentation of the writer(s) and yet often inspire incredible artistic and literary creations.

> The women who appear in biblical stories are often striking characters, distinct personalities who have gone beyond the confines of the tales in which they appear to become important figures in our cultural memory. At the same time, these women are not fleshed-out individuals. Many of them appear in only one story, and that story tells us only the facts that serve the writer's agenda... But these partial images have also been a spur to literary and poetic imagination.[50]

Interpreters certainly are rightly interested in attempting to ascertain the writer's agenda, and legal, wisdom, and hero legend themes as a result often dominate scholarly analysis. The cultural afterlife of biblical texts many times expands the interpretative options of these stories, and this is certainly the case with cultural creations based on the Susanna story. Some of these creations are noted in the analysis below, and there are several excellent general reviews of creative works available for interested readers who wish to delve deeper. For example, Dan W. Clanton surveys interpretations of the Susanna story in the visual arts and music, particularly in the Renaissance period.[51] Fabrizio A. Pennacchietti focuses on the transformations of the

---

49. See Tikva Frymer-Kensky, *Reading the Women of the Bible* (New York: Schocken Books, 2002), pp. xii-xxvii, for a summary of these four types.

50. Frymer-Kensky, *Women of the Bible*, p. 333.

51. Dan W. Clanton, *The Good, the Bold, and the Beautiful: The Story of Susanna and its Renaissance Interpretations* (London: T. & T. Clark, 2006), and 'Susie-Q, Baby I

Susanna story in Arabic and Islamic cultures.[52] A volume edited by Ellen Spolsky contains several essays that explore artistic reinterpretations of Susanna.[53] Anthony C. Swindell concentrates on literary reworkings and identifies multiple themes in these works:

> In terms of diegetic content, the coverage of human experience is very exten-
> sive, including, as it does, the courage of women, corruption in high places,
> marriage in a variety of Western cultures, eroticism, the male gaze, lechery,
> misogyny, instrumental variations in music, the propagandist use of sacred
> stories, women's emancipation, anti-Semitism and the battle for cognitive and
> political freedom.[54]

Victims are the tales of women who suffer at the hands of those in power. This victimization of vulnerable women uncovers the dangers of patriarchal social structures that revolve around male dominance.[55] Several interpreters primarily identify Susanna as a story of sexual violence. Carey A. Moore sees Susanna as a text of sexual violence, of harassment, of attempted rape, of blaming the victim.[56] Susanna is the aggrieved party, she is the woman who is accosted and threatened with attack. She does not acquiesce, she cries out, she resists, and then goes through the ordeal of a legal proceeding where she is put on the defensive. Smith-Christopher recognizes Susanna as the victim of attempted rape, the one who suffers and is marginalized, who then speaks up, cries out, and becomes a symbol of courage and resistance. His interpretation of the book of Daniel and the Greek Additions emphasizes the theme of resistance by the powerless against the oppression of the power-ful.[57] Susanne Scholz highlights the centrality of sexual violence as the key to understanding this narrative lest it be primly classified as a moralistic tale of faith in God to deliver one from difficult circumstances.[58] The history of interpretation and cultural manifestations of the Susanna story have often

Love You', in Clanton, *Daring, Disreputable and Devout: Interpreting the Bible's Women in the Arts and Music* (New York: Continuum, 2009), pp. 157-74.

52. Fabrizio A. Pennacchietti, *Three Mirrors for Two Biblical Ladies: Susanna and the Queen of Sheba in the Eyes of Jews, Christians, and Muslims* (Piscataway, NJ: Gorgias Press, 2006).

53. Ellen Spolsky (ed.), *The Judgment of Susanna: Authority and Witness* (Atlanta, GA: Scholars Press, 1996).

54. Anthony C. Swindell, 'Susanna and a World of Elders', in Swindell, *Reworking the Bible: The Literary Reception-History of Fourteen Biblical Stories* (The Bible in the Modern World, 30; Sheffield: Sheffield Phoenix Press, 2010), pp. 144-59 (159).

55. Frymer-Kensky, *Women of the Bible*, pp. xviii, 91-92.

56. Carey A. Moore, 'Susanna: Sexual Harassment in Ancient Babylon', *BR* 8.3 (1992), pp. 20-29, 52.

57. Smith-Christopher, 'The Additions to Daniel', pp. 171-84, esp. 183-84.

58. Susanne Scholz, *Sacred Witness: Rape in the Hebrew Bible* (Minneapolis: Fortress Press, 2010), pp. 44-51.

cast Susanna in the passive victim role. Jennifer Glancy agrees that this is a story best described as an account of an attempted rape, but that it is often read as a story of failed seduction and that Susanna is partially complicit in the thoughts and actions of the two elders. Readers, particularly male readers, often share the elders' voyeurism, and thus gaze at the beautiful Susanna just like the elders.[59] Of course (wink, wink!), one can understand how they are tempted since she is such a beautiful woman! The issue of gaze is particularly apropos to the visual arts.[60] Mieke Bal and Babette Bohn in particular explore the history of medieval painting and the trajectories of exposure of Susanna at her bath in various stages of undress.[61] Like Glancy, their analyses emphasize the majority of artistic renditions depicting Susanna as at least partially responsible for enflaming the passions and the attack of the elders. Readers can recognize and critically analyze these trajectories, understand their genesis and influence, but choose to resist such leadings. As Clanton helpfully states in his analysis of medieval art:

> In the case of Susanna, once we as readers realize the harmful underlying assumptions and emphases found in the mimetic level of the narrative, and *mutatis mutandis*, subsequent aesthetic and scholarly interpretations, we can begin to resist those assumptions so that we can begin to develop ways to counter them in our own time.[62]

Of course, Susanna is more than a victim. She is also a Victor, the second category of Frymer-Kensky's taxonomy, one who heroically stands her ground and controls her destiny, and thus models appropriate agency in the midst of unjust circumstances.[63] Her resistance is an indictment of community leaders who could act in such a manner, but it is also a statement that sexual harassment and attack is not acceptable.[64] Susanna does cry out, she resists her attackers, and she persists in publicly proclaiming her innocence

---

59. Jennifer A. Glancy, 'The Accused: Susanna and her Readers', *JSOT* 58 (1993), pp. 103-16.

60. Mary D. Garrard, 'Artemisia and Susanna', in Norma Broude and Mary D. Garrard (eds.), *Feminism and Art History: Questioning the Litany* (New York: Westview Press, 1982), pp. 146-71; Margaret Miles, *Carnal Knowing: Female Nakedness and Religious Meaning in the Christian West* (Boston: Beacon Press, 1989).

61. Mieke Bal, 'The Elders and Susanna', *BibInt* 1 (1993), pp. 1-19; Babette Bohn, 'Rape and the Gendered Gaze: Susanna and the Elders in Early Modern Bologna', *BibInt* 9 (2001), pp. 259-86.

62. Clanton, *The Good, the Bold, and the Beautiful*, pp. 181-82.

63. Frymer-Kensky, *Women of the Bible*, pp. xviii, 91.

64. Eric S. Gruen, *Diaspora: Jews Amidst Greeks and Romans* (Cambridge, MA: Harvard University Press, 2002), pp. 171-72, identifies the comedic overtones of the story used to castigate and ridicule the lecherous judges but also notes that 'Susanna fails to qualify fully as a paragon of virtue' and that 'As an example of impeccable purity, Susanna leaves something to be desired'. This blaming the victim mentality is regrettable.

and trust in God for her deliverance.[65] Her response is far from a passive acceptance of her fate, a viewpoint that many interpreters share. The following quote by John Collins is typical of the judgment of many:

> (Susanna) is one of several post-exilic stories that assigns a leading role to women; compare Esther, Ruth and Judith. It could scarcely be called a feminist document, however. Susanna's role is passive, and she must be rescued by Daniel... Nonetheless, the story is remarkable for championing the virtue of a woman over against the corruption of those who were thought to guide the people.[66]

Is the portrayal of Susanna as a passive character in the story accurate? Elma Cornelius argues the rhetoric of Susanna reifies patriarchy, reducing her to a functionary status:

> To me the character Susanna is not really a plausible character in this text. The narrative actually minimizes Susanna even more. She is reduced to a passive human being, simply living her life fearing God, being religious and submissive to men in society and to God... Patriarchy is solid in this text![67]

Pierre J. Jordaan rejects this interpretation with his reading of Susanna as therapeutic narrative. This analysis identifies the clash of the dominant narrative with an alternative narrative that challenges the status quo:

> The narrative therapeutic reading of Susanna posed exciting possibilities. Colliding narratives, the dominant and alternative, were pointed out. It was shown on the one hand how there was discrimination against women in an oppressive society and on the other hand how this was challenged and turned around... An individual—even a woman—may rise above it.[68]

Using Speech-Act theory, Eugene Coetzer argues that Susanna's crying out when confronted by the elders and her prayer during the trial shows her tenacity, fortitude, and agency:

> Susanna is indeed a story of doing things with words. We find the lustful judges actually being impotent. Their words are empty and do not have the ability to have an effect. On the contrary, Susanna and Daniel function together as a steady structure that uses the truth to affect not only the outcome of the trial but the future of justice.[69]

---

65. Smith-Christopher, 'Additions to Daniel', pp. 175, 181.

66. John J. Collins, *Daniel: A Commentary on the Book of Daniel* (Hermeneia; Minneapolis: Fortress Press, 1993), p. 438.

67. Elma Cornelius, 'The Woman in "Susanna": An Understanding of the Rhetoric of "Susanna"', *Acta patristica et byzantina* 19 (2008), pp. 97-109 (104-105).

68. Pierre Jordaan, 'Reading Susanna as Therapeutic Narrative', *Journal for Semitics* 17 (2008), pp. 114-28 (127).

69. Eugene Coetzer, 'Performing Susanna: Speech Acts and Other Performative Elements in Susanna', in Johann Cook (ed.), *Septuagint and Reception* (VTSup, 127; Leiden: E.J. Brill, 2009), pp. 347-60.

Utilizing a simplified Greimassian Narrative Analysis developed by Nicole Ereraert-Desmedt, Dichk M. Kanonge identifies Susanna as the main focus of the text:

> In brief, the narrative level consists of revealing the functions of actants and observing their courses in the unfolding of a narrative… The function of these is to reveal the signifying organisation of a text. In *Susanna* it is revealed that Susanna is the subject of the narrative, responsible for the main programme. The elders are the opponents, introducing an opposed programme. Daniel is Susanna's helper.[70]

Even the servants function in the narrative to highlight the importance of Susanna. Robin Gallaher Branch and Pierre J. Jordaan note:

> Servants appear in verses 17, 19, 26, 27. They are significant in the text because of their function (serving Susanna) and in terms of their reaction to the charge against her (shock)… Let us pause for a moment on the servants' reaction. It reinforces the character of Susanna.[71]

Glancy also observes that it is the servants, not the family members, that express shock and thereby protect Susanna and her family from public acknowledgment of their shame.[72] It is clear that Susanna is the focus of the narrative as demonstrated in several ways by these interpreters, and is vindicated. While other concerns such as corrupt leadership and the wisdom of young Daniel are important subplots in the text, Susanna is the main focus of the story.

Frymer-Kensky's third category, Virgins, encapsulates Hebrew Bible stories concerning questions of marriage, intermarriage, ethnicity, and boundaries.[73] These stories explore the borders of gender, male and female sexuality, and the social, political, and personal implications of intimate relationships. An excellent resource that explores these issues with superb analysis and command of relevant sources is the volume by William Loader on *Pseudepigrapha and Sexuality*.[74] His judgment is that Susanna depicts appropriate and inappropriate attitudes and behavior for both male and

---

70. Dichk M. Kanonge, 'Reading Narratives in the Septuagint: A Discourse on Method', in Cook (ed.), *Septuagint and Reception*, pp. 361-81 (376).

71. Pierre Jordaan and Robin Gallaher Branch, 'The Significance of Secondary Characters in Susanna, Judith, and the Additions to Esther in the Septuagint', *Acta patristica et byzantina* 20 (2009), pp. 389-416 (396-97).

72. Jennifer A. Glancy, 'The Mistress–Slave Dialectic: Paradoxes of Slavery in Three LXX Narratives', *JSOT* 72 (1996), pp. 71-87 (80).

73. Frymer-Kensky *Women of the Bible*, p. xix.

74. William Loader, *The Pseudepigrapha on Sexuality: Attitudes towards Sexuality in Apocalypses, Testaments, Wisdom and Related Literature* (Grand Rapids: Eerdmans, 2011).

female sexuality.[75] Nothing in the text suggests that female sexual attractiveness is problematic, despite the history of interpretation of the text. Males who do not take responsibility for their sexual responses in combination with the lack of appropriate leadership of the community come under close scrutiny and approbation.[76] The story then becomes a statement of the appropriate boundaries for interpersonal relationships and responsible leadership. Interpreters such as Susan Sered and Samuel Cooper point out and sometimes lament the fact that the book of Susanna reifies the status quo concerning patriarchy, that she is overshadowed by Daniel who is the true hero of the story, and that her lot is simply to return to the home of her husband, Joakim, who is basically an absent figure in this story.[77] Tal Ilan also notes that from a feminist point of view this may be a disappointing text for not directly championing female leadership and agency; however, it is a text that questions patriarchy.

> If this book is not a piece of propaganda for women's leadership, it certainly undermines the assumption underlying the opposite point of view, namely that men are made to rule over women. It does so by pointing out the wickedness and high-handed behavior of some male rulers on the one hand, and the righteousness and sexual innocence of some women on the other. The stage is set for a possible role reversal.[78]

This disappointment concerning the return to patriarchy misses the point of how impressive a character Susanna is in this time period. Brown Takcz points out that her reaction to the Elders in the garden demonstrates her exemplary character and her considerable religious learning.[79] Eugene Coetzer argues that Susanna must have been a popular story precisely because it dealt with 'hot topics' (leadership, sexuality) in an engaging manner.[80] In terms of sexual and gender roles, Kanonge rightly notes that the main point of the story of Susanna is identity:

> The data of the text provide an answer to the question by insisting that neither gender nor age are criteria for defining Jewishness. Being Jewish depends exclusively on commitment to the Law of Moses. By rejecting gender as

75. Loader, 'Susanna', in Loader, *Pseudepigrapha on Sexuality*, pp. 214-36 (235).

76. Helene Koehl, 'Suzanne subversive a son corps défendant. Quand le jeune s'oppose à l'institution', *ETR* 84 (2009), pp. 537-51.

77. Susan Sered and Samuel Cooper, 'Sexuality and Social Control: Anthropological Reflections on the Book of Susanna', in Spolsky (ed.), *Judgment of Susanna*, pp. 43-55 (54-55).

78. Tal Ilan, *Integrating Women into Second Temple History* (Texts and Studies in Ancient Judaism, 76, Tübingen: Mohr Siebeck, 1999), pp. 49-50.

79. Catherine Brown Tkacz, 'A Biblical Woman's Paraphrase of King David: Susanna's Refusal of the Elders', *Downside Review* 128.450 (2010), pp. 39-51 (46).

80. Coetzer, 'Performing Susanna', p. 350.

criterion for defining Jewishness and by praising a woman as a true Jew, challenging the assumptions of the leading class of men, the story of Susanna makes a strong case for gender equality... Only the Jew who practises the Law of Moses is real Jew. To be more precise, anyone—man, woman, or even a youth—who lives by the Law of Moses, as Susanna does, is a real Jew.[81]

Susanna is a strong, independent character who embodies power and independence in the midst of an extremely troubling event in a hostile patriarchal environment.

Frymer-Kensky's final category of Voice explores those stories where women function in the role of spokesperson for God. Through words and actions, sometimes functioning as oracles, these women act out or proclaim a message that the community needs to hear.[82] Susanna speaks to the elders when she is accosted, she shrieks and cries out to resist her attackers, and she prays out loud before the assembly of the elders and the community. Toni Craven notes that the Apocryphal/Deuterocanonical books record several examples of women's prayers, something relatively rare in the Hebrew Bible.[83] This prayer is important, and has resulted in the trajectory of Susanna as the representation of the wise and virtuous woman who trusts in God, and God's chosen one, Daniel, for her deliverance. Chris de Wet has identified four symbolic functions of the Susanna story in early Christian iconography: chastity; martyrdom; wisdom and virtue; and Holy Woman, a gender parallel to Peter Brown's characterization of the 'Holy Man', the monastic ideal.[84] Such characterizations are important in the history of interpretation but have the tendency to reduce the role of Susanna to one of the minor characters of the narrative, essential to move along the plot to the important garden scene and then subsequent trial before Daniel. Coetzer helps us understand the forceful significance of Susanna's voice in her refusal of the elders.

> She opposes the elders with another speech act. Here Susanna is a moral example to other female characters in the Septuagint. Eve is persuaded even before speaking, Bathsheba does not say a thing, and Judith and Esther use their bodies rather than reason to accomplish their political goals. This is not the case with Susanna, however, as she is one tough woman.[85]

81.   Kanonge, 'Reading Narratives in the Septuagint', pp. 380-81.

82.   Frymer-Kensky, *Women of the Bible*, pp. xxi, 327-30.

83.   Toni Craven, 'From Whence Will My Help Come? Women and Prayer in the Apocryphal/Deuterocanonical Books', in M. Patrick Graham *et al.* (eds.), *Worship in the Hebrew Bible: Essays in Honor of John T. Willis* (Sheffield: Sheffield Academic Press, 1999), pp. 95-109.

84.   Chris L. de Wet, 'The Reception of the Susanna Narrative (Dan. XIII; LXX) in Early Christianity', in Cook (ed.), *Septuagint and Reception*, pp. 229-44 (242).

85.   Coetzer, 'Performing Susanna', p. 356.

Tough woman indeed! Pierre Jordaan notes that the dominant narrative of this story (the treatment of women in an unjust legal environment) is in tension with a challenging narrative (the conduct of an accused woman who resists with her voice). It is Susanna who is the agent of change, challenging social mores that women's voices do not count and that their bodies are inferior.[86] Her voice cannot be reduced, as it is argued even today, to calling for the virtues of chastity and martyrdom.

Cristina L.H. Traina explores the use of the Susanna narrative in contemporary Roman Catholic interpretation to reify the moral absolute of sexual purity, even to the point of martyrdom. She argues:

> John Paul II's labeling of Susana as a potential martyr, bound on pain of loss of soul to refuse the judges in the name of faith, is thus flawed in several ways. It flies in the face of contemporary experience by employing definitions of adultery and rape that are virtually meaningless in contemporary western culture; it misuses personalism, ignoring both the judges' objectification of Susanna and their substantial power over her; it draws inappropriate distinctions between physical and other sorts of violence; and it misapplies the rule of double effect and overlooks the rule of cooperation, both important tools of the moral tradition it purports to uphold.[87]

Susanna's voice is loud and strong, a voice that can inspire those who yearn for justice in the face of physical and psychological assault.[88]

Conclusion

The Daniel and Susanna texts have been muted and misused in a variety of ways in the long history of biblical interpretation. These are not texts to reify and reinforce the status quo, but texts meant to raise questions and cause discomfort. Feminist interpretations of these materials can help correct the silencing of important messages contained in these texts and help bring about a world that is more in tune with concerns for peace, justice, and equality. The book of Daniel provides numerous resources for challenging claims to power, authority, and hegemony that continue to thwart those who work for peace, justice, and equality in all areas of life. Susanna is so much more than a story that illustrates divine blessings for faithful behavior. Tkacz asserts that many feminist theologians and biblical scholars continue

86. Jordaan, 'Therapeutic Narrative', p. 114.

87. Cristina L.H. Traina, 'Oh, Susanna: The New Absolutism and Natural Law', *JAAR* 65 (1997), pp. 371-401 (385-86).

88. Ulrike Bail, 'Susanna verläßt Hollywood: Eine feministische Auslegung von Dan 13', in Ulrike Bail and Renate Jost (eds.), *Gott an den Rändern: Sozialgeschichtliche Perspektiven auf die Bibel* (Gütersloh: Kaiser Verlag, 1996), pp. 91-98.

to portray Susanna as passive rather than an agent of power and change.[89] She sees this as a form of neosexism:

> The effect of these feminist analyses is neosexist: the biblical Susanna is a learned, effective, self-assured woman, relayed to us in a text presumably written down by a man, and honored and emulated by men and women for centuries.[90]

A judgment of neosexism is overly simplistic. Feminist analysis has alerted readers of the dangers of reading this text as confirming patriarchal structures of society, of applauding passive acceptance of one's fate in the face of evil, of simply enduring injustice, even threatened and real physical abuse, as a sign of virtue and purity. As illustrated in this survey, feminist interpreters have explored this text from many angles, noting ways this text has been used and misused. One of the challenges of future feminist explorations of the Susanna narrative is to challenge historical and literary readings that mute the devastation of sexual harassment and violence, and minimize the destructive effect of victimization and powerlessness. Scholz gets it right:

> Susanna's story then has a liberating effect: encouraging women to fiercely, forcefully, and uncompromisingly resist violent advances from men in their communities and lives. Then the story becomes a resistance tale that reminds readers, female and male, of the prevalence of acquaintance rapes even in biblical literature.[91]

Daniel and Susanna are tales of empowerment and resistance, and future feminist forays into this literature are most welcome indeed.

89. Catherine Brown Tkacz, 'Silencing Susanna: Neosexism and the Denigration of Women', *Intercollegiate Review* 34 (1998), pp. 31-47 (34).

90. Tkacz, 'Silencing Susanna', p. 36.

91. Scholz, *Sacred Witness*, p 50.

INDEX OF AUTHORS

CPSIA information can be obtained
at www.ICGtesting.com
Printed in the USA
LVHW011951010720
659482LV00004B/71

9 781910 928318